Alice 19th ™

volume 5 *Jealousy*

Alice 19th
volume 5 Jealousy
shôjo edition

STORY & ART BY
Yû Watase

English Adaptation/Lance Caselman
Translation/JN Productions
Touch-Up Art & Lettering/Walden Wong
Cover Design & Layout/Judi Roubideaux
Editor/Frances E. Wall

Managing Editor/Annette Roman
Editor in Chief/Alvin Lu
Director of Production/Noboru Watanabe
Sr. Director of Licensing & Acquisitions/Rika Inouye
V.P. of Sales & Marketing/Liza Coppola
Executive Vice President/Hyoe Narita
Publisher/Seiji Horibuchi

Printed in Canada

Published by VIZ, LLC
P.O. Box 77010 · San Francisco, CA 94107

10 9 8 7 6 5 4 3 2
First printing, June 2004
Second printing, October 2004

www.viz.com

volume 5 *Jealousy*

story and art by Yû Watase

Alice 19th™

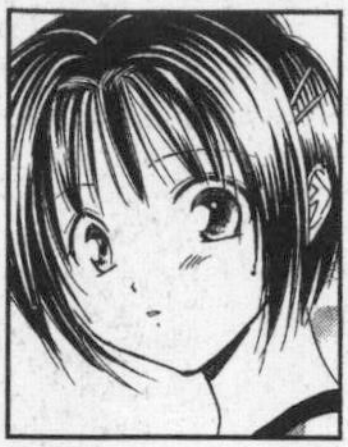

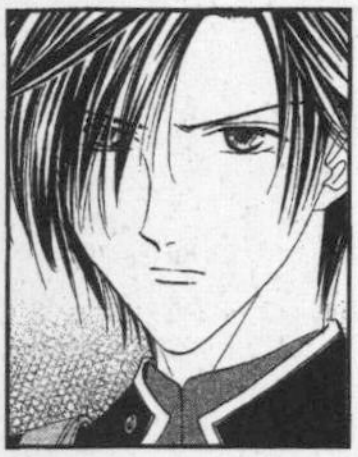

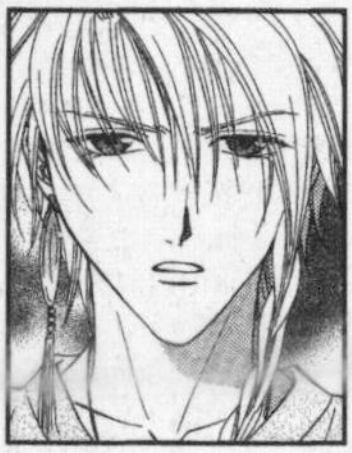

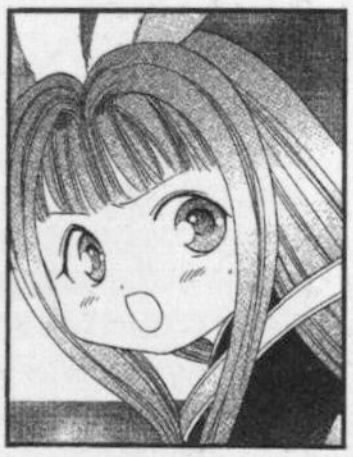

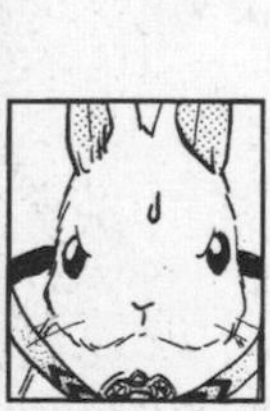

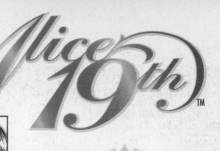

Story thus far

Mayura is possessed by Darva, the ruler of evil; her power has increased dramatically, and she's still out for revenge on Alice. She has taken over the Tokyo Metropolitan Building and unleashed a Barrier of Evil over Tokyo, enabling her to control the city's inhabitants by manipulating the Mara in their hearts.

The Lotsuan Council in Scandinavia sends the Mirror of Lota, which has the power to grant all wishes and desires to the Lotis Master who uses it, to Kyô and Alice. They accept the gift and vow to fulfill their calling to become true Lotis Masters. Chris, a young Lotis Master from England dispatched by the Lotsuan Council, shows up suddenly with his butler and pet swallow in tow. Chris buys a house to serve as a new Lotsuan HQ, where all the new Lotis Masters will live together. Alice is nervous about moving in with Chris, Frey, and especially Kyô, because after several romantic moments with Kyô, it's getting harder and harder to hold her feelings in check!

Mayura, still using the Tokyo Metropolitan Building as her base, sends servants of Mara to Kyô's house in an effort to use his aunt and uncle as tools of Mara against Kyô...

CHAPTER 4 UNREQUITED LOVE

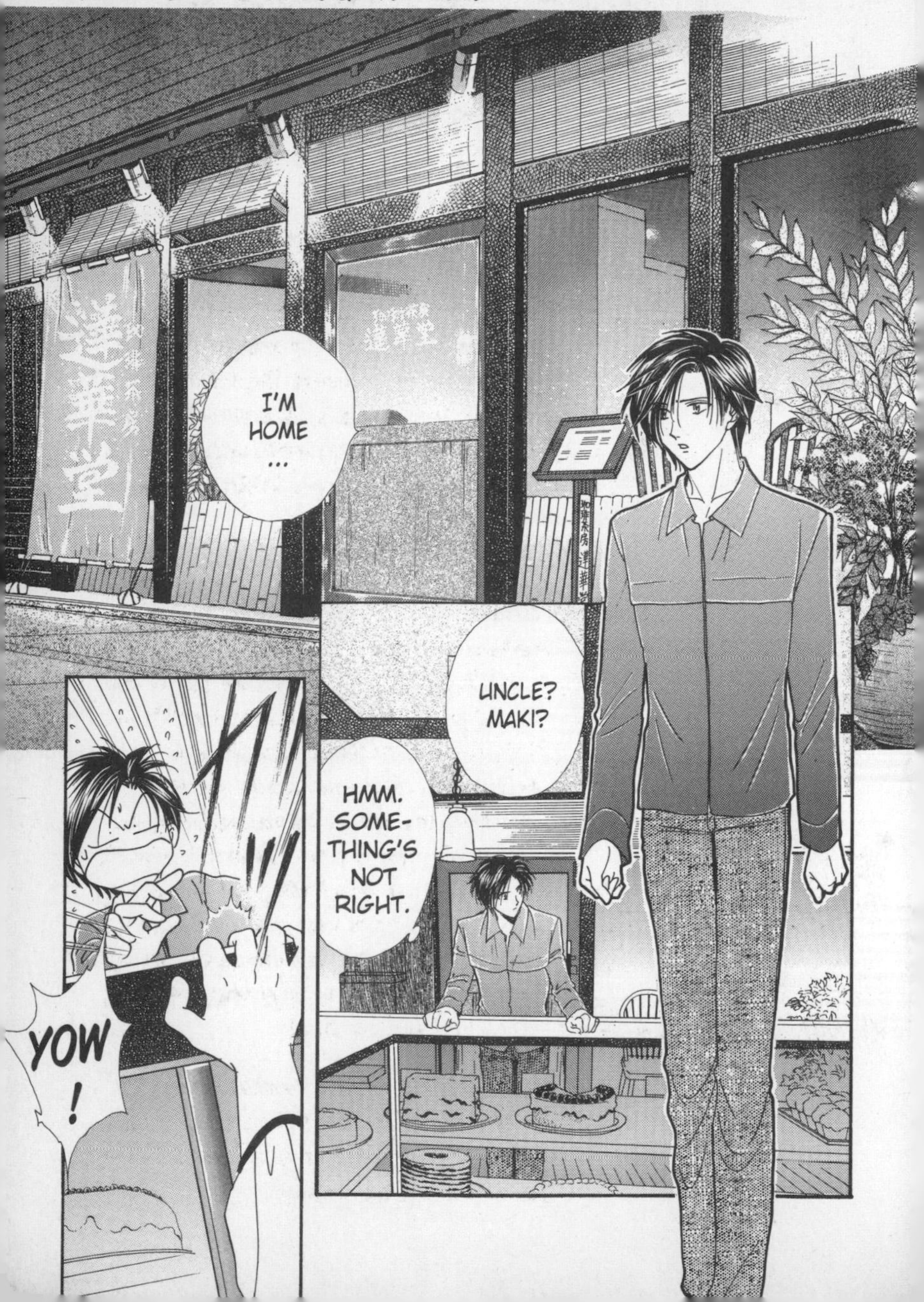
I'M HOME ...
UNCLE? MAKI?
HMM. SOMETHING'S NOT RIGHT.
YOW!

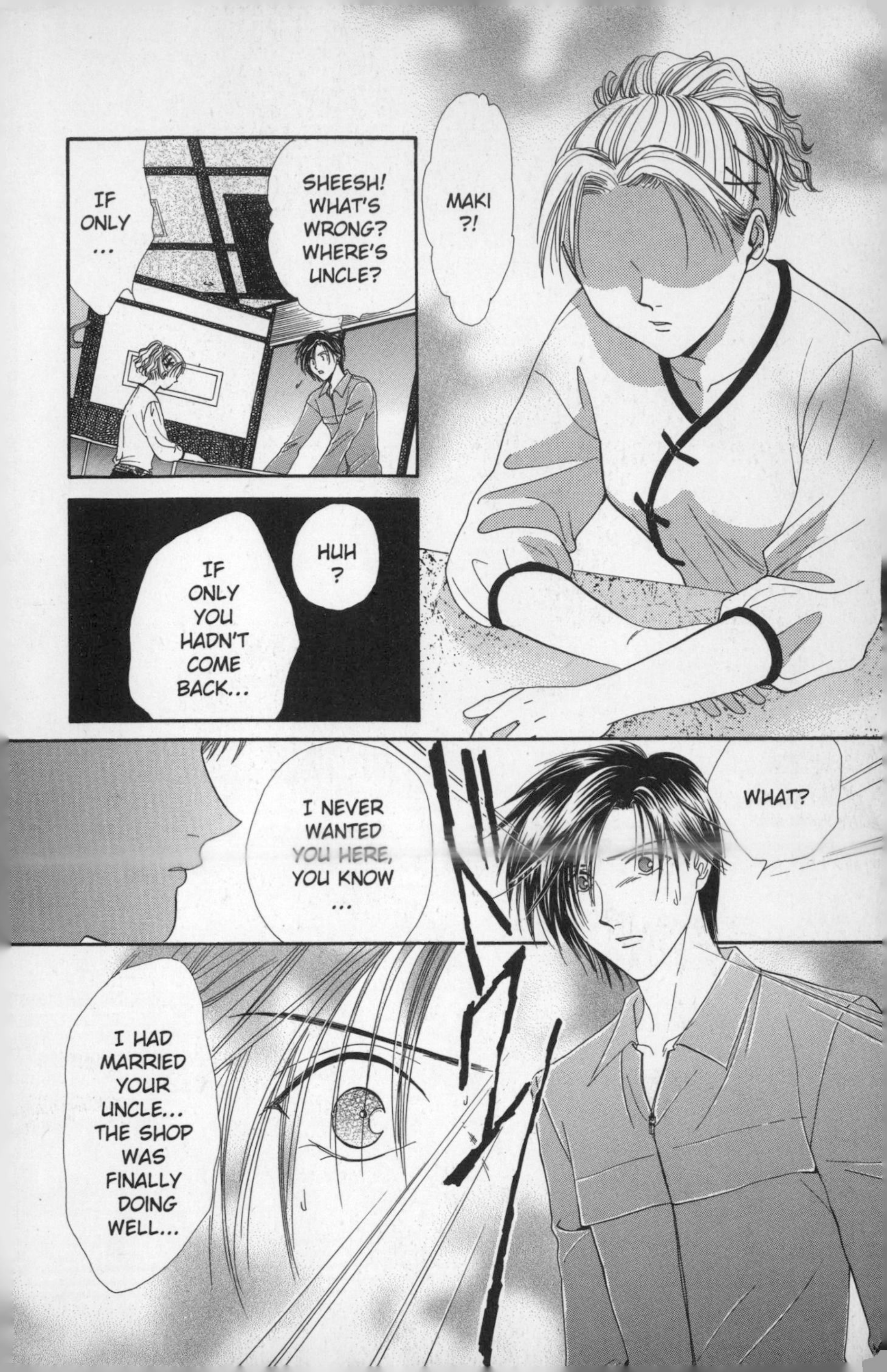

MAKI ?!
SHEESH! WHAT'S WRONG? WHERE'S UNCLE?
IF ONLY ...
HUH ?
IF ONLY YOU HADN'T COME BACK...
I NEVER WANTED YOU HERE, YOU KNOW ...
WHAT?
I HAD MARRIED YOUR UNCLE... THE SHOP WAS FINALLY DOING WELL...

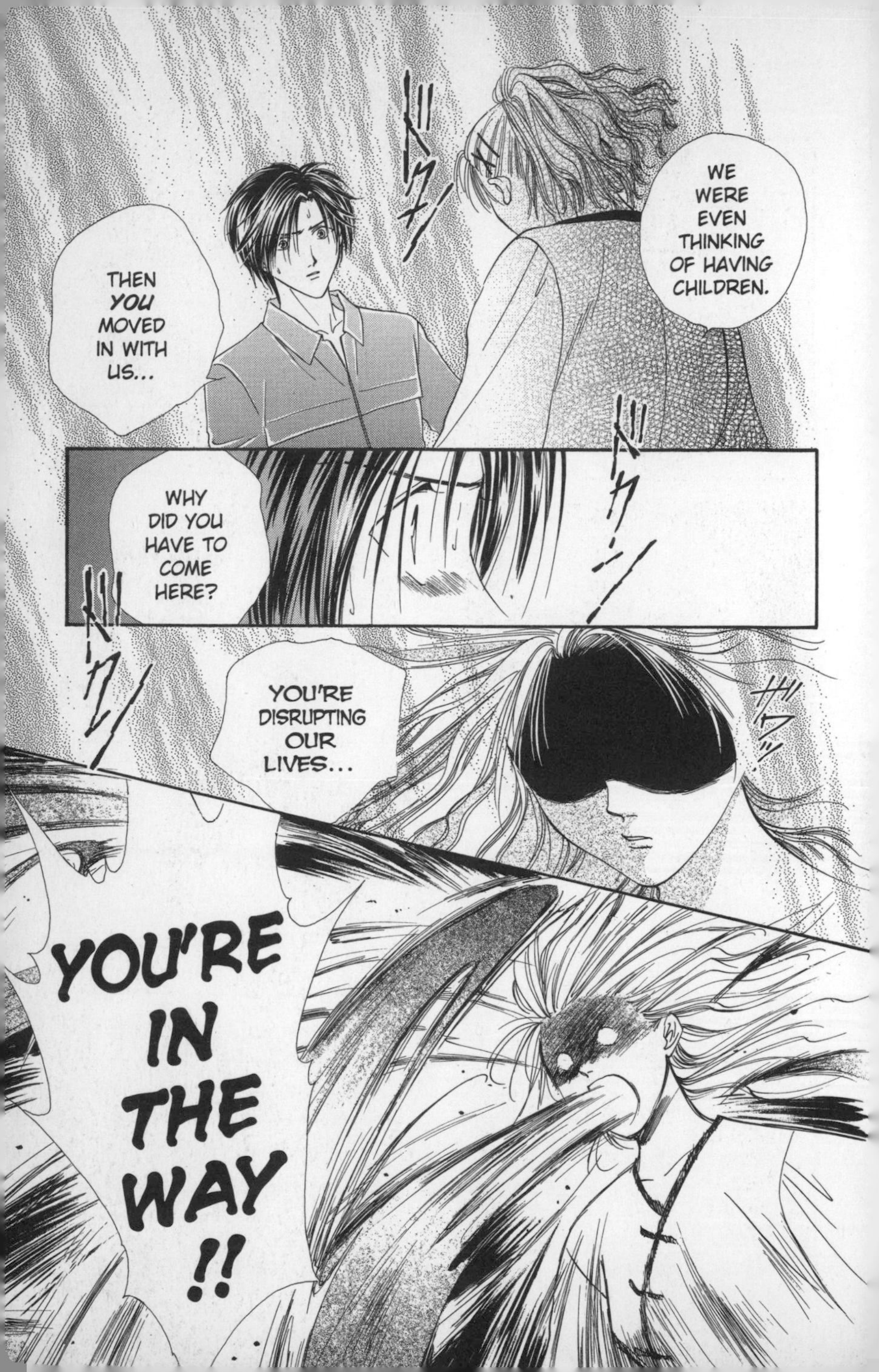
WE WERE EVEN THINKING OF HAVING CHILDREN.
THEN *YOU* MOVED IN WITH US...
WHY DID YOU HAVE TO COME HERE?
YOU'RE DISRUPTING OUR LIVES...
YOU'RE IN THE WAY!!

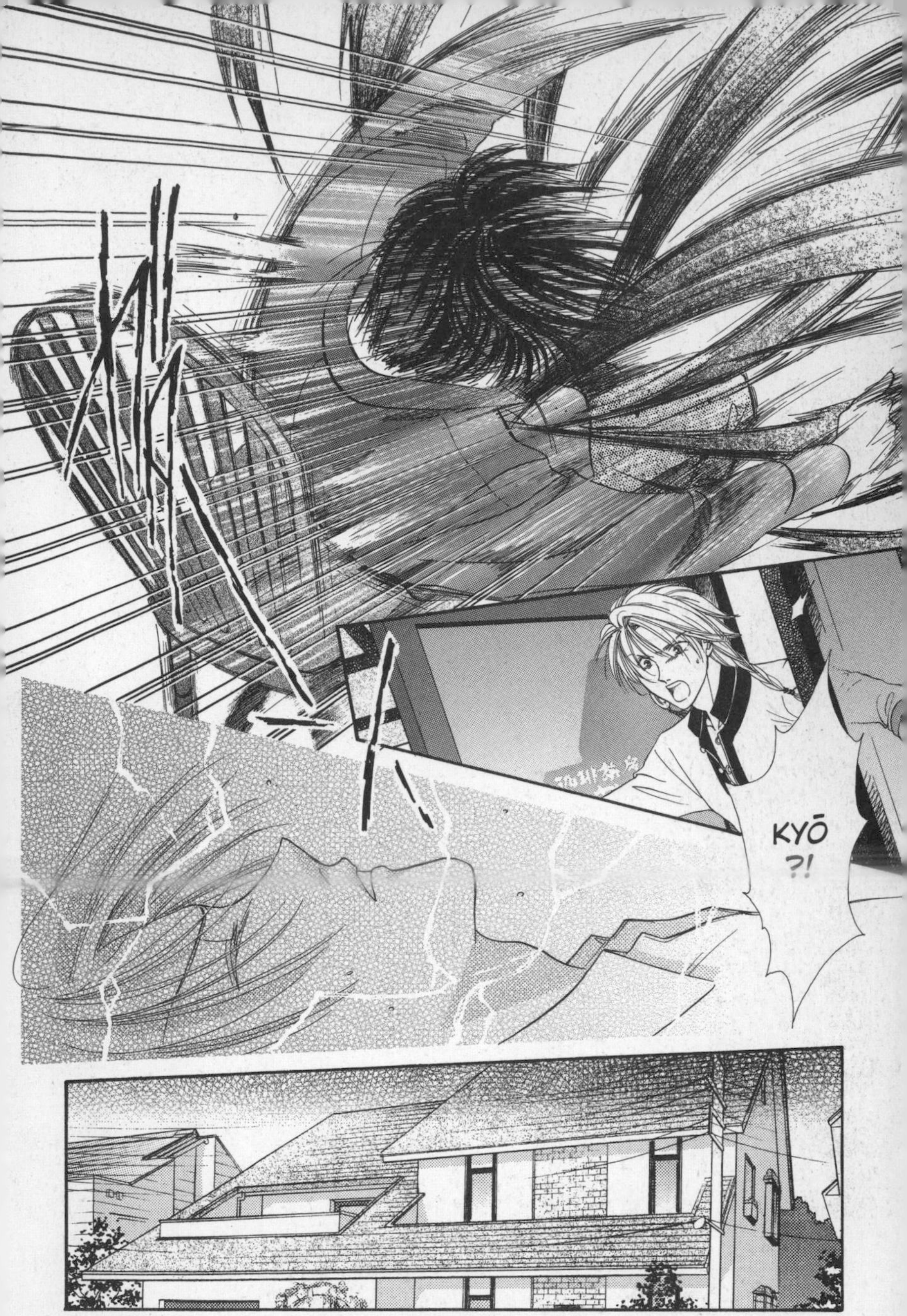
KYŌ
?!

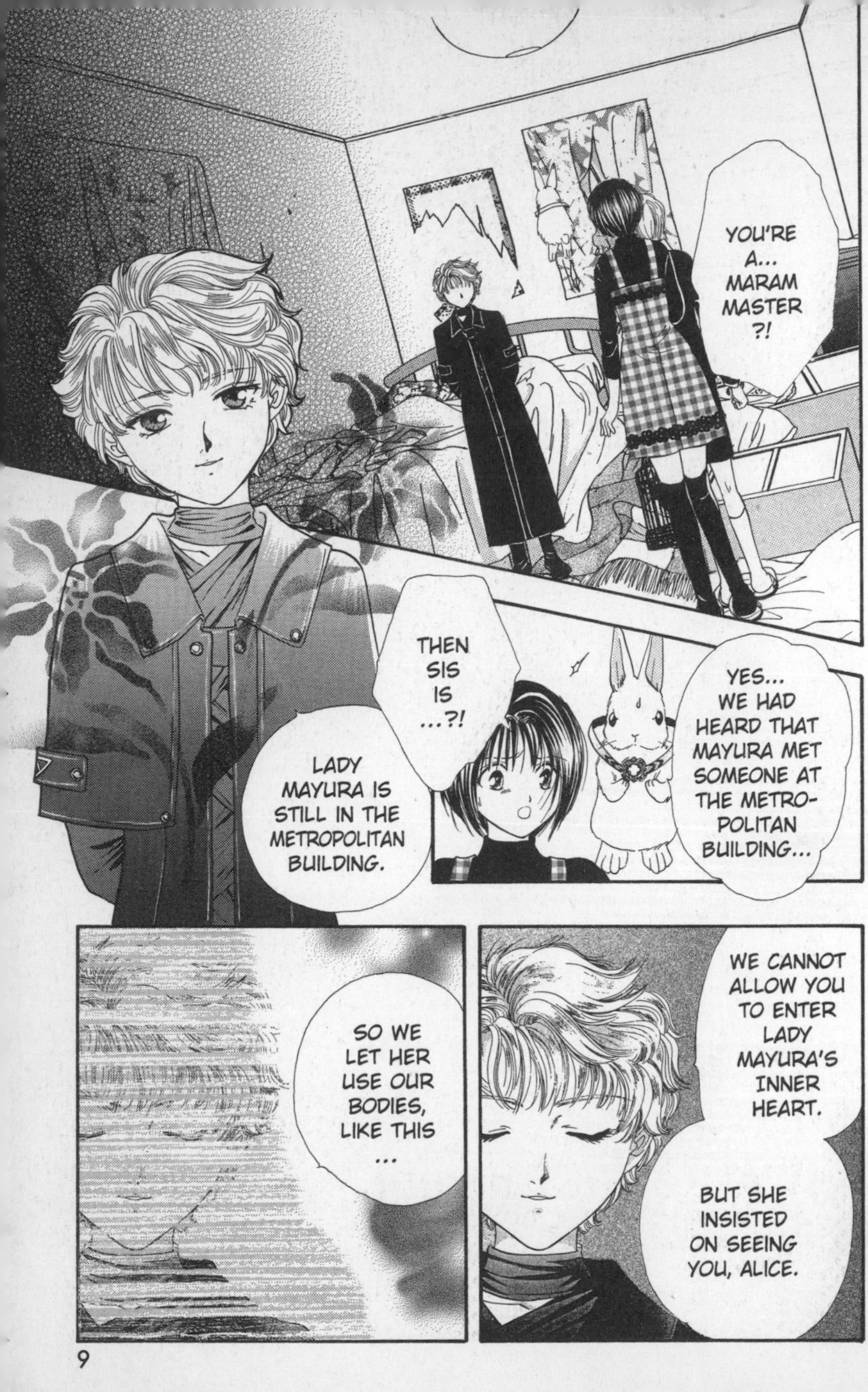
YOU'RE A... MARAM MASTER ?!
YES... WE HAD HEARD THAT MAYURA MET SOMEONE AT THE METRO-POLITAN BUILDING...
THEN SIS IS ...?!
LADY MAYURA IS STILL IN THE METROPOLITAN BUILDING.
WE CANNOT ALLOW YOU TO ENTER LADY MAYURA'S INNER HEART.
BUT SHE INSISTED ON SEEING YOU, ALICE.
SO WE LET HER USE OUR BODIES, LIKE THIS ...

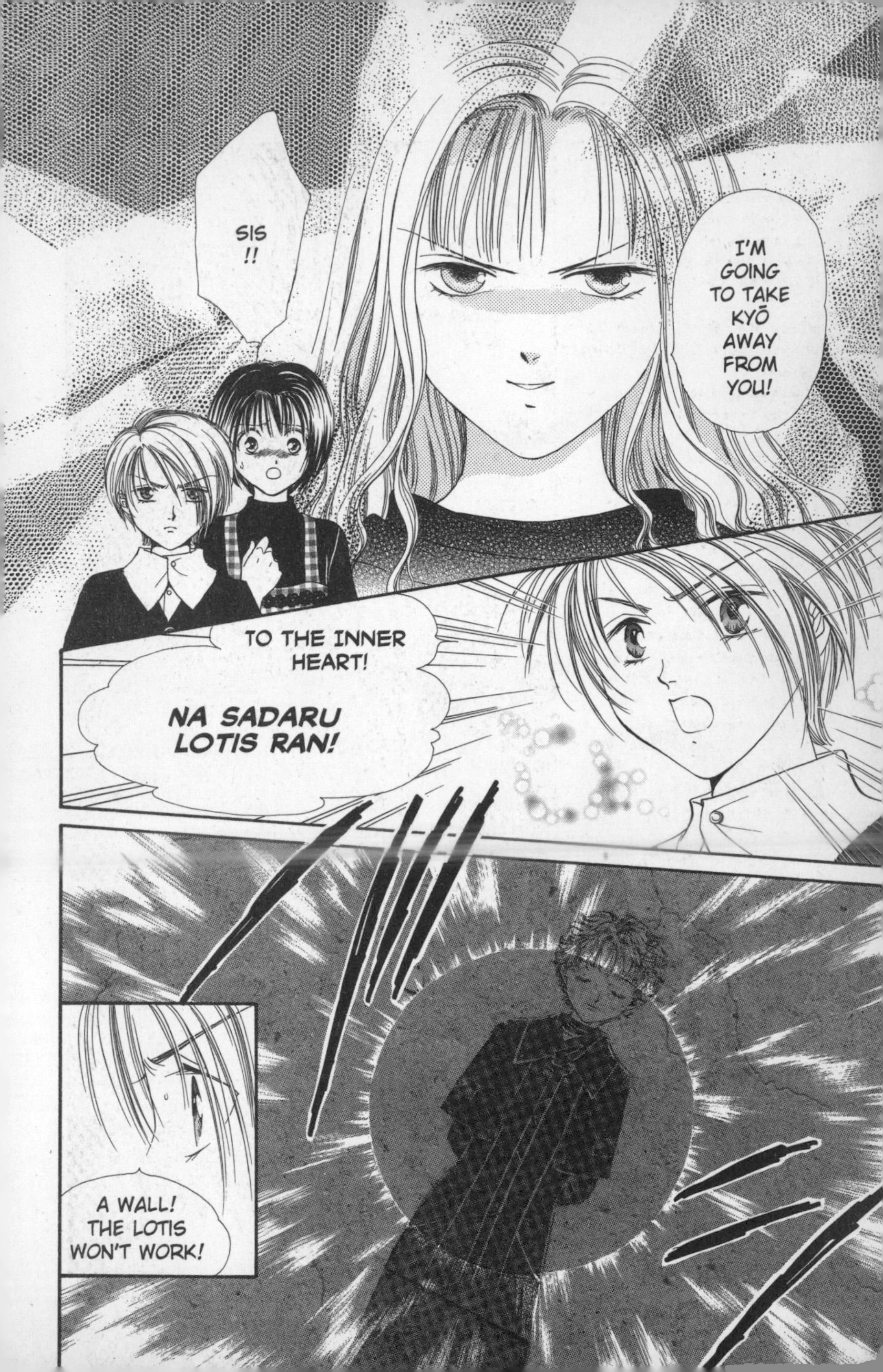

I'M GOING TO TAKE KYŌ AWAY FROM YOU!
SIS !!
TO THE INNER HEART!
NA SADARU LOTIS RAN!
A WALL! THE LOTIS WON'T WORK!

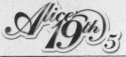

Ugh. Hot!! (I'm writing this on 9/2.)
Somehow my brain has shrunken beyond the sea-urchin-egg stage to the size of an amoeba. I don't want to keep writing, but I will. (Heh, heh)

Alice 19th has finally made it to Volume 5! Mayura's really losing it, huh?
Alice and Kyō are both the sincere type, so this is a real calamity!
Oh, yeah. The costumes changed in the last volume. Frey and the other Sacred Guides always wear fancy robes... vestments! But Alice and Kyō wear them in their hearts, so their vestments aren't usually visible. Only Lotis Masters or Maram Masters can see them. Well, I haven't made it clear what's reality and what's illusion, so you can interpret things however you want.
And this is a fantasy, so... (Don't run from it!)
In drawing this, though, Alice seems too meek for a heroine, so I'm having trouble.
On the other hand, the sympathy from the readers for Alice is the strongest for any character so far. Maybe more readers can identify with her....
Oh, the other day my assistant said, "It might be fun to make an Alice 19th card game!" (Smile) Maybe with 24 Lotis cards. When the swallow card stands alone, it's weak, but combined with a Chris card, it becomes powerful!
Or maybe each player could become a Master. Something like that. Talks were going on for an eventual Fushigi Yûgi game...

I wish some company would make one for me.

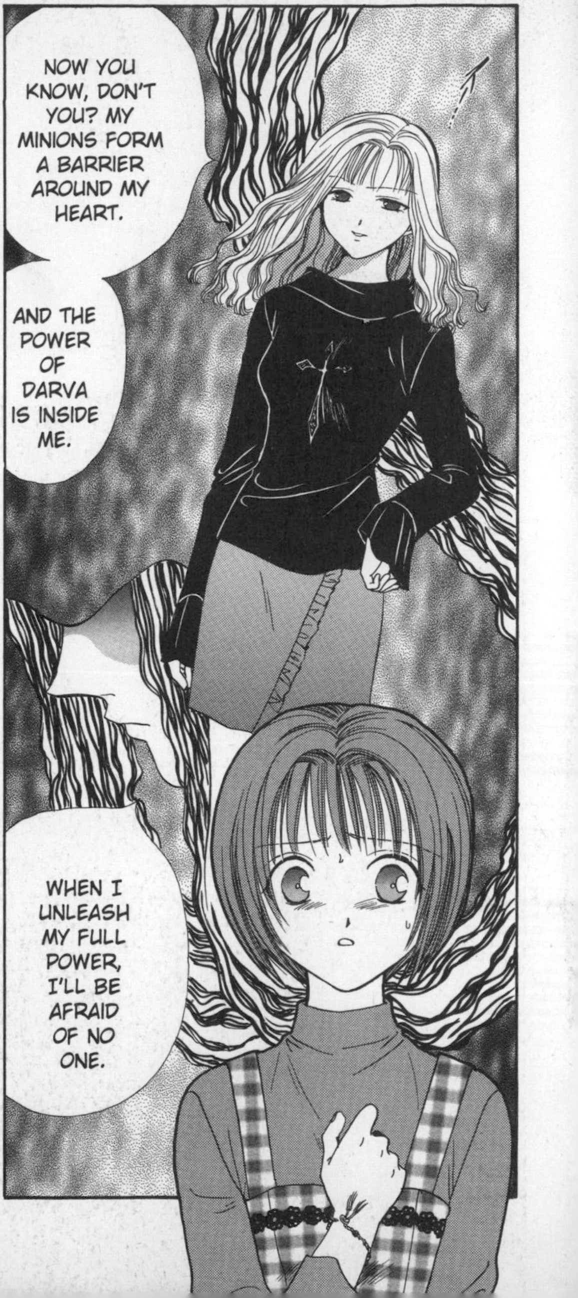
NOW YOU KNOW, DON'T YOU? MY MINIONS FORM A BARRIER AROUND MY HEART.
AND THE POWER OF DARVA IS INSIDE ME.
WHEN I UNLEASH MY FULL POWER, I'LL BE AFRAID OF NO ONE.

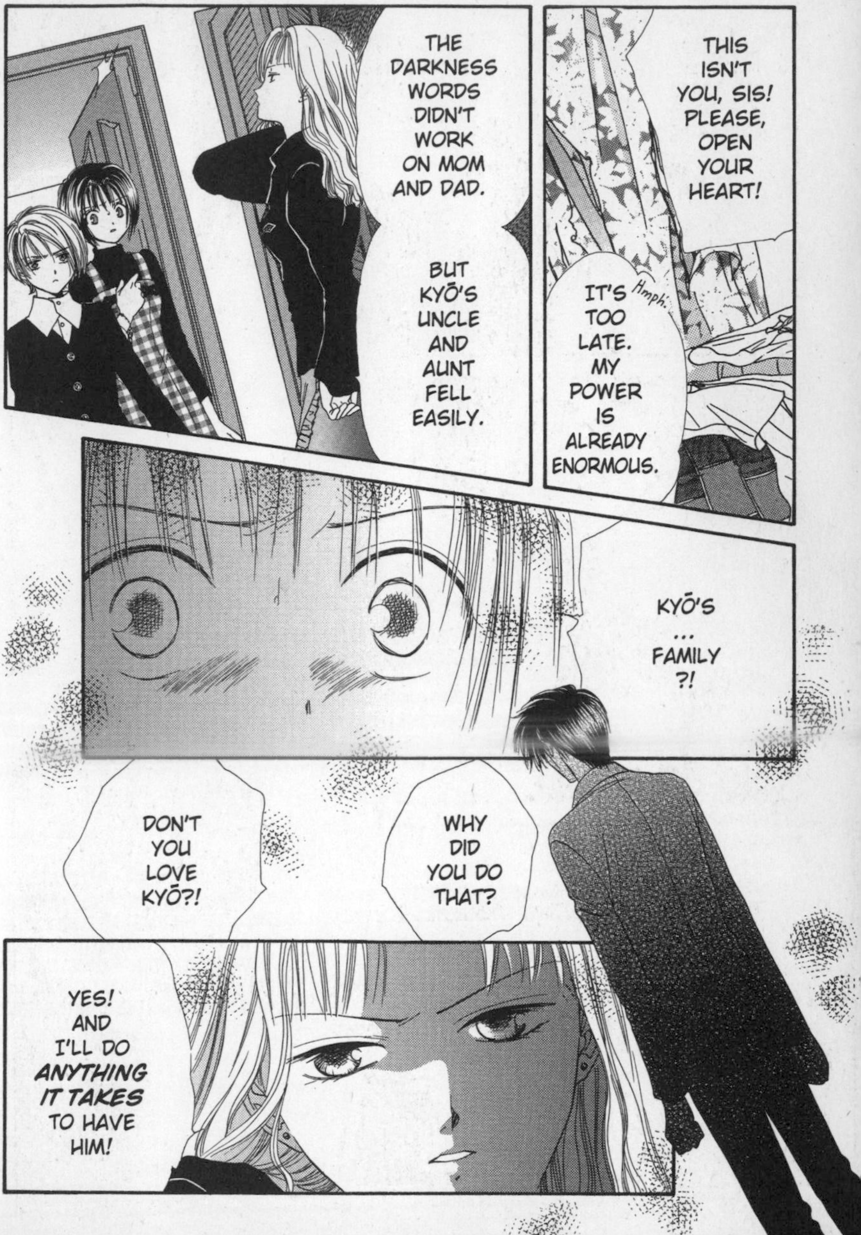
THIS ISN'T YOU, SIS! PLEASE, OPEN YOUR HEART!
Hmph.
IT'S TOO LATE. MY POWER IS ALREADY ENORMOUS.
THE DARKNESS WORDS DIDN'T WORK ON MOM AND DAD.
BUT KYŌ'S UNCLE AND AUNT FELL EASILY.
KYŌ'S ... FAMILY ?!
WHY DID YOU DO THAT?
DON'T YOU LOVE KYŌ?!
YES! AND I'LL DO *ANYTHING IT TAKES* TO HAVE HIM!

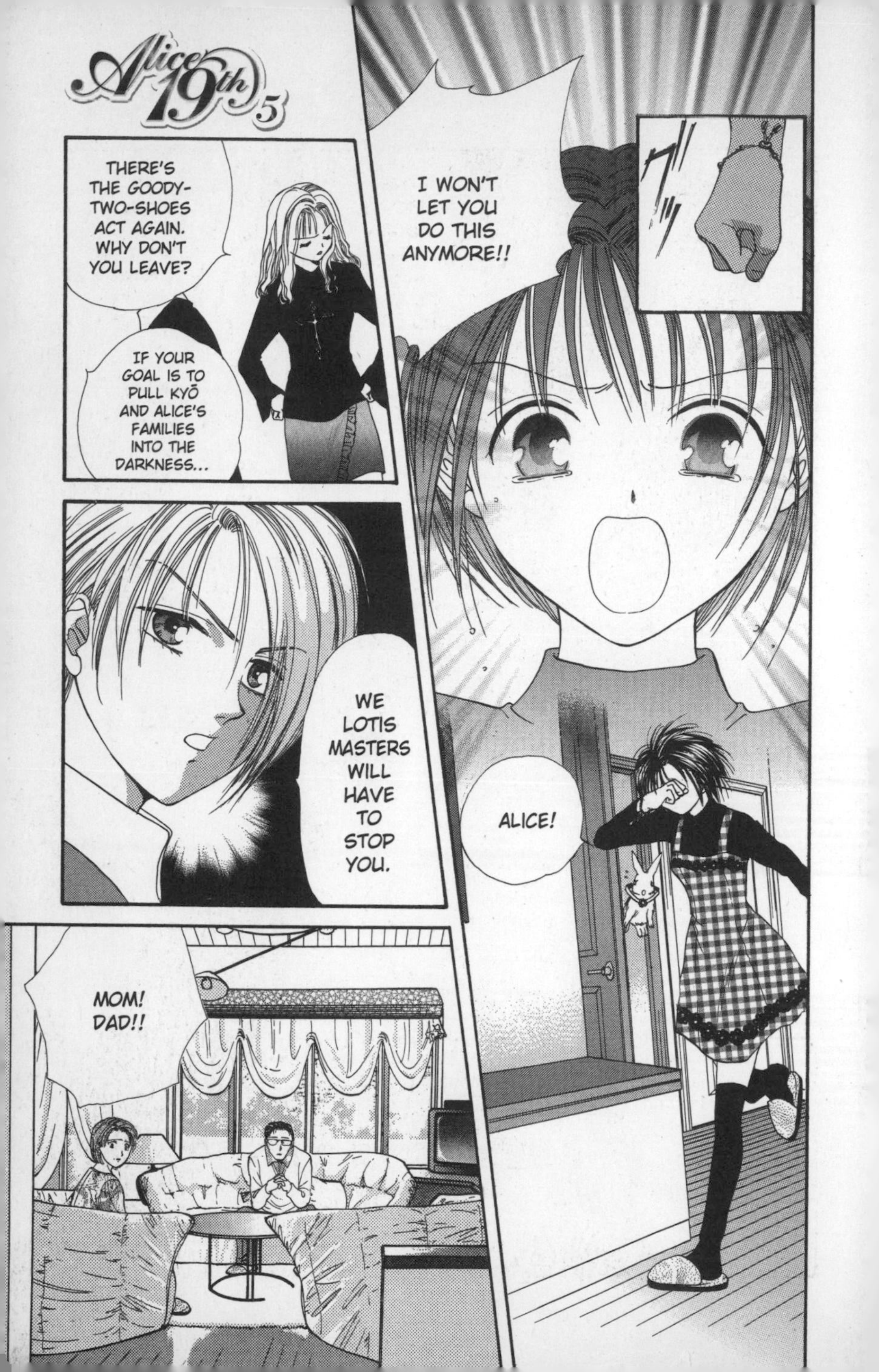
I WON'T LET YOU DO THIS ANYMORE!!
THERE'S THE GOODY-TWO-SHOES ACT AGAIN. WHY DON'T YOU LEAVE?
IF YOUR GOAL IS TO PULL KYŌ AND ALICE'S FAMILIES INTO THE DARKNESS...
WE LOTIS MASTERS WILL HAVE TO STOP YOU.
ALICE!
MOM! DAD!!

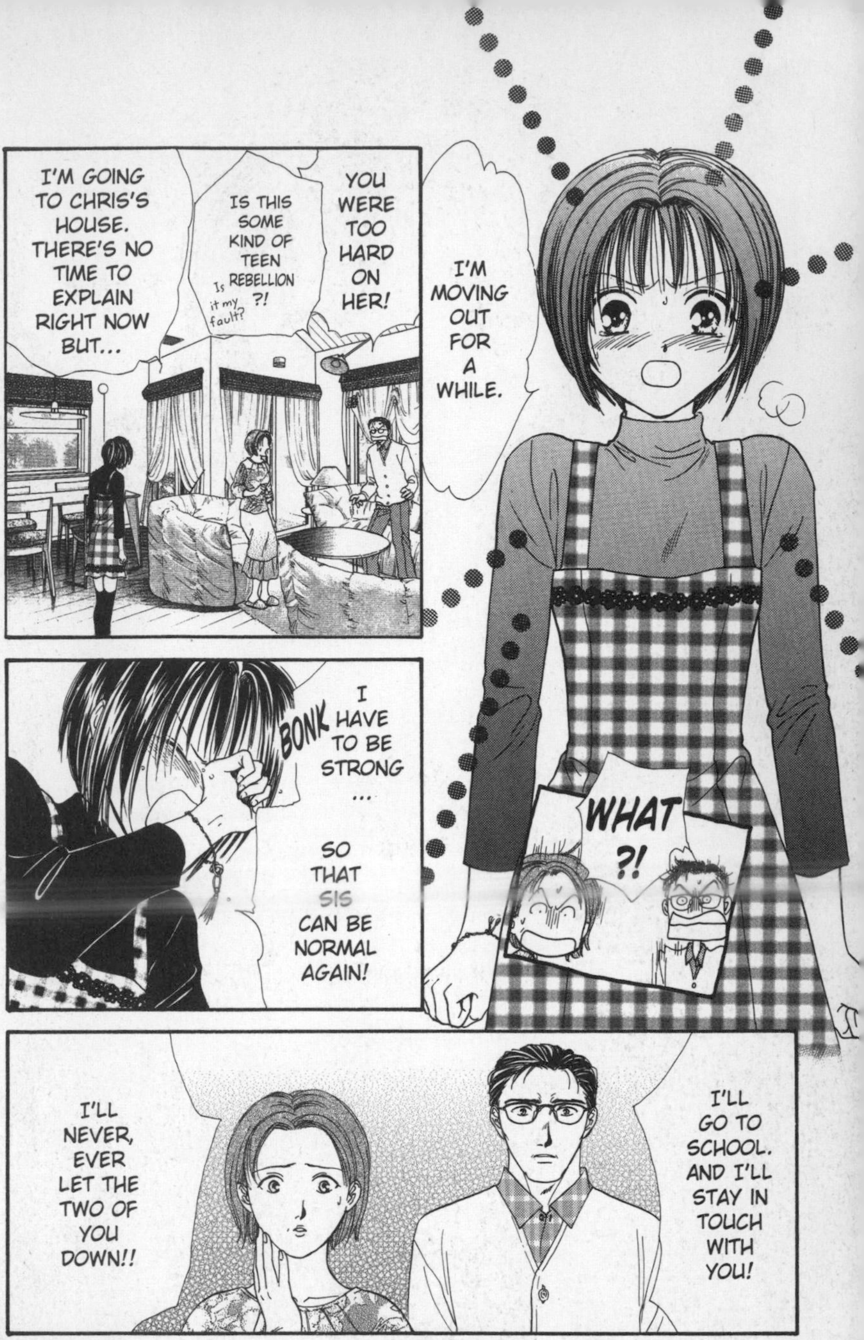
I'M MOVING OUT FOR A WHILE.
WHAT ?!
YOU WERE TOO HARD ON HER!
IS THIS SOME KIND OF TEEN REBELLION ?!
Is it my fault?
I'M GOING TO CHRIS'S HOUSE. THERE'S NO TIME TO EXPLAIN RIGHT NOW BUT...
BONK
I HAVE TO BE STRONG ...
SO THAT SIS CAN BE NORMAL AGAIN!
I'LL GO TO SCHOOL. AND I'LL STAY IN TOUCH WITH YOU!
I'LL NEVER, EVER LET THE TWO OF YOU DOWN!!

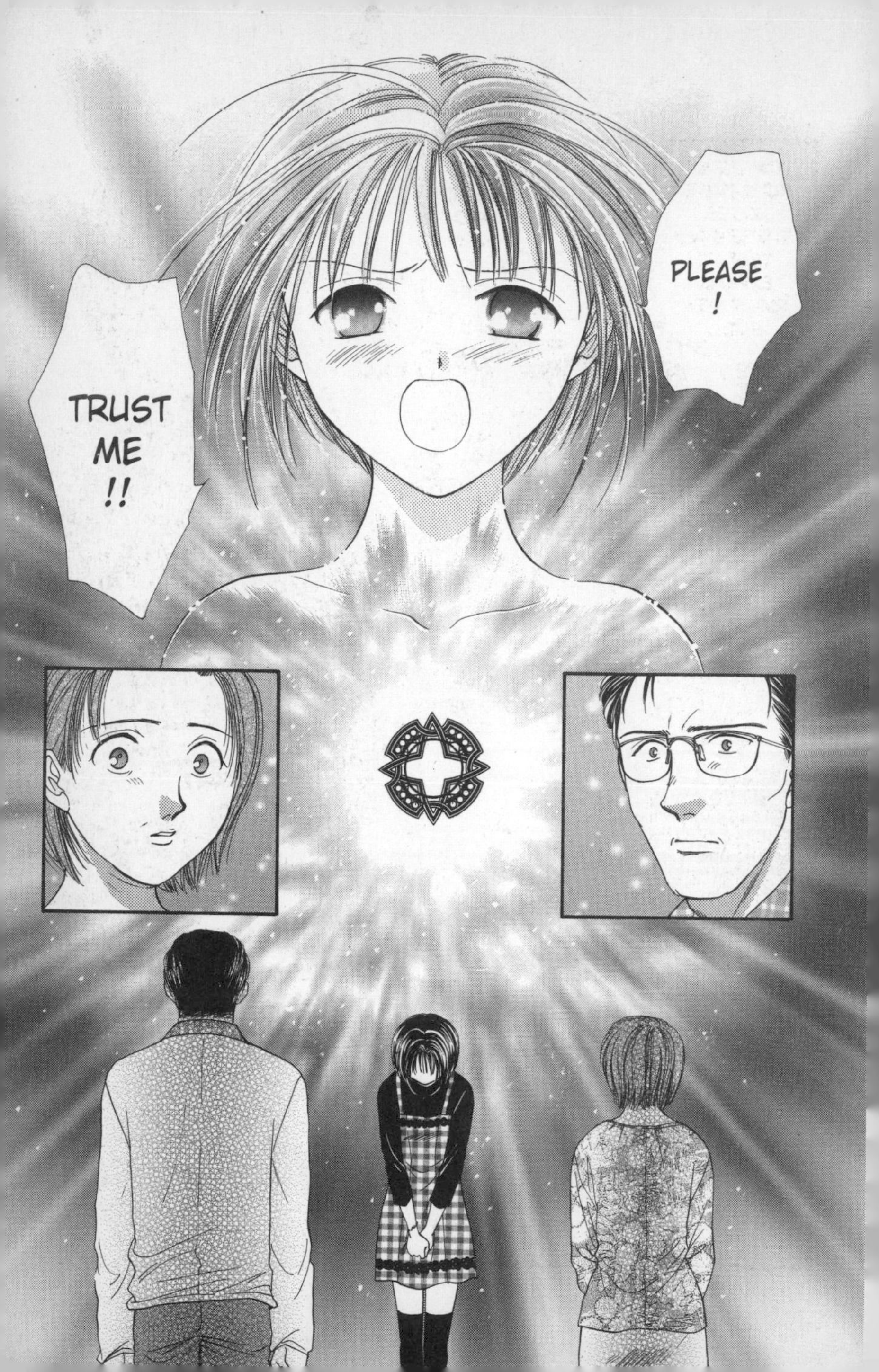
PLEASE!
TRUST ME!!

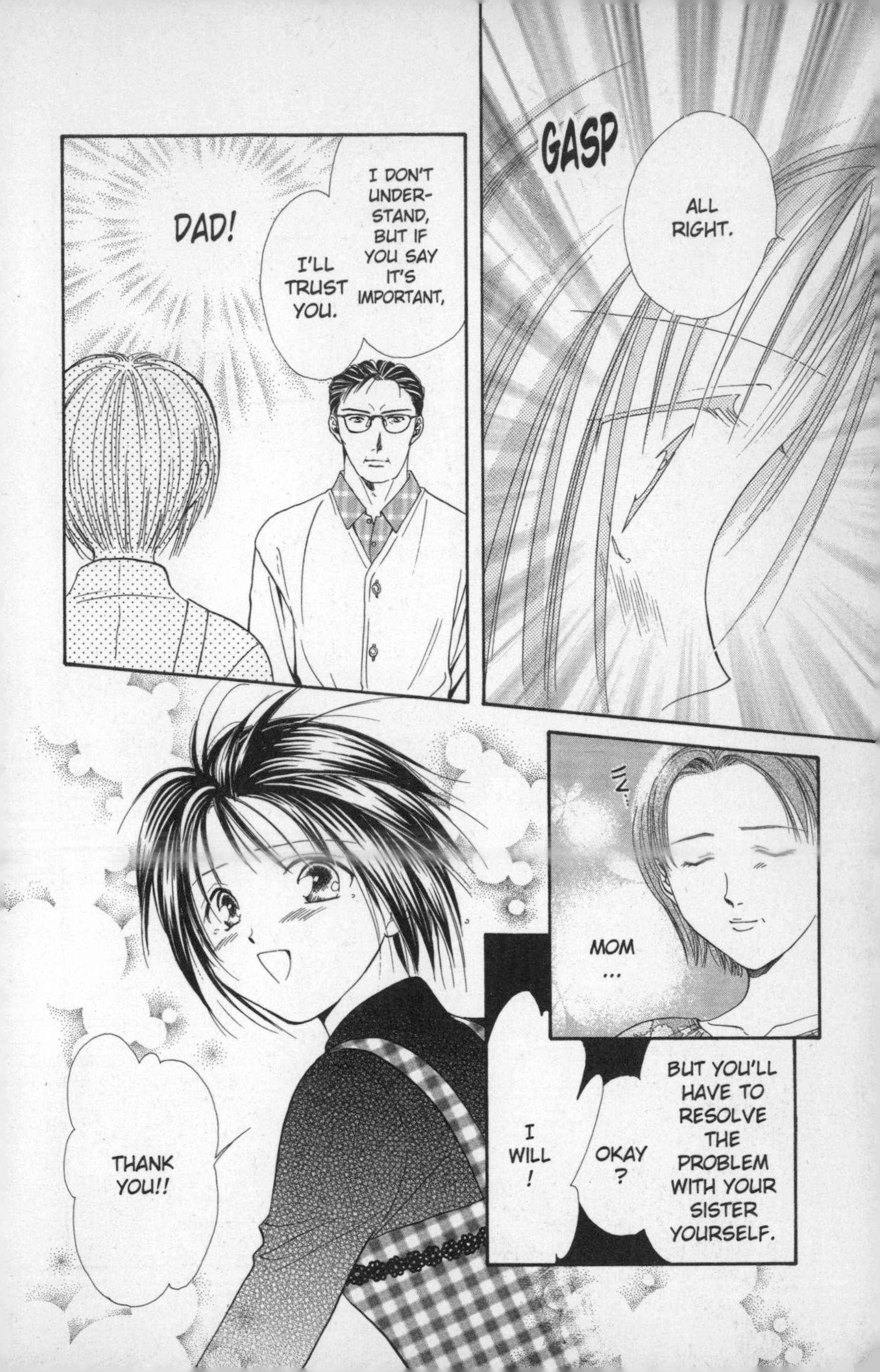

GASP
ALL RIGHT.
DAD!
I DON'T UNDER-STAND, BUT IF YOU SAY IT'S IMPORTANT,
I'LL TRUST YOU.
MOM ...
BUT YOU'LL HAVE TO RESOLVE THE PROBLEM WITH YOUR SISTER YOURSELF.
OKAY ?
I WILL !
THANK YOU!!

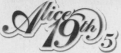

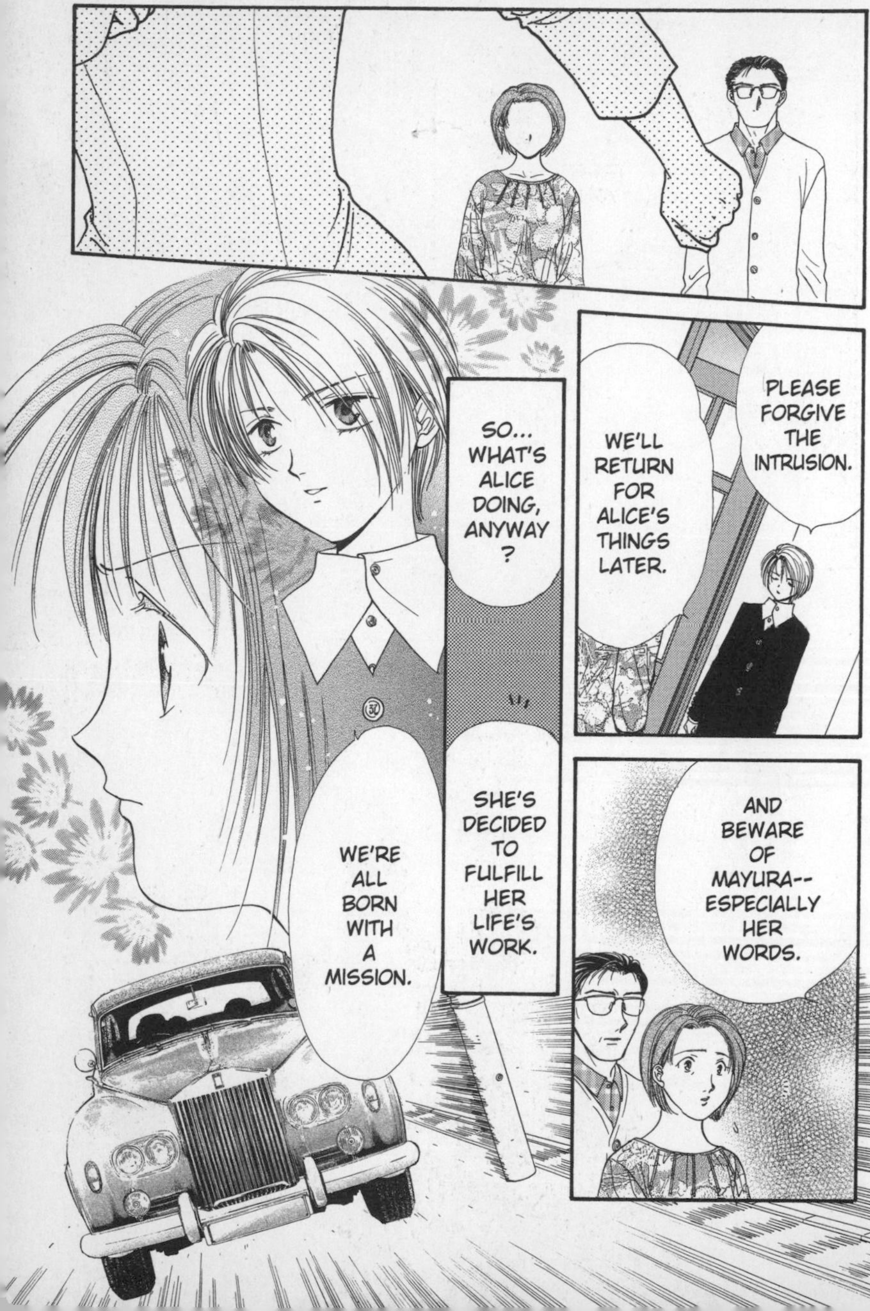
PLEASE FORGIVE THE INTRUSION.
WE'LL RETURN FOR ALICE'S THINGS LATER.
AND BEWARE OF MAYURA-- ESPECIALLY HER WORDS.
SO... WHAT'S ALICE DOING, ANYWAY?
SHE'S DECIDED TO FULFILL HER LIFE'S WORK.
WE'RE ALL BORN WITH A MISSION.

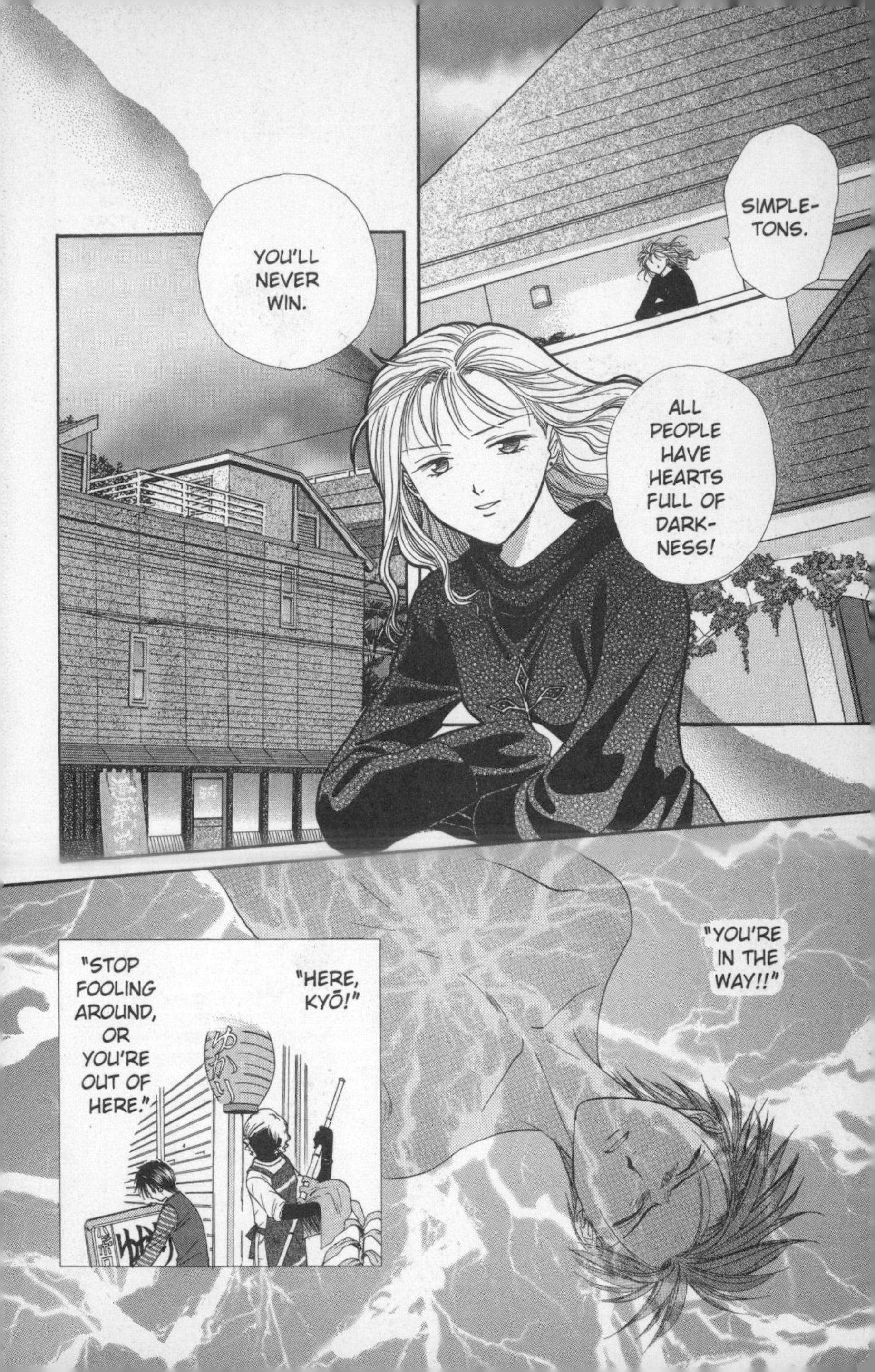
SIMPLE-TONS.
ALL PEOPLE HAVE HEARTS FULL OF DARK-NESS!
YOU'LL NEVER WIN.
"YOU'RE IN THE WAY!!"
"HERE, KYŌ!"
"STOP FOOLING AROUND, OR YOU'RE OUT OF HERE."

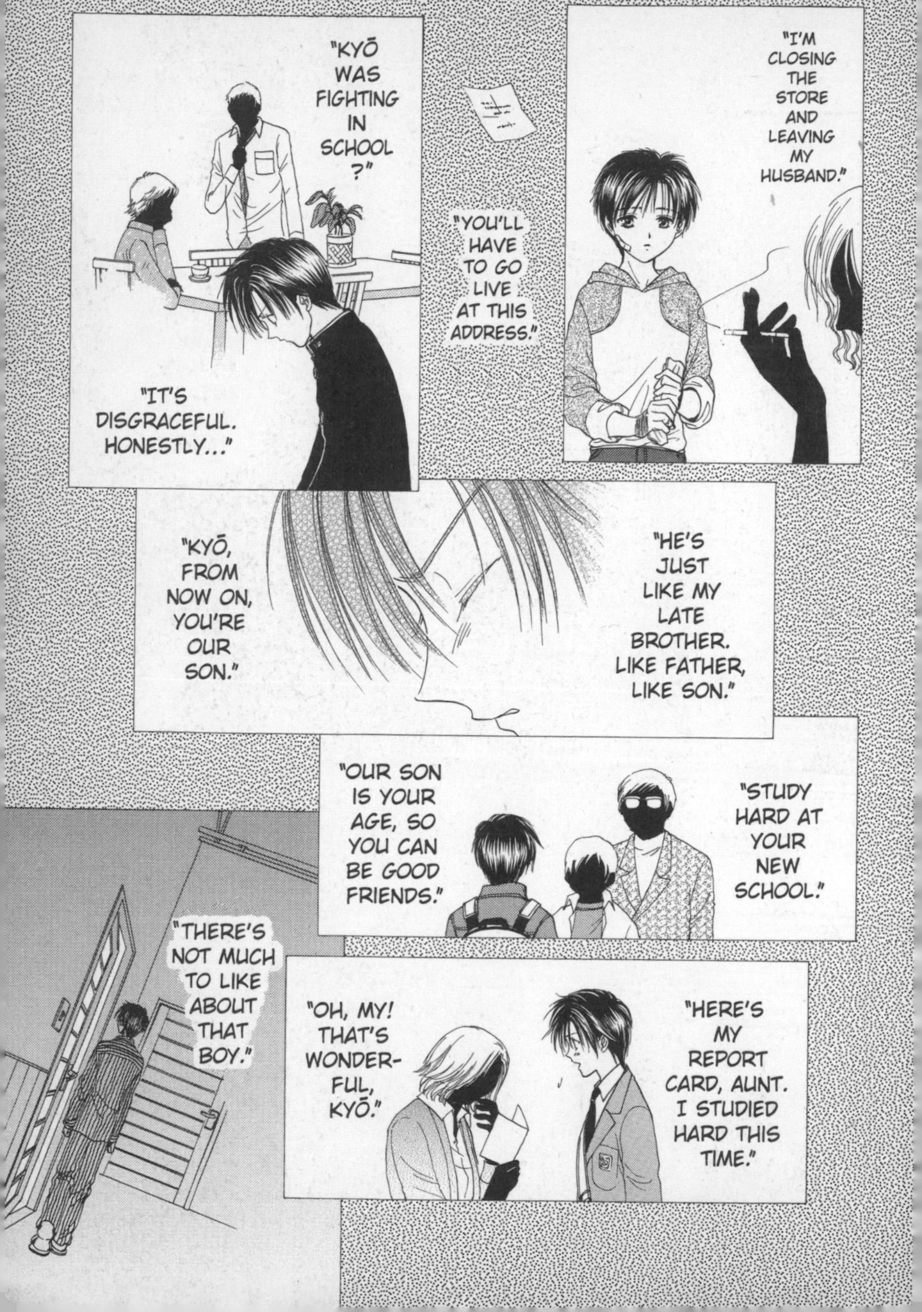
"I'M CLOSING THE STORE AND LEAVING MY HUSBAND."
"YOU'LL HAVE TO GO LIVE AT THIS ADDRESS."
"KYŌ WAS FIGHTING IN SCHOOL?"
"IT'S DISGRACEFUL. HONESTLY..."
"HE'S JUST LIKE MY LATE BROTHER. LIKE FATHER, LIKE SON."
"KYŌ, FROM NOW ON, YOU'RE OUR SON."
"STUDY HARD AT YOUR NEW SCHOOL."
"OUR SON IS YOUR AGE, SO YOU CAN BE GOOD FRIENDS."
"HERE'S MY REPORT CARD, AUNT. I STUDIED HARD THIS TIME."
"OH, MY! THAT'S WONDERFUL, KYŌ."
"THERE'S NOT MUCH TO LIKE ABOUT THAT BOY."

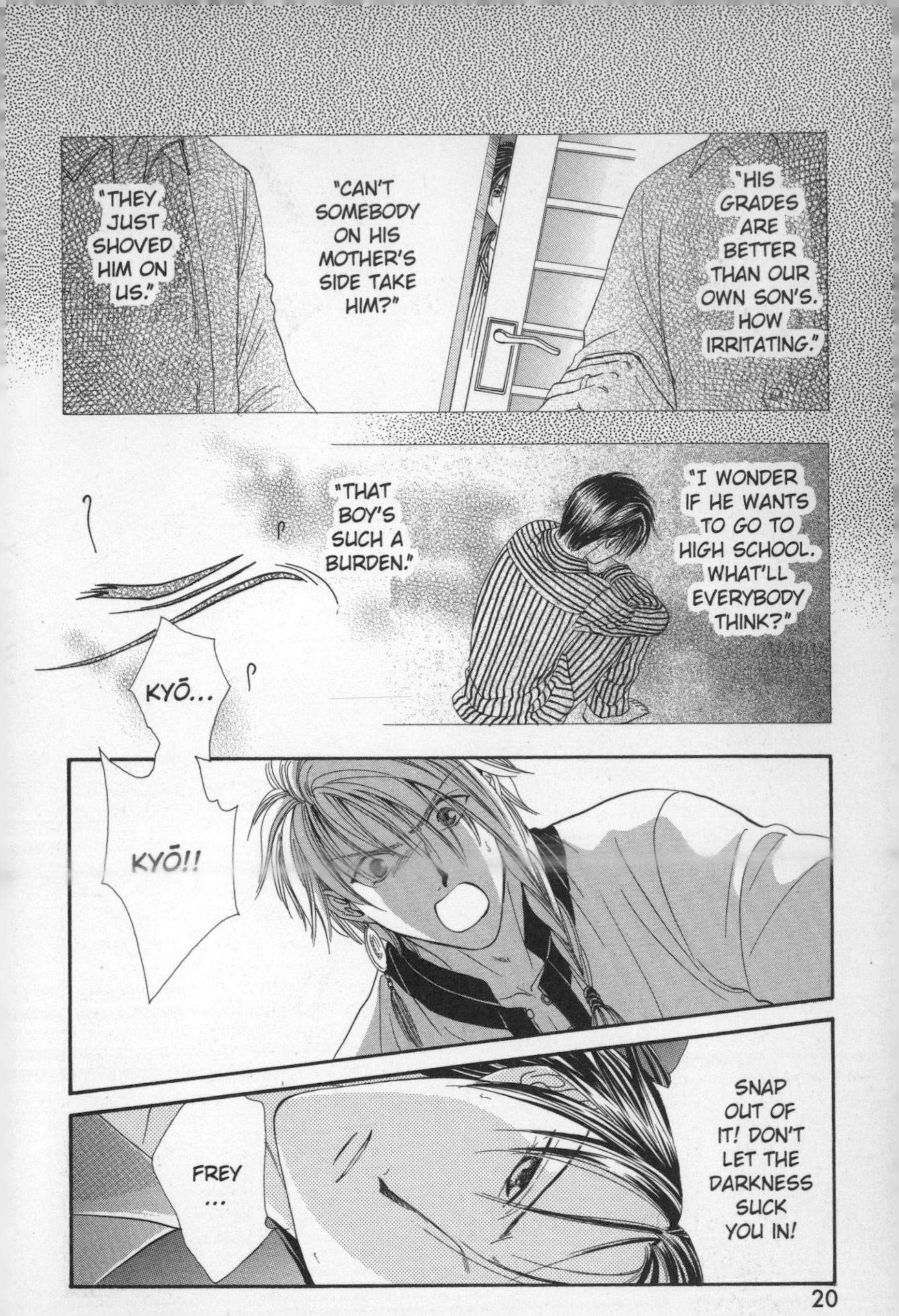
"HIS GRADES ARE BETTER THAN OUR OWN SON'S. HOW IRRITATING."
"CAN'T SOMEBODY ON HIS MOTHER'S SIDE TAKE HIM?"
"THEY JUST SHOVED HIM ON US."
"I WONDER IF HE WANTS TO GO TO HIGH SCHOOL. WHAT'LL EVERYBODY THINK?"
"THAT BOY'S SUCH A BURDEN."
KYŌ...
KYŌ!!
SNAP OUT OF IT! DON'T LET THE DARKNESS SUCK YOU IN!
FREY ...

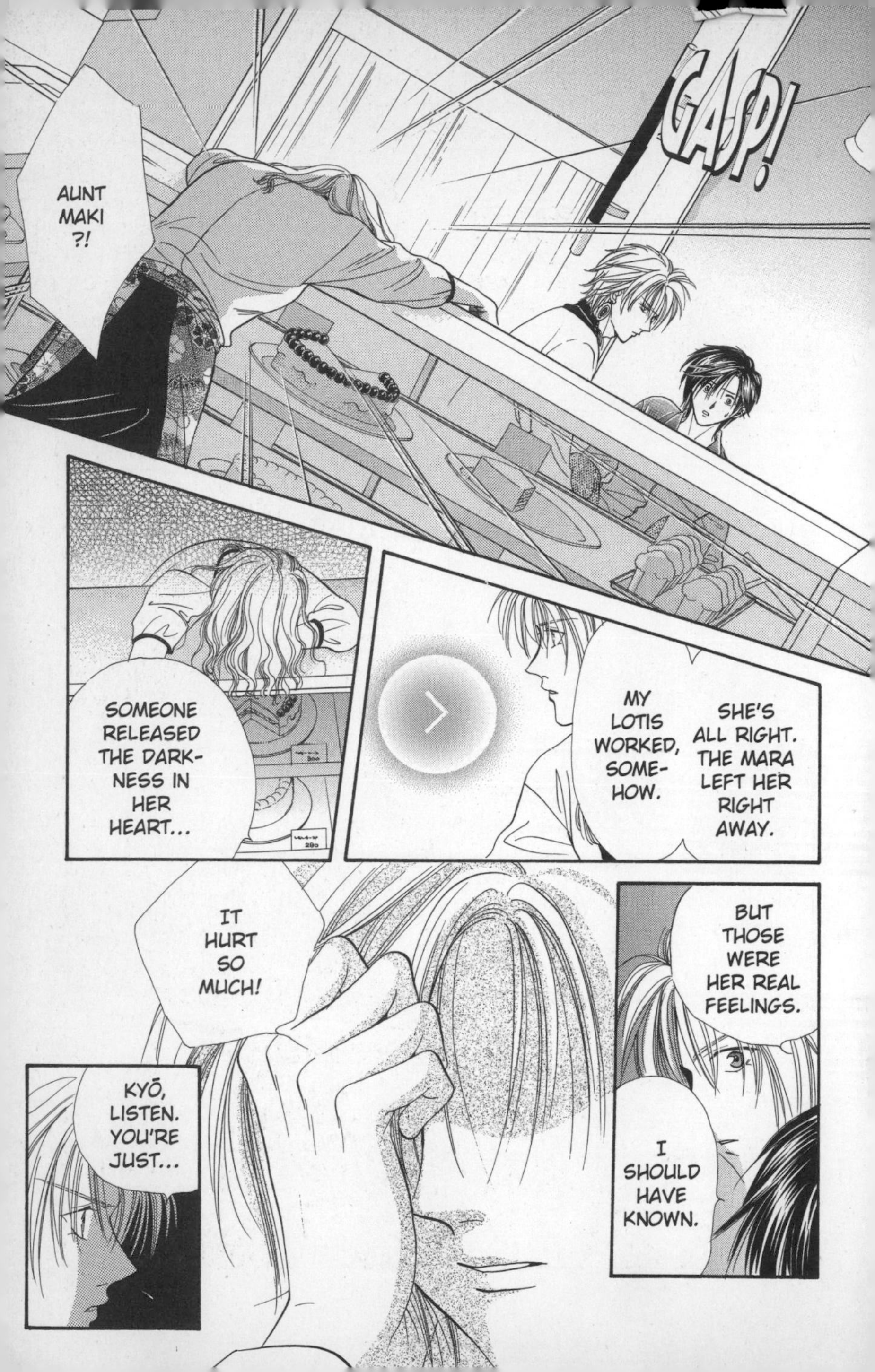
GASP!
AUNT MAKI ?!
SHE'S ALL RIGHT. THE MARA LEFT HER RIGHT AWAY.
MY LOTIS WORKED, SOME-HOW.
SOMEONE RELEASED THE DARK-NESS IN HER HEART...
BUT THOSE WERE HER REAL FEELINGS.
I SHOULD HAVE KNOWN.
IT HURT SO MUCH!
KYŌ, LISTEN. YOU'RE JUST...

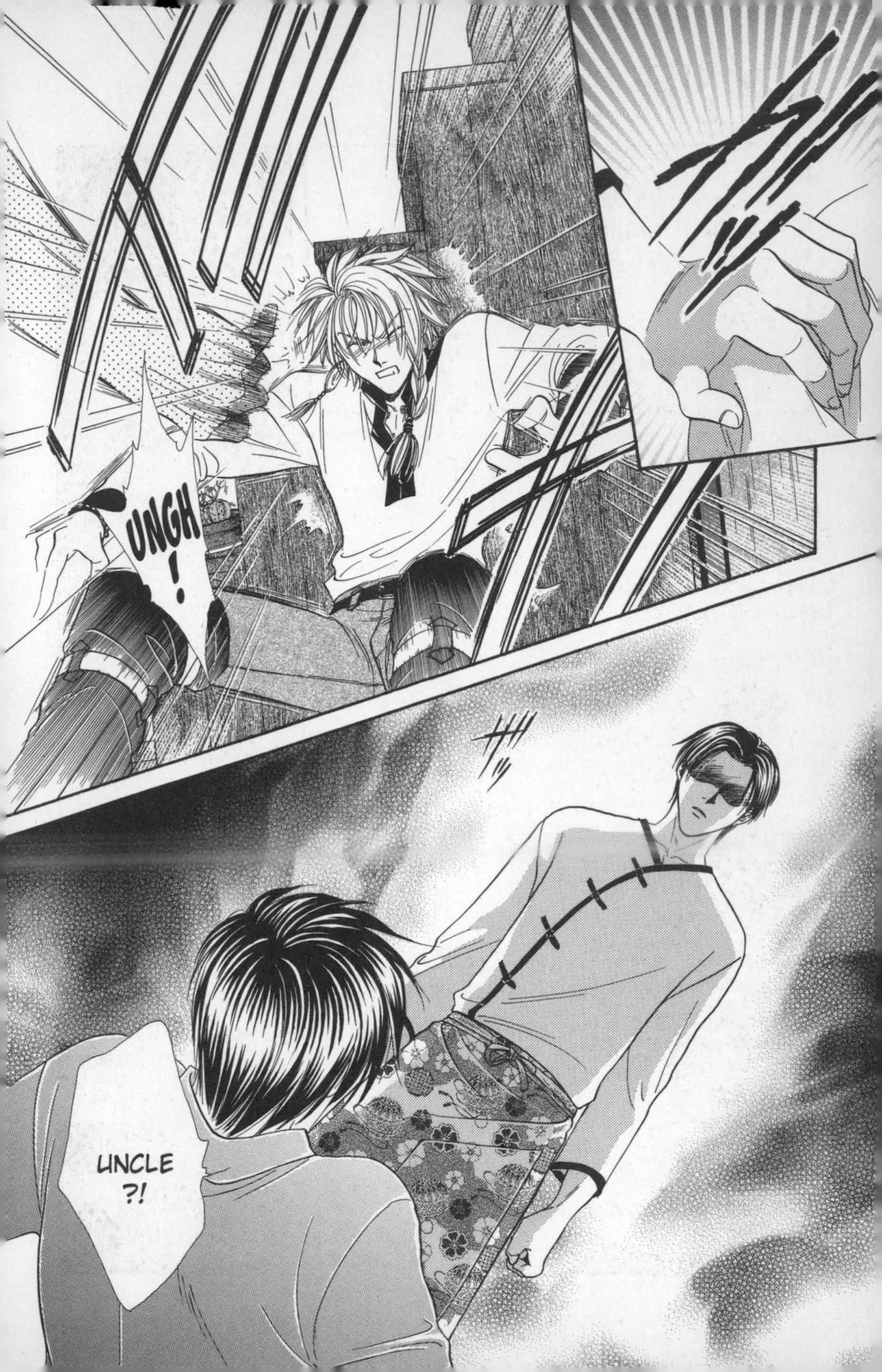
UNGH
!
UNCLE
?!

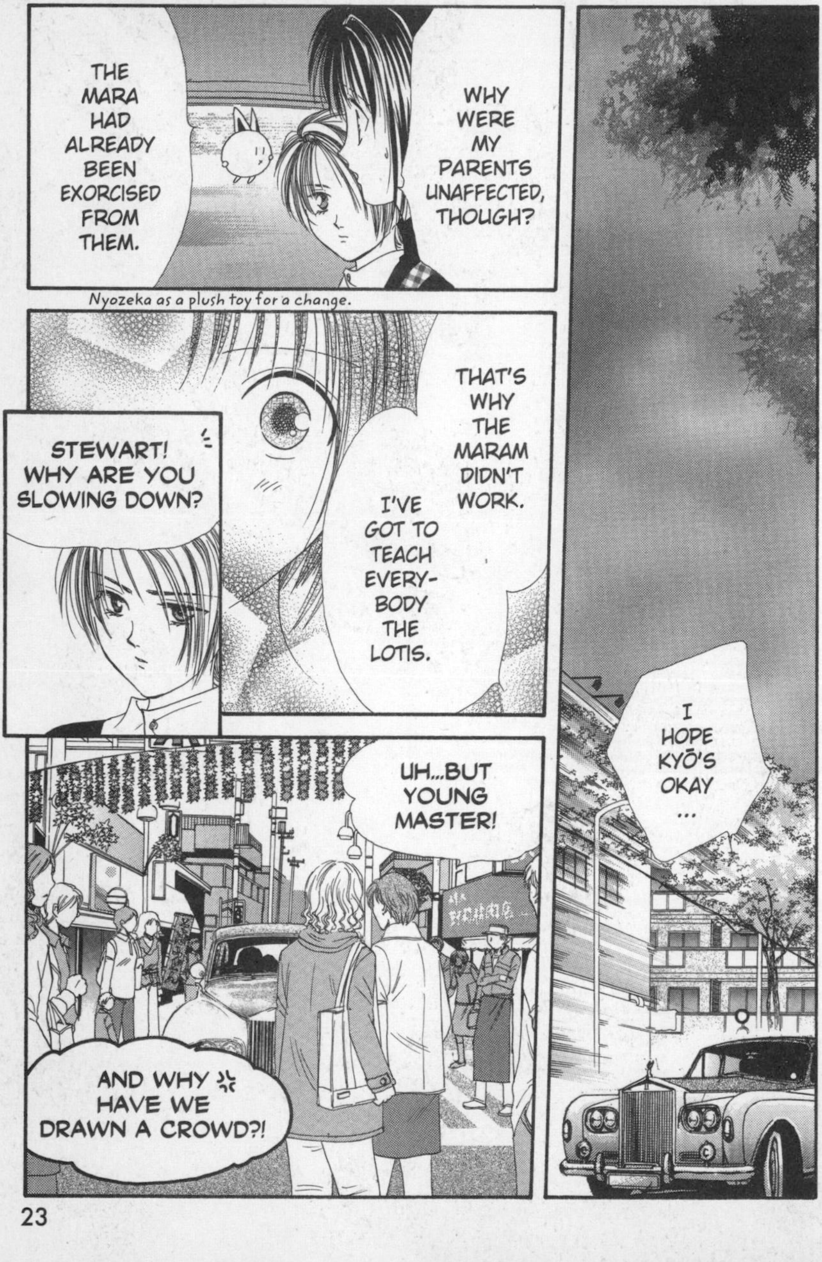
I HOPE KYŌ'S OKAY ...
WHY WERE MY PARENTS UNAFFECTED, THOUGH?
THE MARA HAD ALREADY BEEN EXORCISED FROM THEM.
Nyozeka as a plush toy for a change.
THAT'S WHY THE MARAM DIDN'T WORK.
I'VE GOT TO TEACH EVERYBODY THE LOTIS.
STEWART! WHY ARE YOU SLOWING DOWN?
UH...BUT YOUNG MASTER!
AND WHY HAVE WE DRAWN A CROWD?!

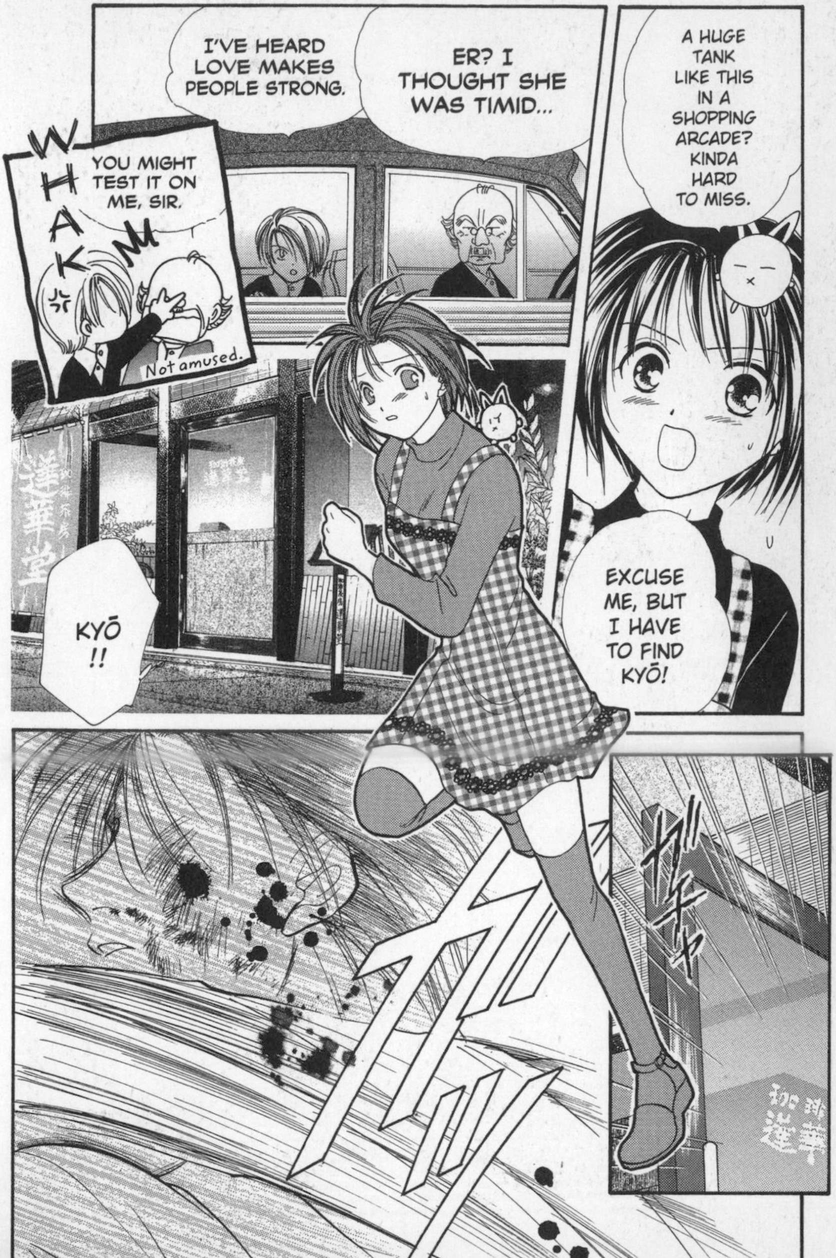
A HUGE TANK LIKE THIS IN A SHOPPING ARCADE? KINDA HARD TO MISS.
EXCUSE ME, BUT I HAVE TO FIND KYŌ!
ER? I THOUGHT SHE WAS TIMID...
I'VE HEARD LOVE MAKES PEOPLE STRONG.
WHAKM
YOU MIGHT TEST IT ON ME, SIR.
Not amused.
KYŌ !!

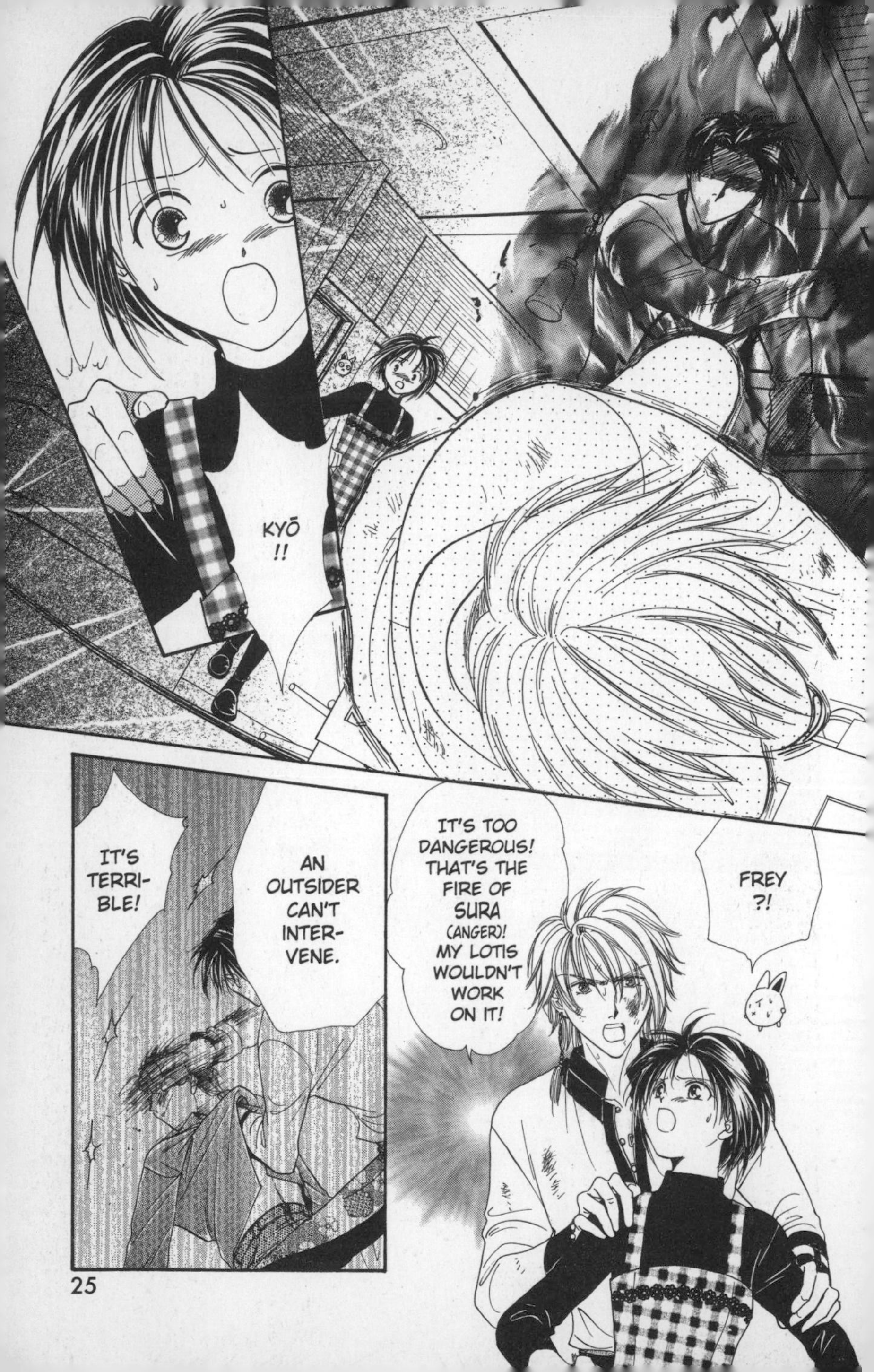
KYŌ !!
FREY ?!
IT'S TOO DANGEROUS! THAT'S THE FIRE OF SURA (ANGER)! MY LOTIS WOULDN'T WORK ON IT!
AN OUTSIDER CAN'T INTER-VENE.
IT'S TERRI-BLE!

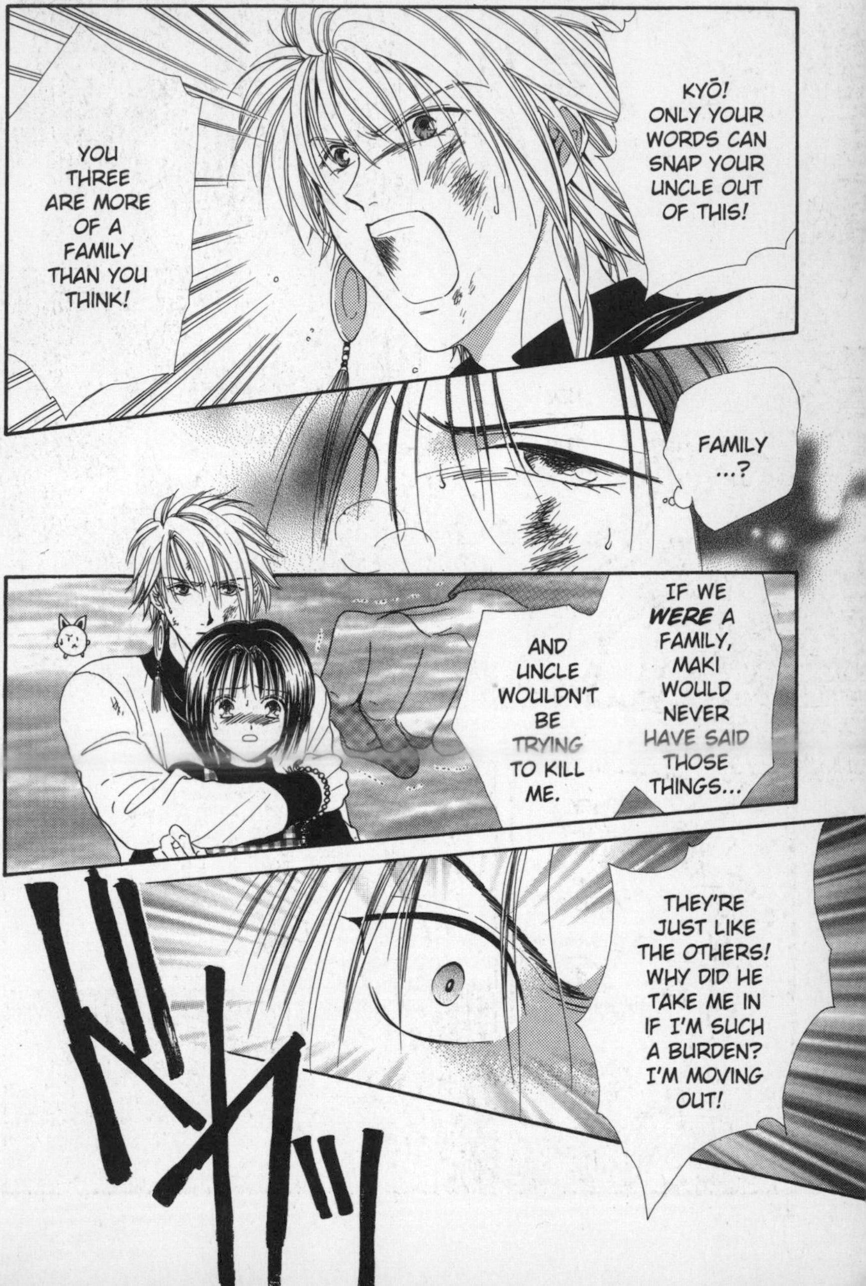
KYŌ! ONLY YOUR WORDS CAN SNAP YOUR UNCLE OUT OF THIS!
YOU THREE ARE MORE OF A FAMILY THAN YOU THINK!
FAMILY ...?
IF WE *WERE* A FAMILY, MAKI WOULD NEVER HAVE SAID THOSE THINGS...
AND UNCLE WOULDN'T BE TRYING TO KILL ME.
THEY'RE JUST LIKE THE OTHERS! WHY DID HE TAKE ME IN IF I'M SUCH A BURDEN? I'M MOVING OUT!

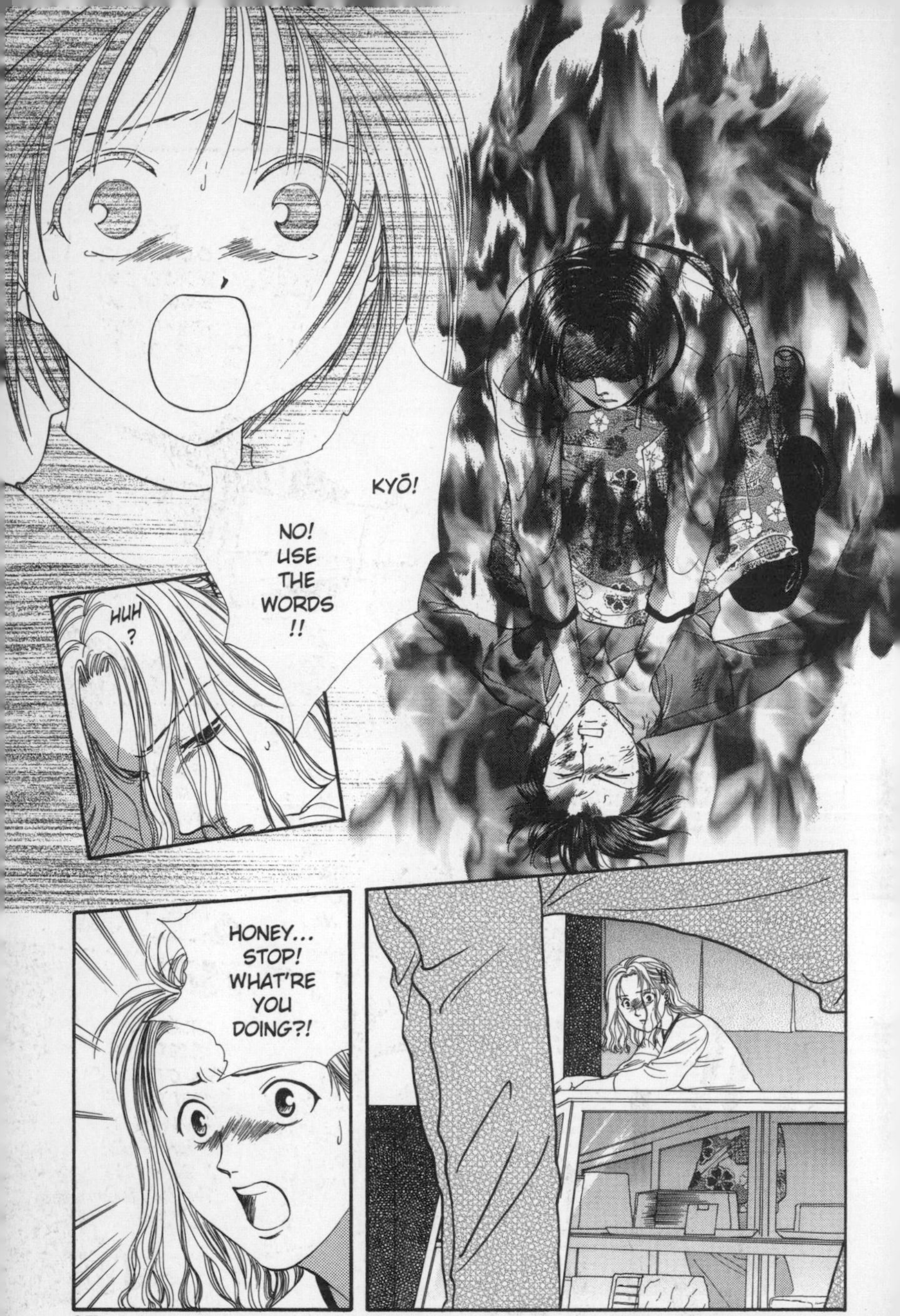
KYŌ!
NO! USE THE WORDS !!
HUH ?
HONEY... STOP! WHAT'RE YOU DOING?!

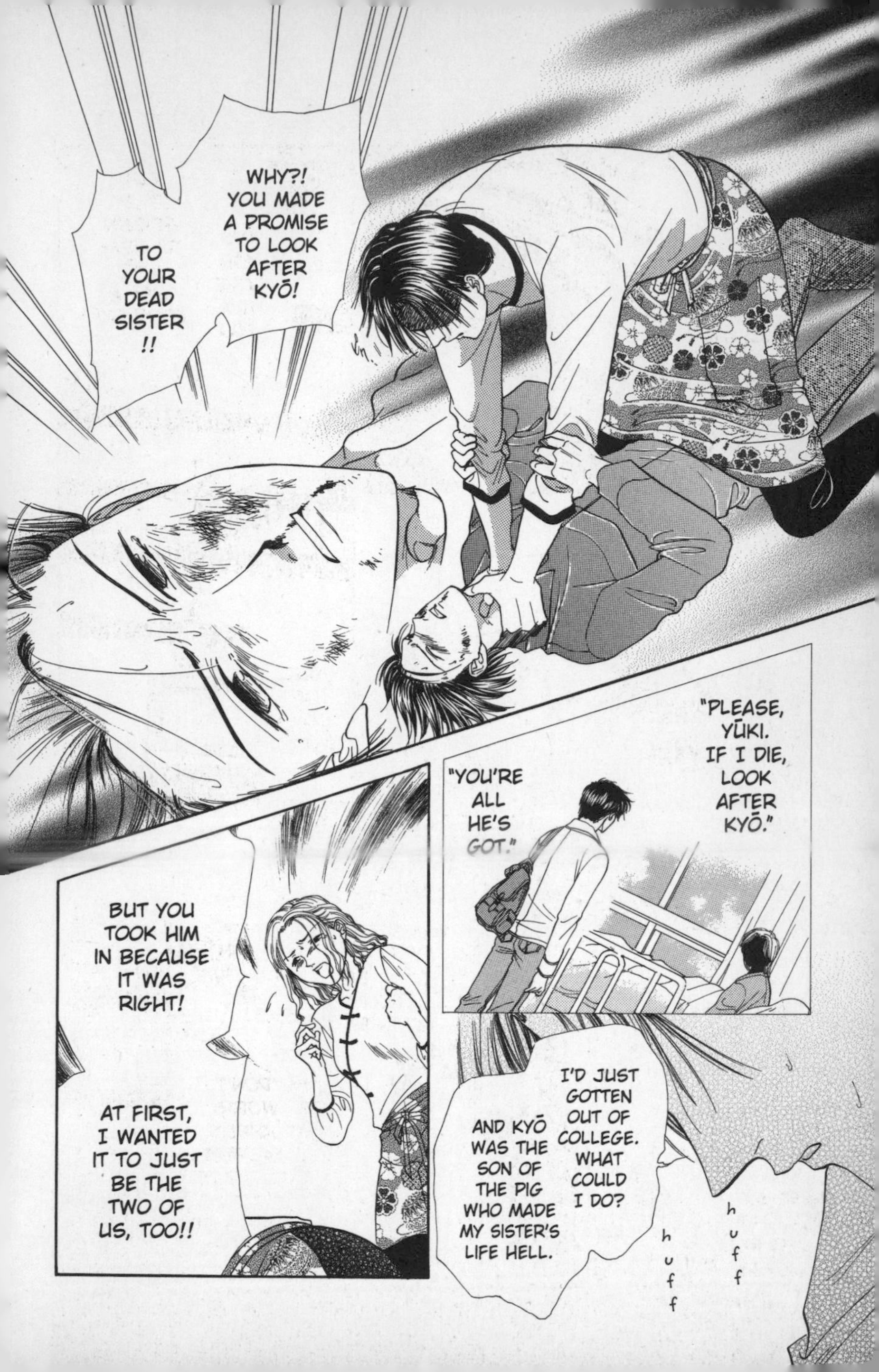
WHY?! YOU MADE A PROMISE TO LOOK AFTER KYŌ!
TO YOUR DEAD SISTER !!
"PLEASE, YŪKI. IF I DIE, LOOK AFTER KYŌ."
"YOU'RE ALL HE'S GOT."
I'D JUST GOTTEN OUT OF COLLEGE. WHAT COULD I DO?
AND KYŌ WAS THE SON OF THE PIG WHO MADE MY SISTER'S LIFE HELL.
huff
huff
BUT YOU TOOK HIM IN BECAUSE IT WAS RIGHT!
AT FIRST, I WANTED IT TO JUST BE THE TWO OF US, TOO!!

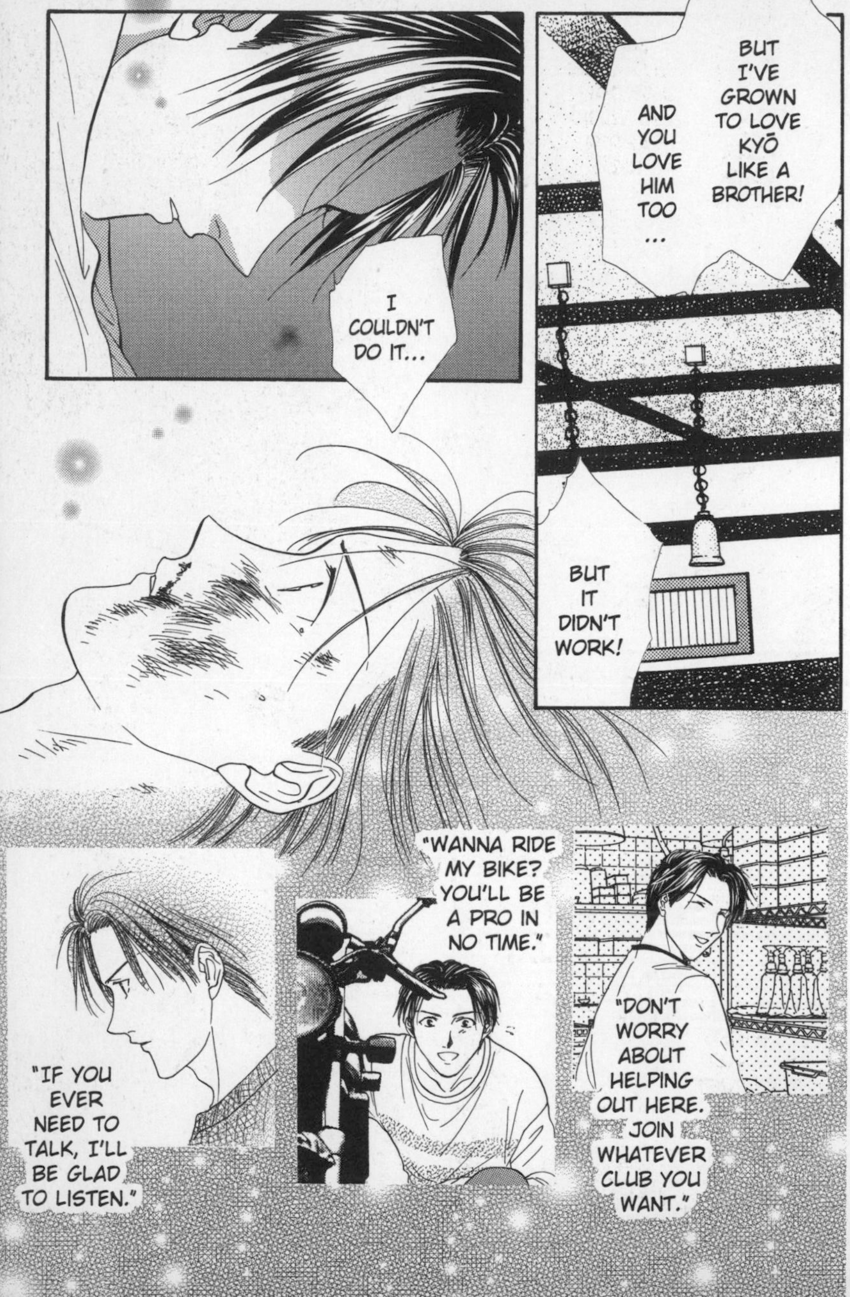
BUT I'VE GROWN TO LOVE KYŌ LIKE A BROTHER!
AND YOU LOVE HIM TOO ...
BUT IT DIDN'T WORK!
I COULDN'T DO IT...
"DON'T WORRY ABOUT HELPING OUT HERE. JOIN WHATEVER CLUB YOU WANT."
"WANNA RIDE MY BIKE? YOU'LL BE A PRO IN NO TIME."
"IF YOU EVER NEED TO TALK, I'LL BE GLAD TO LISTEN."

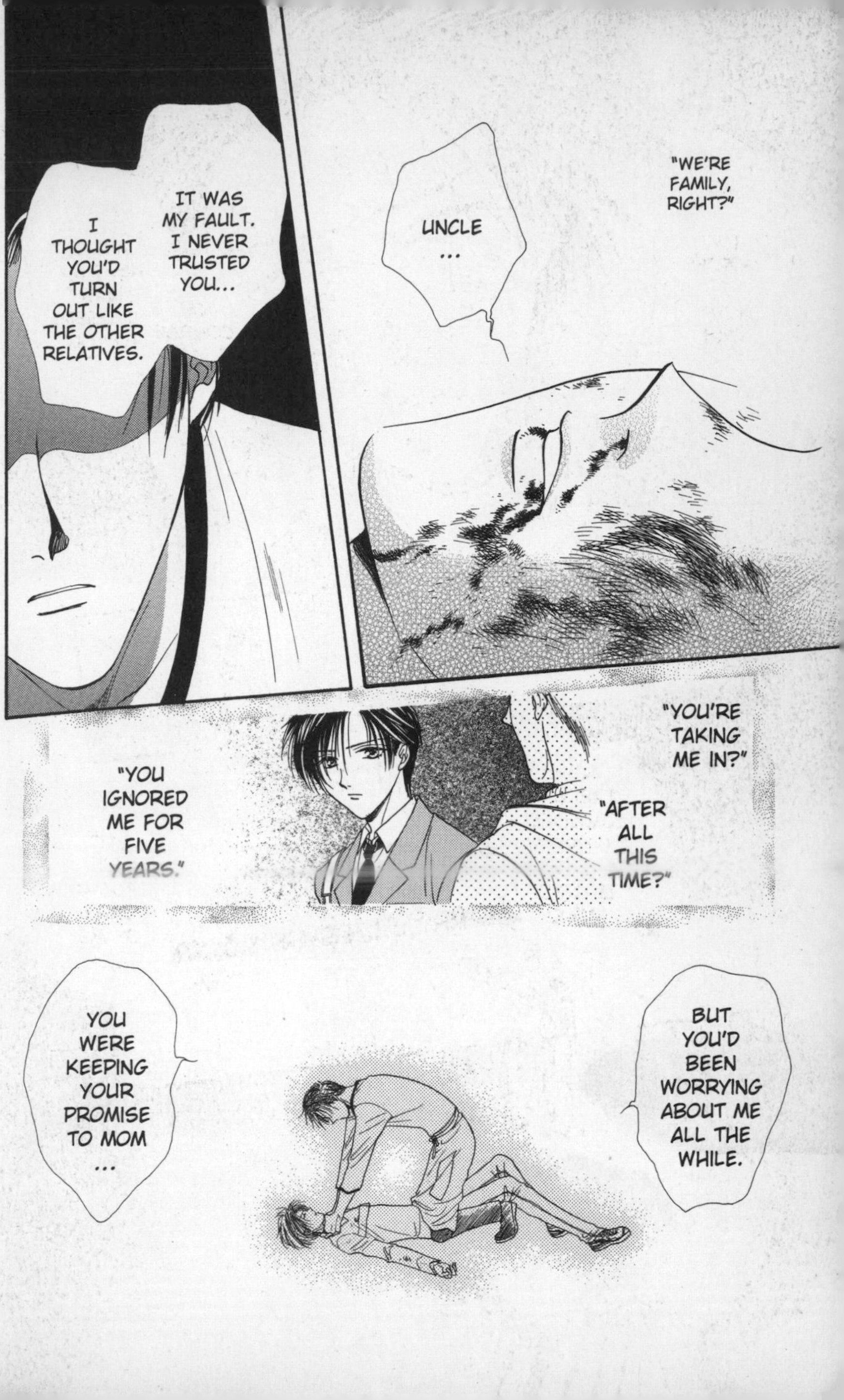
"WE'RE FAMILY, RIGHT?"
UNCLE ...
IT WAS MY FAULT. I NEVER TRUSTED YOU...
I THOUGHT YOU'D TURN OUT LIKE THE OTHER RELATIVES.
"YOU'RE TAKING ME IN?"
"AFTER ALL THIS TIME?"
"YOU IGNORED ME FOR FIVE YEARS."
BUT YOU'D BEEN WORRYING ABOUT ME ALL THE WHILE.
YOU WERE KEEPING YOUR PROMISE TO MOM ...

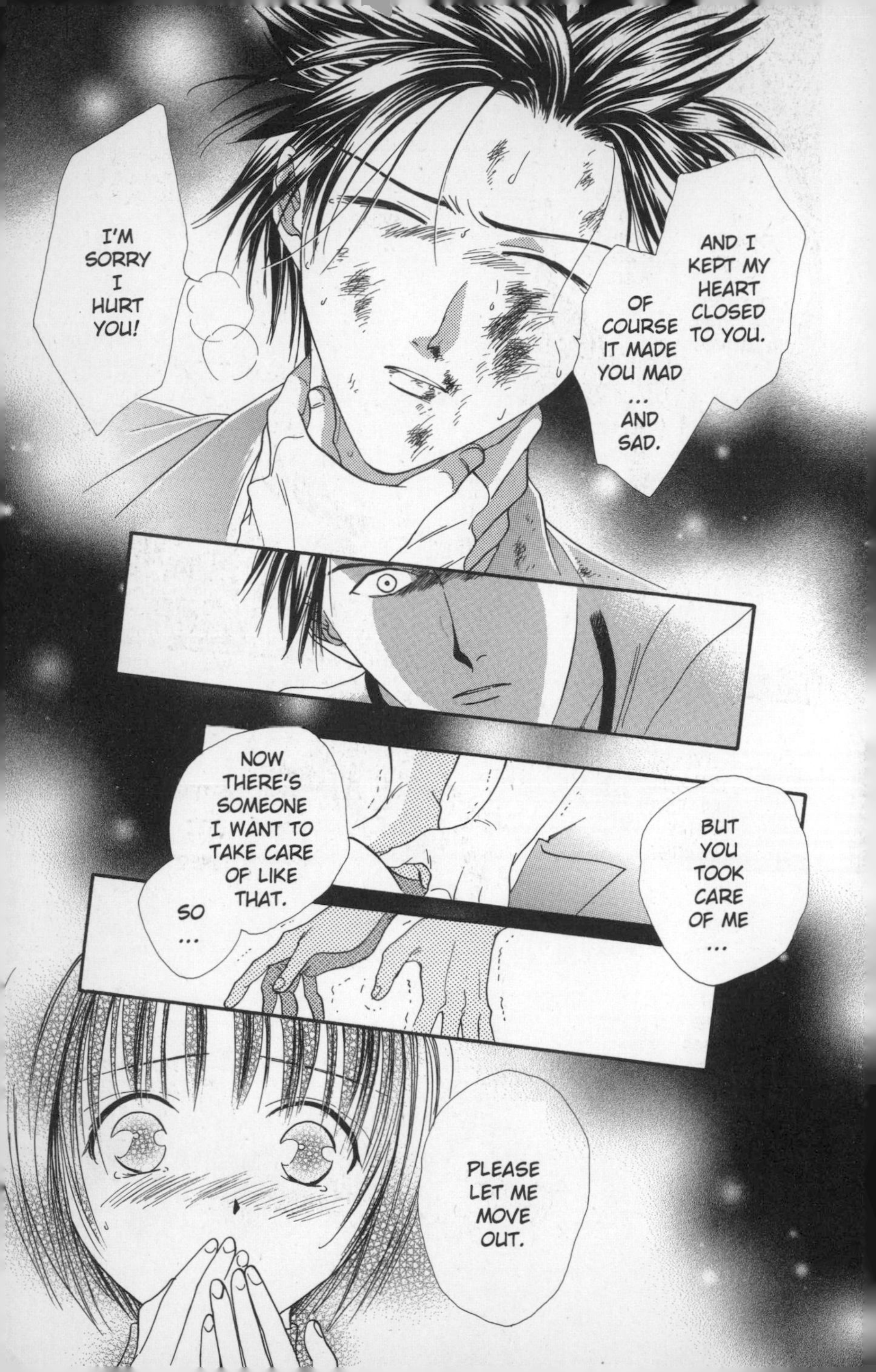
AND I KEPT MY HEART CLOSED TO YOU.
OF COURSE IT MADE YOU MAD ... AND SAD.
I'M SORRY I HURT YOU!
BUT YOU TOOK CARE OF ME ...
NOW THERE'S SOMEONE I WANT TO TAKE CARE OF LIKE THAT.
SO ...
PLEASE LET ME MOVE OUT.

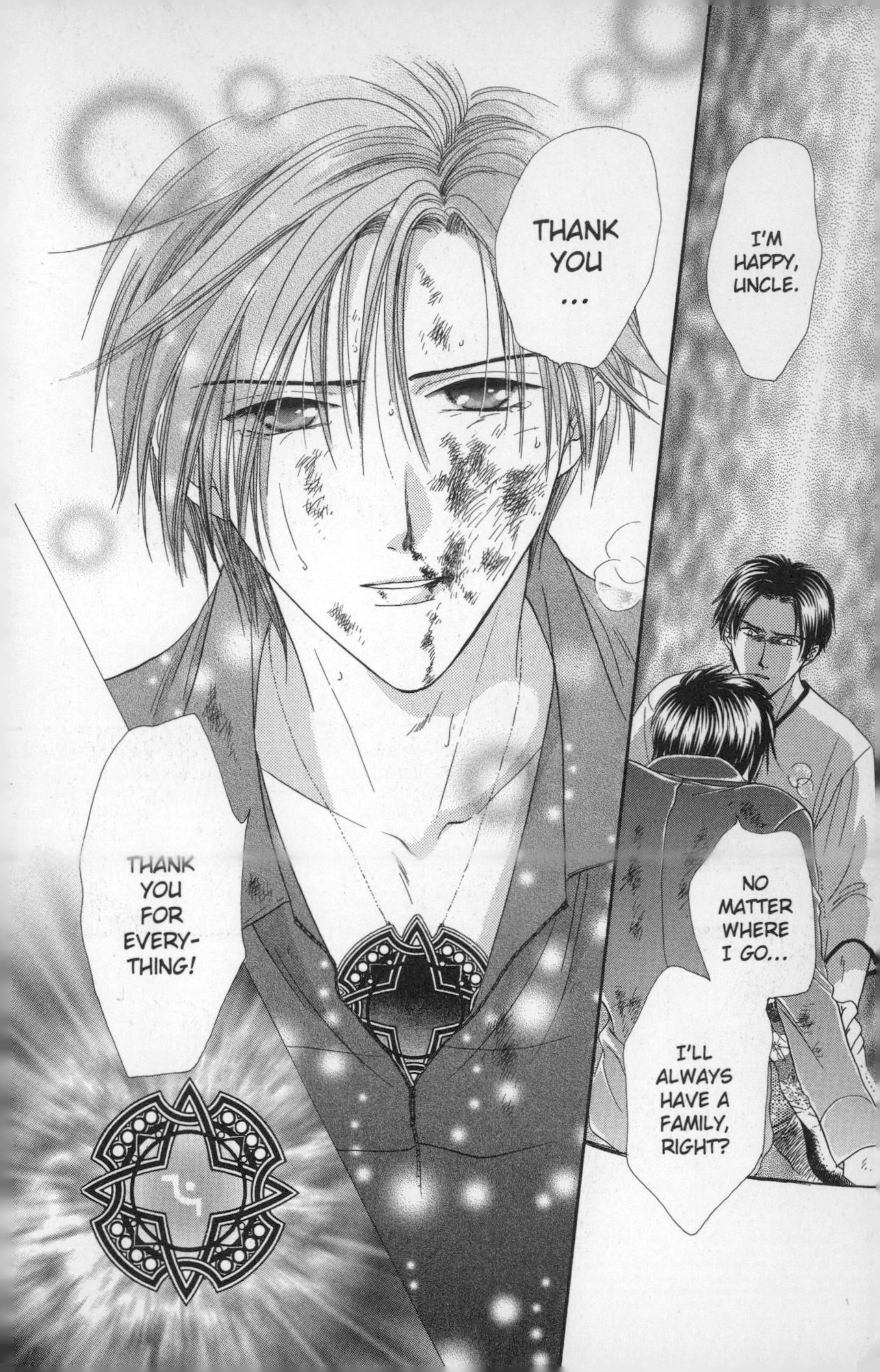
I'M HAPPY, UNCLE.
NO MATTER WHERE I GO...
I'LL ALWAYS HAVE A FAMILY, RIGHT?
THANK YOU ...
THANK YOU FOR EVERY-THING!

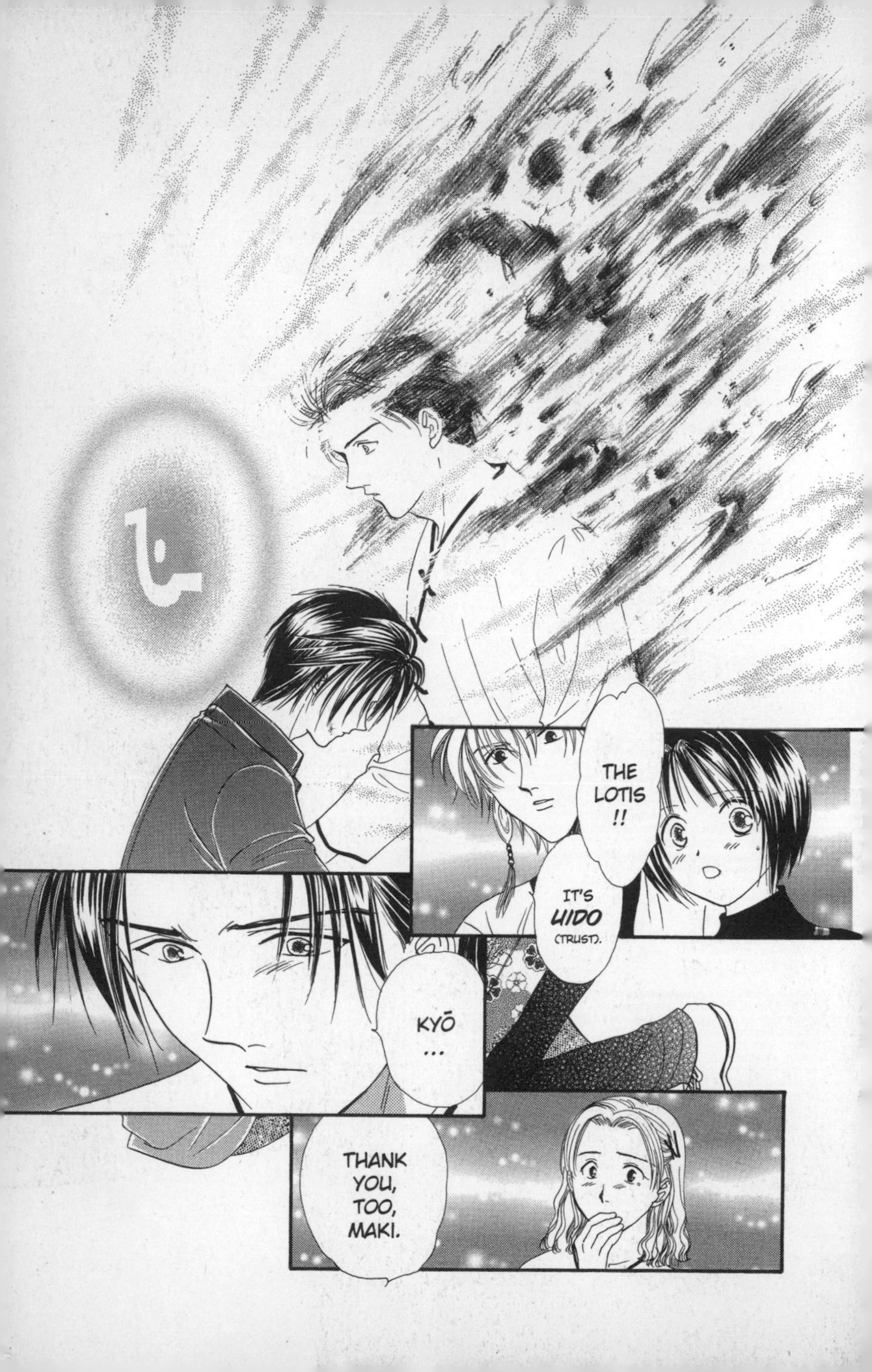
THE LOTIS !!
IT'S UIDO (TRUST).
KYŌ ...
THANK YOU, TOO, MAKI.

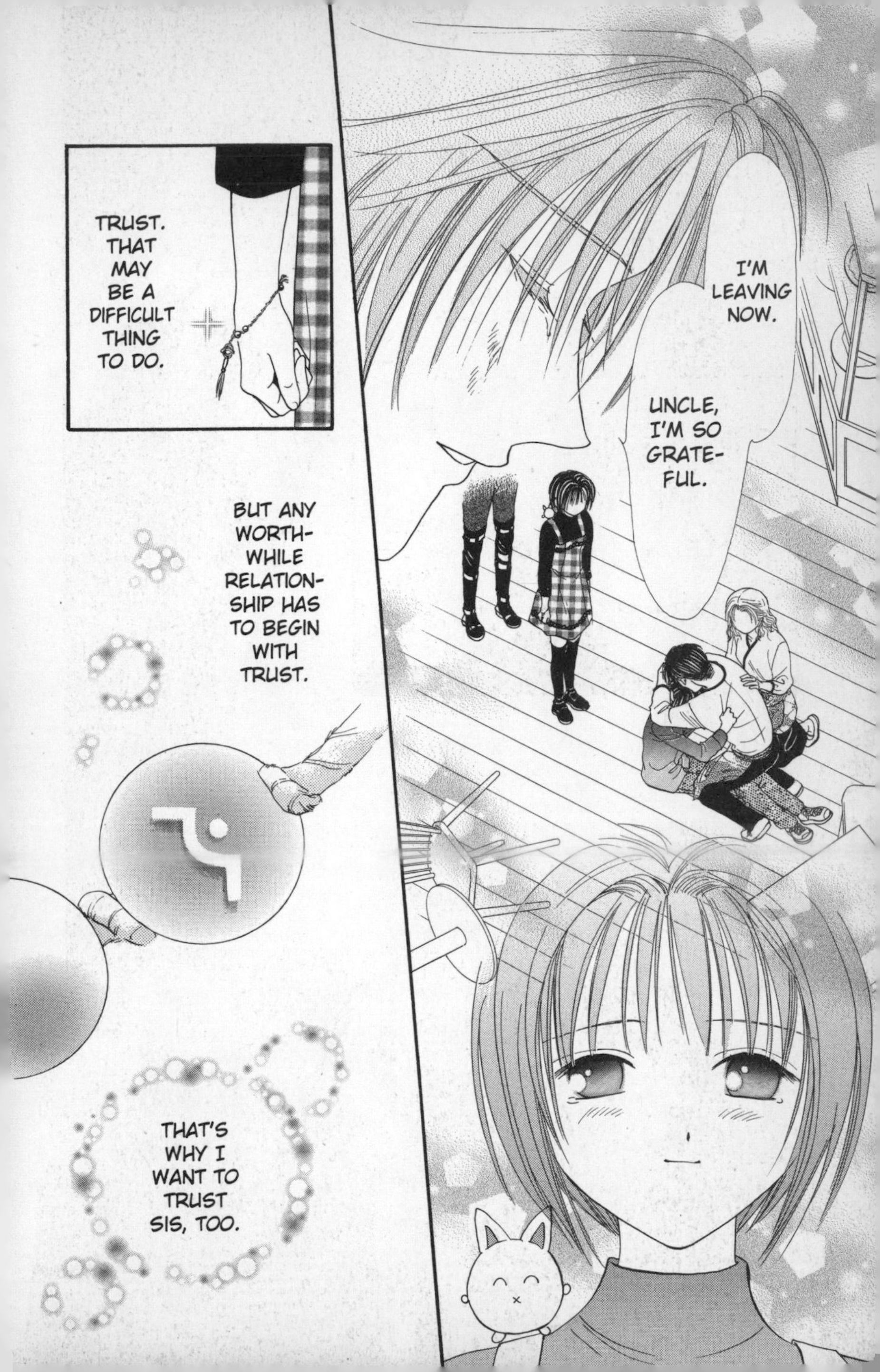
I'M LEAVING NOW.
UNCLE, I'M SO GRATEFUL.
TRUST. THAT MAY BE A DIFFICULT THING TO DO.
BUT ANY WORTHWHILE RELATIONSHIP HAS TO BEGIN WITH TRUST.
THAT'S WHY I WANT TO TRUST SIS, TOO.

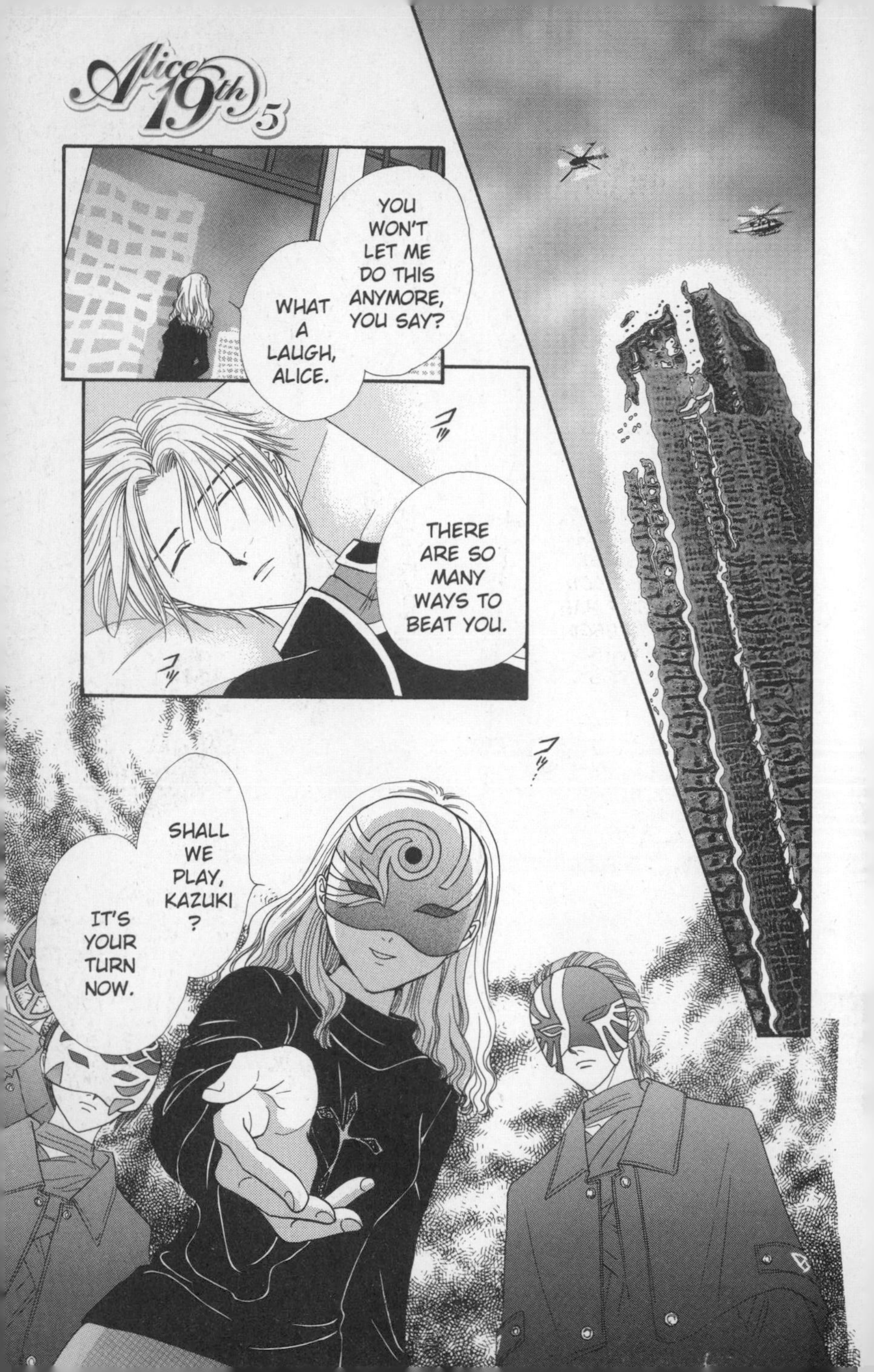
YOU WON'T LET ME DO THIS ANYMORE, YOU SAY?
WHAT A LAUGH, ALICE.
THERE ARE SO MANY WAYS TO BEAT YOU.
SHALL WE PLAY, KAZUKI?
IT'S YOUR TURN NOW.

❋AGE: 19

❋HEIGHT: 182 CM (ALMOST 6 FEET)

❋SIGN: GEMINI

❋BLOOD TYPE: B

❋HOBBIES: MAKING JAM, GARDENING

❋HOMELAND: NORWAY

❋DISTINGUISHING FEATURE: BRAID ON LEFT SIDE OF HEAD. THIS STYLE IS CHARACTERISTIC OF THE LOTSUAN LEGION OF SACRED GUIDES OF THE NORTHERN EUROPEAN ORDER, TO WHICH HE BELONGS. FOLLOWERS OF THE FIRST GUIDE WHO TAUGHT THE LOTIS IN THIS REGION ADOPTED HIS BRAID OUT OF REVERENCE FOR THEIR MASTER.

❋OUTWARDLY, A CHEERFUL YOUNG RASCAL WHO LIKES GIRLS. THOUGH HE SEEMS FLIGHTY, HE HAS A SERIOUS SIDE AND GOOD SENSE.

❋HIS ABILITIES AS A LOTIS MASTER ARE INDISPUTABLE.

❋HE SEEMS TO BE INFATUATED WITH ALICE, BUT HE IS ABOVE ALL DEDICATED TO HELPING HER DEFEAT DARVA. HE HAS A SECRET IN HIS PAST...

FREY WEILHAUSEN

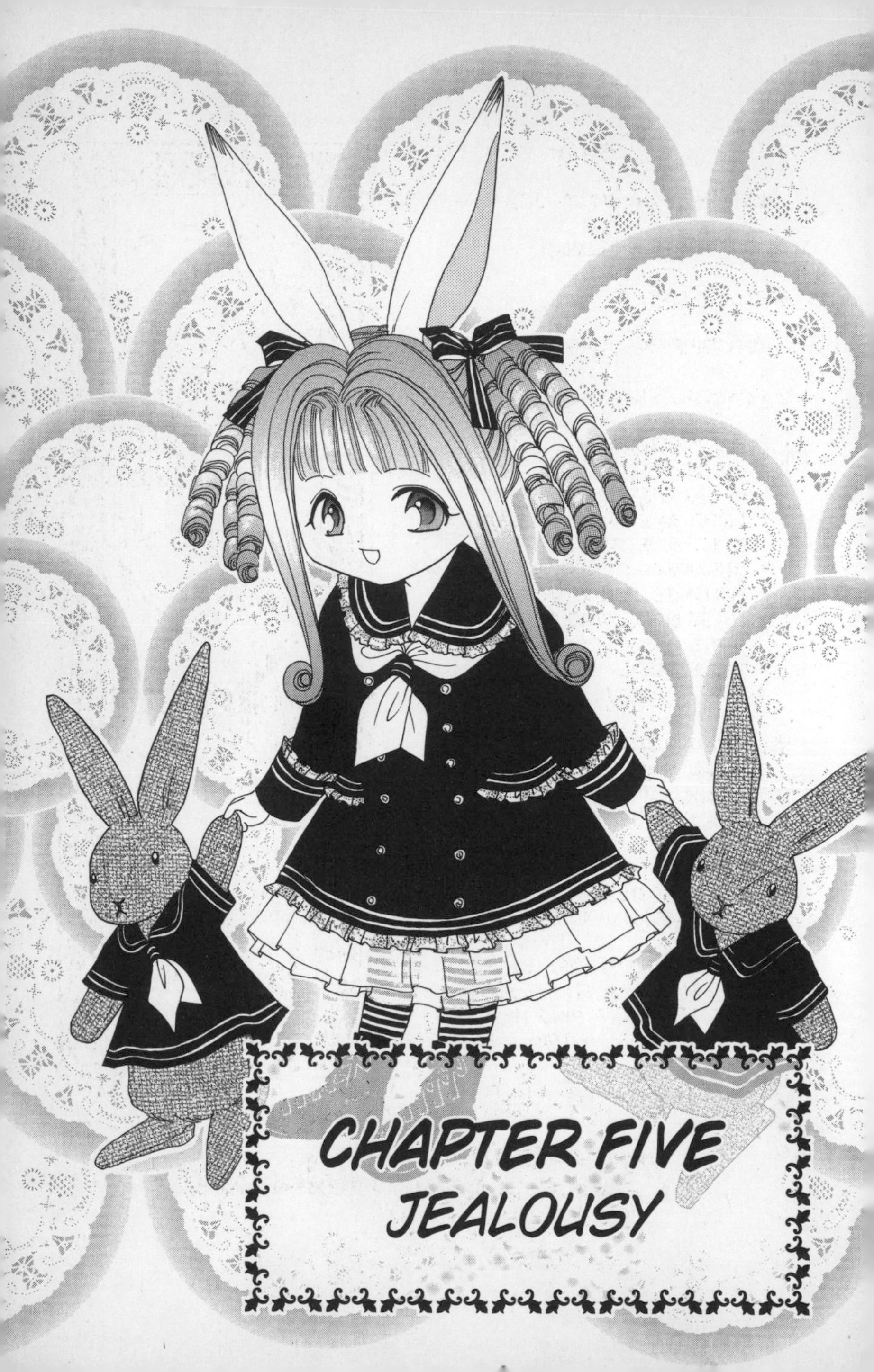
CHAPTER FIVE
JEALOUSY

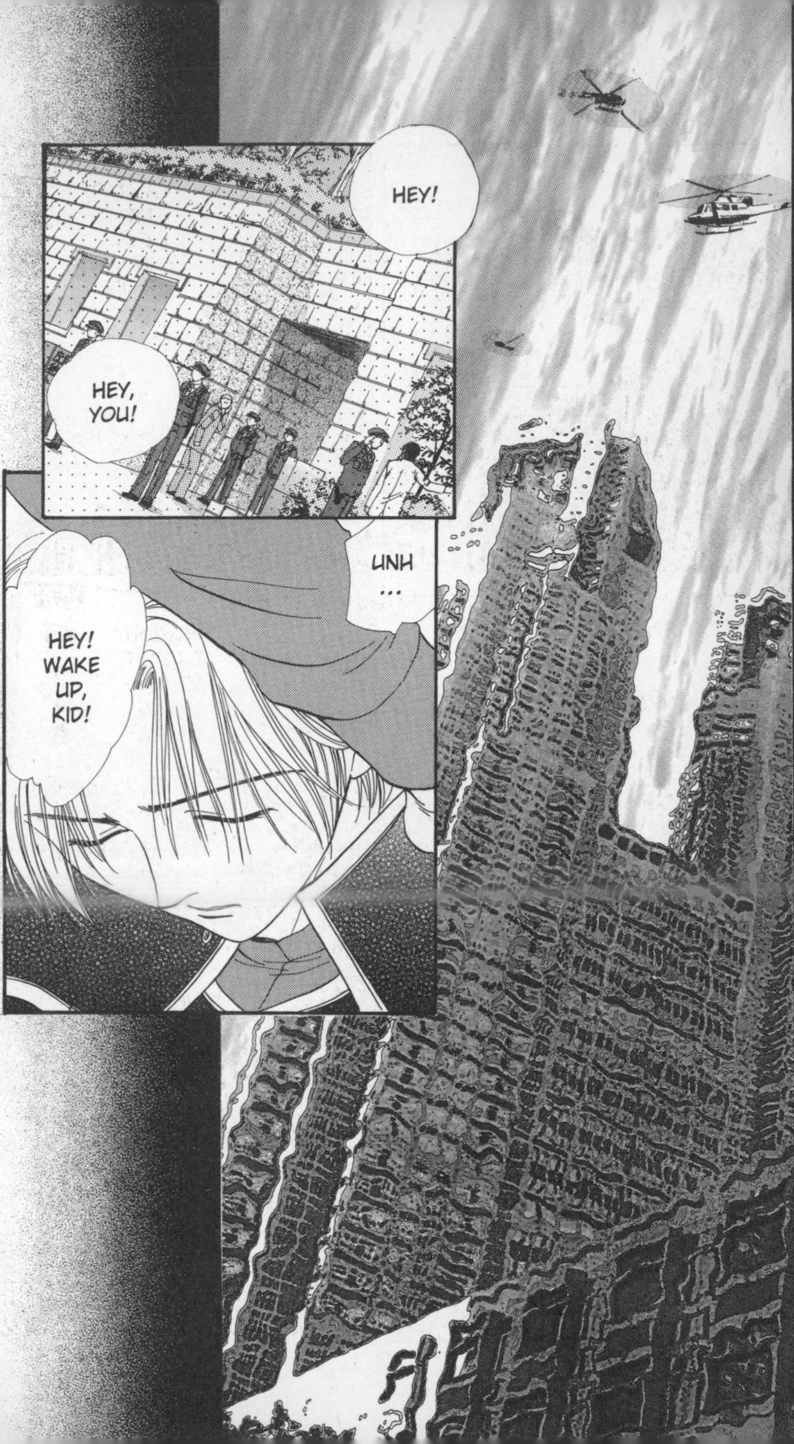
HEY!
HEY, YOU!
UNH ...
HEY! WAKE UP, KID!

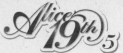

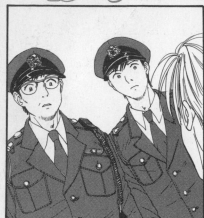

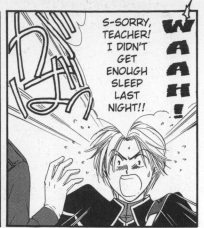

WAAAH!
S-SORRY, TEACHER! I DIDN'T GET ENOUGH SLEEP LAST NIGHT!!
WAIT!
I'M INNOCENT! I DIDN'T DO ANY-THING WRONG!!
YOU WERE ASLEEP!
HUH? WHERE AM I?
HOW'D YOU GET IN HERE?!
THE AREA AROUND THE METRO-POLITAN BUILDING IS A CRIME SCENE! DON'T YOU KNOW IT'S OFF-LIMITS, SON?
DUH
HUH?

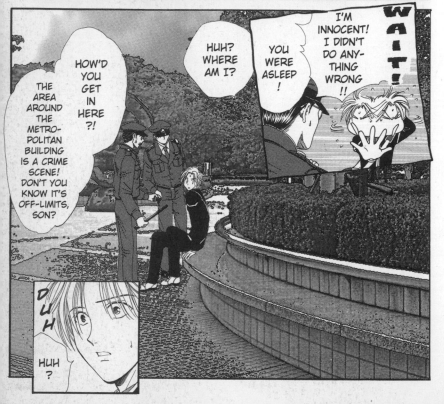

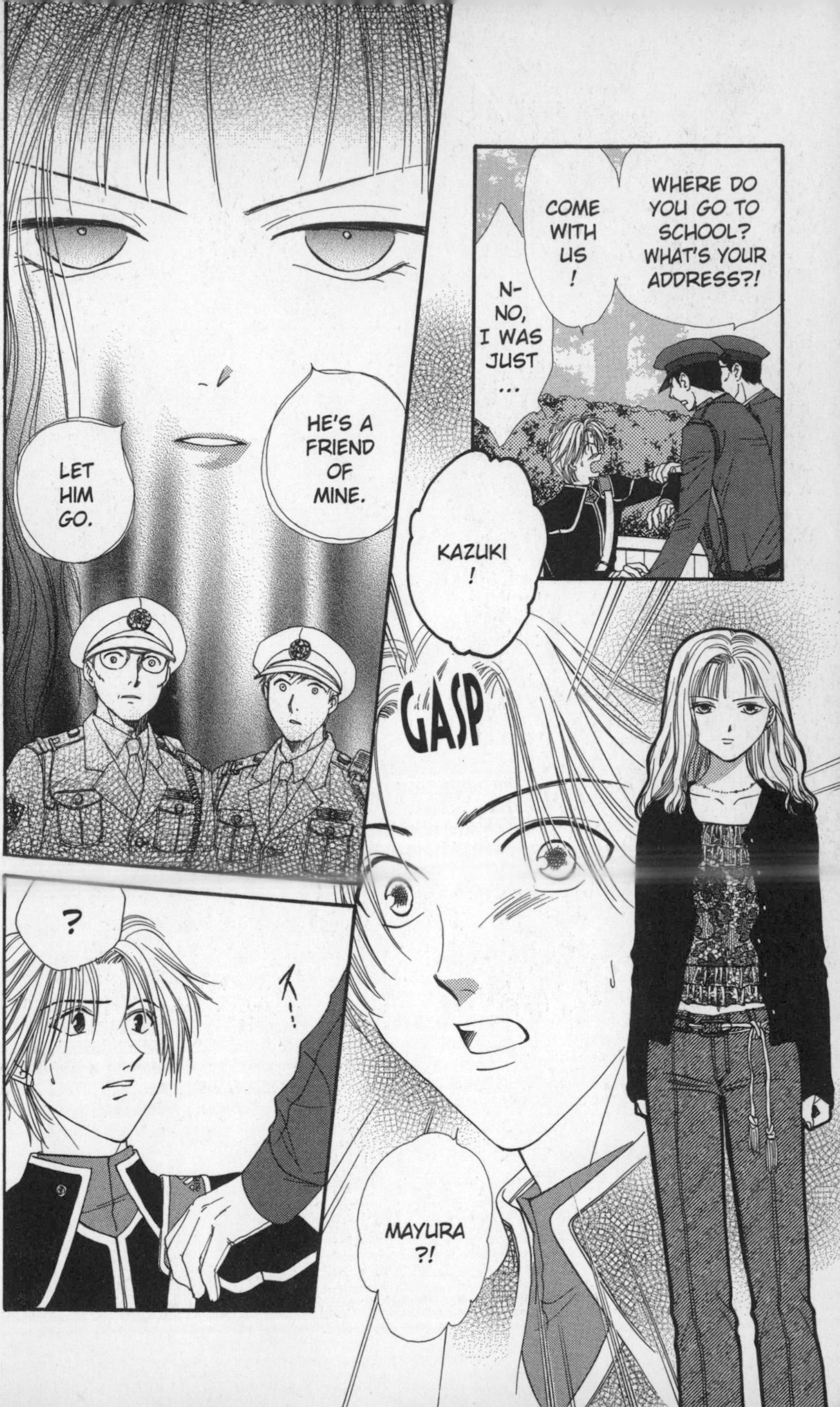
WHERE DO YOU GO TO SCHOOL? WHAT'S YOUR ADDRESS?!
COME WITH US!
N-NO, I WAS JUST...
KAZUKI!
GASP
MAYURA?!
HE'S A FRIEND OF MINE.
LET HIM GO.
?

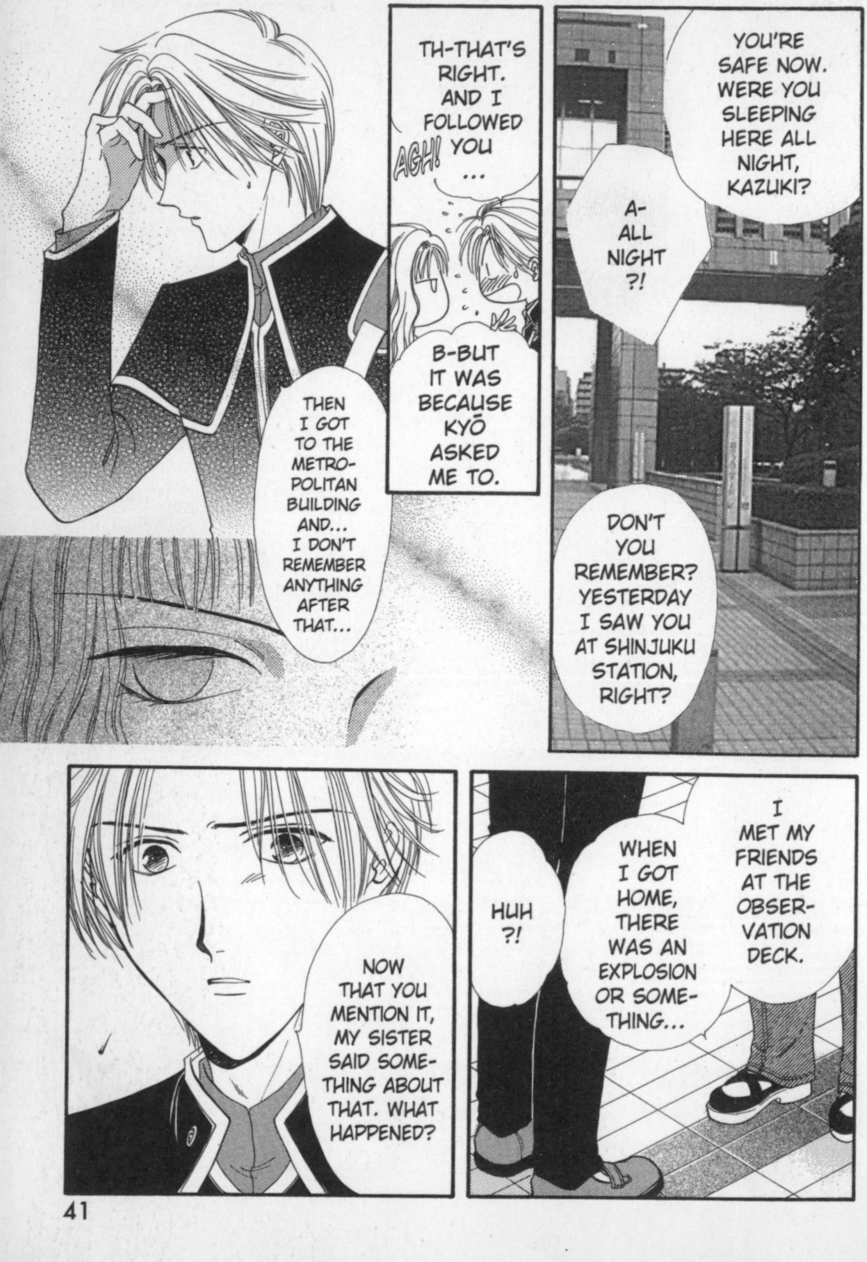
YOU'RE SAFE NOW. WERE YOU SLEEPING HERE ALL NIGHT, KAZUKI?
A-ALL NIGHT?!
DON'T YOU REMEMBER? YESTERDAY I SAW YOU AT SHINJUKU STATION, RIGHT?
TH-THAT'S RIGHT. AND I FOLLOWED YOU ...
AGH!
B-BUT IT WAS BECAUSE KYŌ ASKED ME TO.
THEN I GOT TO THE METRO-POLITAN BUILDING AND... I DON'T REMEMBER ANYTHING AFTER THAT...
I MET MY FRIENDS AT THE OBSER-VATION DECK.
WHEN I GOT HOME, THERE WAS AN EXPLOSION OR SOME-THING...
HUH?!
NOW THAT YOU MENTION IT, MY SISTER SAID SOME-THING ABOUT THAT. WHAT HAPPENED?

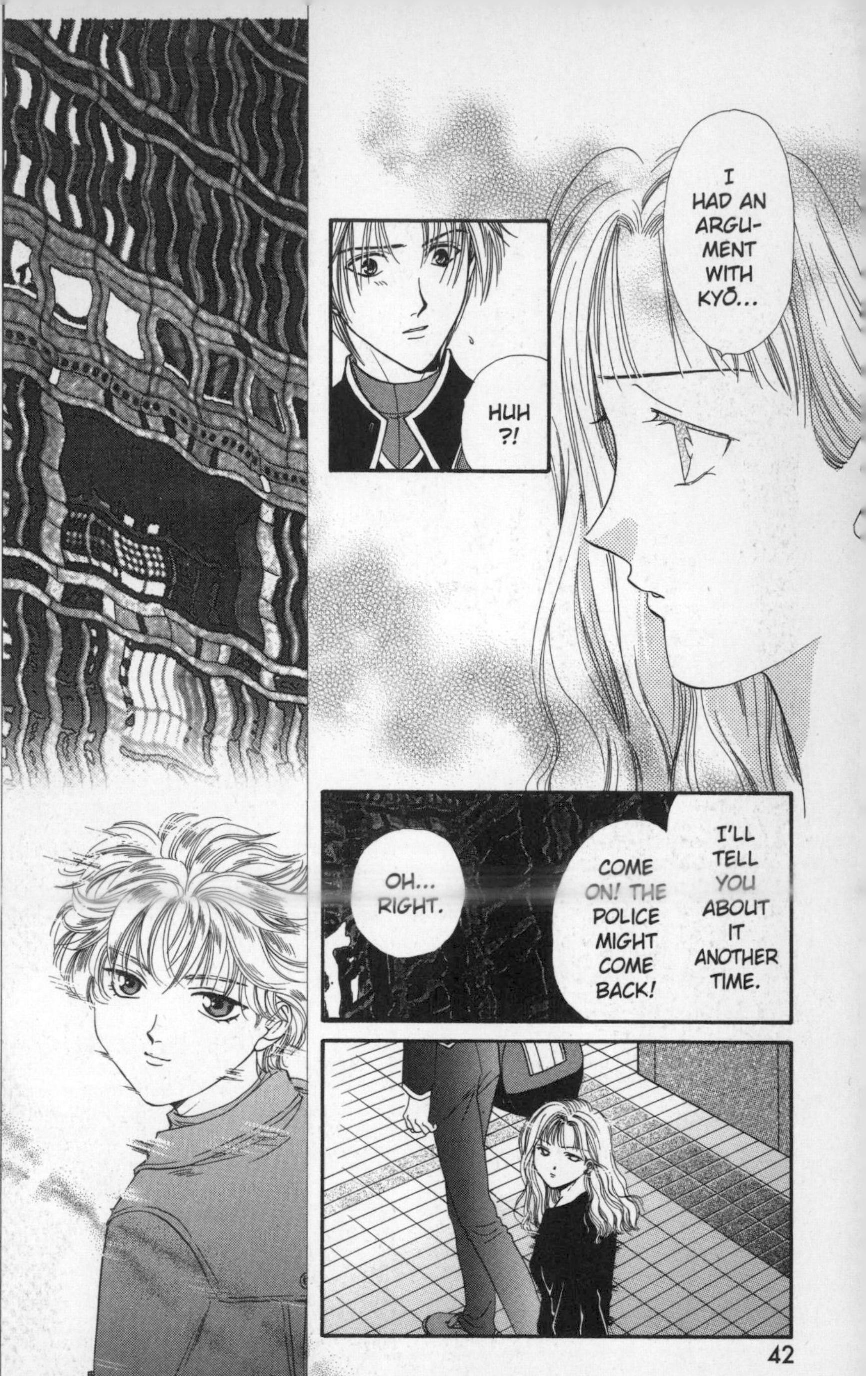
I HAD AN ARGUMENT WITH KYŌ...
HUH ?!
I'LL TELL YOU ABOUT IT ANOTHER TIME.
COME ON! THE POLICE MIGHT COME BACK!
OH... RIGHT.

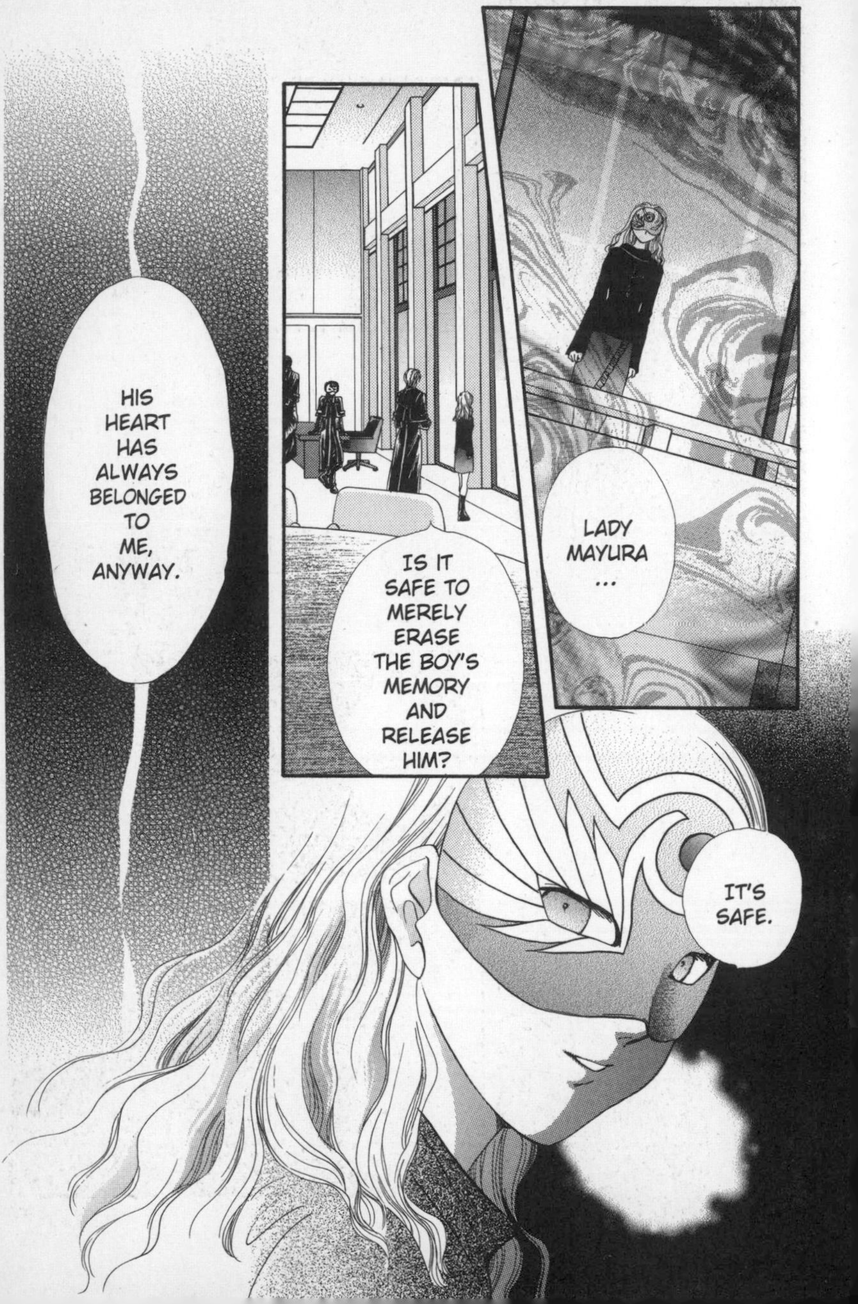
LADY MAYURA ...
IS IT SAFE TO MERELY ERASE THE BOY'S MEMORY AND RELEASE HIM?
IT'S SAFE.
HIS HEART HAS ALWAYS BELONGED TO ME, ANYWAY.

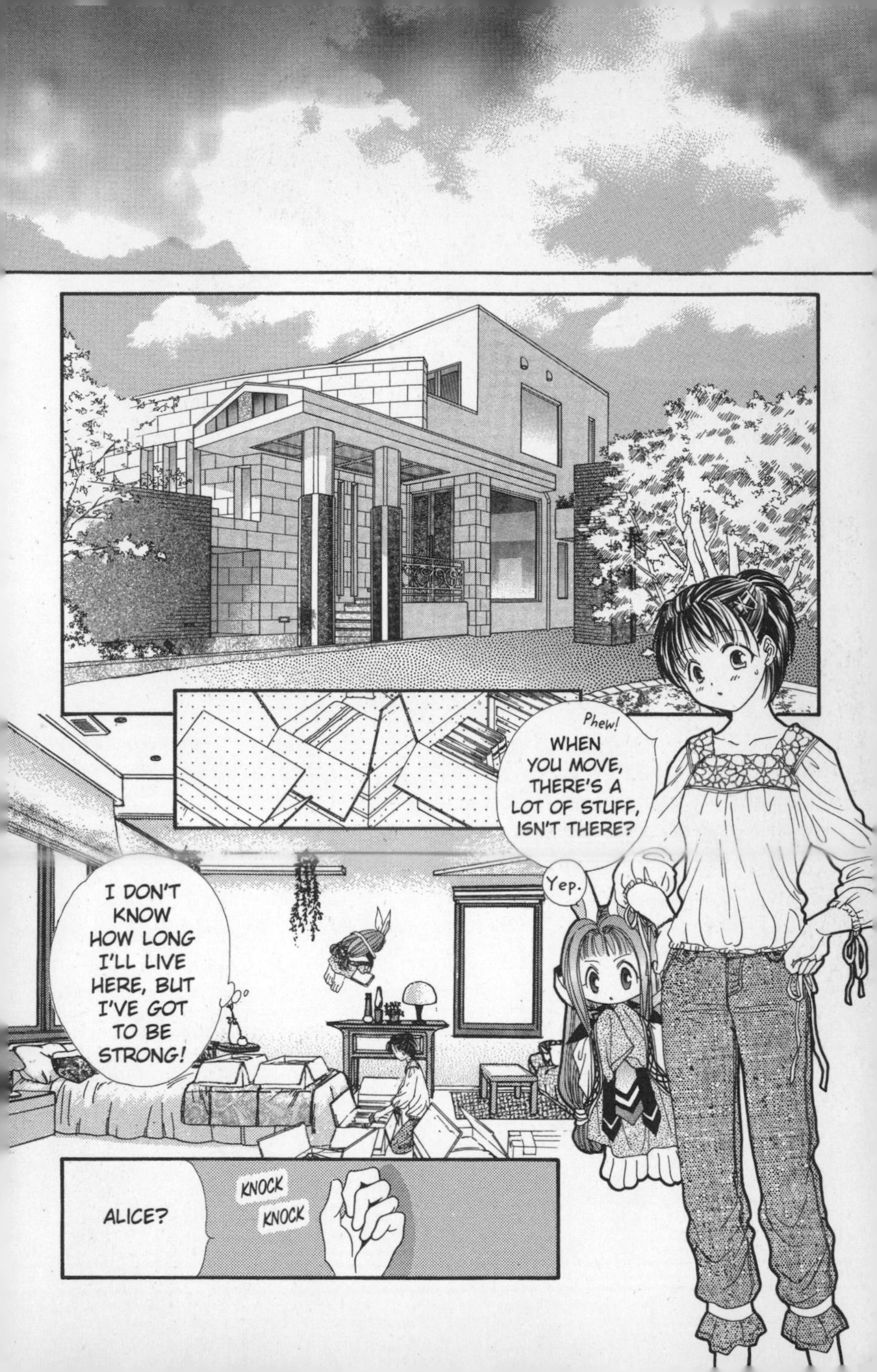
Phew!
WHEN YOU MOVE, THERE'S A LOT OF STUFF, ISN'T THERE?
Yep.
I DON'T KNOW HOW LONG I'LL LIVE HERE, BUT I'VE GOT TO BE STRONG!
KNOCK
KNOCK
ALICE?

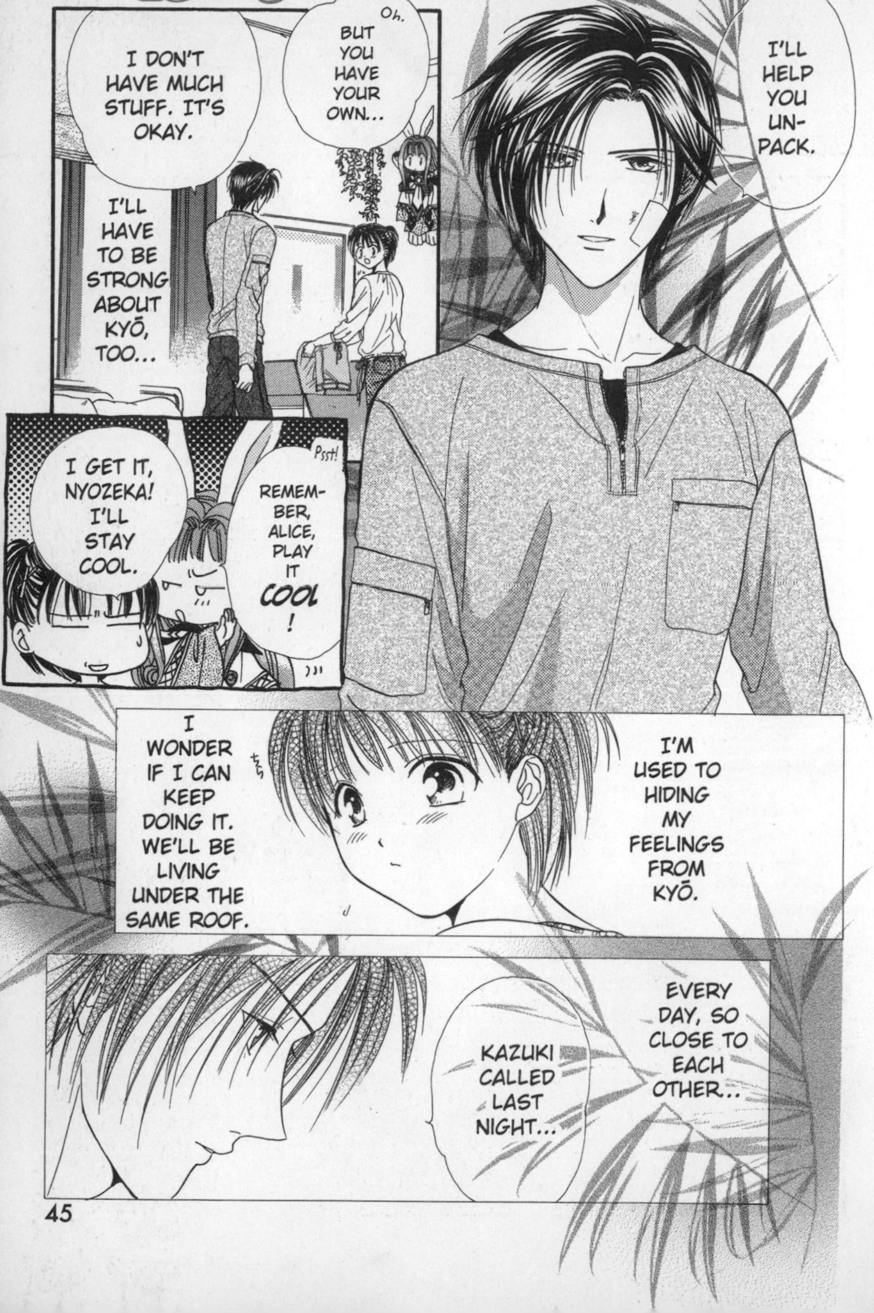
I'LL HELP YOU UN-PACK.
Oh. BUT YOU HAVE YOUR OWN...
I DON'T HAVE MUCH STUFF. IT'S OKAY.
I'LL HAVE TO BE STRONG ABOUT KYŌ, TOO...
Psst!
REMEM-BER, ALICE, PLAY IT COOL!
I GET IT, NYOZEKA! I'LL STAY COOL.
I'M USED TO HIDING MY FEELINGS FROM KYŌ.
I WONDER IF I CAN KEEP DOING IT. WE'LL BE LIVING UNDER THE SAME ROOF.
EVERY DAY, SO CLOSE TO EACH OTHER...
KAZUKI CALLED LAST NIGHT...

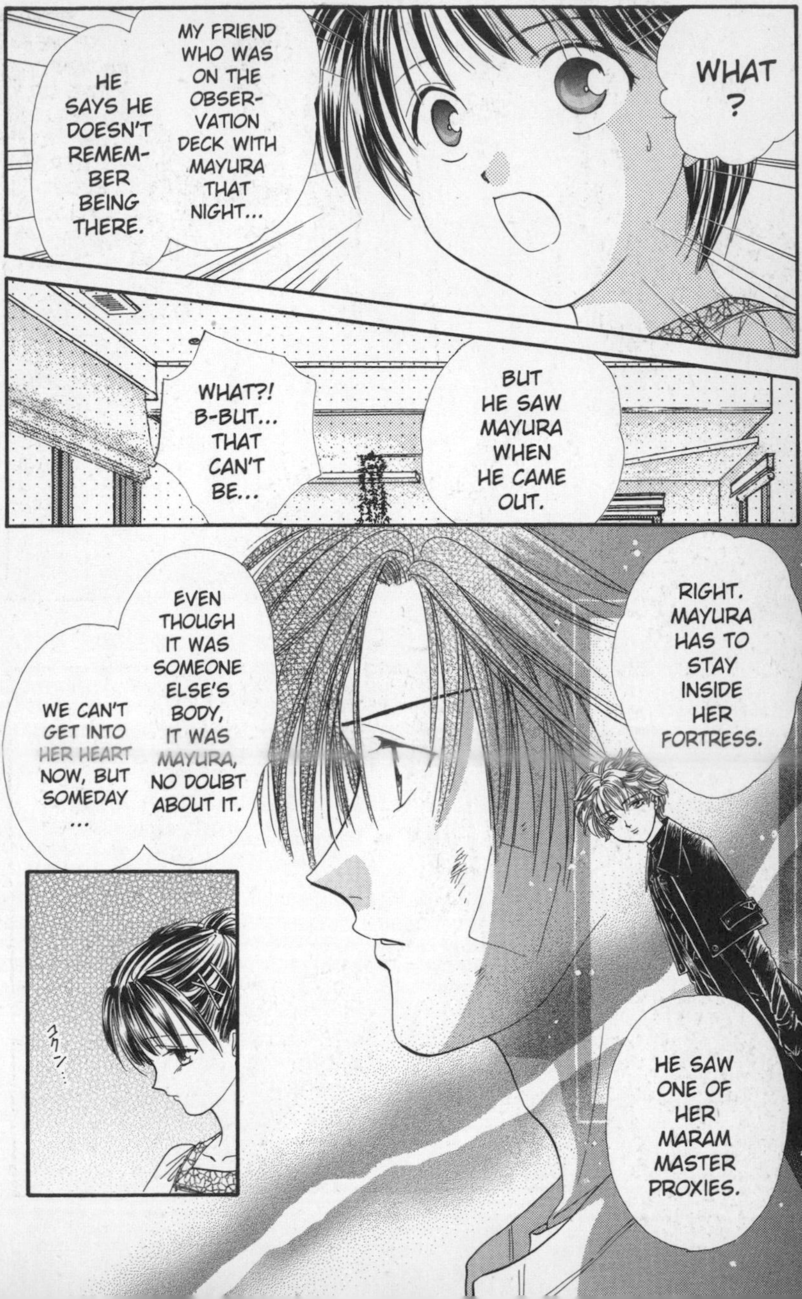
WHAT?
MY FRIEND WHO WAS ON THE OBSERVATION DECK WITH MAYURA THAT NIGHT...
HE SAYS HE DOESN'T REMEMBER BEING THERE.
BUT HE SAW MAYURA WHEN HE CAME OUT.
WHAT?! B-BUT... THAT CAN'T BE...
RIGHT. MAYURA HAS TO STAY INSIDE HER FORTRESS.
HE SAW ONE OF HER MARAM MASTER PROXIES.
EVEN THOUGH IT WAS SOMEONE ELSE'S BODY, IT WAS MAYURA, NO DOUBT ABOUT IT.
WE CAN'T GET INTO HER HEART NOW, BUT SOMEDAY...

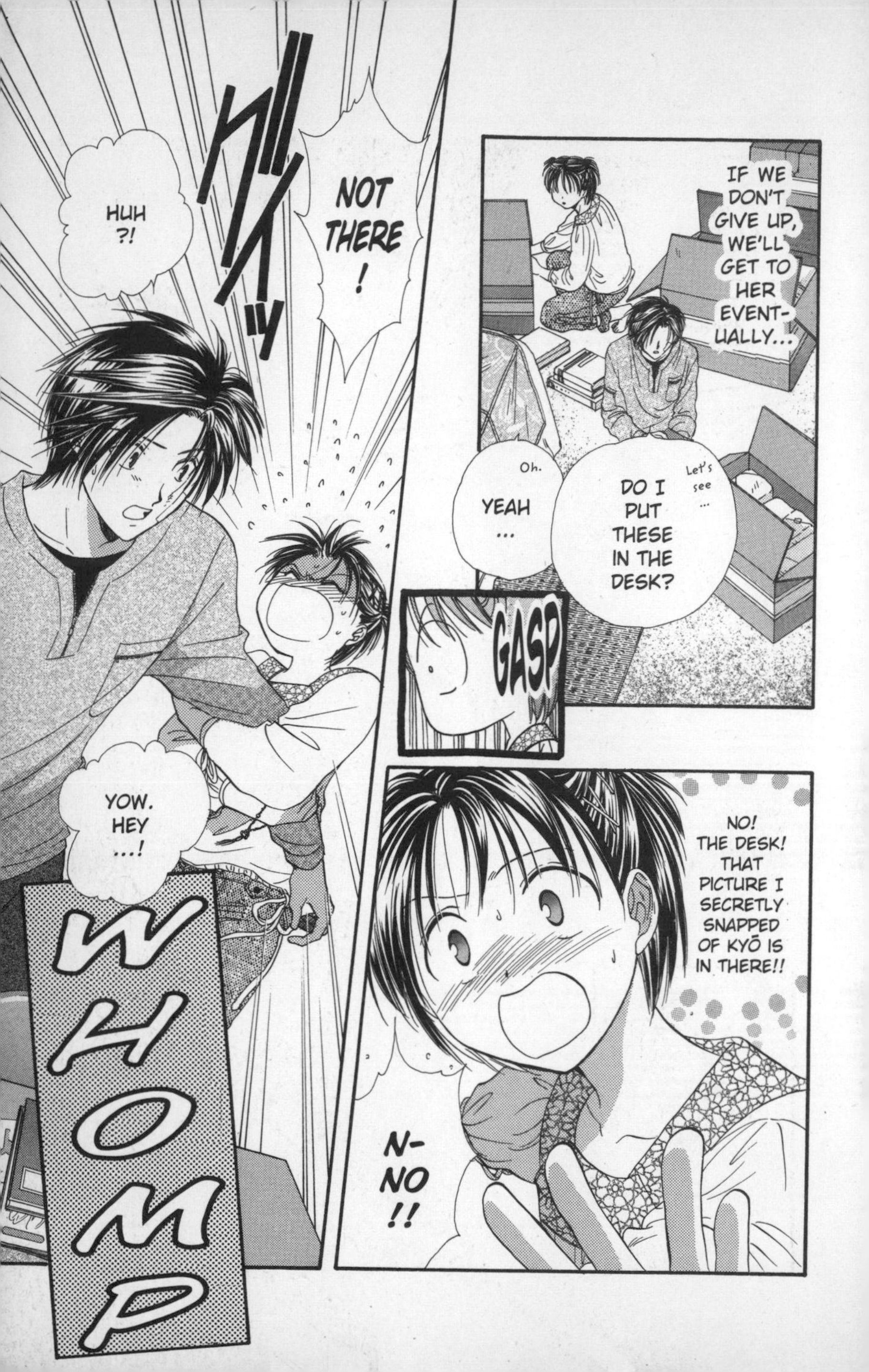
IF WE DON'T GIVE UP, WE'LL GET TO HER EVENT-UALLY...
Let's see ...
DO I PUT THESE IN THE DESK?
Oh.
YEAH ...
GASP
NO! THE DESK! THAT PICTURE I SECRETLY SNAPPED OF KYŌ IS IN THERE!!
N-NO!!
NOT THERE!
HUH ?!
YOW. HEY ...!
WHOMP

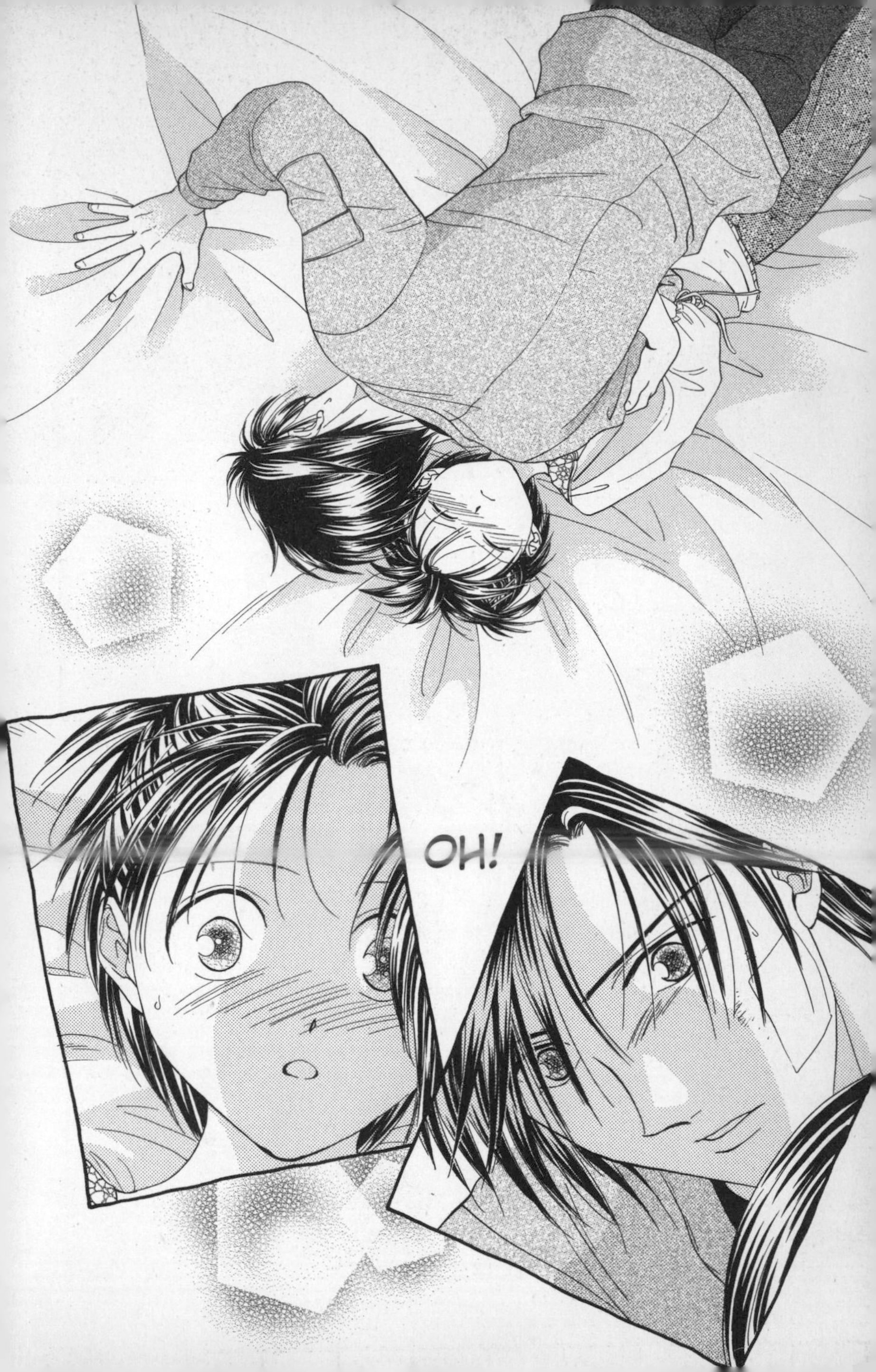
OH!

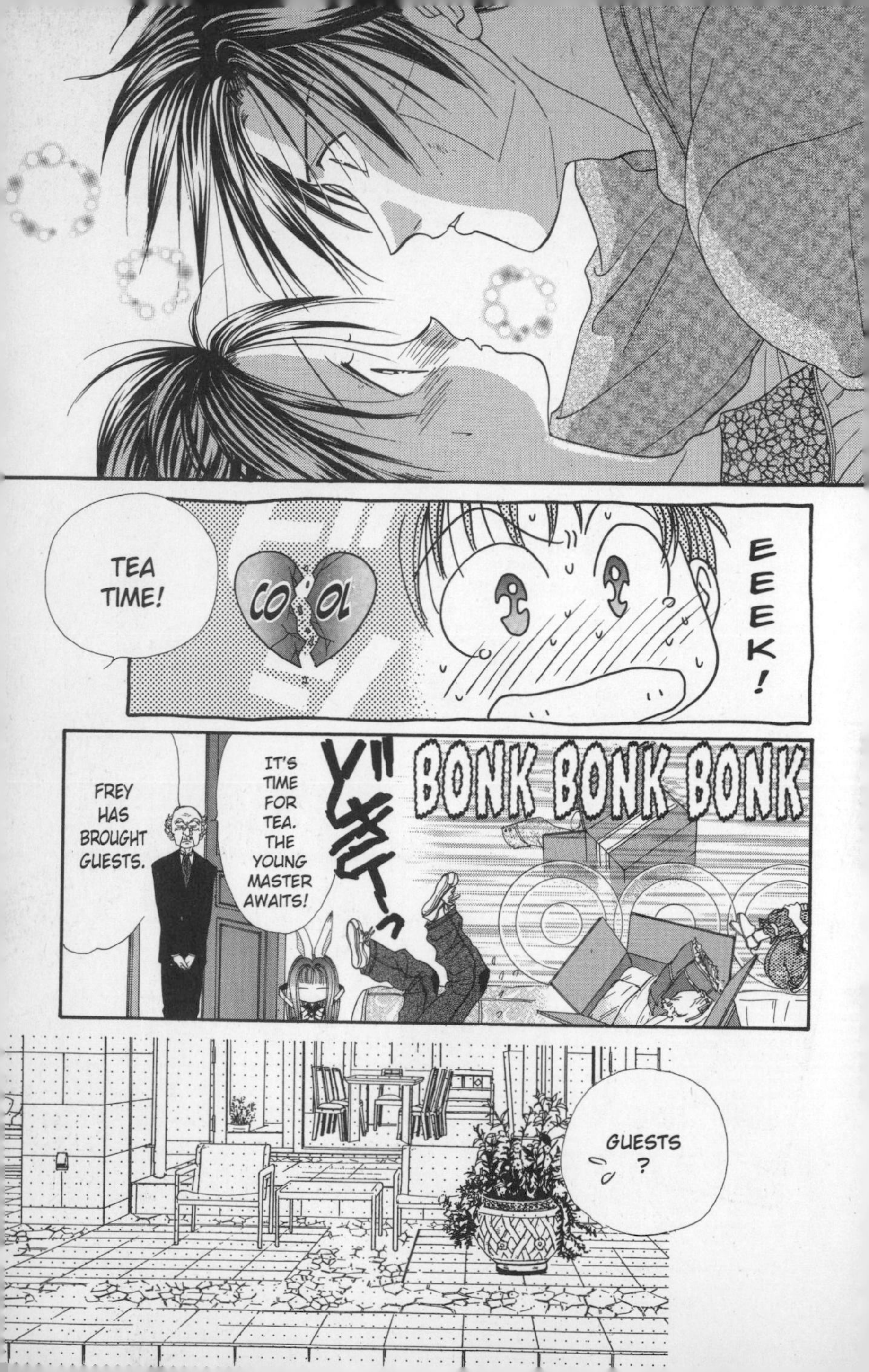
EEEK!
CO OL
TEA TIME!
BONK BONK BONK
IT'S TIME FOR TEA. THE YOUNG MASTER AWAITS!
FREY HAS BROUGHT GUESTS.
GUESTS ?

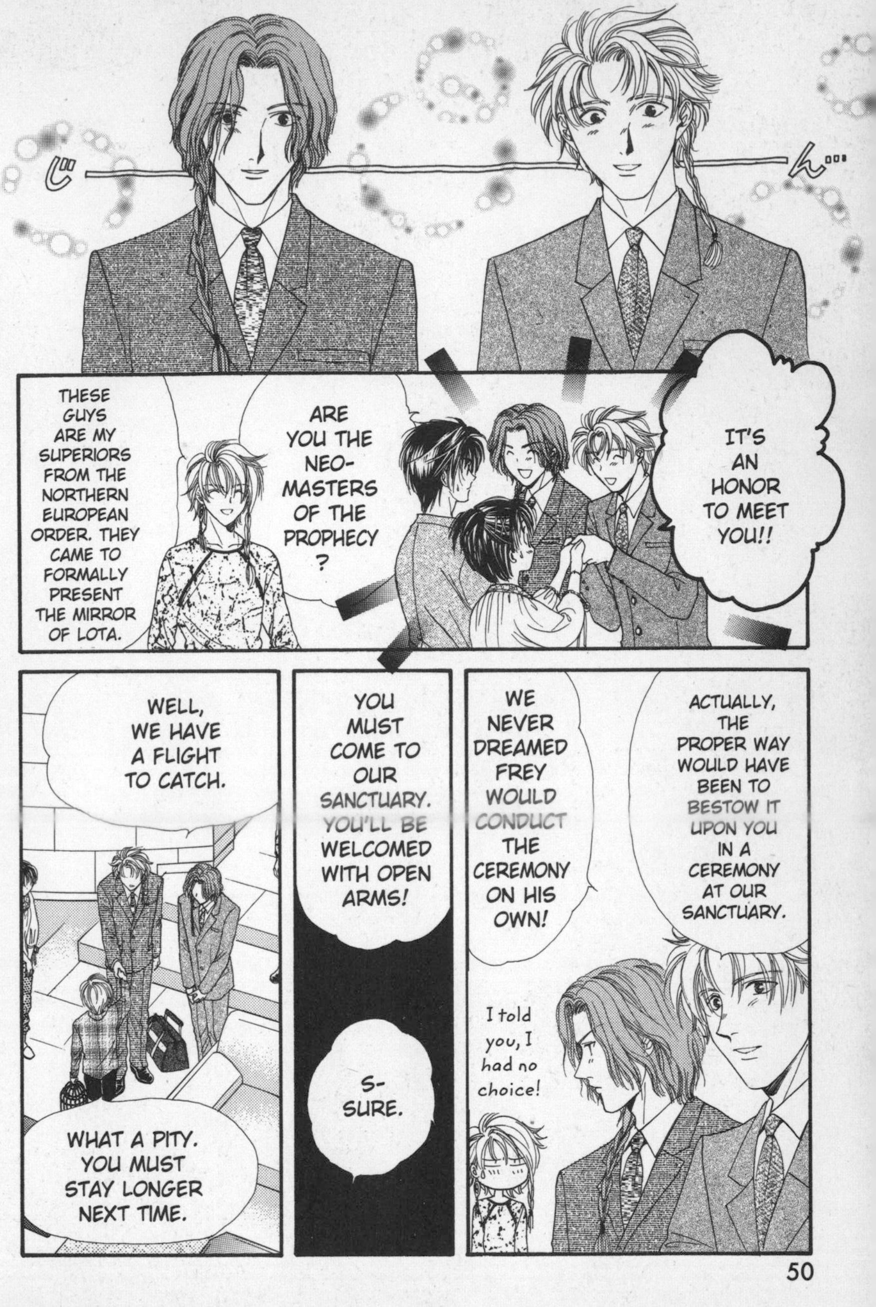
じ—ん…
IT'S AN HONOR TO MEET YOU!!
ARE YOU THE NEO-MASTERS OF THE PROPHECY?
THESE GUYS ARE MY SUPERIORS FROM THE NORTHERN EUROPEAN ORDER. THEY CAME TO FORMALLY PRESENT THE MIRROR OF LOTA.
ACTUALLY, THE PROPER WAY WOULD HAVE BEEN TO BESTOW IT UPON YOU IN A CEREMONY AT OUR SANCTUARY.
WE NEVER DREAMED FREY WOULD CONDUCT THE CEREMONY ON HIS OWN!
I told you, I had no choice!
YOU MUST COME TO OUR SANCTUARY. YOU'LL BE WELCOMED WITH OPEN ARMS!
S-SURE.
WELL, WE HAVE A FLIGHT TO CATCH.
WHAT A PITY. YOU MUST STAY LONGER NEXT TIME.

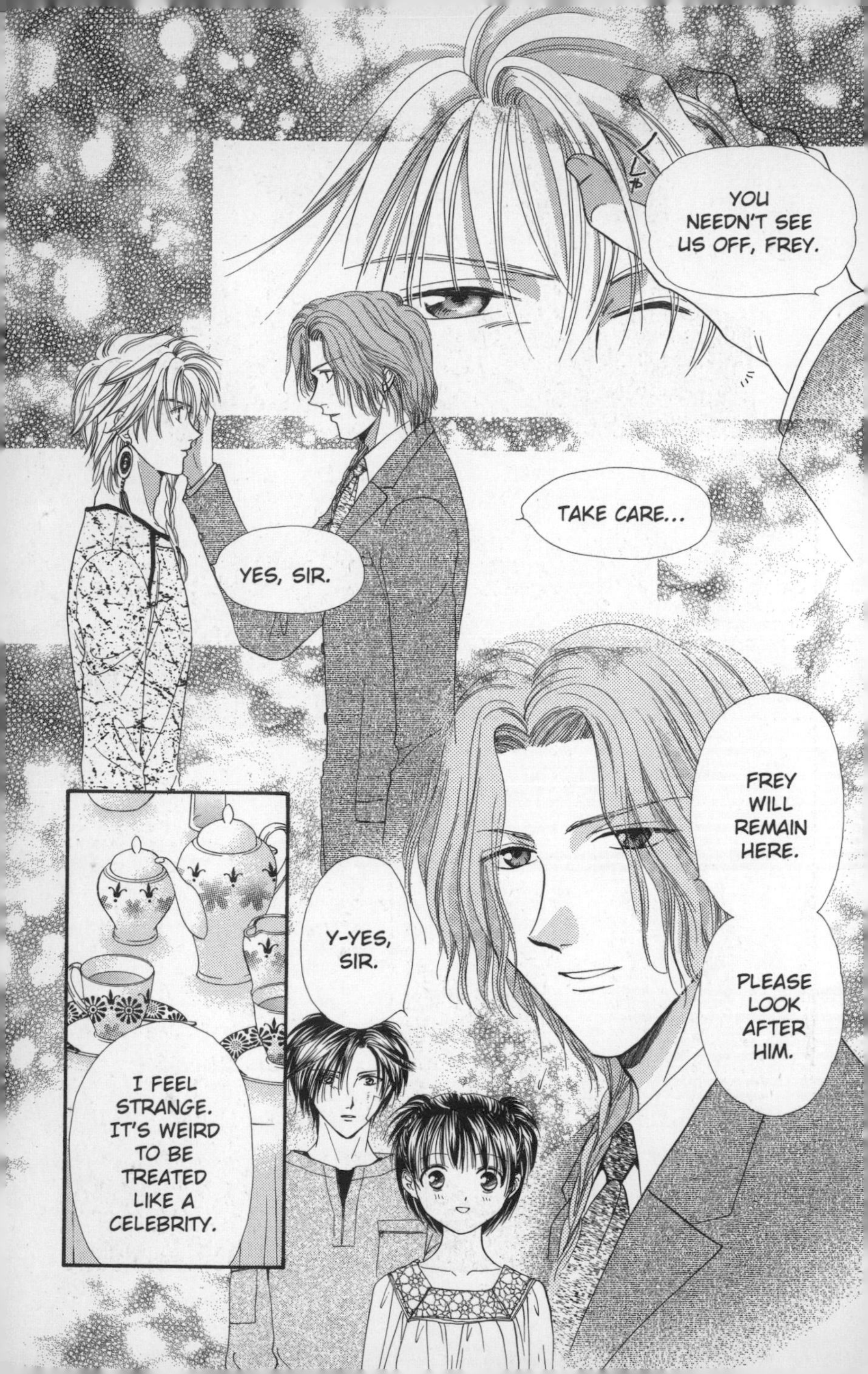
YOU NEEDN'T SEE US OFF, FREY.
TAKE CARE...
YES, SIR.
FREY WILL REMAIN HERE.
PLEASE LOOK AFTER HIM.
Y-YES, SIR.
I FEEL STRANGE. IT'S WEIRD TO BE TREATED LIKE A CELEBRITY.

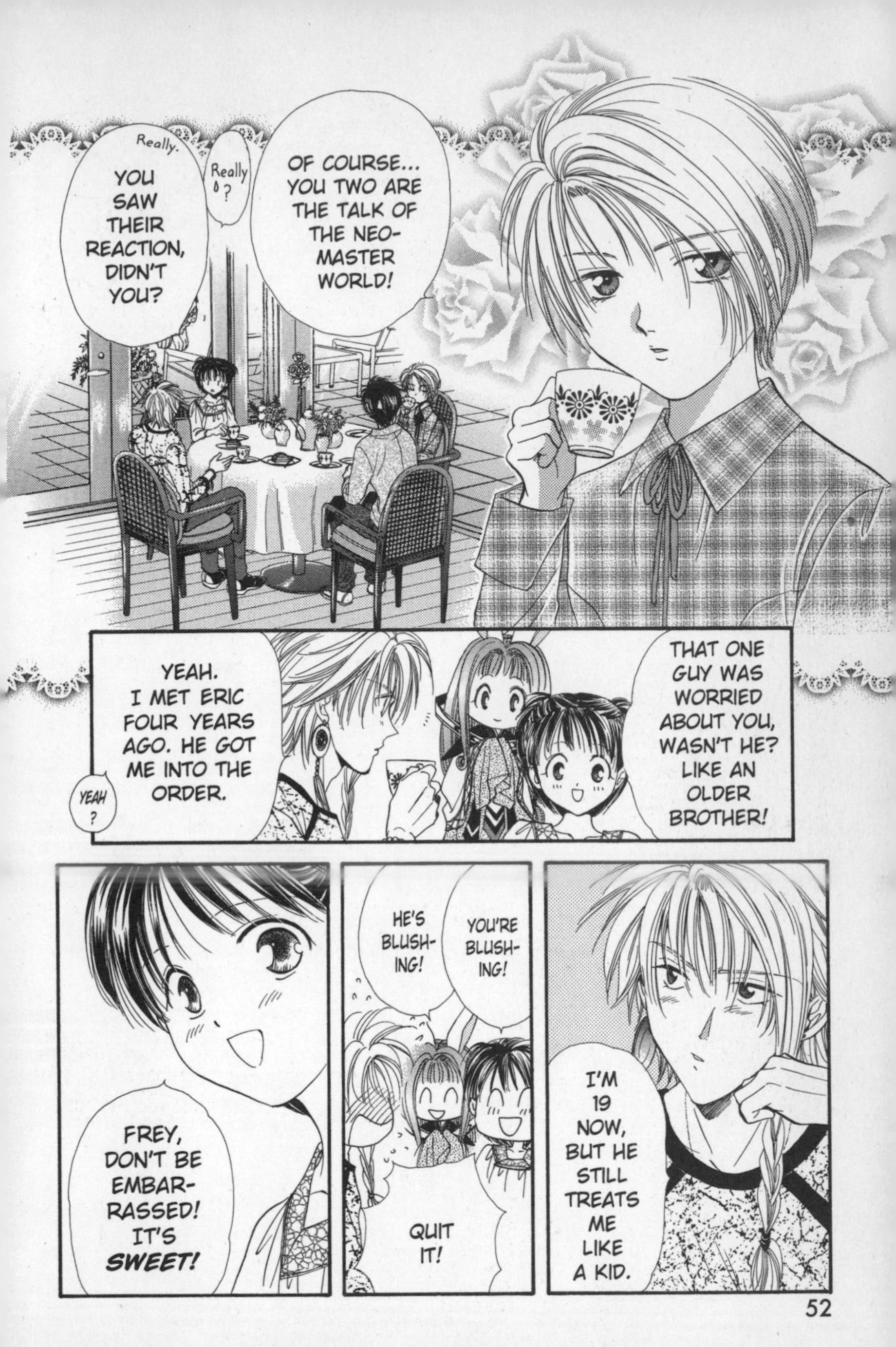
OF COURSE... YOU TWO ARE THE TALK OF THE NEO-MASTER WORLD!
Really?
Really.
YOU SAW THEIR REACTION, DIDN'T YOU?
THAT ONE GUY WAS WORRIED ABOUT YOU, WASN'T HE? LIKE AN OLDER BROTHER!
YEAH. I MET ERIC FOUR YEARS AGO. HE GOT ME INTO THE ORDER.
YEAH?
I'M 19 NOW, BUT HE STILL TREATS ME LIKE A KID.
YOU'RE BLUSHING!
HE'S BLUSHING!
QUIT IT!
FREY, DON'T BE EMBARRASSED! IT'S *SWEET!*

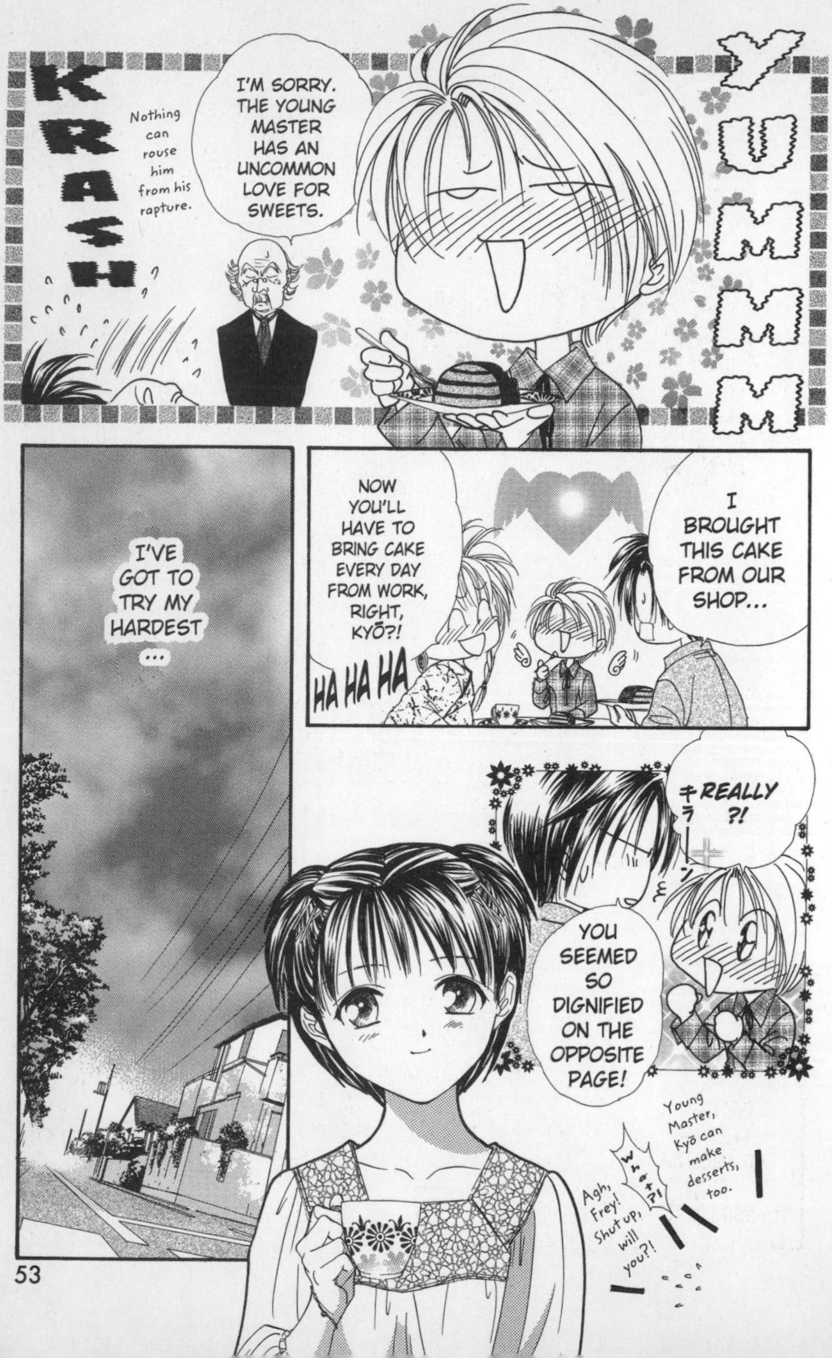
YUMMM
I'M SORRY. THE YOUNG MASTER HAS AN UNCOMMON LOVE FOR SWEETS.
Nothing can rouse him from his rapture.
KRASH
I BROUGHT THIS CAKE FROM OUR SHOP...
NOW YOU'LL HAVE TO BRING CAKE EVERY DAY FROM WORK, RIGHT, KYŌ?!
HA HA HA
REALLY ?!
キラーン
YOU SEEMED SO DIGNIFIED ON THE OPPOSITE PAGE!
Young Master, Kyō can make desserts, too.
What?!
Agh, Frey! Shut up, will you?!
I'VE GOT TO TRY MY HARDEST ...

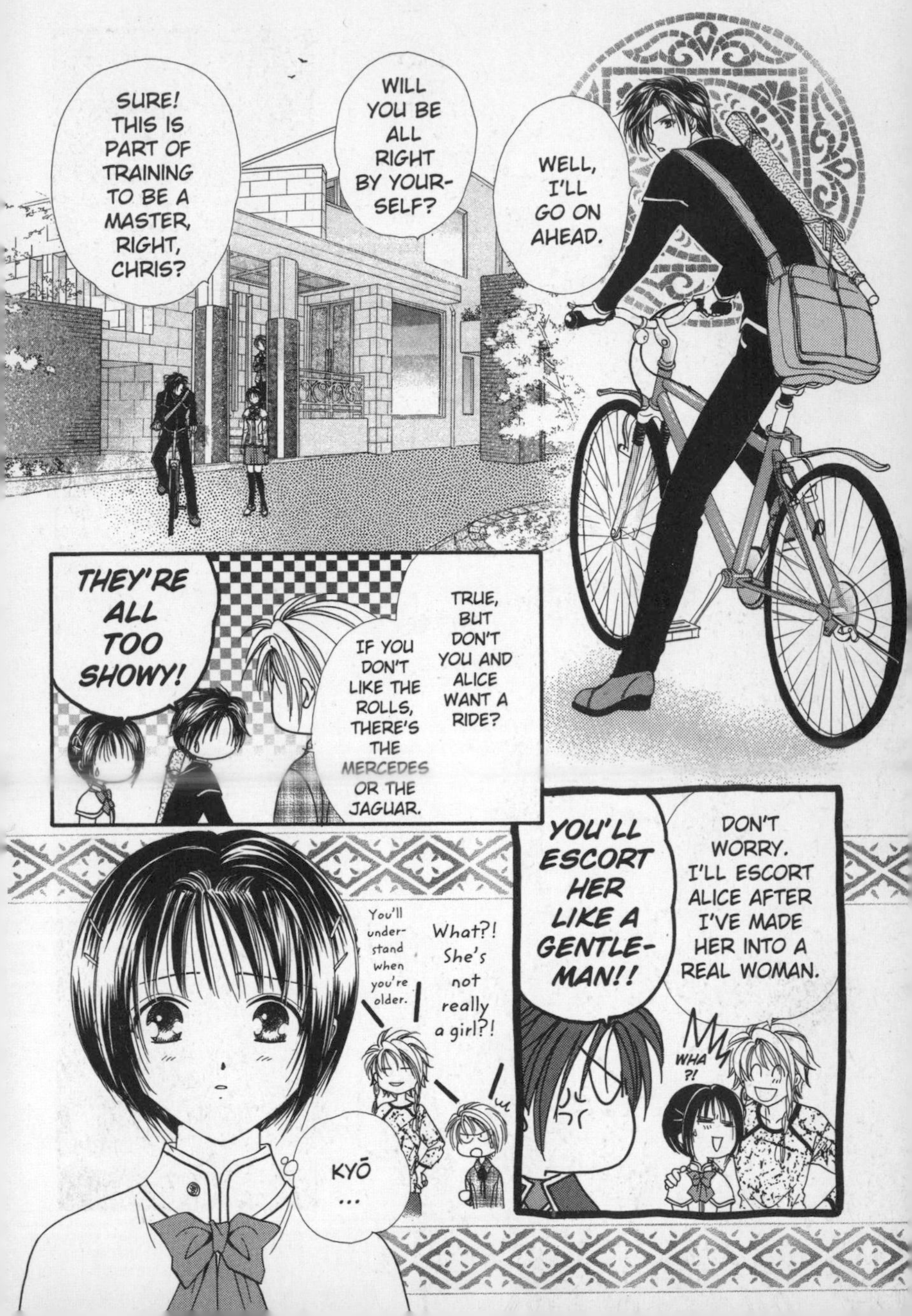
WELL, I'LL GO ON AHEAD.
WILL YOU BE ALL RIGHT BY YOURSELF?
SURE! THIS IS PART OF TRAINING TO BE A MASTER, RIGHT, CHRIS?
TRUE, BUT DON'T YOU AND ALICE WANT A RIDE?
IF YOU DON'T LIKE THE ROLLS, THERE'S THE MERCEDES OR THE JAGUAR.
THEY'RE ALL TOO SHOWY!
DON'T WORRY. I'LL ESCORT ALICE AFTER I'VE MADE HER INTO A REAL WOMAN.
YOU'LL ESCORT HER LIKE A GENTLEMAN!!
WHA ?!
What?! She's not really a girl?!
You'll understand when you're older.
KYŌ ...

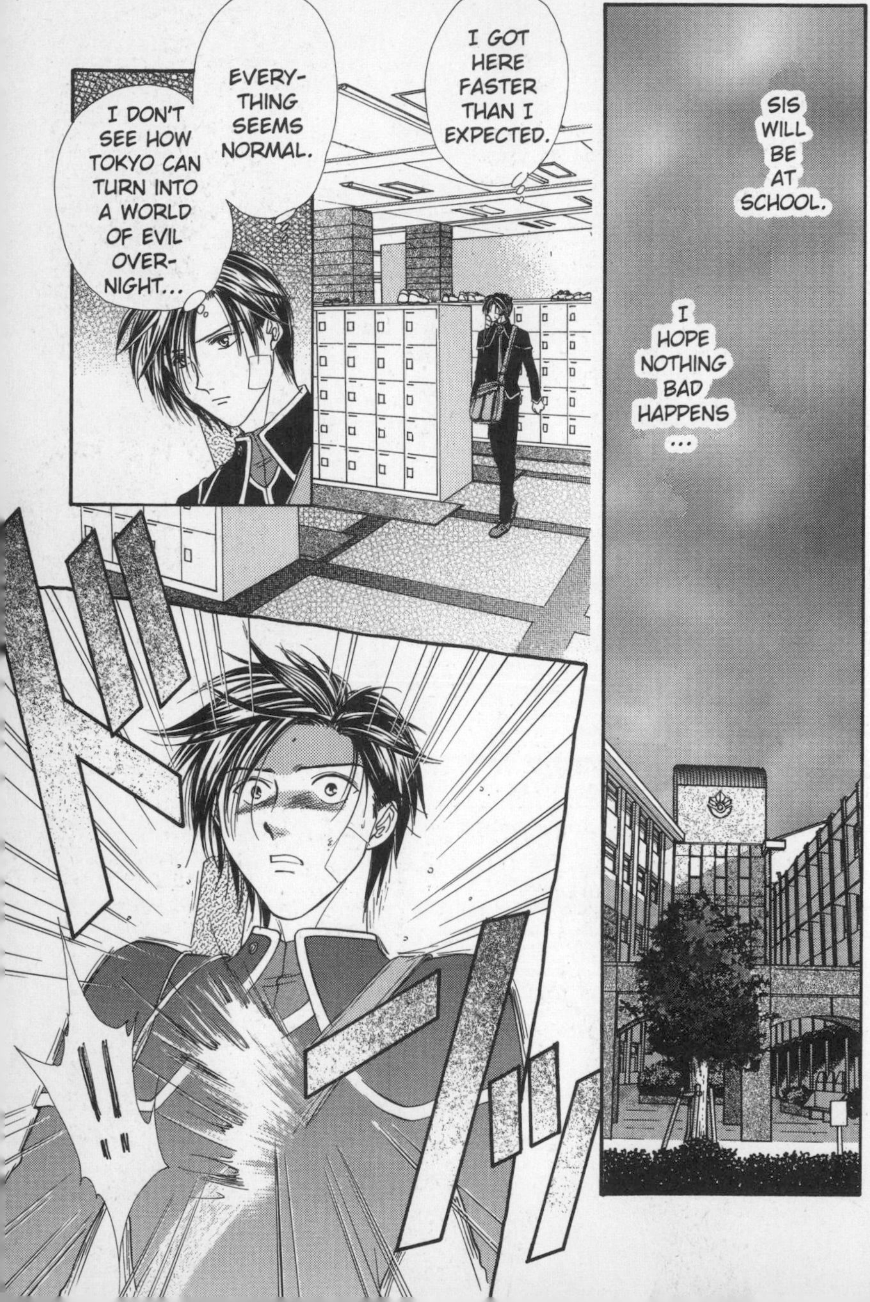
SIS WILL BE AT SCHOOL.
I HOPE NOTHING BAD HAPPENS...
I GOT HERE FASTER THAN I EXPECTED.
EVERY-THING SEEMS NORMAL.
I DON'T SEE HOW TOKYO CAN TURN INTO A WORLD OF EVIL OVER-NIGHT...

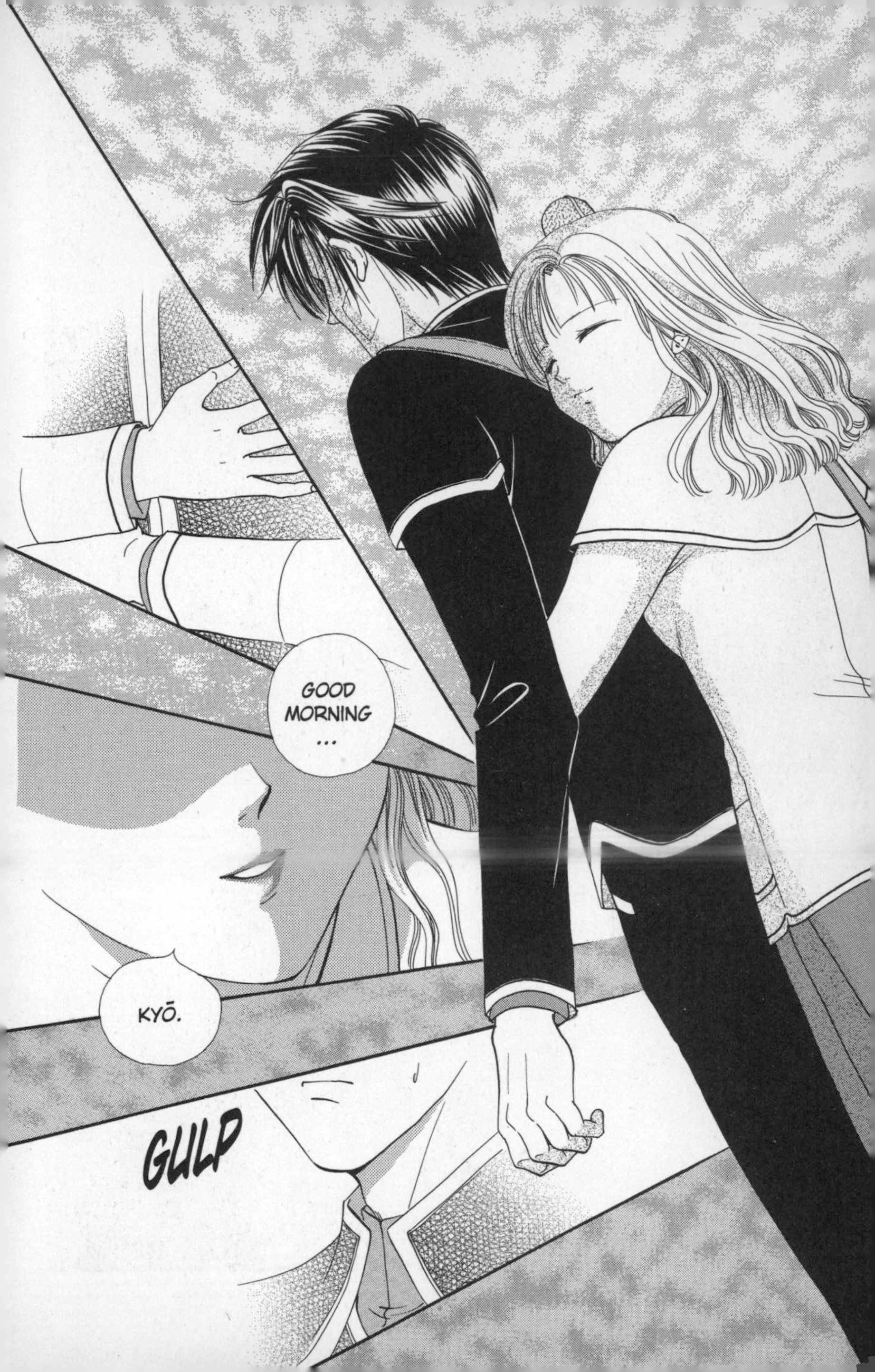
GOOD MORNING ...
KYŌ.
GULP

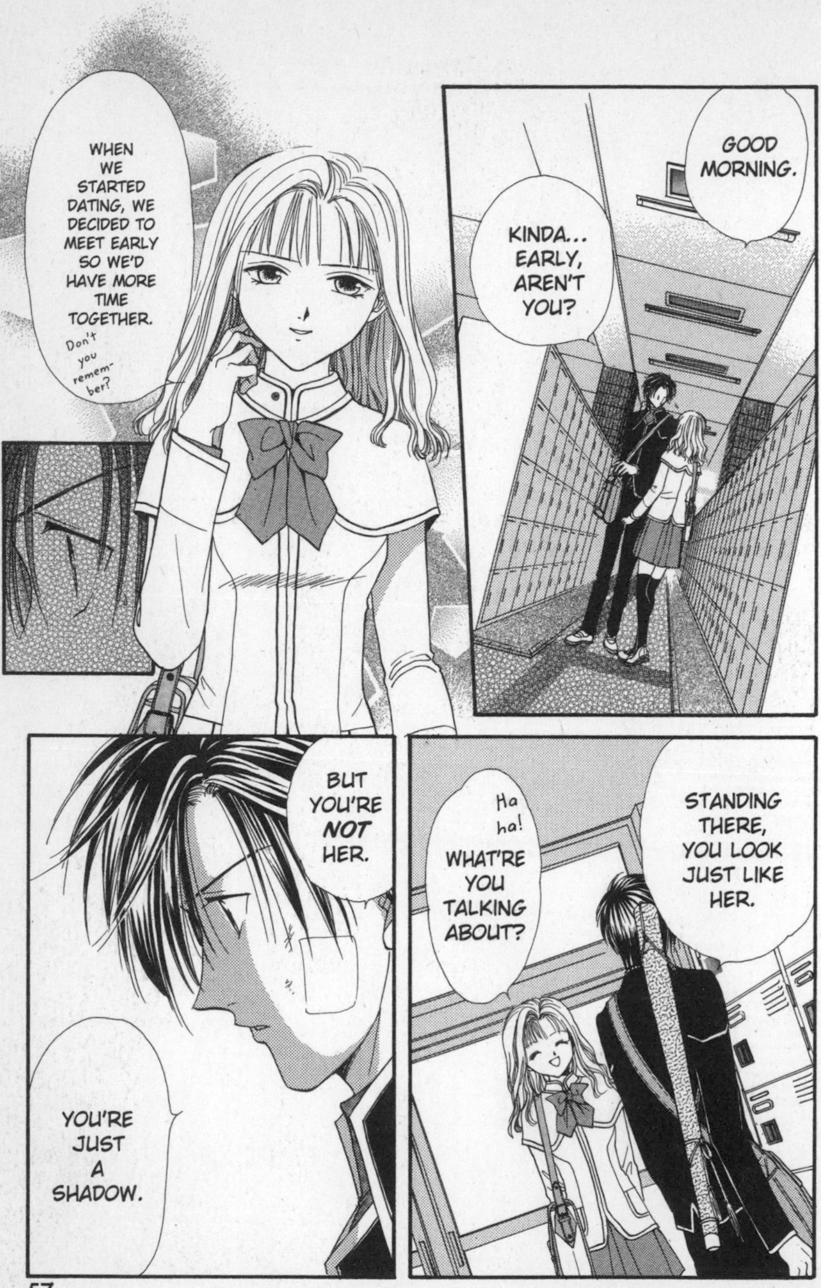
GOOD MORNING.
KINDA... EARLY, AREN'T YOU?
WHEN WE STARTED DATING, WE DECIDED TO MEET EARLY SO WE'D HAVE MORE TIME TOGETHER.
Don't you remem-ber?
STANDING THERE, YOU LOOK JUST LIKE HER.
Ha ha!
WHAT'RE YOU TALKING ABOUT?
BUT YOU'RE *NOT* HER.
YOU'RE JUST A SHADOW.

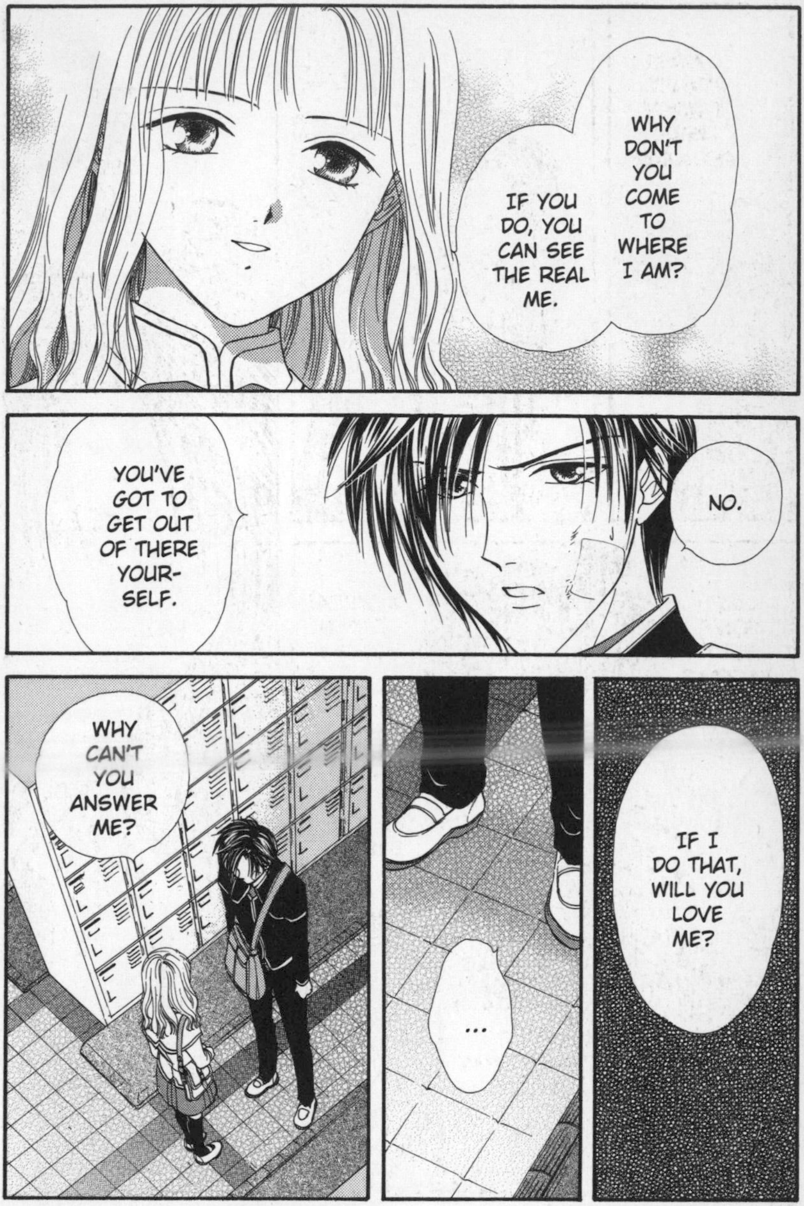
WHY DON'T YOU COME TO WHERE I AM?
IF YOU DO, YOU CAN SEE THE REAL ME.
NO.
YOU'VE GOT TO GET OUT OF THERE YOUR-SELF.
IF I DO THAT, WILL YOU LOVE ME?
...
WHY CAN'T YOU ANSWER ME?

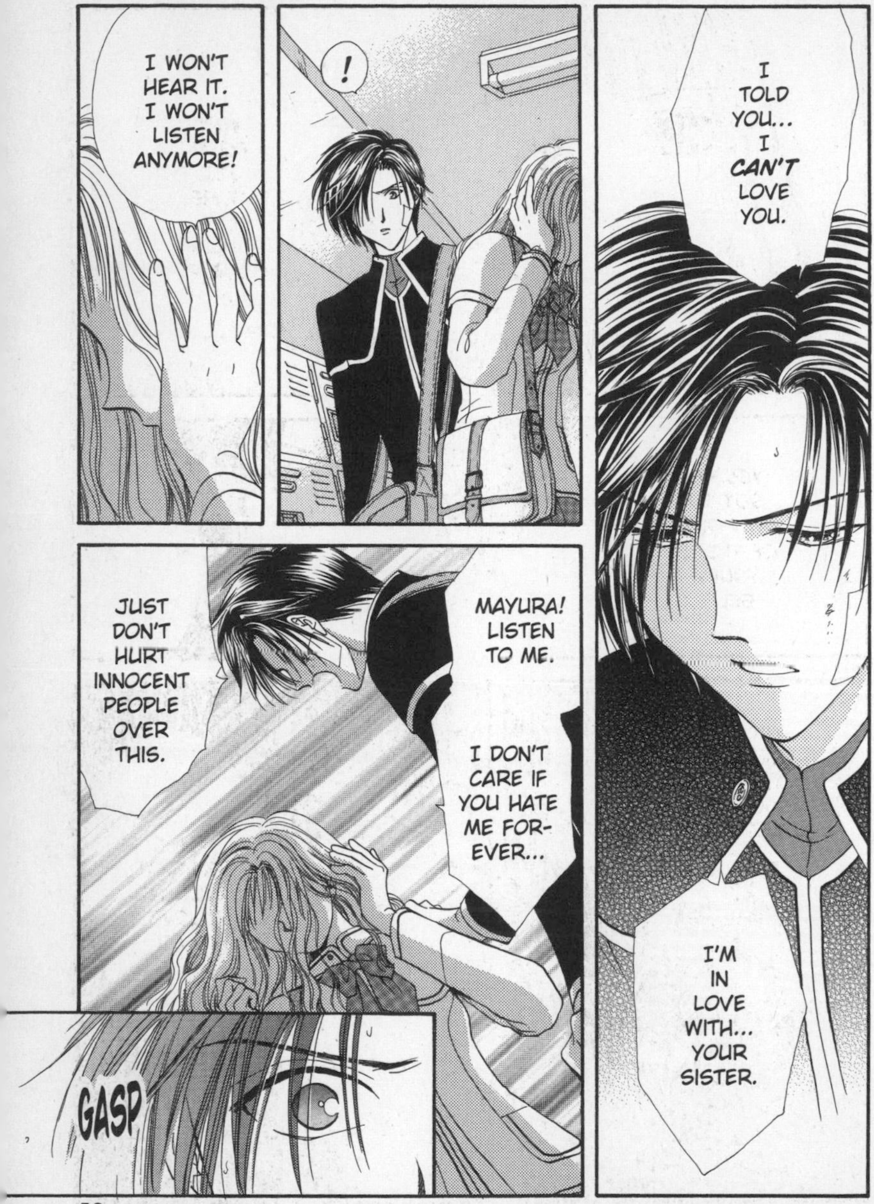
I TOLD YOU... I *CAN'T* LOVE YOU.
I'M IN LOVE WITH... YOUR SISTER.
!
I WON'T HEAR IT. I WON'T LISTEN ANYMORE!
MAYURA! LISTEN TO ME.
I DON'T CARE IF YOU HATE ME FOR-EVER...
JUST DON'T HURT INNOCENT PEOPLE OVER THIS.
GASP

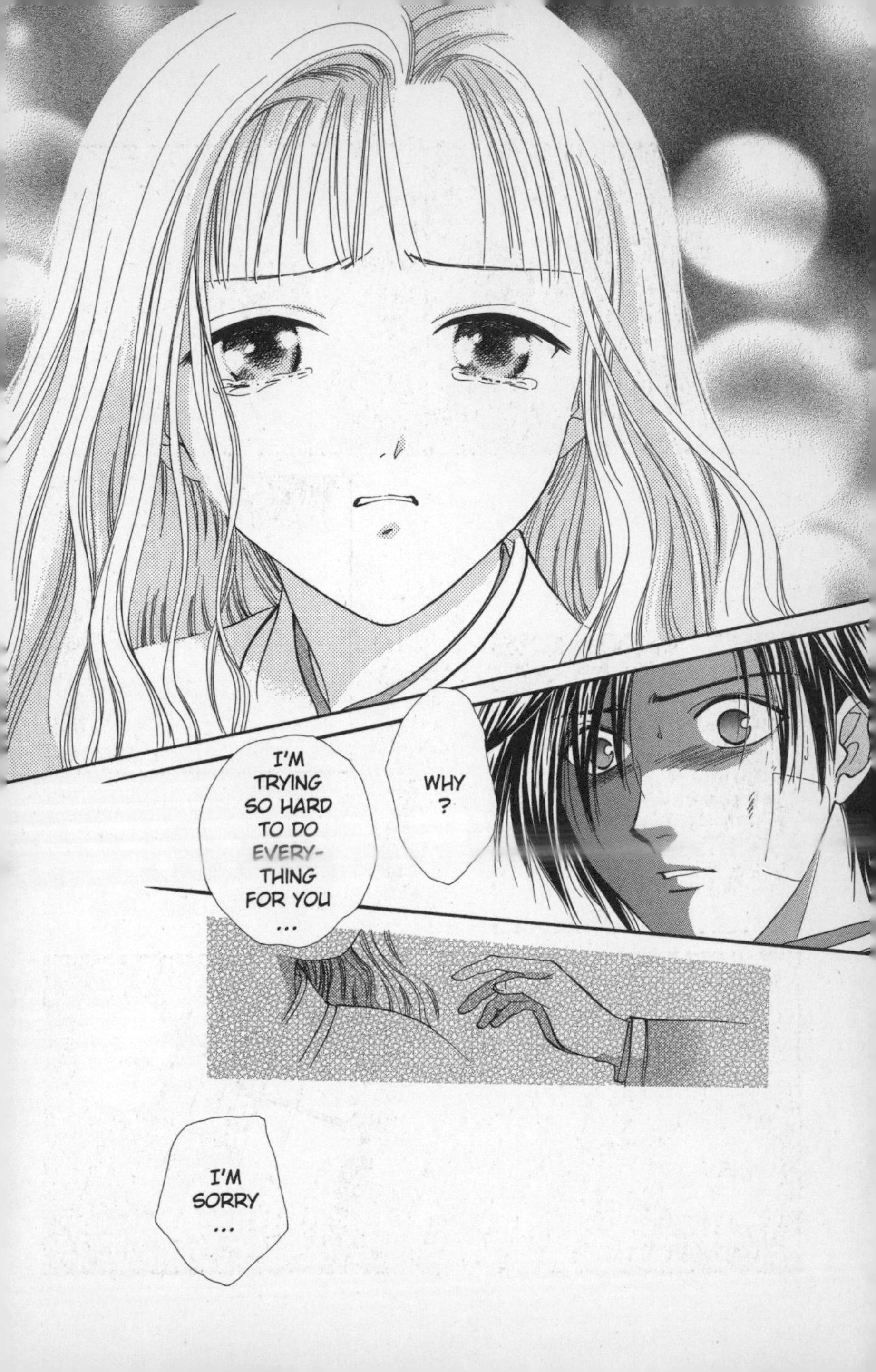
WHY?
I'M TRYING SO HARD TO DO EVERY-THING FOR YOU...
I'M SORRY...

I'M SORRY !!

SEE ?

...

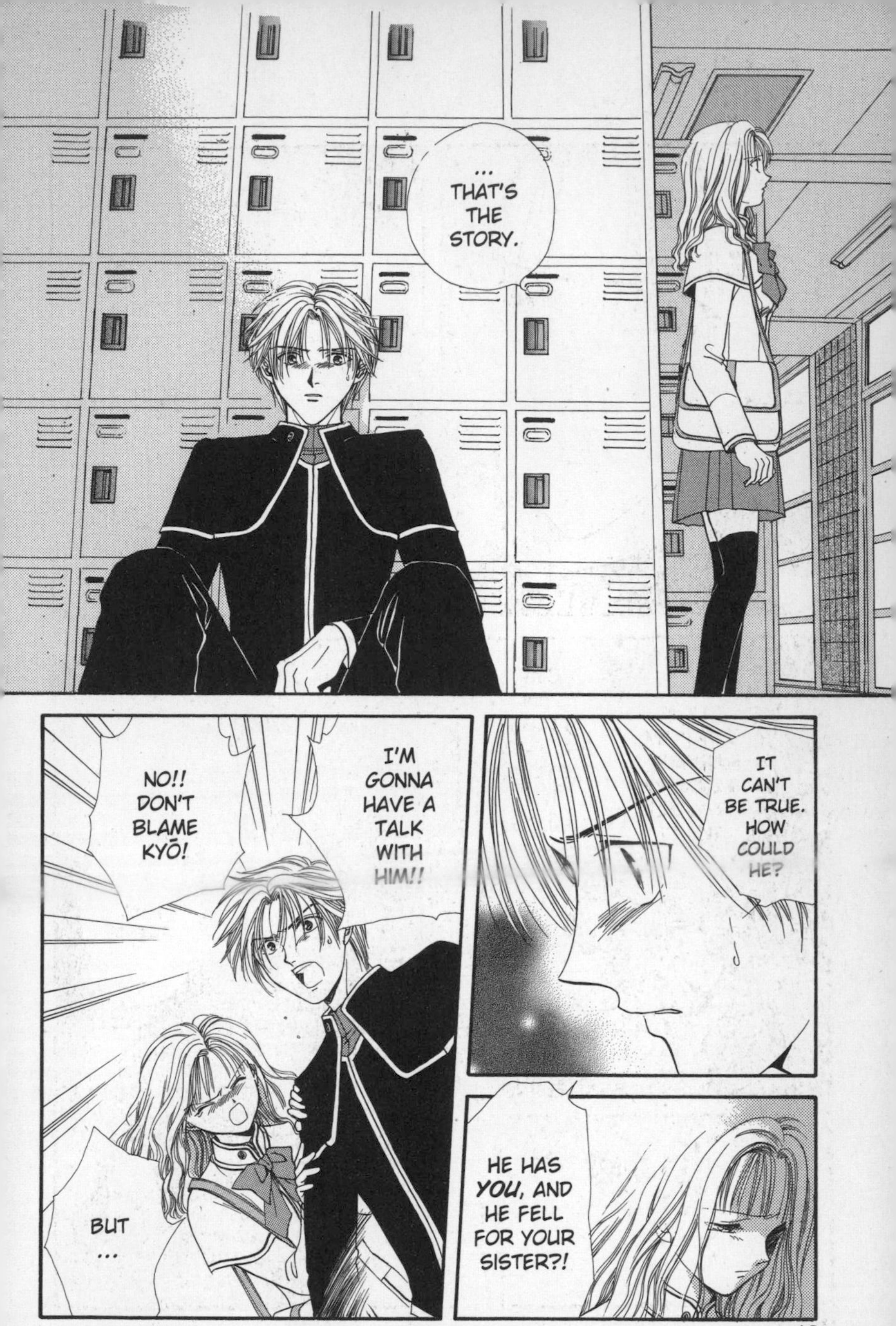
... THAT'S THE STORY.
IT CAN'T BE TRUE. HOW COULD HE?
HE HAS *YOU*, AND HE FELL FOR YOUR SISTER?!
I'M GONNA HAVE A TALK WITH HIM!!
NO!! DON'T BLAME KYŌ!
BUT ...

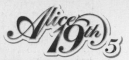

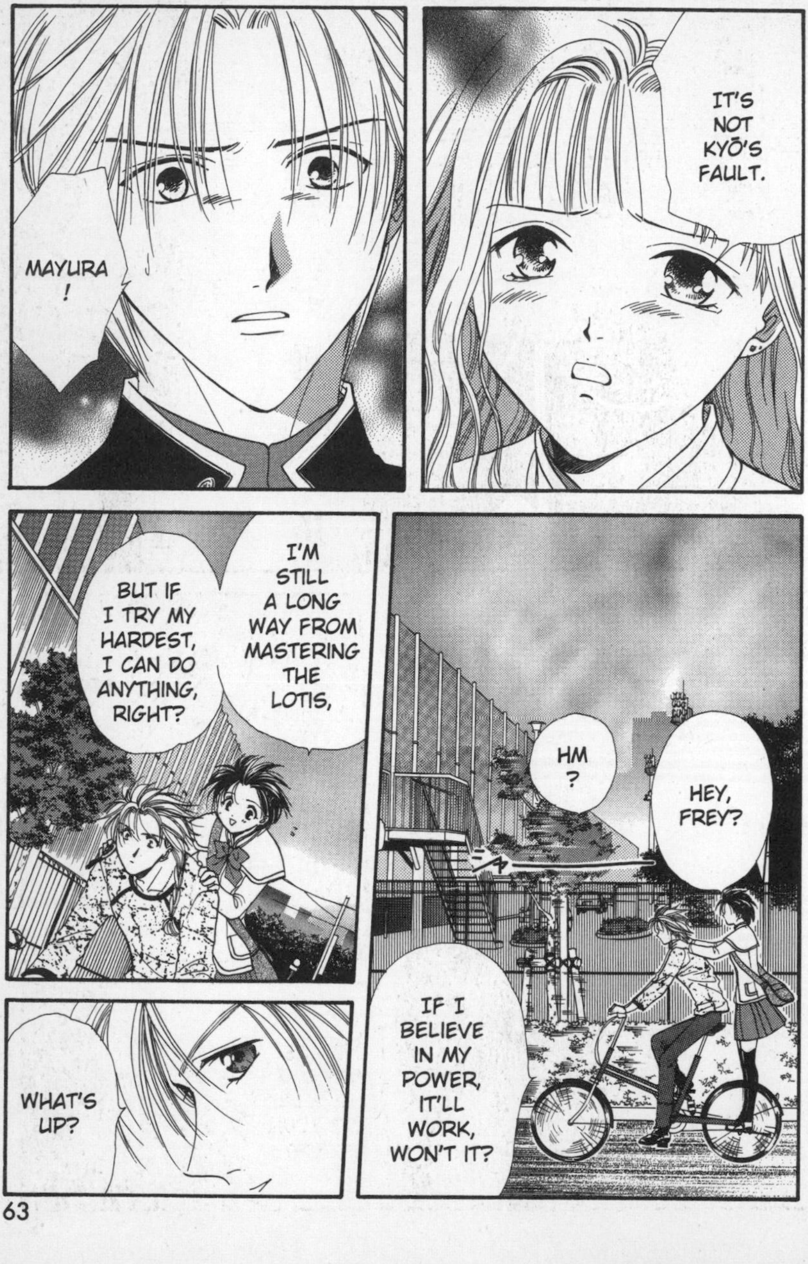
IT'S NOT KYŌ'S FAULT.
MAYURA!
HEY, FREY?
HM?
IF I BELIEVE IN MY POWER, IT'LL WORK, WON'T IT?
I'M STILL A LONG WAY FROM MASTERING THE LOTIS,
BUT IF I TRY MY HARDEST, I CAN DO ANYTHING, RIGHT?
WHAT'S UP?

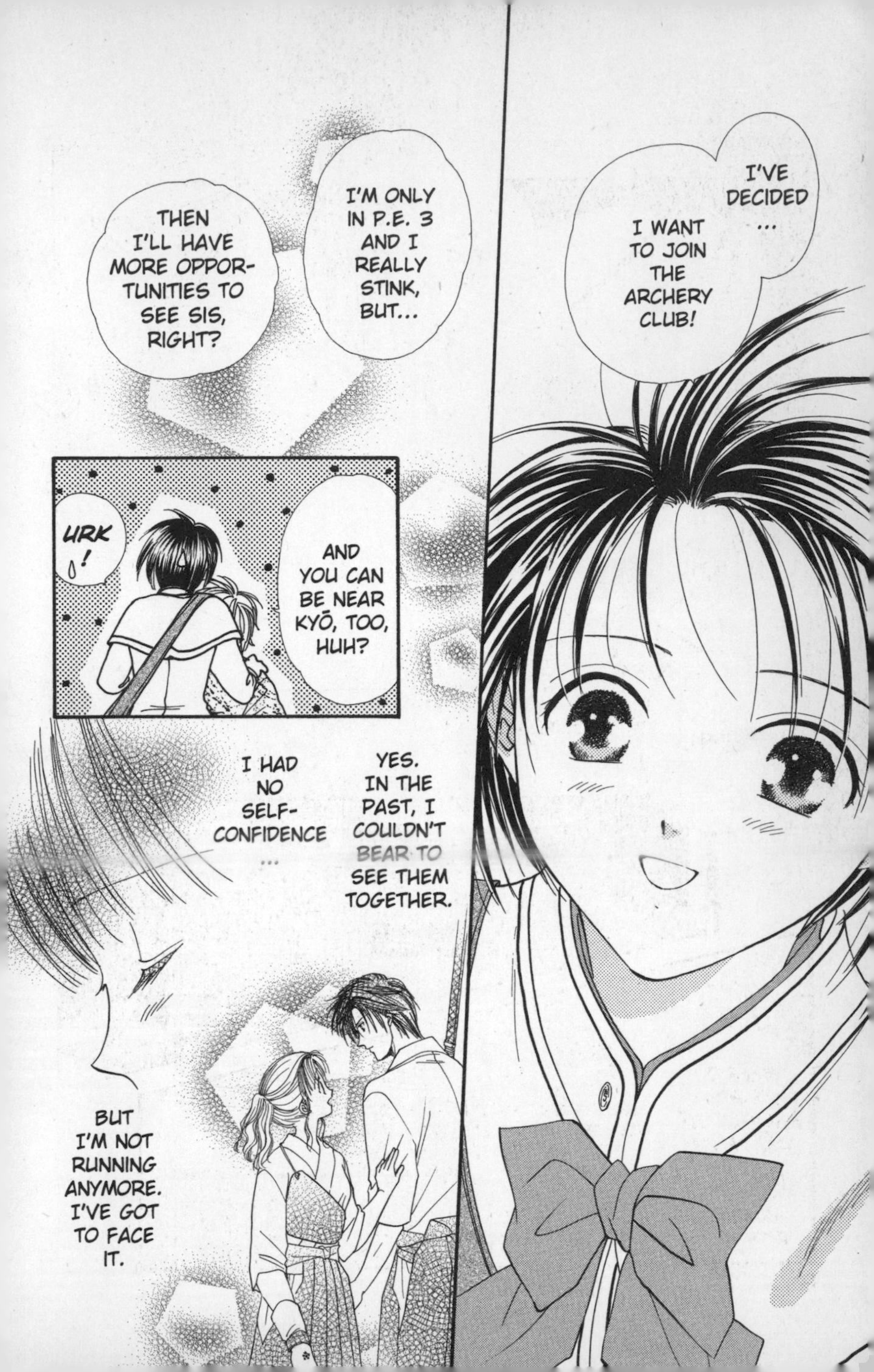
I'VE DECIDED ...
I WANT TO JOIN THE ARCHERY CLUB!
I'M ONLY IN P.E. 3 AND I REALLY STINK, BUT...
THEN I'LL HAVE MORE OPPOR-TUNITIES TO SEE SIS, RIGHT?
AND YOU CAN BE NEAR KYŌ, TOO, HUH?
URK!
YES. IN THE PAST, I COULDN'T BEAR TO SEE THEM TOGETHER.
I HAD NO SELF-CONFIDENCE ...
BUT I'M NOT RUNNING ANYMORE. I'VE GOT TO FACE IT.

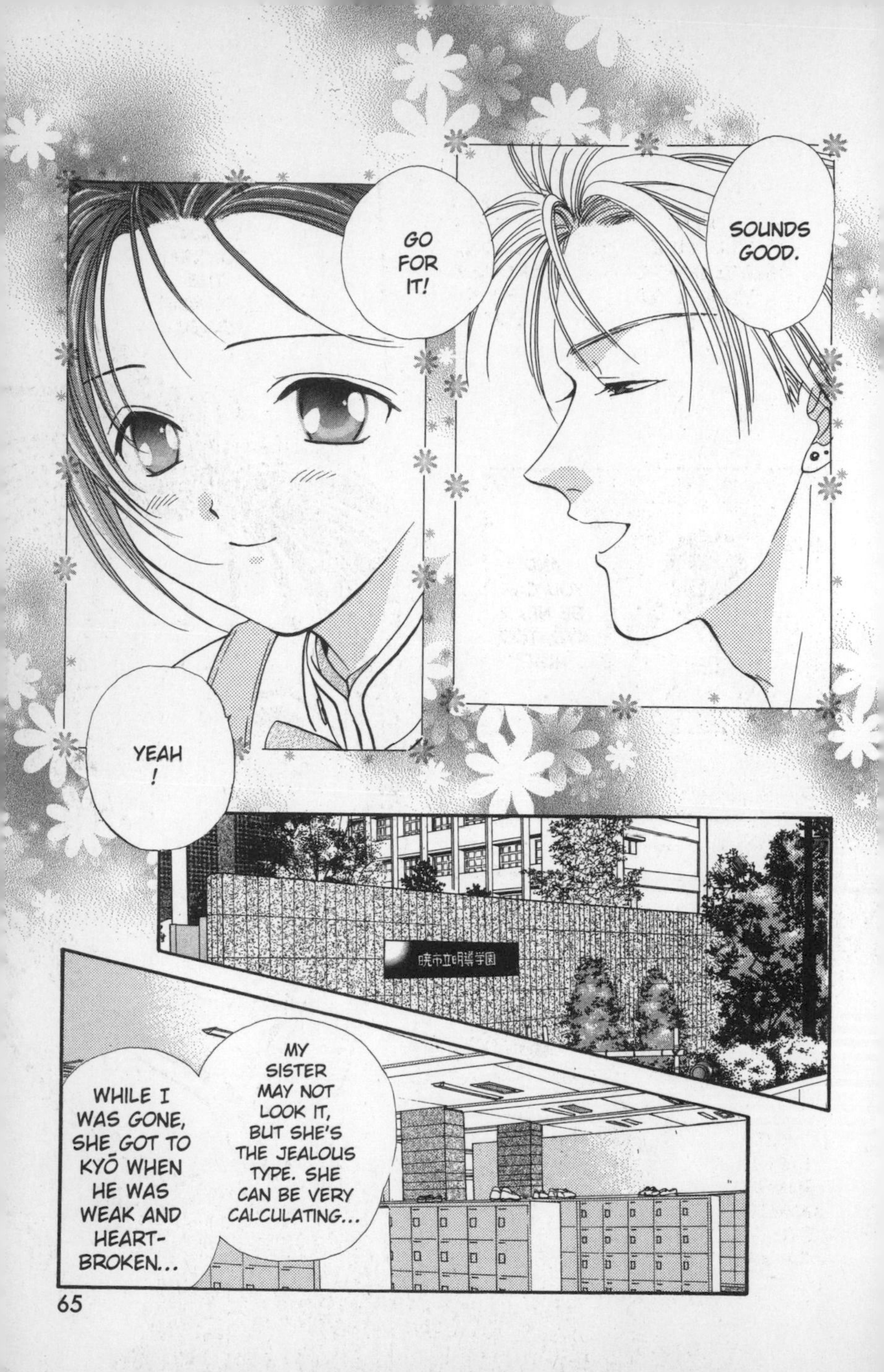
SOUNDS GOOD.
GO FOR IT!
YEAH!
暁市立明導学園
MY SISTER MAY NOT LOOK IT, BUT SHE'S THE JEALOUS TYPE. SHE CAN BE VERY CALCULATING...
WHILE I WAS GONE, SHE GOT TO KYŌ WHEN HE WAS WEAK AND HEART-BROKEN...

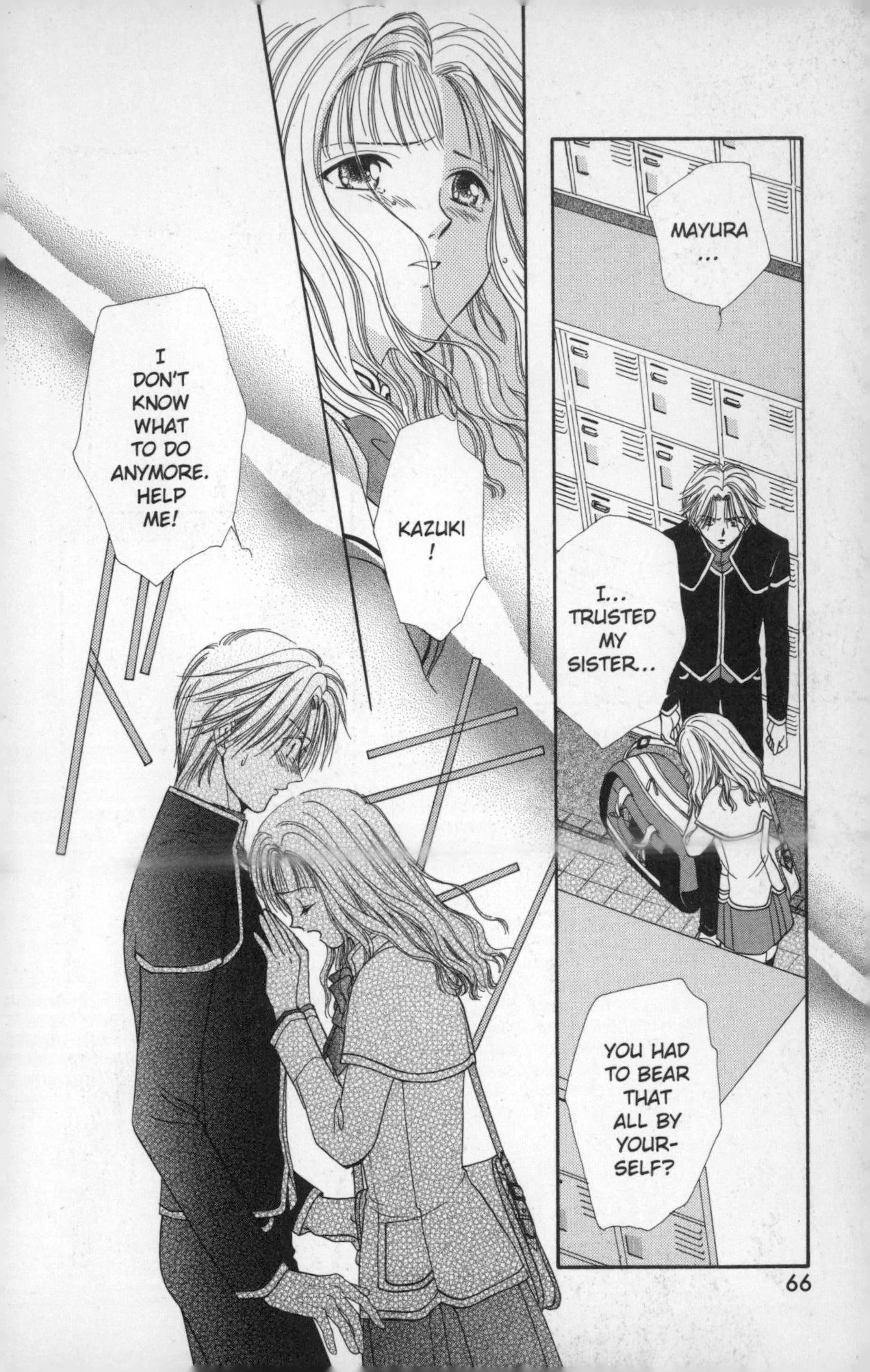
MAYURA ...
I... TRUSTED MY SISTER...
YOU HAD TO BEAR THAT ALL BY YOUR-SELF?
KAZUKI!
I DON'T KNOW WHAT TO DO ANYMORE. HELP ME!

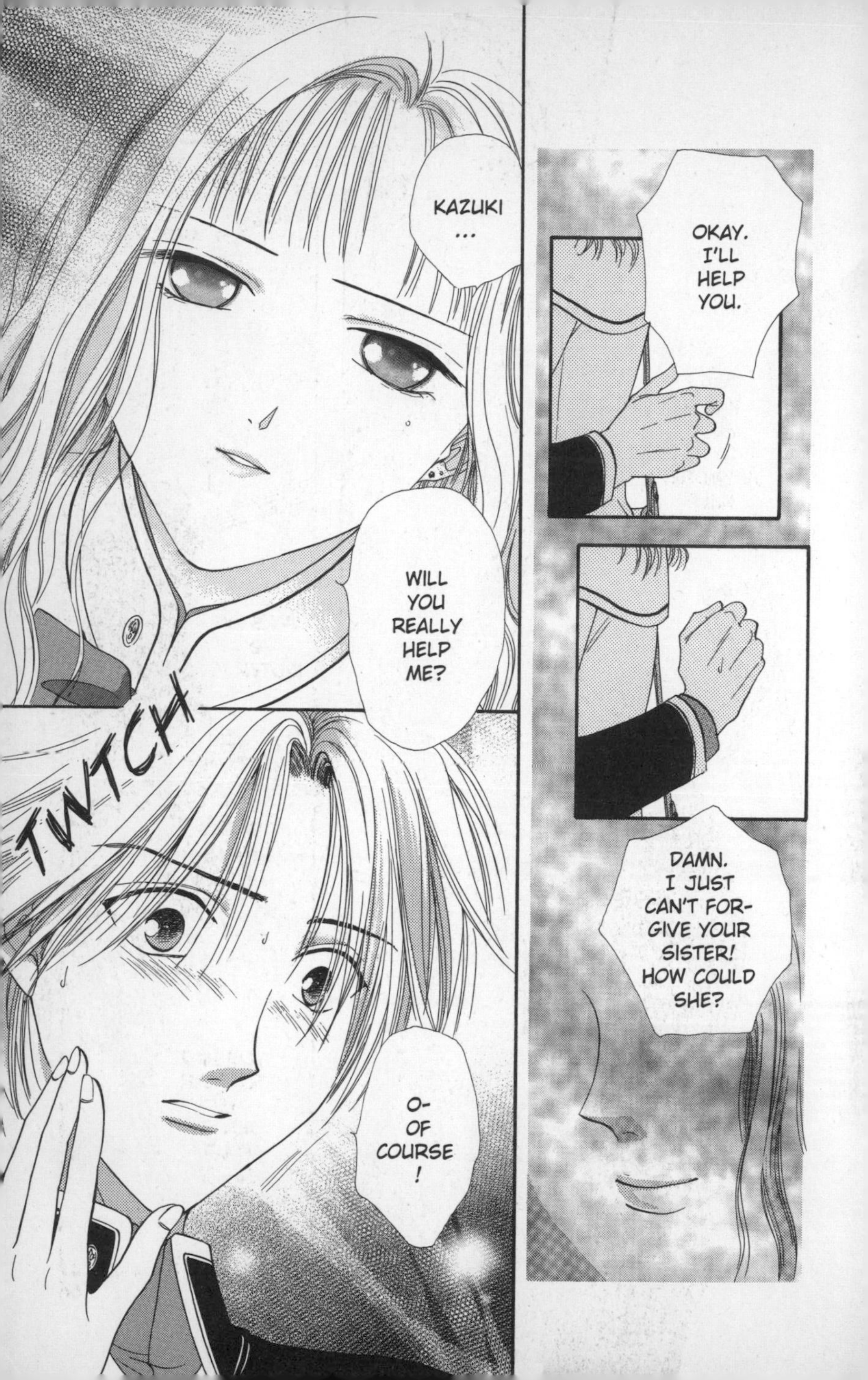
OKAY. I'LL HELP YOU.
DAMN. I JUST CAN'T FOR-GIVE YOUR SISTER! HOW COULD SHE?
KAZUKI ...
WILL YOU REALLY HELP ME?
TWITCH
O-OF COURSE!

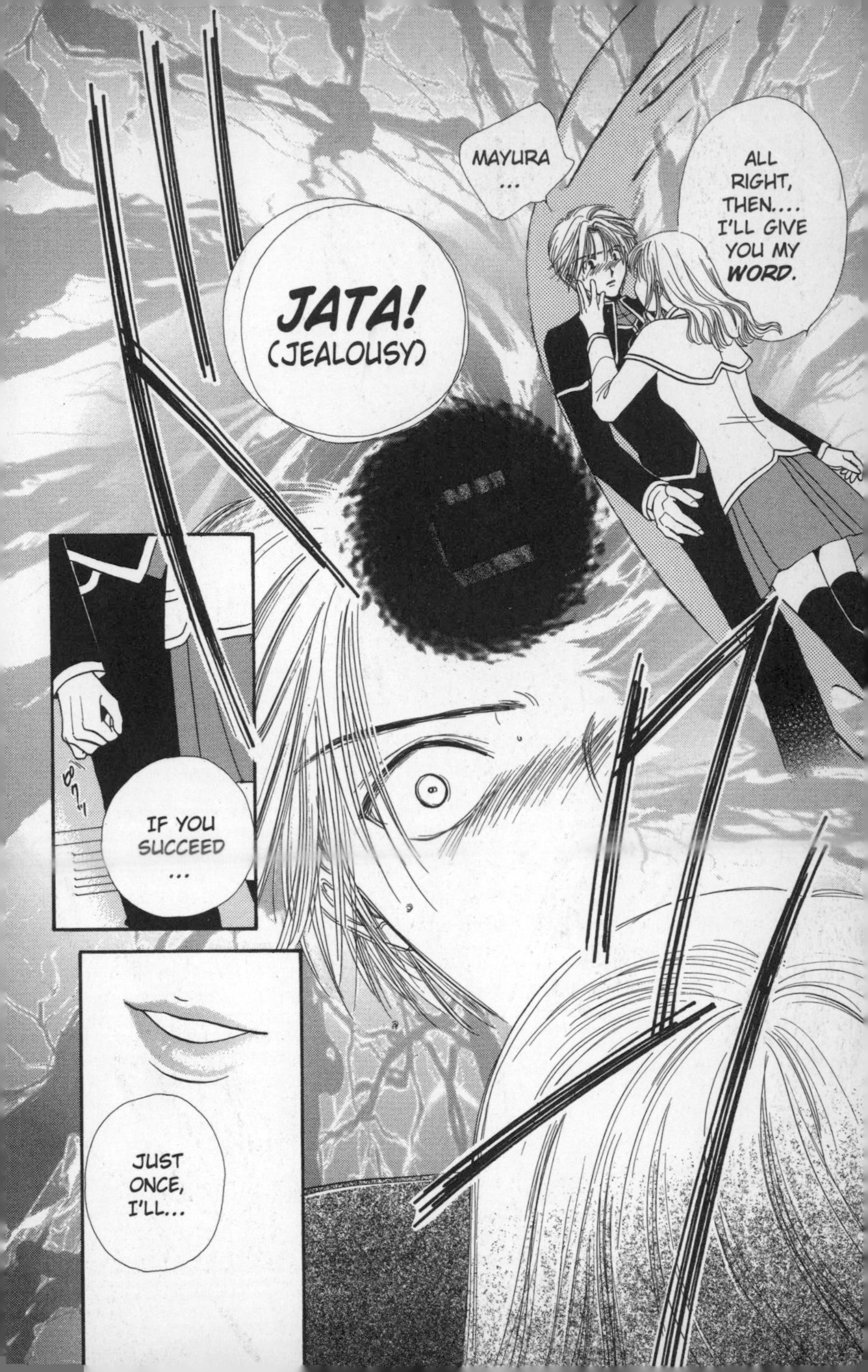
ALL RIGHT, THEN.... I'LL GIVE YOU MY WORD.
MAYURA...
JATA! (JEALOUSY)
IF YOU SUCCEED...
JUST ONCE, I'LL...

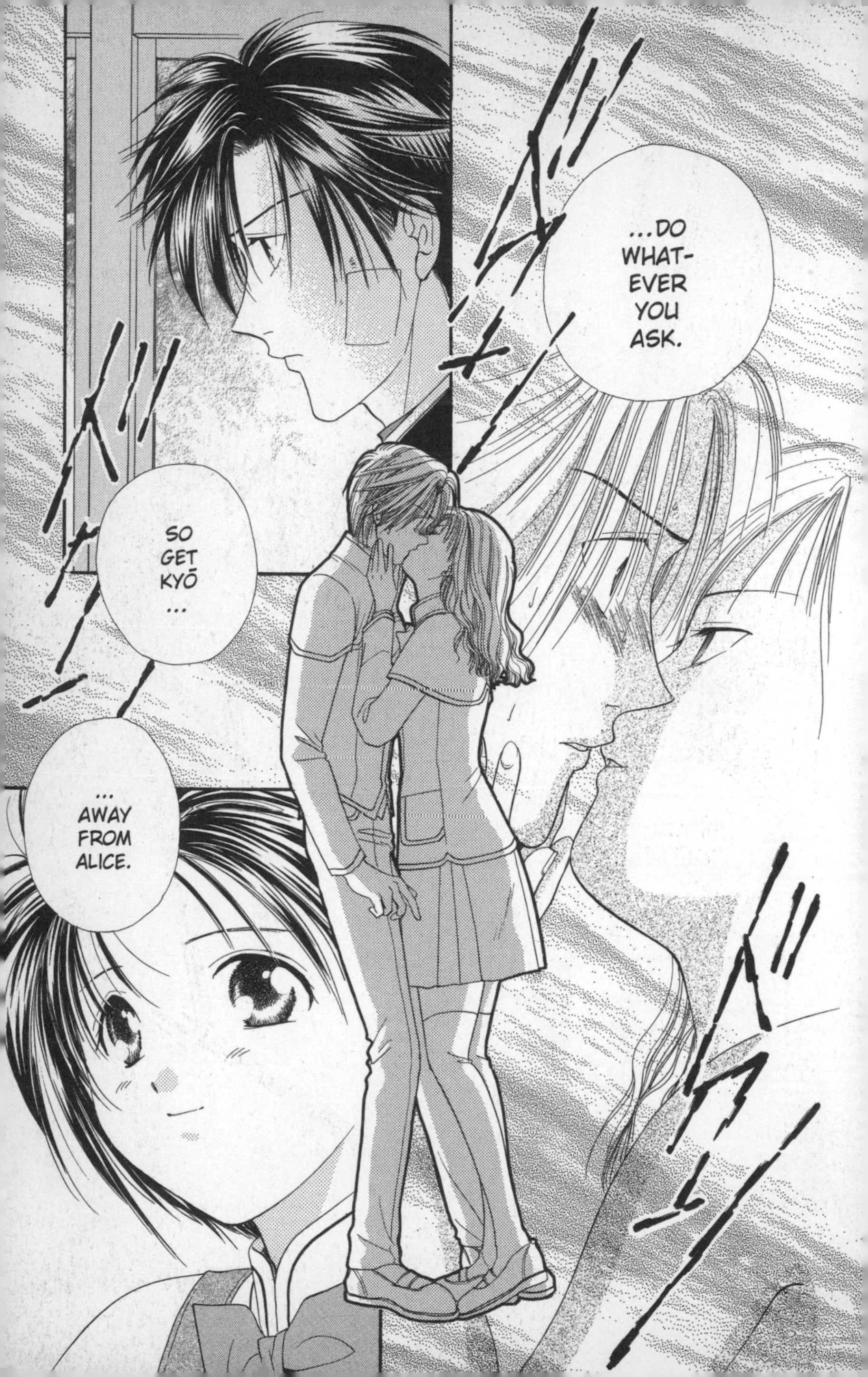
...DO WHATEVER YOU ASK.
SO GET KYŌ ...
... AWAY FROM ALICE.

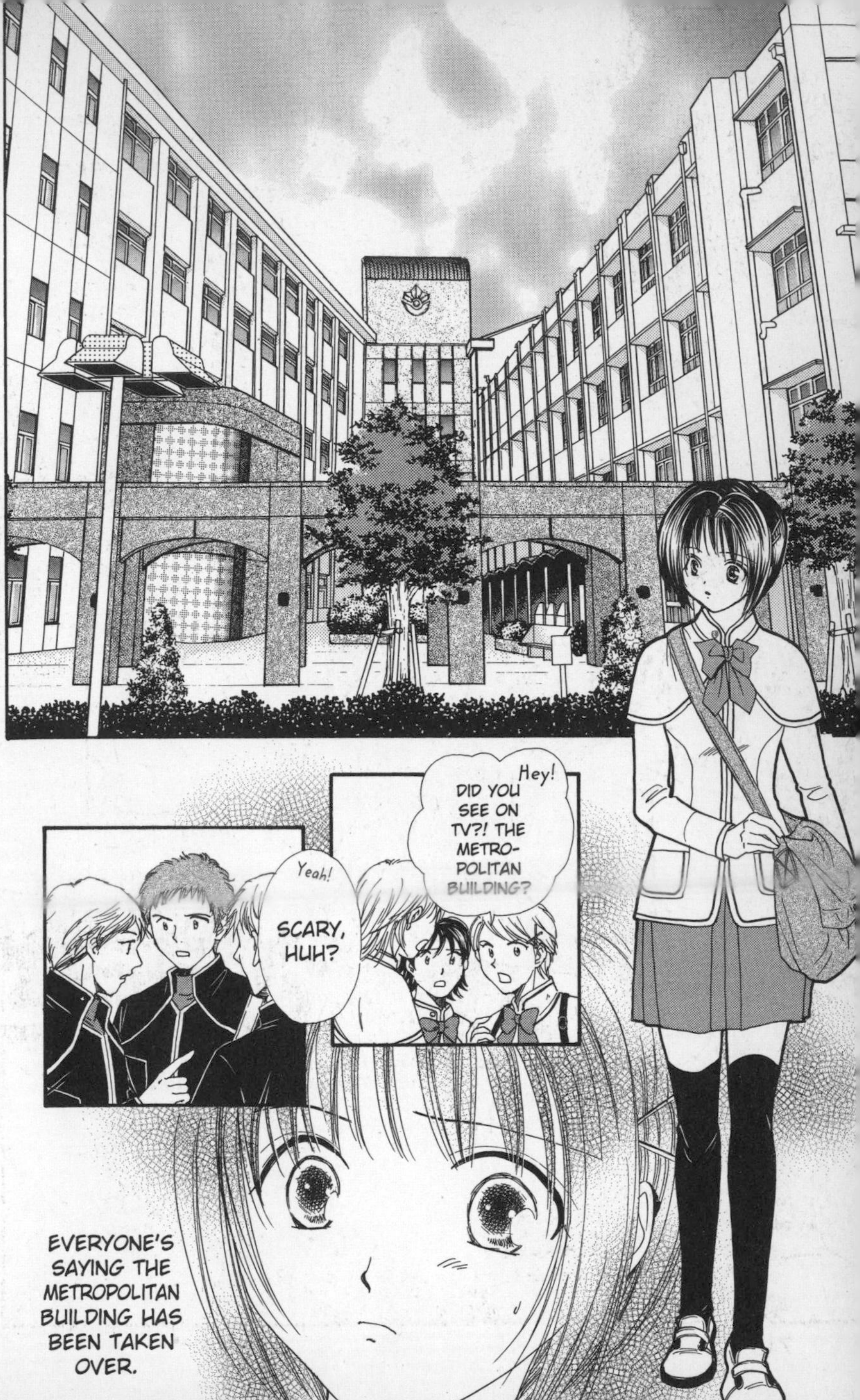
Hey!
DID YOU SEE ON TV?! THE METRO-POLITAN BUILDING?
Yeah!
SCARY, HUH?
EVERYONE'S SAYING THE METROPOLITAN BUILDING HAS BEEN TAKEN OVER.

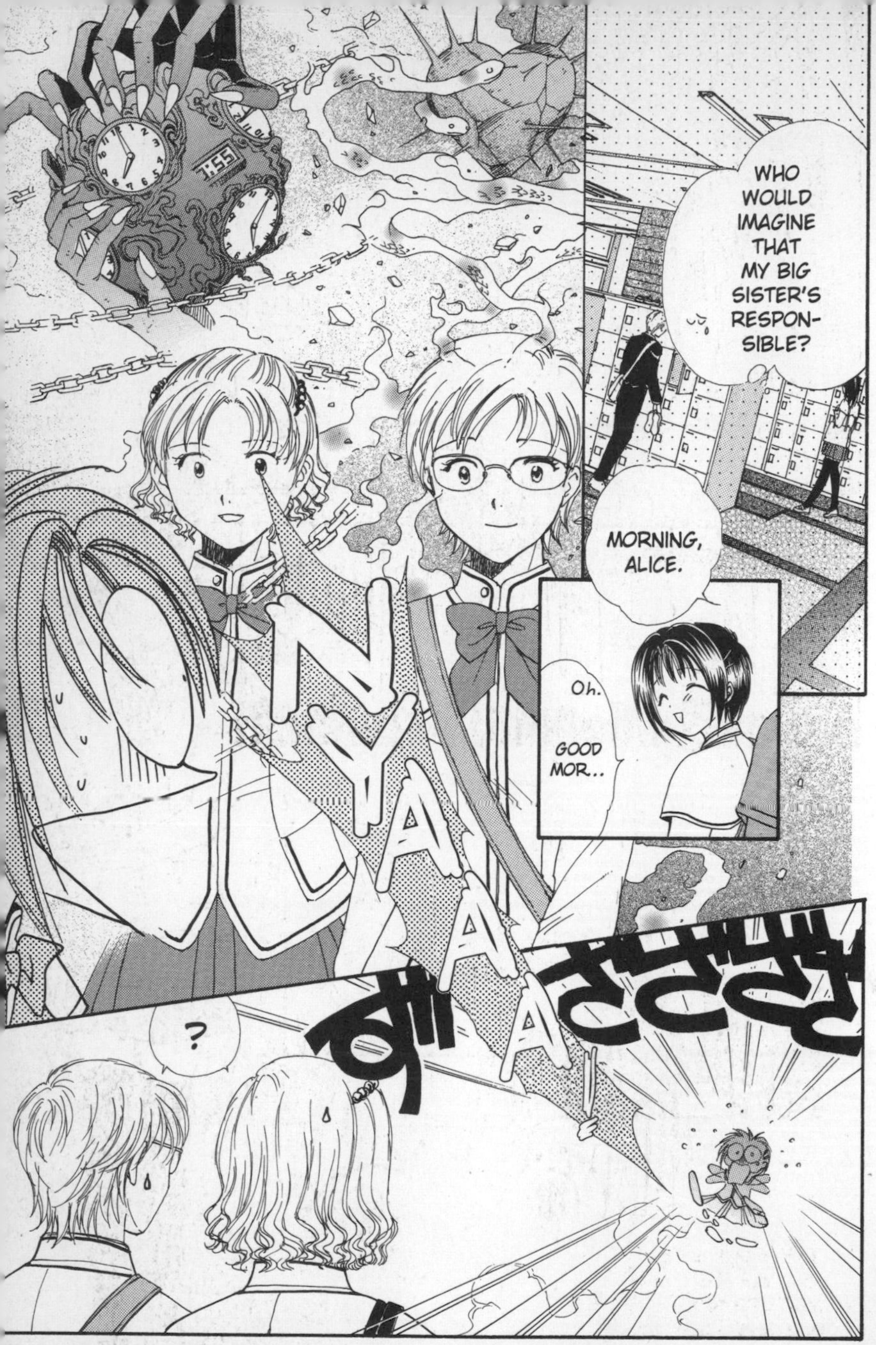
WHO WOULD IMAGINE THAT MY BIG SISTER'S RESPON-SIBLE?
MORNING, ALICE.
Oh.
GOOD MOR..
NYAAAA
?

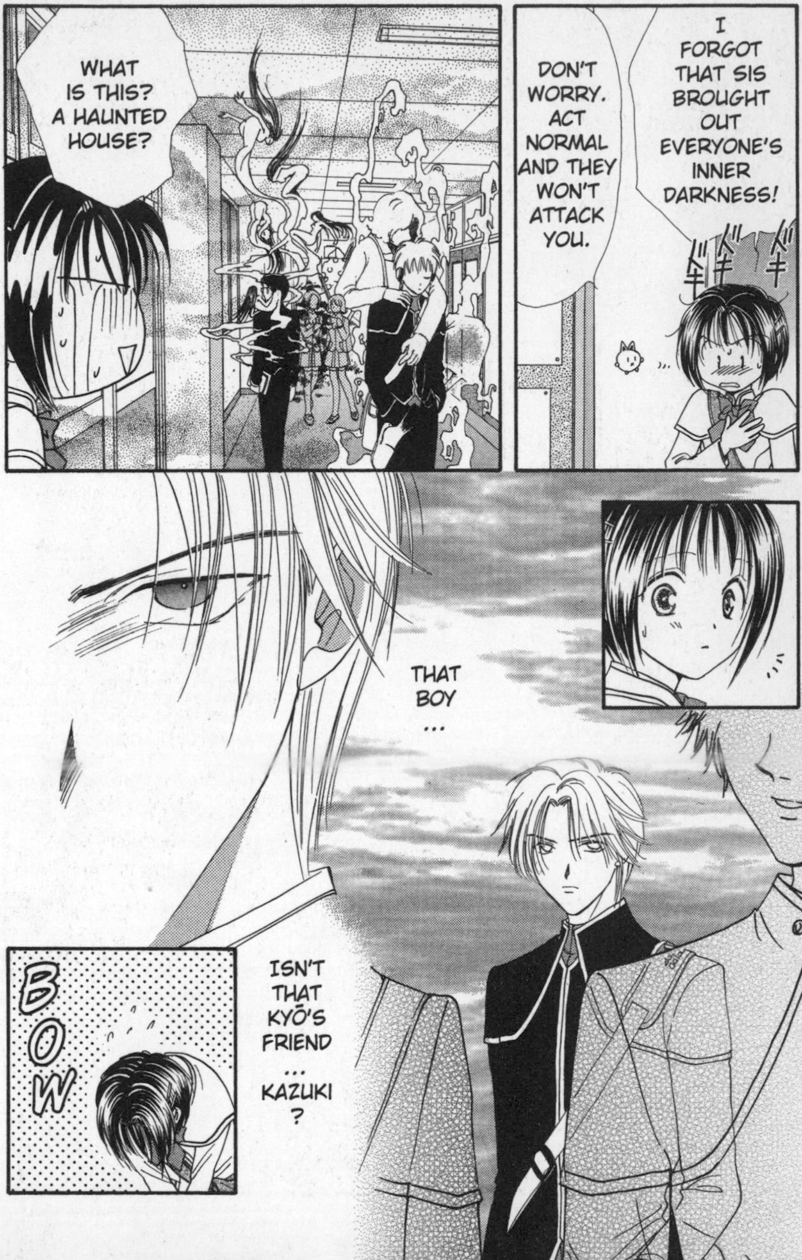
I FORGOT THAT SIS BROUGHT OUT EVERYONE'S INNER DARKNESS!
DON'T WORRY. ACT NORMAL AND THEY WON'T ATTACK YOU.
WHAT IS THIS? A HAUNTED HOUSE?
THAT BOY ...
ISN'T THAT KYŌ'S FRIEND ... KAZUKI ?
BOW

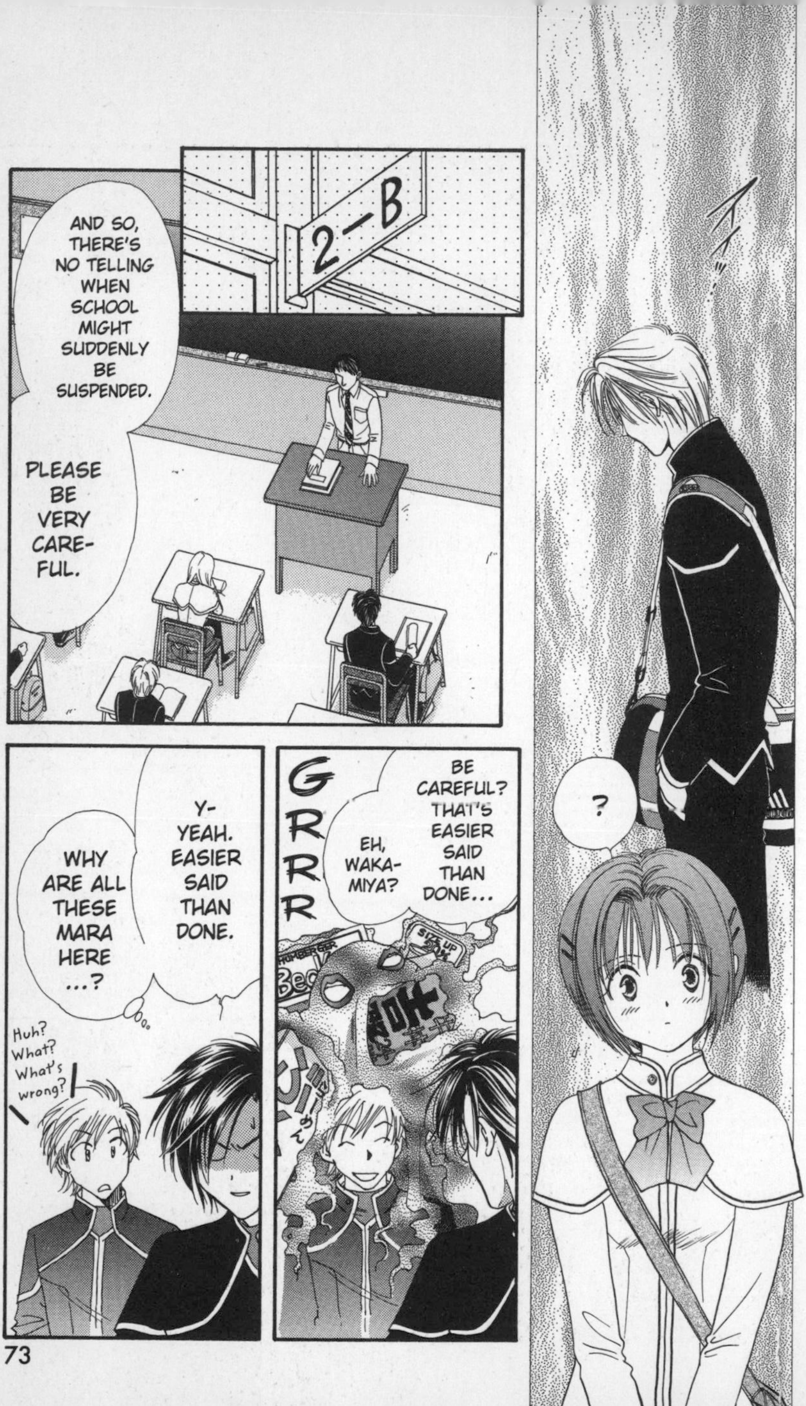
?
2-B
AND SO, THERE'S NO TELLING WHEN SCHOOL MIGHT SUDDENLY BE SUSPENDED.
PLEASE BE VERY CAREFUL.
GRRR
BE CAREFUL? THAT'S EASIER SAID THAN DONE...
EH, WAKA-MIYA?
Y-YEAH. EASIER SAID THAN DONE.
WHY ARE ALL THESE MARA HERE ...?
Huh? What? What's wrong?

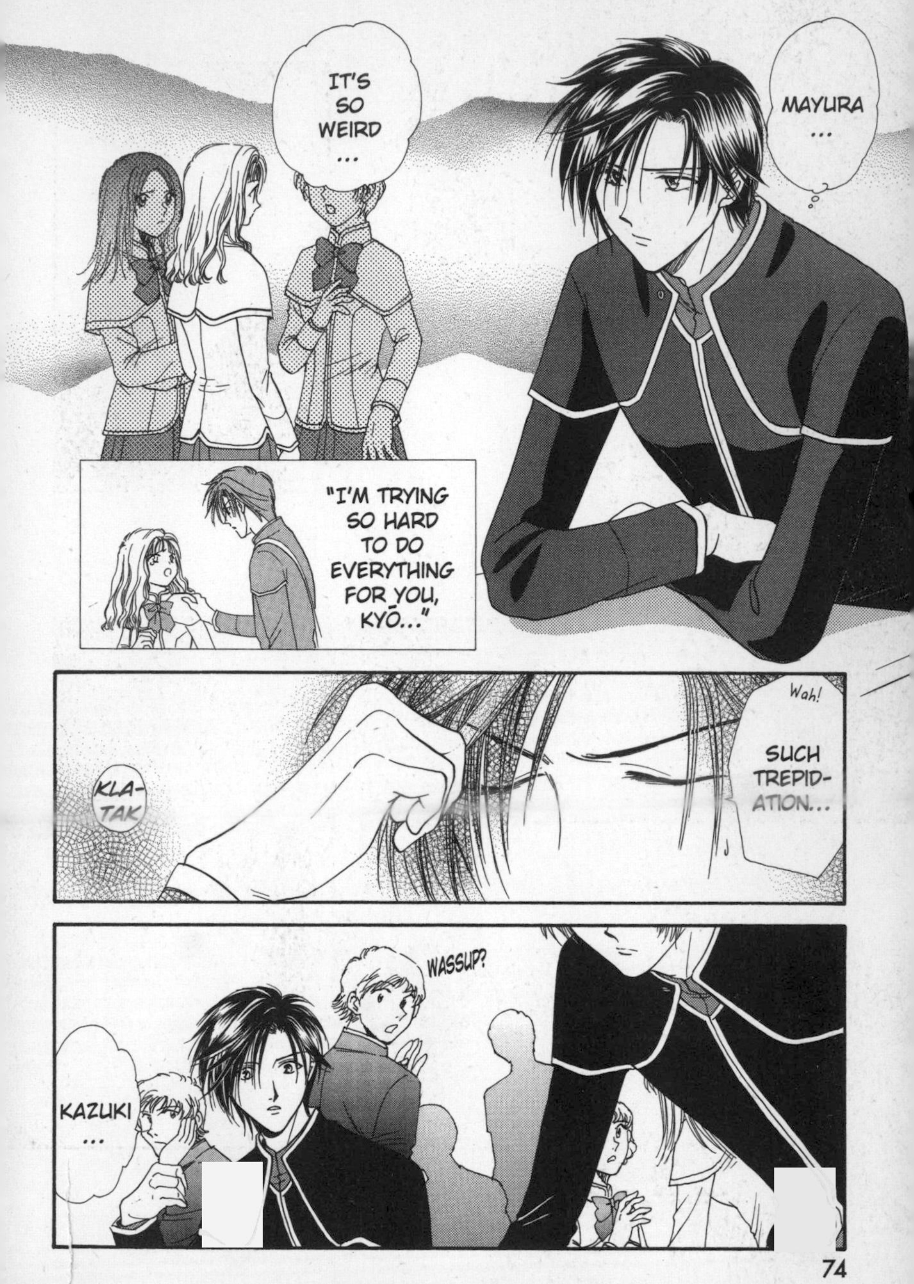
MAYURA ...
IT'S SO WEIRD ...
"I'M TRYING SO HARD TO DO EVERYTHING FOR YOU, KYŌ..."
Wah!
SUCH TREPID-ATION...
KLA-TAK
WASSUP?
KAZUKI ...

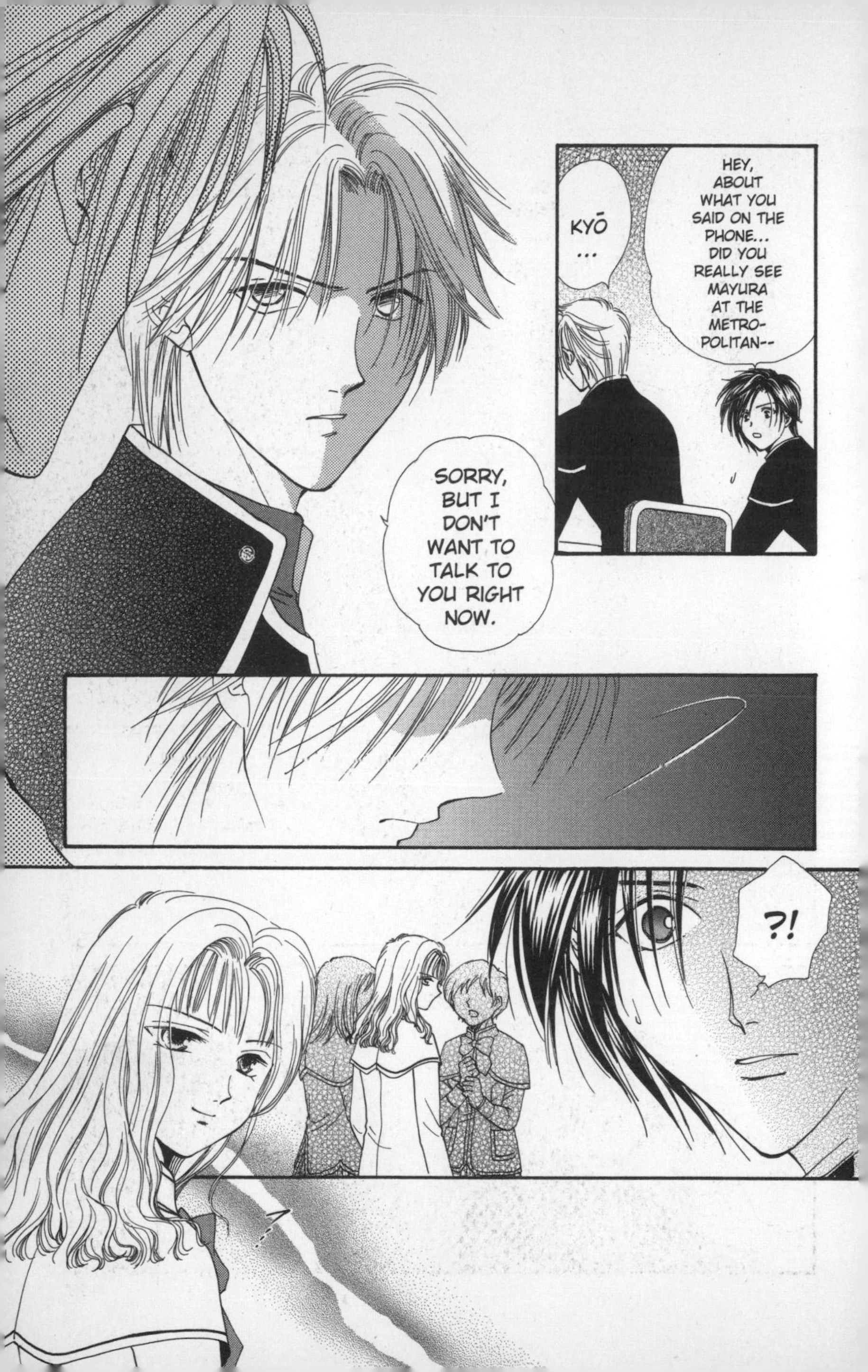
HEY, ABOUT WHAT YOU SAID ON THE PHONE... DID YOU REALLY SEE MAYURA AT THE METRO-POLITAN--
KYŌ ...
SORRY, BUT I DON'T WANT TO TALK TO YOU RIGHT NOW.
?!

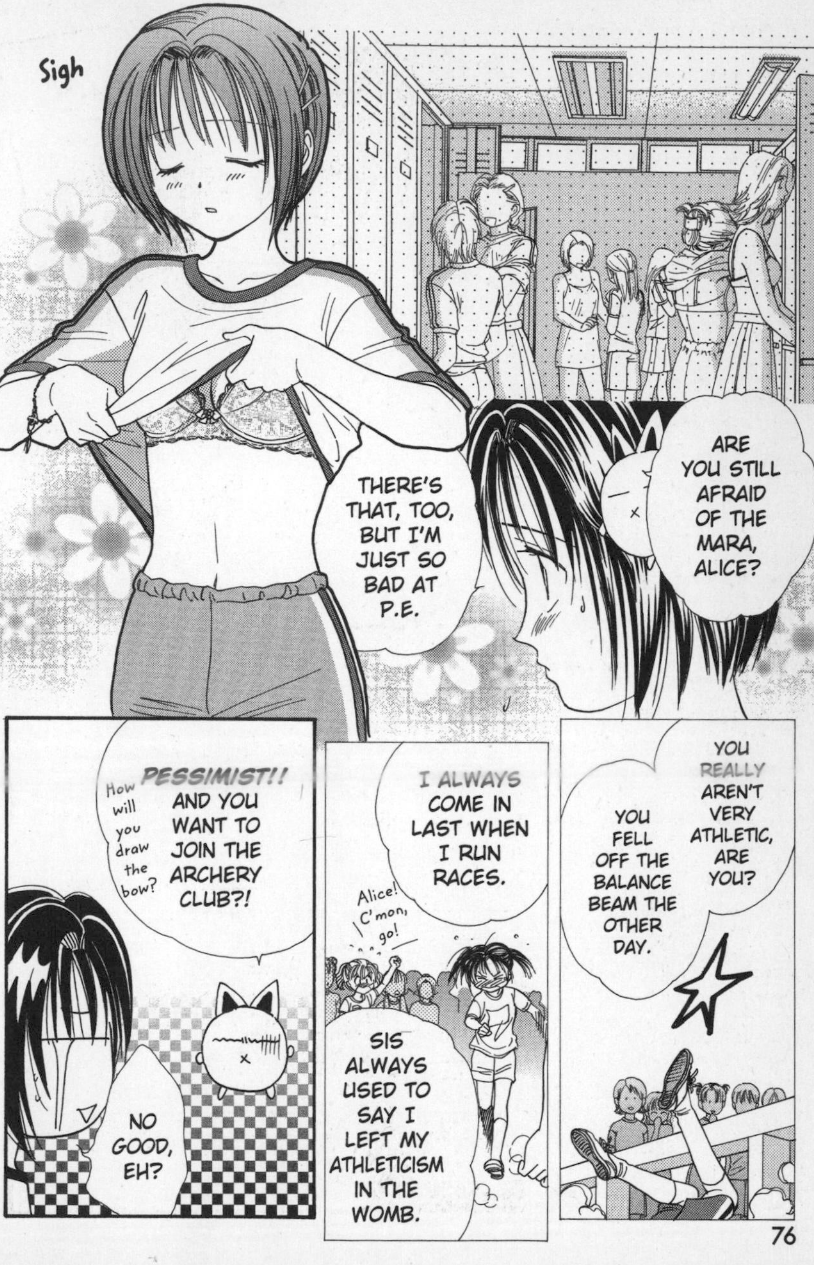
Sigh
ARE YOU STILL AFRAID OF THE MARA, ALICE?
THERE'S THAT, TOO, BUT I'M JUST SO BAD AT P.E.
YOU REALLY AREN'T VERY ATHLETIC, ARE YOU?
YOU FELL OFF THE BALANCE BEAM THE OTHER DAY.
I ALWAYS COME IN LAST WHEN I RUN RACES.
Alice! C'mon, go!
SIS ALWAYS USED TO SAY I LEFT MY ATHLETICISM IN THE WOMB.
PESSIMIST!! AND YOU WANT TO JOIN THE ARCHERY CLUB?!
How will you draw the bow?
NO GOOD, EH?

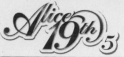

To those of you who came to the Summer Fest autograph session again, thank you! (I read all of your letters.) I do it every year, but I still get nervous. Especially when I have to draw in front of everybody!! I just drip with perspiration. It's not my occupation to do public drawings, anyway.
All kinds of goods have come out, haven't they? Sales of Fushigi Yûgi posters are still being continued from last year. Of the illustrations being used this year, only a few are from my illustration collections, but maybe it's good that others are being used. Although they were originally done for calendars. I wonder if animation artists do these, too?
Music... These days, I like the .hack//SIGN background music. I listen to it when I set up my storyboard and put the sweeping images to great use. I've seen only a few of the shows on TV, though. But the music is really great! I've got to get the second CD. But I can't watch the anime on a regular basis.
I videotape 12 Kingdoms and Whistle! for my assistant (who doesn't have satellite TV), though. I've only read volumes 1 and 2 of the original 12 Kingdoms (and that was two years ago), but the anime is interesting! It's different from the manga, but it's well done, too. When I see it, I think, "Eee!! I wanna do a Chinese story," and get all excited. Somehow only the fetish-oriented anime get all the attention, and I don't care for them, but down-to-earth works are good!
Whistle! is good, too, the original. The characters are refreshing! There are lots of good Shonen Manga. Another one that I enjoy is Atashinchi. And so here was another meager 1/3.
See you again in Volume 6 on the stands (in Japan) in January 2003!

I KNOW, JUST USE THE LOTIS!
IS THAT ALLOWED ?!
YOU'VE ONLY USED IT TO FIGHT MARA SO FAR.
What a waste.
?
IF YOU USE SOME-THING LIKE SAKUA (INTELLIGENCE), YOU'LL LEARN FASTER AND YOUR GRADES WILL IMPROVE.
HUH?! TEACH THEM TO ME, QUICK! BEFORE A TEST!
FOOL!
BONK
DIDN'T I TELL YOU THAT YOU COULD MASTER ANYTHING IF YOU TRY HARD ENOUGH ?!

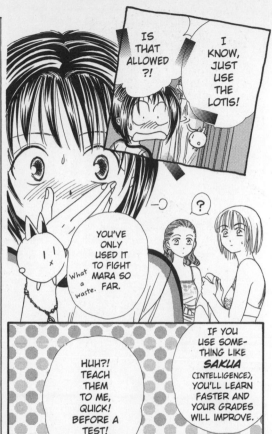

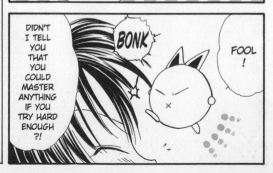

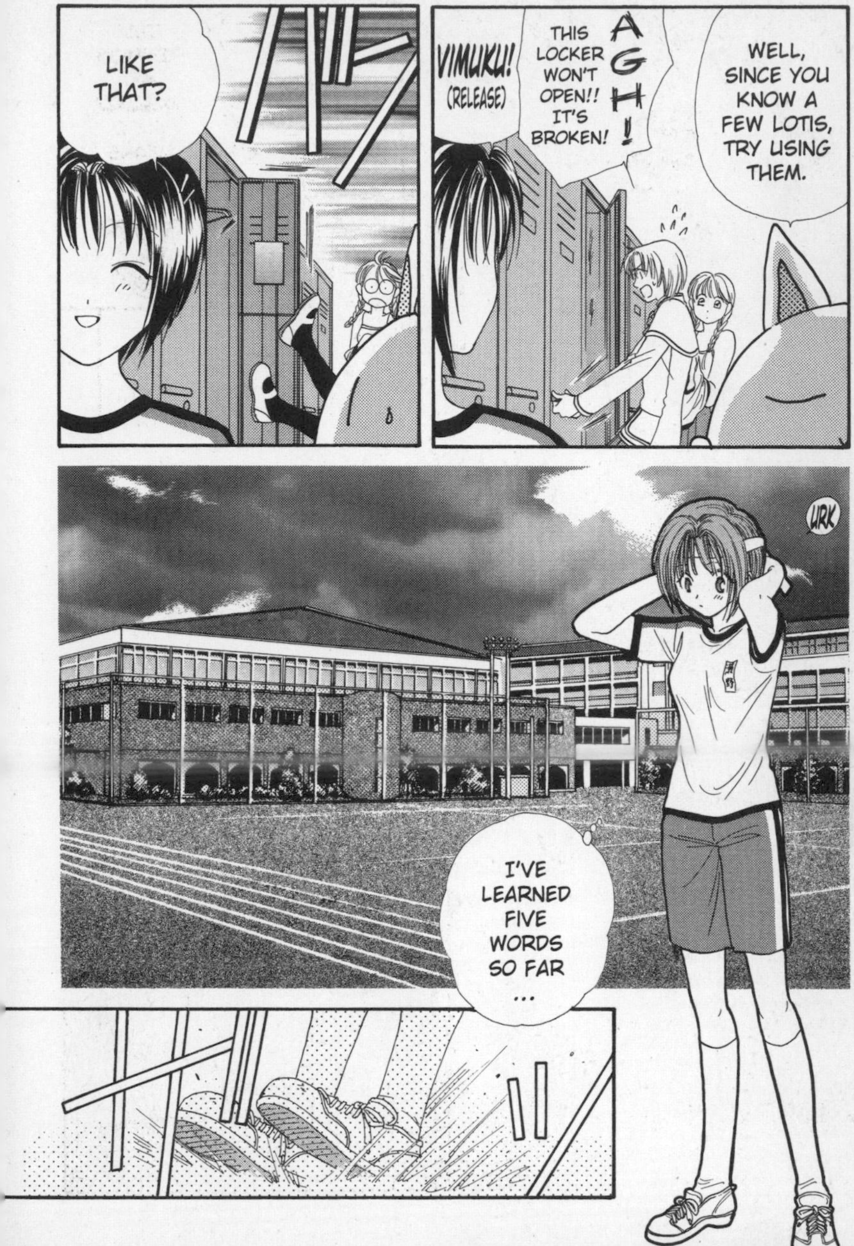
WELL, SINCE YOU KNOW A FEW LOTIS, TRY USING THEM.
AGH!
THIS LOCKER WON'T OPEN!! IT'S BROKEN!
VIMUKU! (RELEASE)
LIKE THAT?
URK
I'VE LEARNED FIVE WORDS SO FAR ...

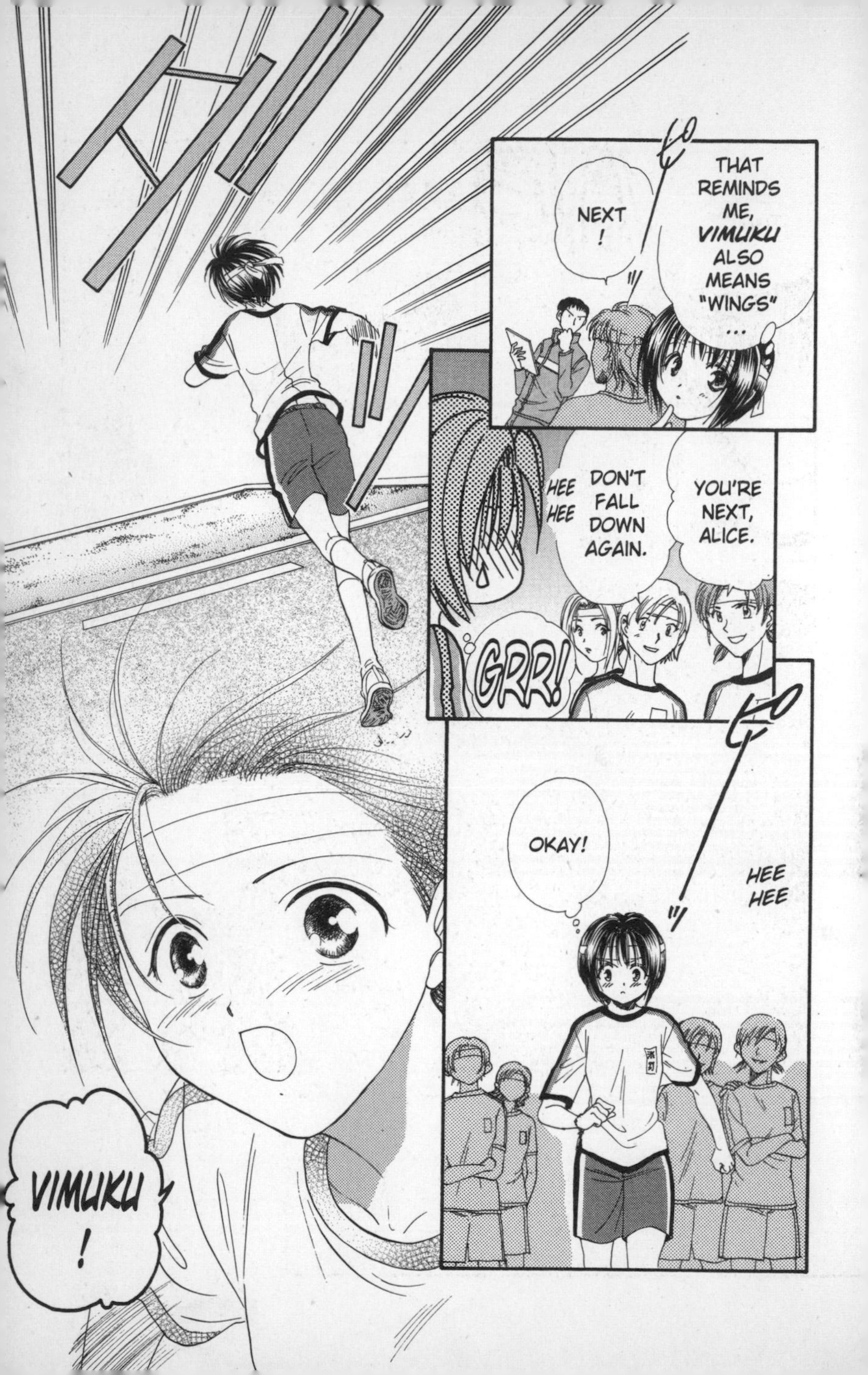

THAT REMINDS ME, VIMUKU ALSO MEANS "WINGS"...
NEXT!
YOU'RE NEXT, ALICE.
DON'T FALL DOWN AGAIN.
HEE HEE
GRR!
HEE HEE
OKAY!
VIMUKU!

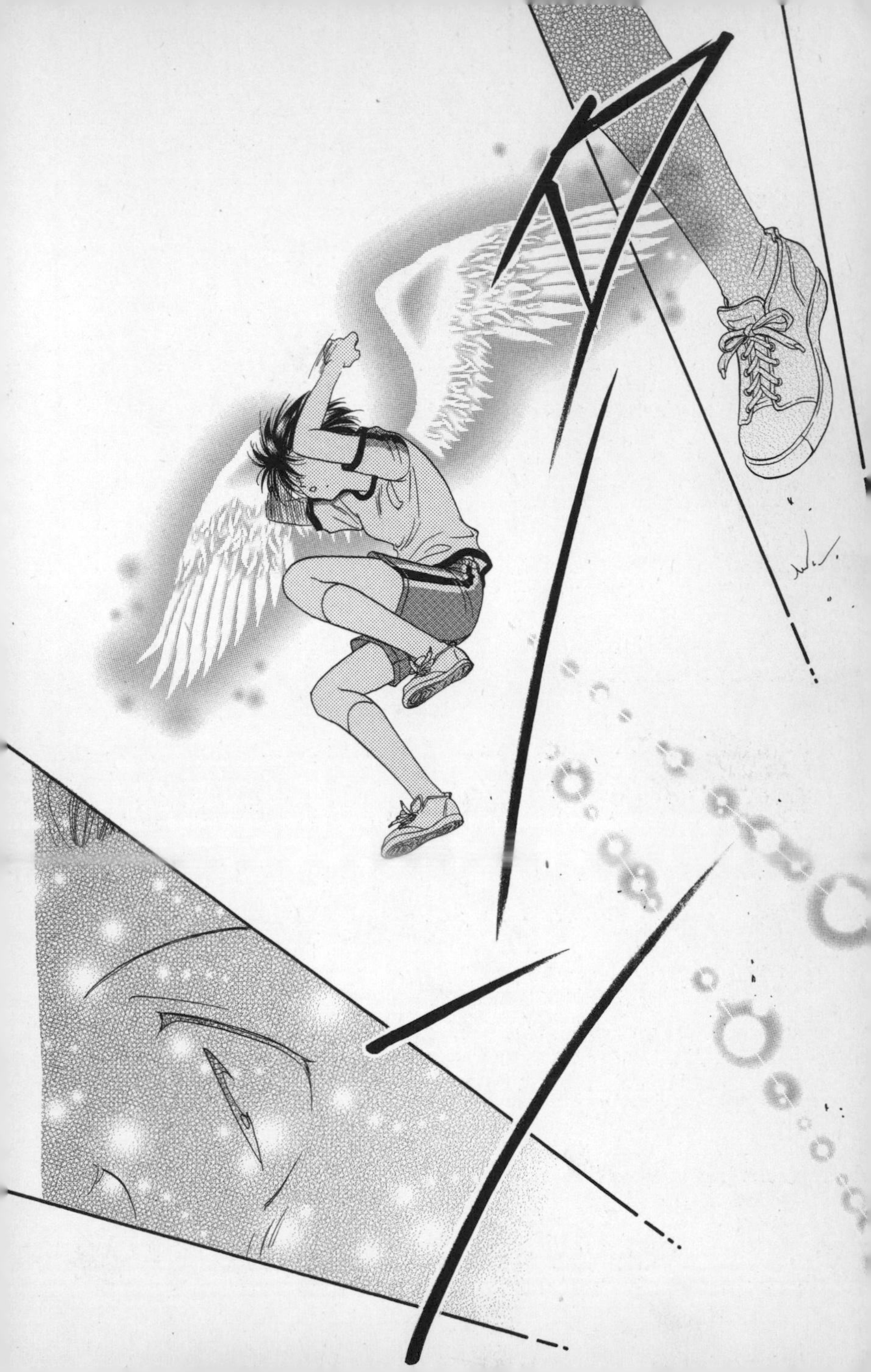

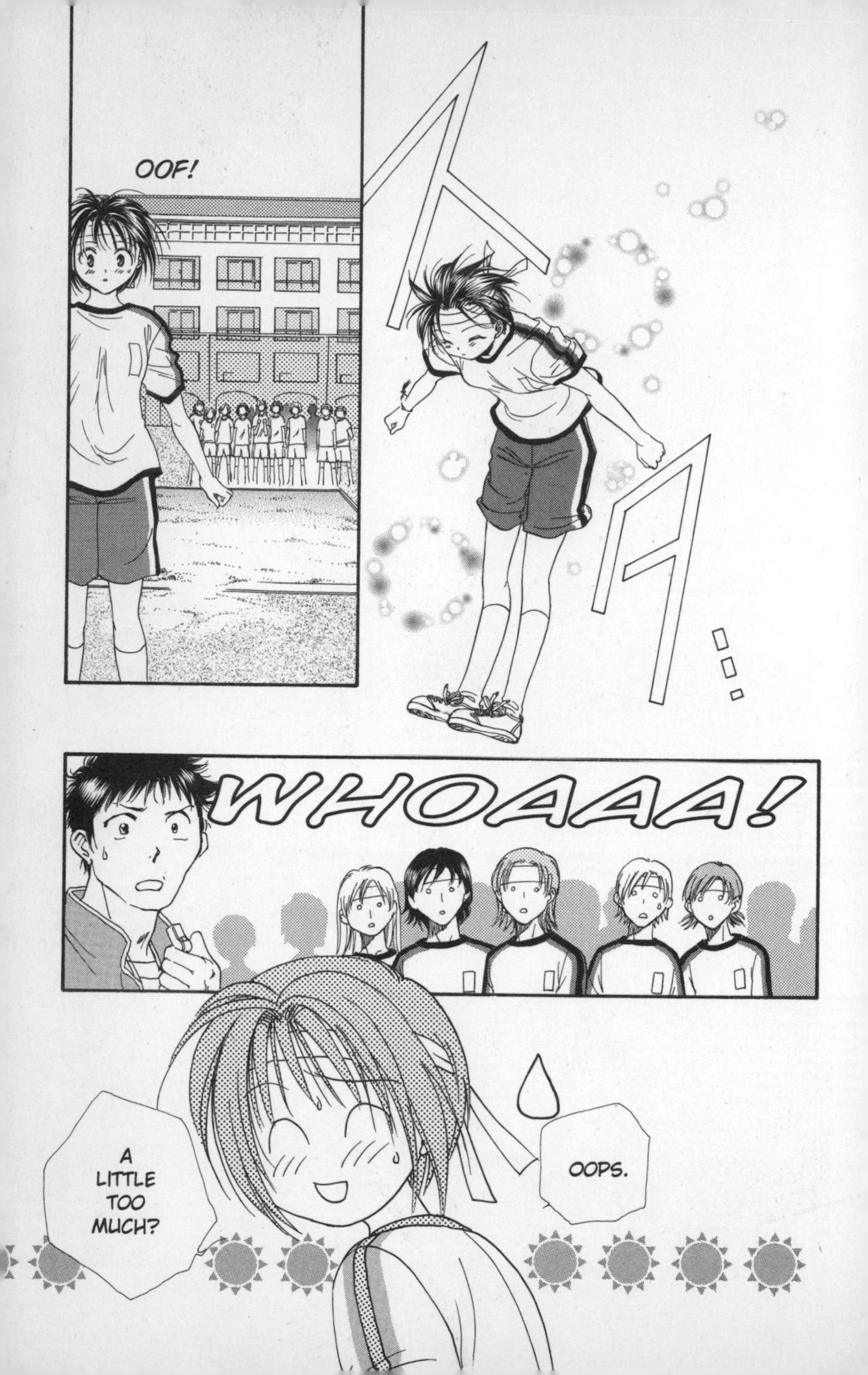
OOF!
WHOAAA!
OOPS.
A LITTLE TOO MUCH?

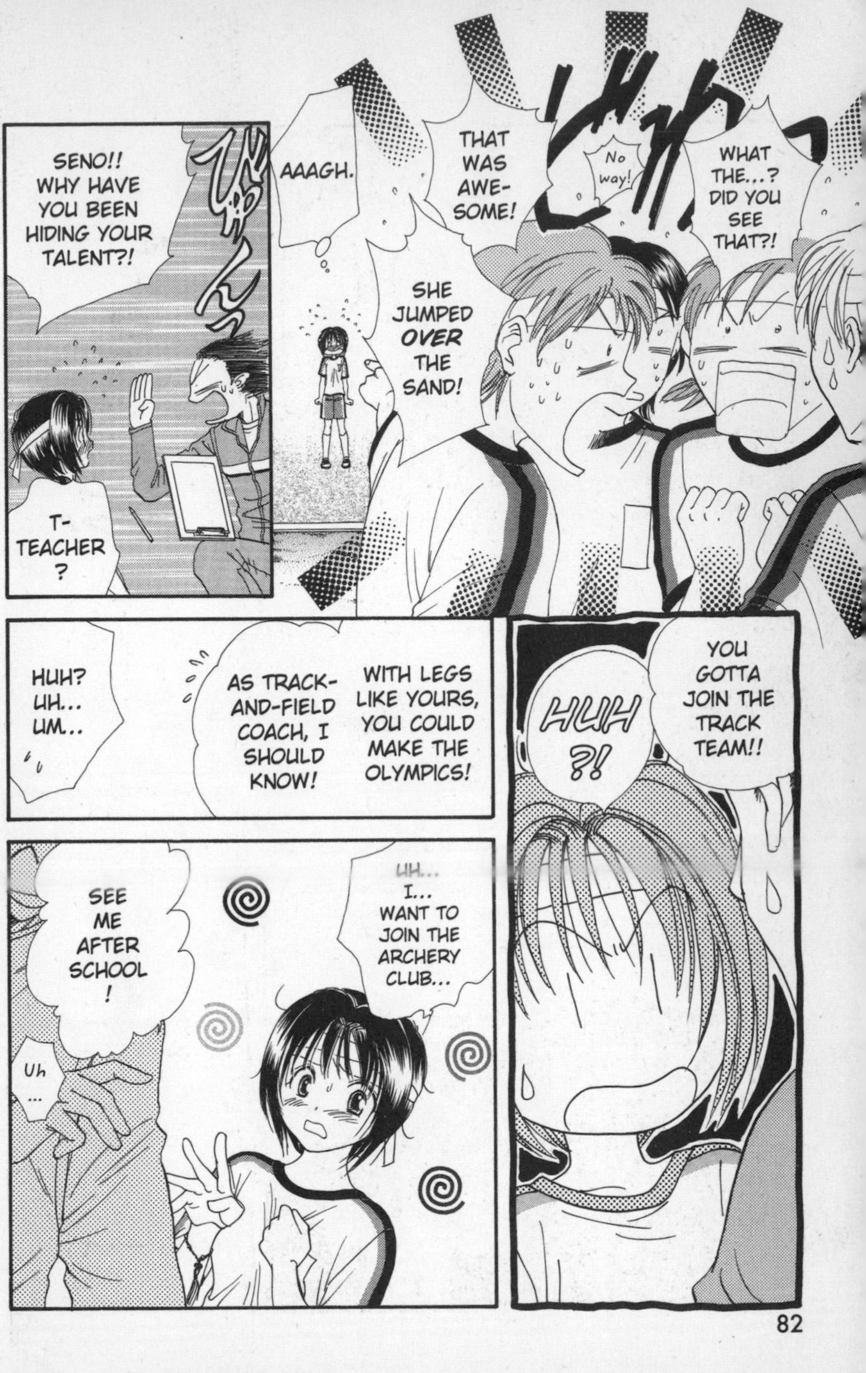
WHAT THE...? DID YOU SEE THAT?!
No way!
THAT WAS AWE-SOME!
AAAGH.
SHE JUMPED OVER THE SAND!
SENO!! WHY HAVE YOU BEEN HIDING YOUR TALENT?!
T-TEACHER?
YOU GOTTA JOIN THE TRACK TEAM!!
HUH?!
WITH LEGS LIKE YOURS, YOU COULD MAKE THE OLYMPICS!
AS TRACK-AND-FIELD COACH, I SHOULD KNOW!
HUH? UH... UM...
UH... I... WANT TO JOIN THE ARCHERY CLUB...
SEE ME AFTER SCHOOL!
Uh ...

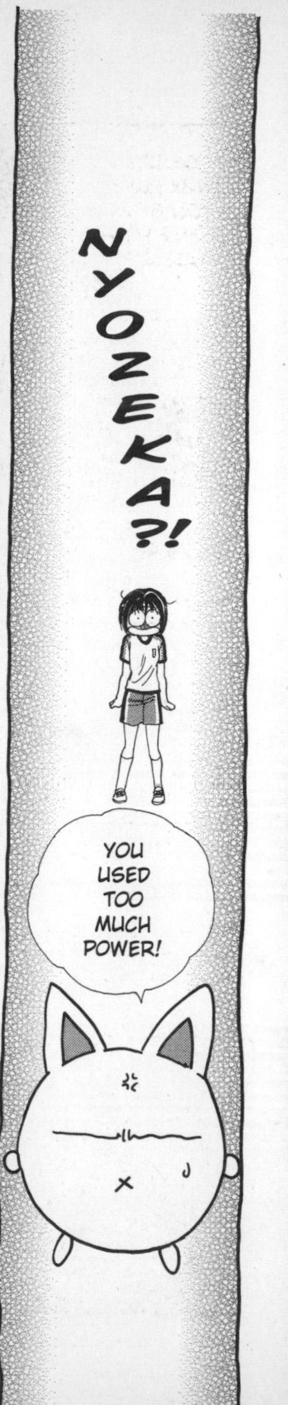
NYOZEKA?!
YOU USED TOO MUCH POWER!

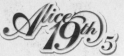

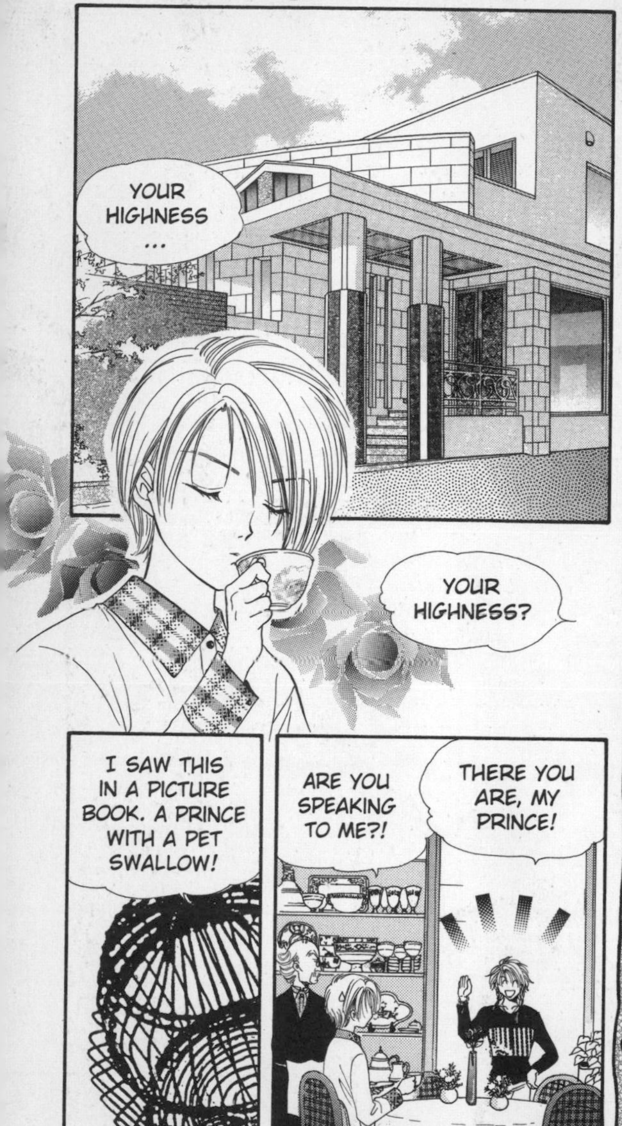
YOUR HIGHNESS ...
YOUR HIGHNESS?
THERE YOU ARE, MY PRINCE!
ARE YOU SPEAKING TO ME?!
I SAW THIS IN A PICTURE BOOK. A PRINCE WITH A PET SWALLOW!

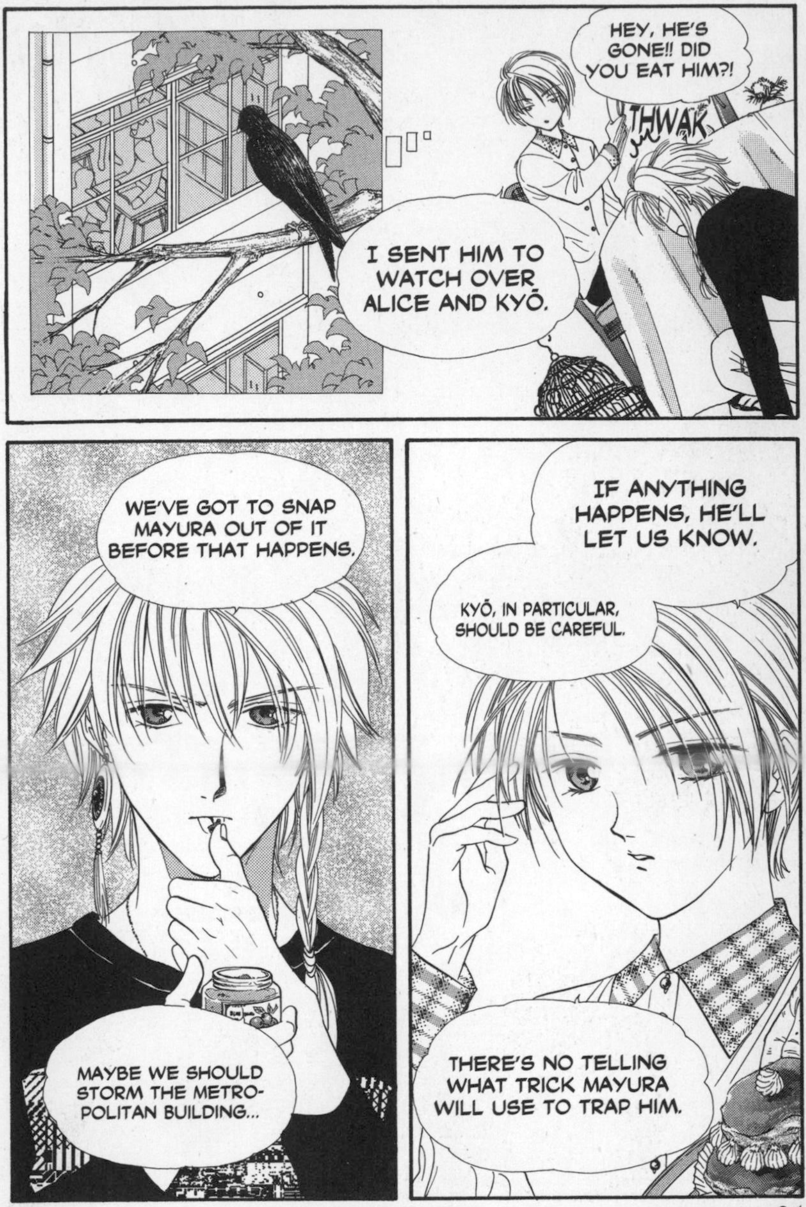
HEY, HE'S GONE!! DID YOU EAT HIM?!
THWAK
I SENT HIM TO WATCH OVER ALICE AND KYŌ.
IF ANYTHING HAPPENS, HE'LL LET US KNOW.
KYŌ, IN PARTICULAR, SHOULD BE CAREFUL.
THERE'S NO TELLING WHAT TRICK MAYURA WILL USE TO TRAP HIM.
WE'VE GOT TO SNAP MAYURA OUT OF IT BEFORE THAT HAPPENS.
MAYBE WE SHOULD STORM THE METRO-POLITAN BUILDING...

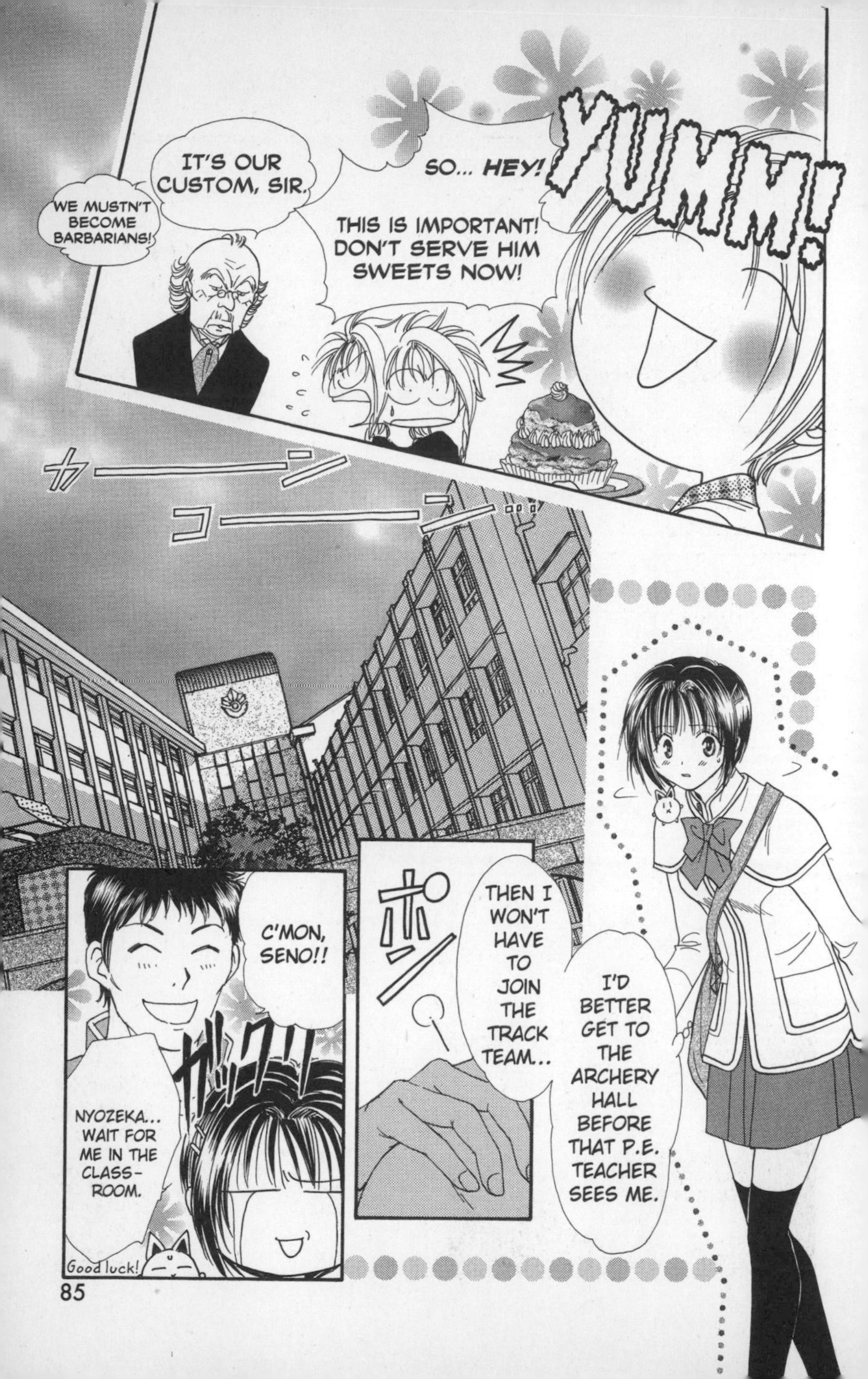
YUMM!
SO... HEY!
THIS IS IMPORTANT! DON'T SERVE HIM SWEETS NOW!
IT'S OUR CUSTOM, SIR.
WE MUSTN'T BECOME BARBARIANS!
カーーン
コーーン…
I'D BETTER GET TO THE ARCHERY HALL BEFORE THAT P.E. TEACHER SEES ME.
THEN I WON'T HAVE TO JOIN THE TRACK TEAM...
ポン
C'MON, SENO!!
NYOZEKA... WAIT FOR ME IN THE CLASS-ROOM.
Good luck!

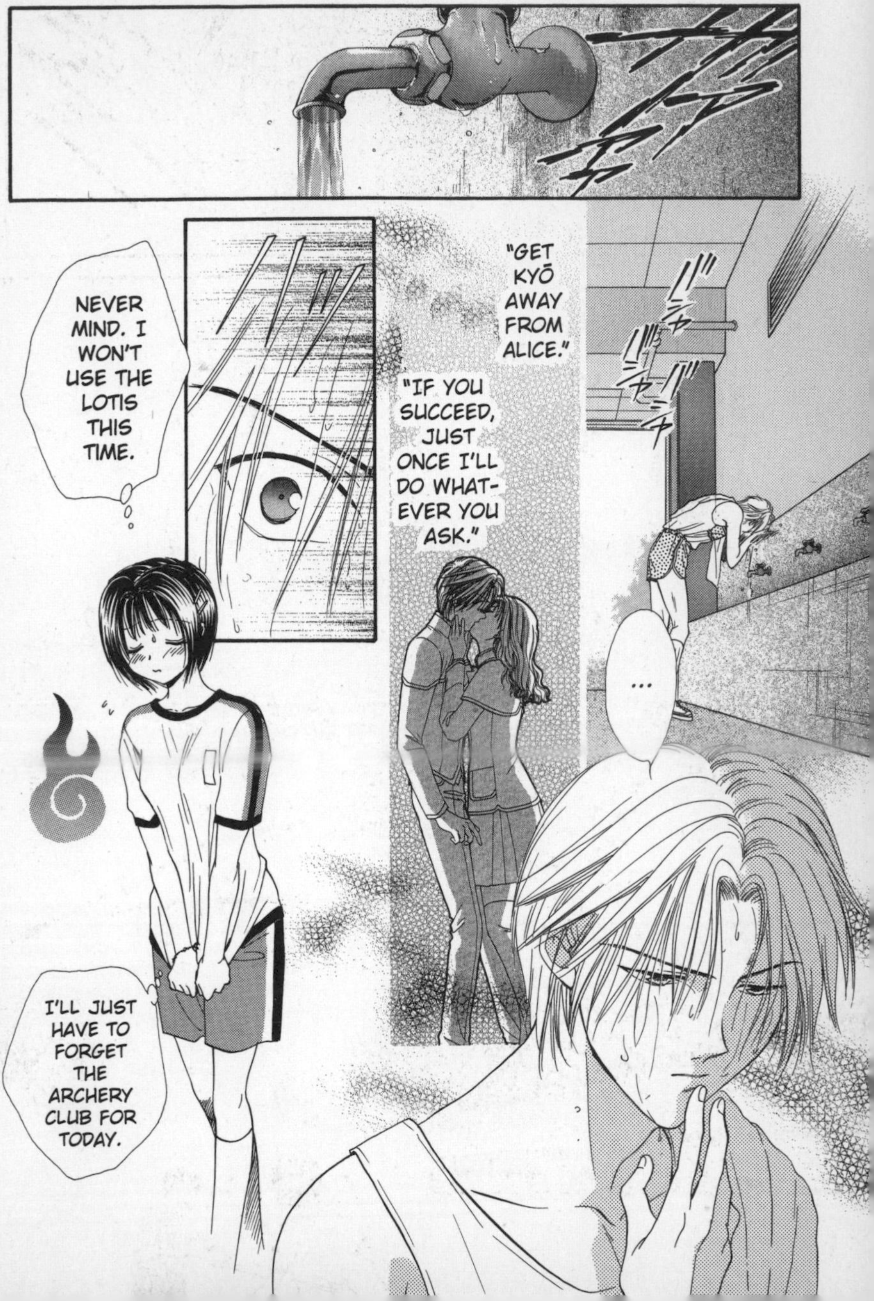
"GET KYŌ AWAY FROM ALICE."
"IF YOU SUCCEED, JUST ONCE I'LL DO WHATEVER YOU ASK."
...
NEVER MIND. I WON'T USE THE LOTIS THIS TIME.
I'LL JUST HAVE TO FORGET THE ARCHERY CLUB FOR TODAY.

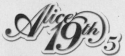

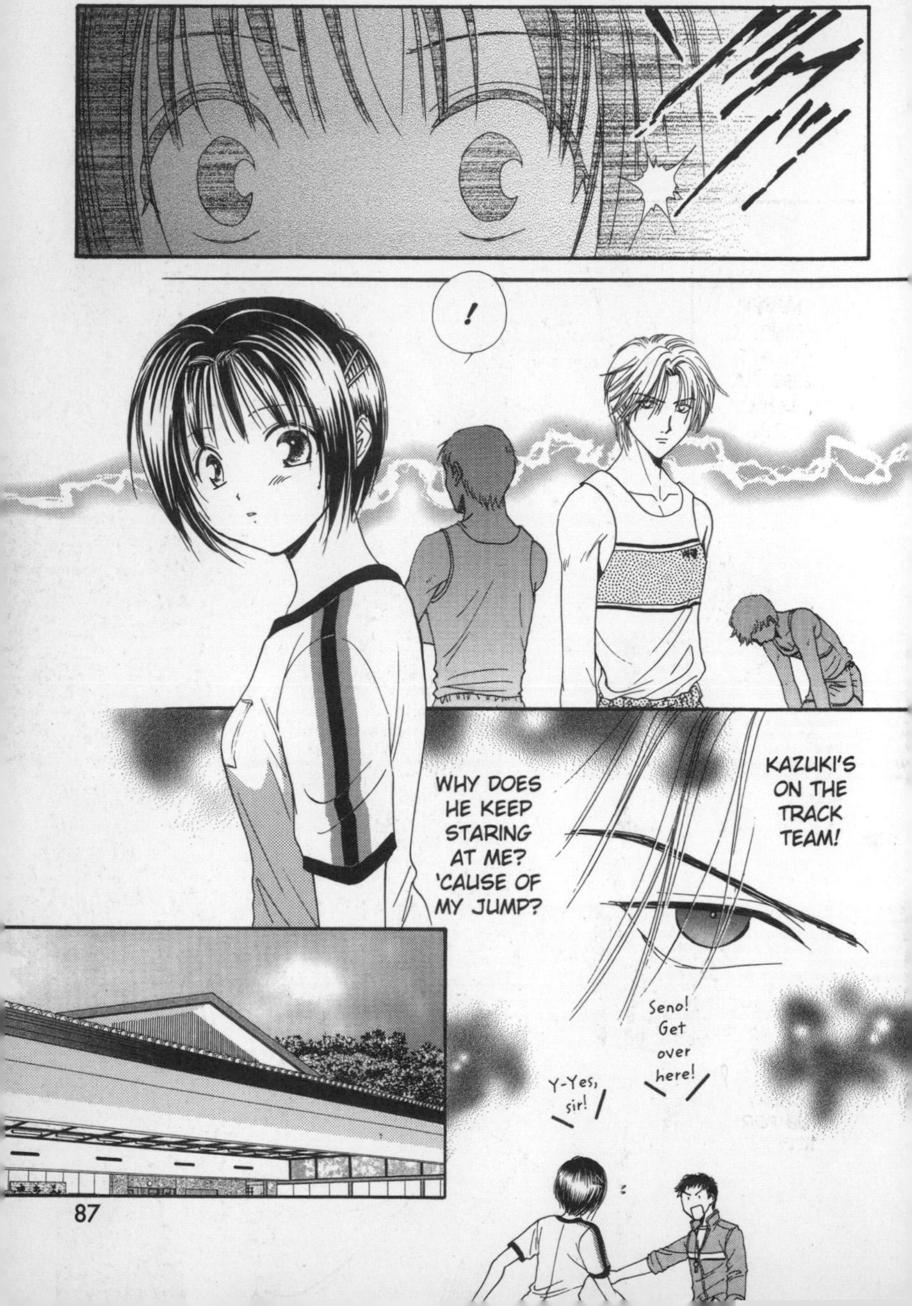
!
KAZUKI'S ON THE TRACK TEAM!
WHY DOES HE KEEP STARING AT ME? 'CAUSE OF MY JUMP?
Seno! Get over here!
Y-Yes, sir!

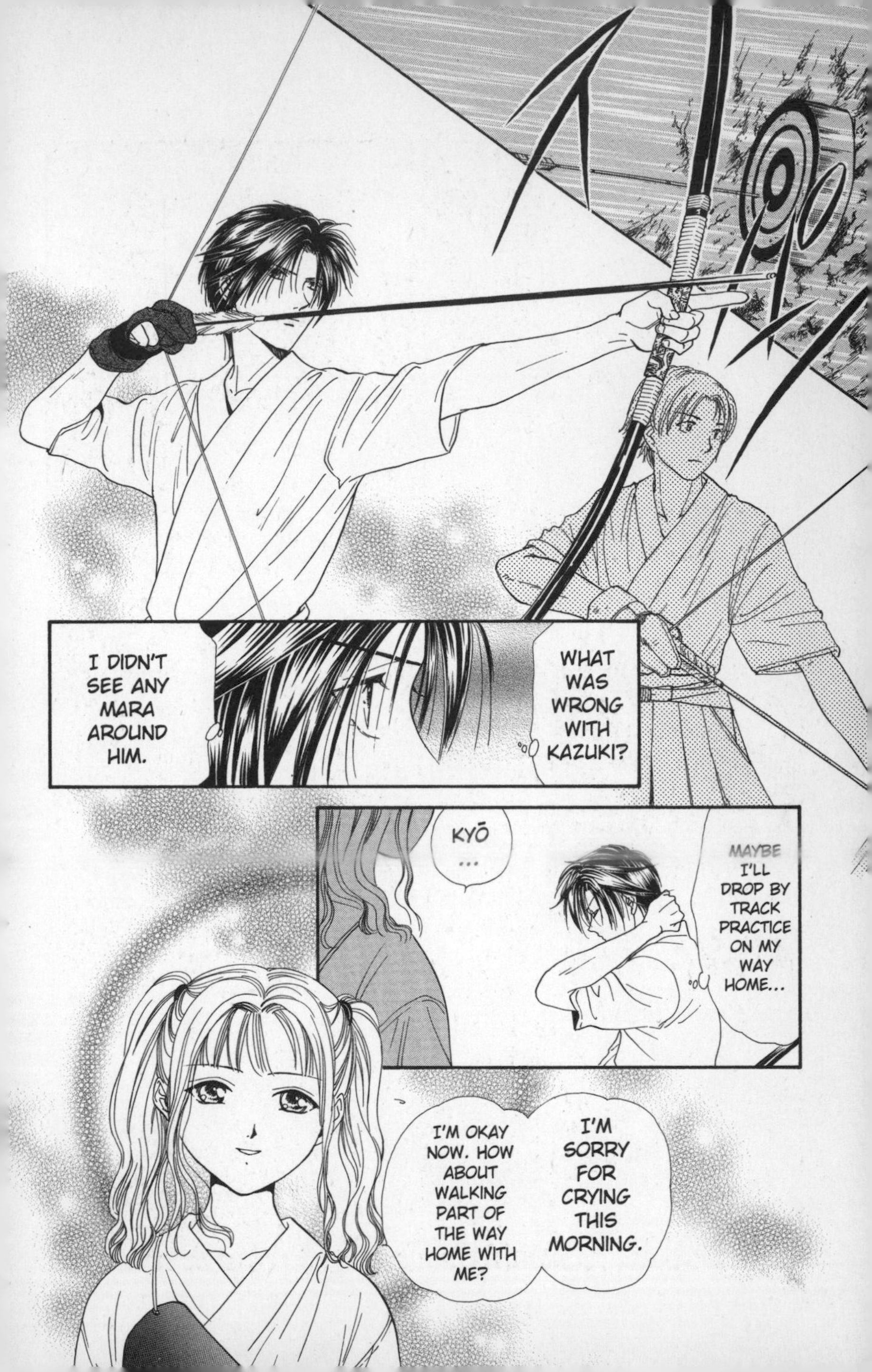
WHAT WAS WRONG WITH KAZUKI?
I DIDN'T SEE ANY MARA AROUND HIM.
MAYBE I'LL DROP BY TRACK PRACTICE ON MY WAY HOME...
KYŌ ...
I'M SORRY FOR CRYING THIS MORNING.
I'M OKAY NOW. HOW ABOUT WALKING PART OF THE WAY HOME WITH ME?

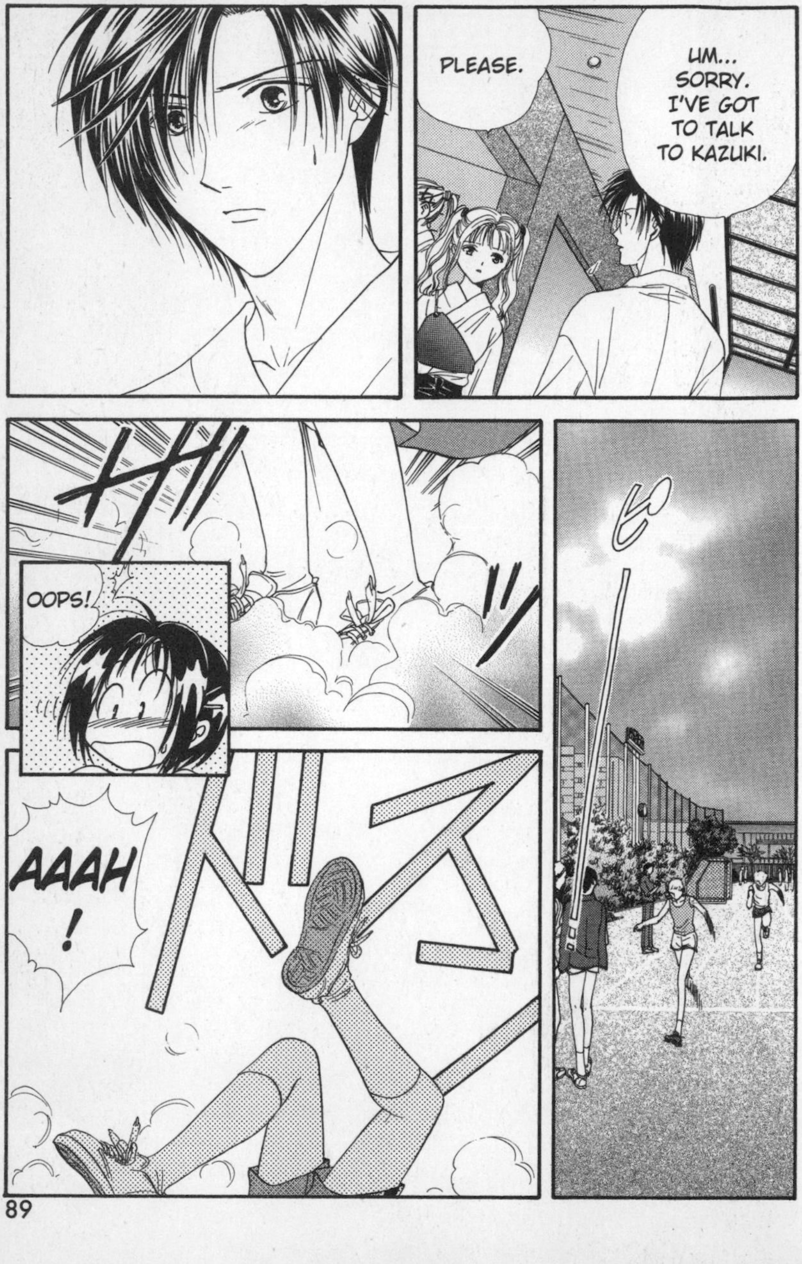
UM... SORRY. I'VE GOT TO TALK TO KAZUKI.
PLEASE.
OOPS!
AAAH!

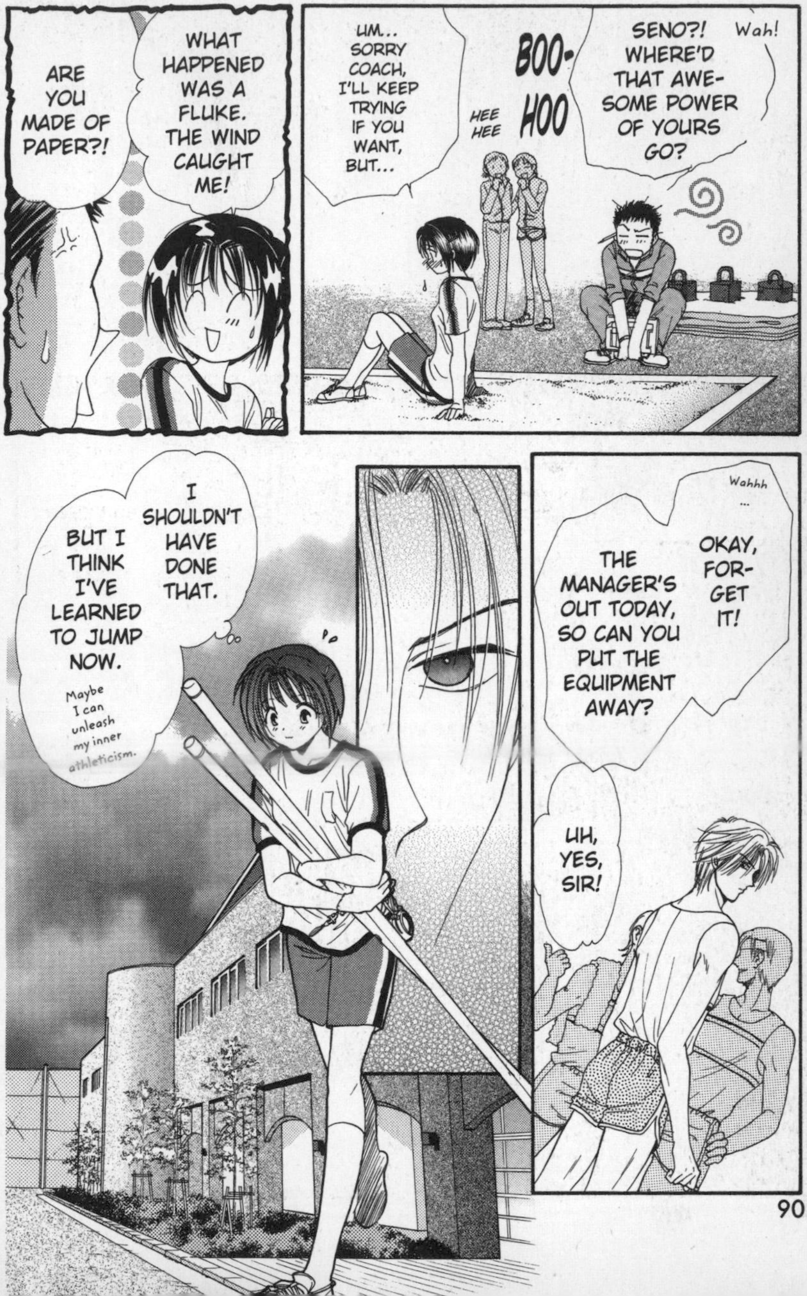
Wah!
SENO?! WHERE'D THAT AWE-SOME POWER OF YOURS GO?
BOO-HOO
HEE HEE
UM... SORRY COACH, I'LL KEEP TRYING IF YOU WANT, BUT...
WHAT HAPPENED WAS A FLUKE. THE WIND CAUGHT ME!
ARE YOU MADE OF PAPER?!
Wahhh ...
OKAY, FOR-GET IT!
THE MANAGER'S OUT TODAY, SO CAN YOU PUT THE EQUIPMENT AWAY?
UH, YES, SIR!
I SHOULDN'T HAVE DONE THAT.
BUT I THINK I'VE LEARNED TO JUMP NOW.
Maybe I can unleash my inner athleticism.

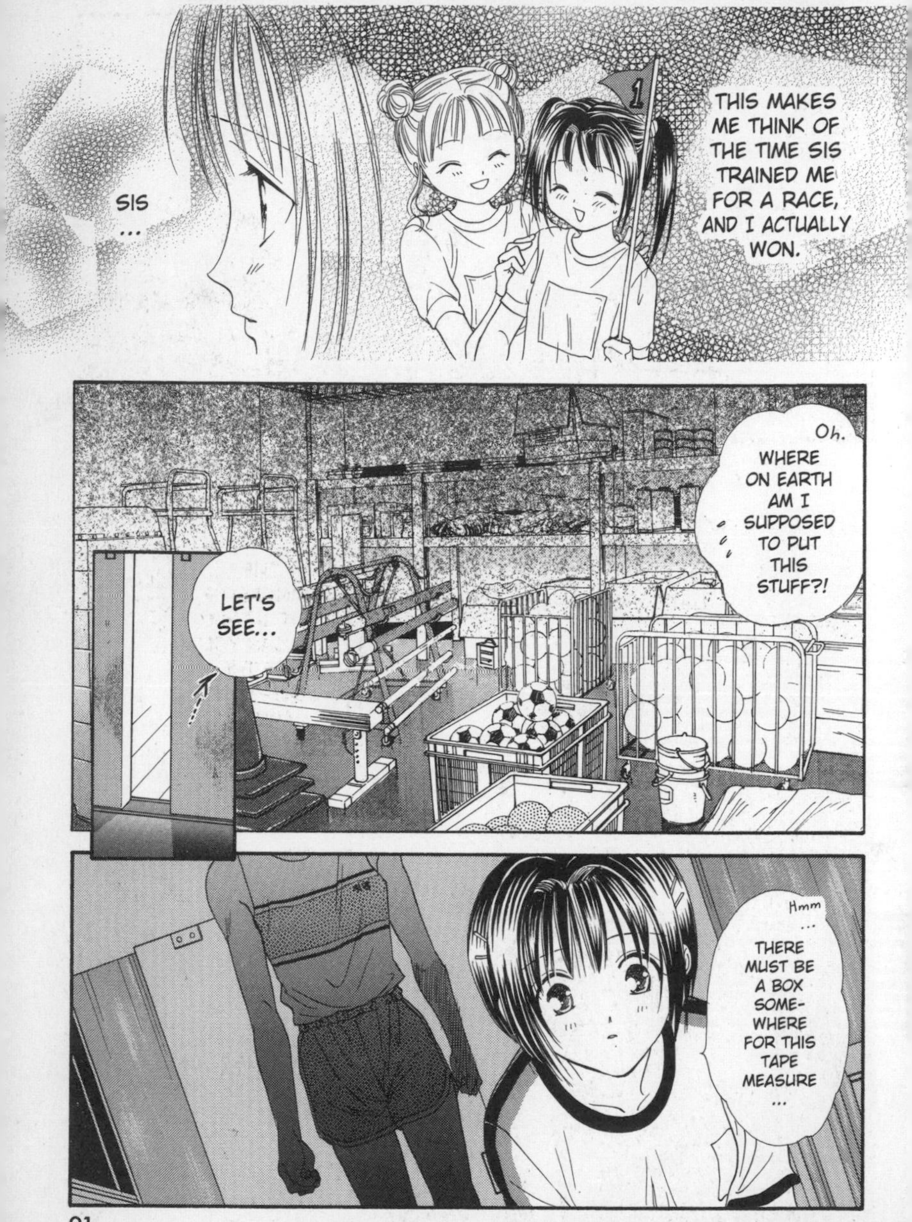
THIS MAKES ME THINK OF THE TIME SIS TRAINED ME FOR A RACE, AND I ACTUALLY WON.
SIS ...
Oh.
WHERE ON EARTH AM I SUPPOSED TO PUT THIS STUFF?!
LET'S SEE...
Hmm ...
THERE MUST BE A BOX SOME-WHERE FOR THIS TAPE MEASURE ...

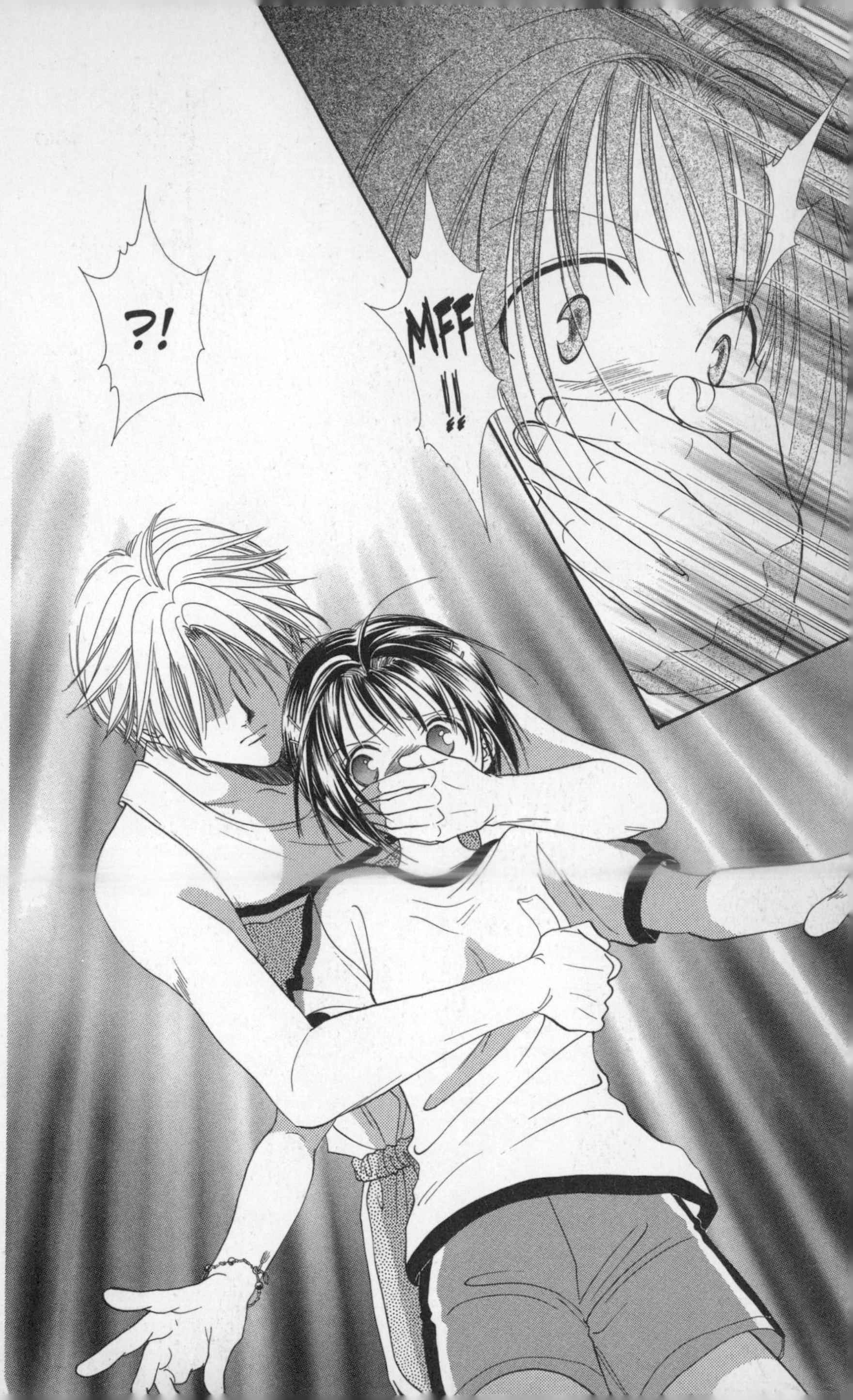
MFF !!
?!

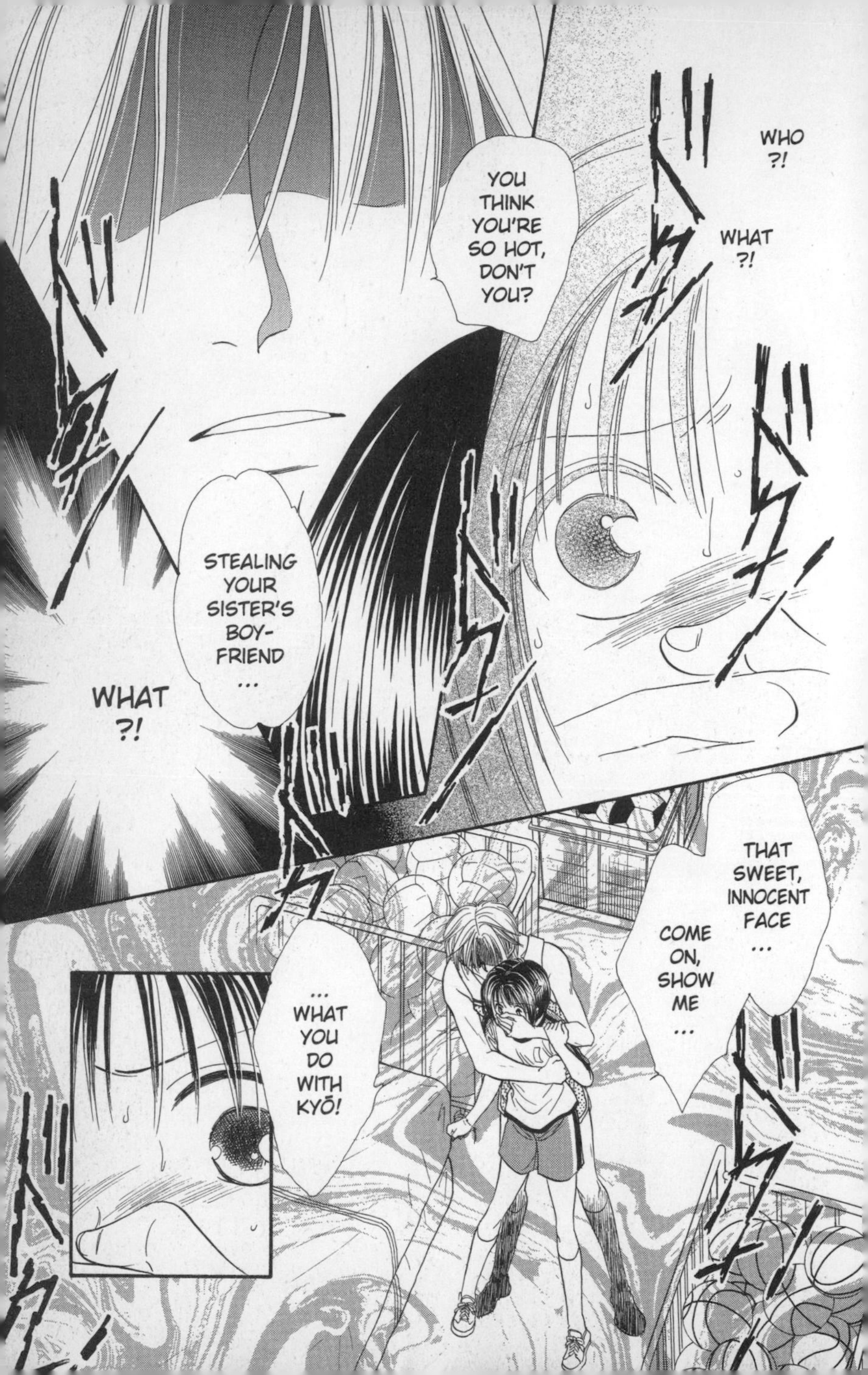
WHO ?!
WHAT ?!
YOU THINK YOU'RE SO HOT, DON'T YOU?
STEALING YOUR SISTER'S BOY-FRIEND ...
WHAT ?!
THAT SWEET, INNOCENT FACE ...
COME ON, SHOW ME ...
... WHAT YOU DO WITH KYŌ!

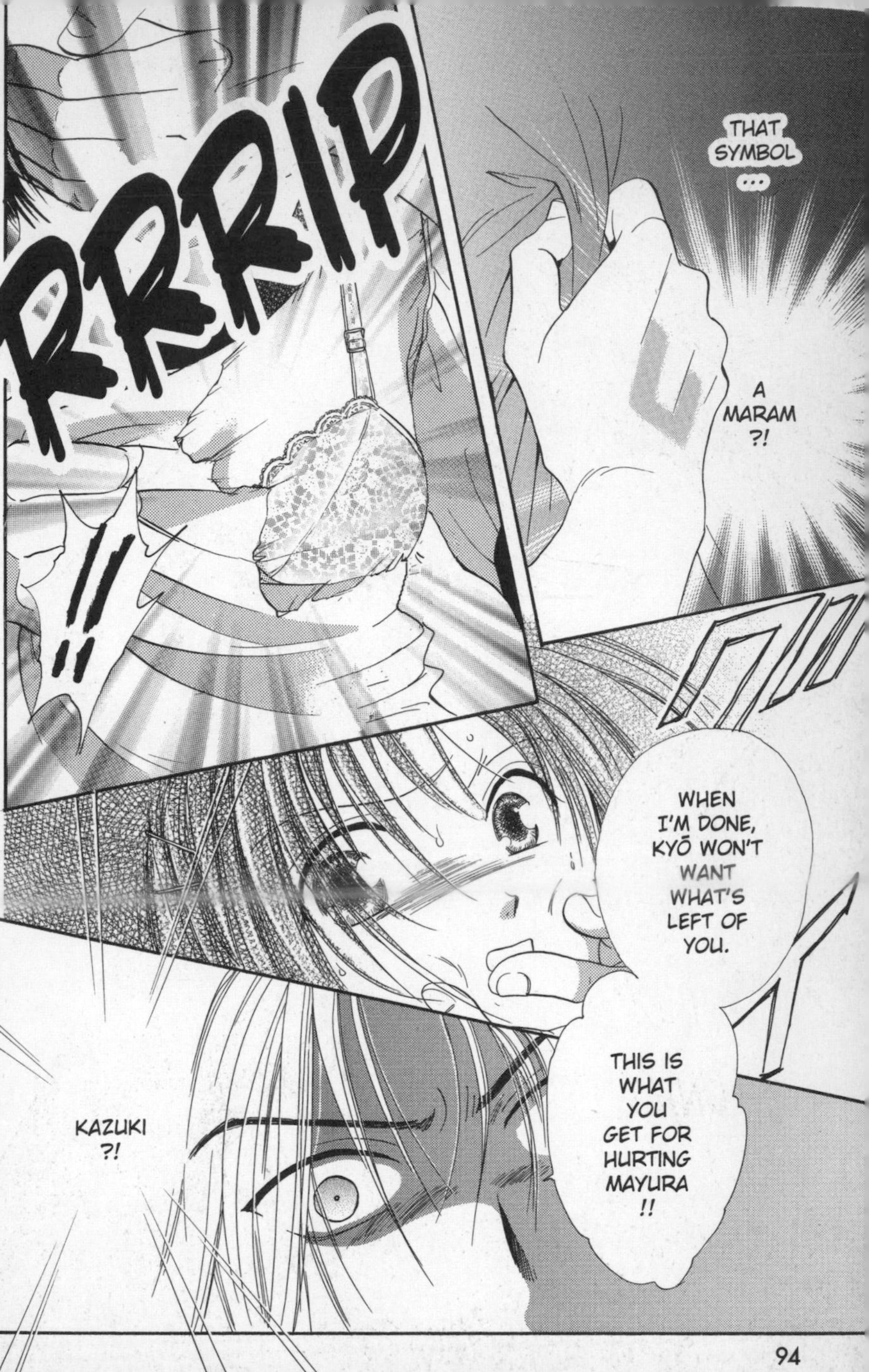
THAT SYMBOL ...
A MARAM ?!
RRRIP
!!
WHEN I'M DONE, KYŌ WON'T WANT WHAT'S LEFT OF YOU.
THIS IS WHAT YOU GET FOR HURTING MAYURA !!
KAZUKI ?!

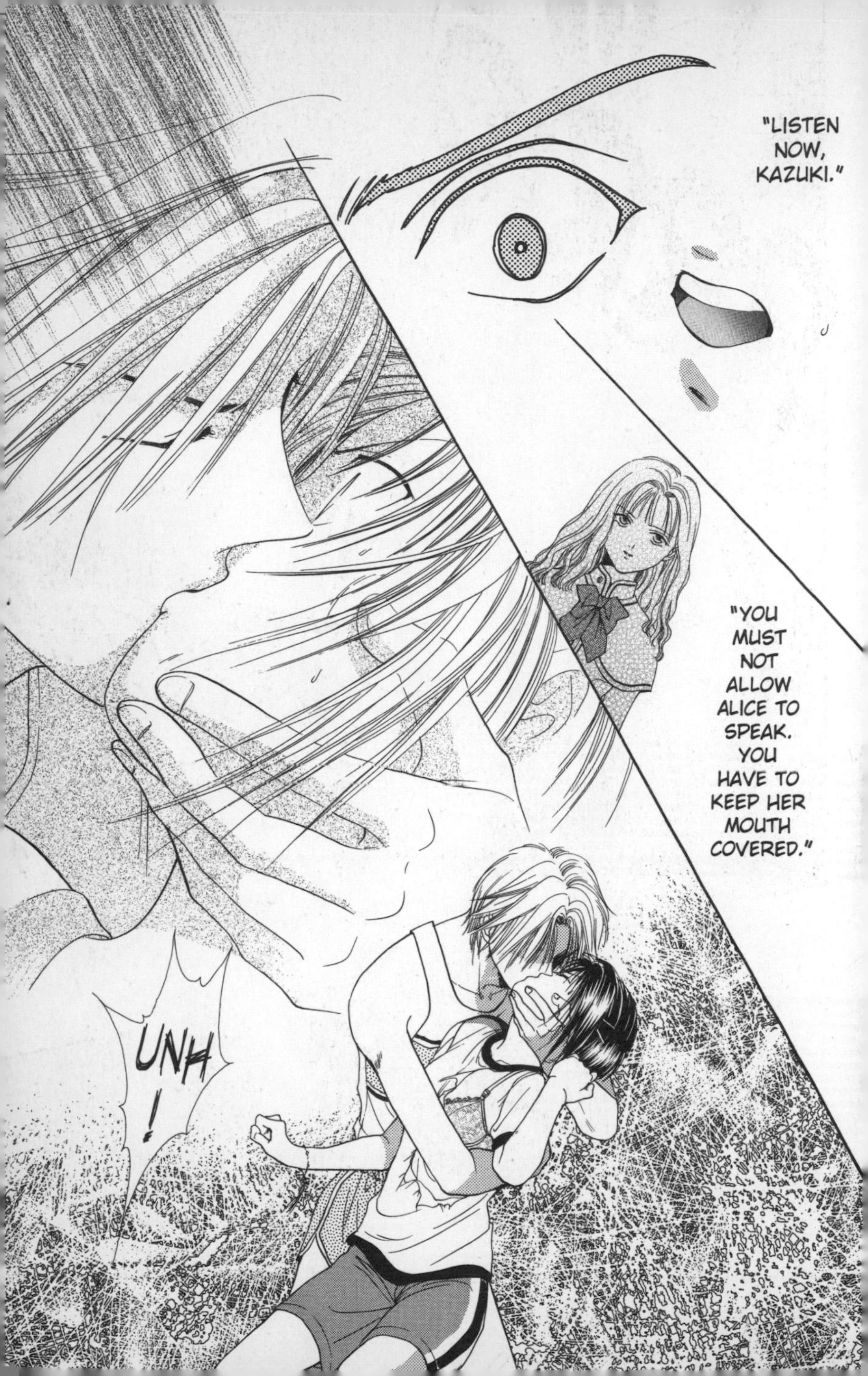
"LISTEN NOW, KAZUKI."
"YOU MUST NOT ALLOW ALICE TO SPEAK. YOU HAVE TO KEEP HER MOUTH COVERED."
UNH!

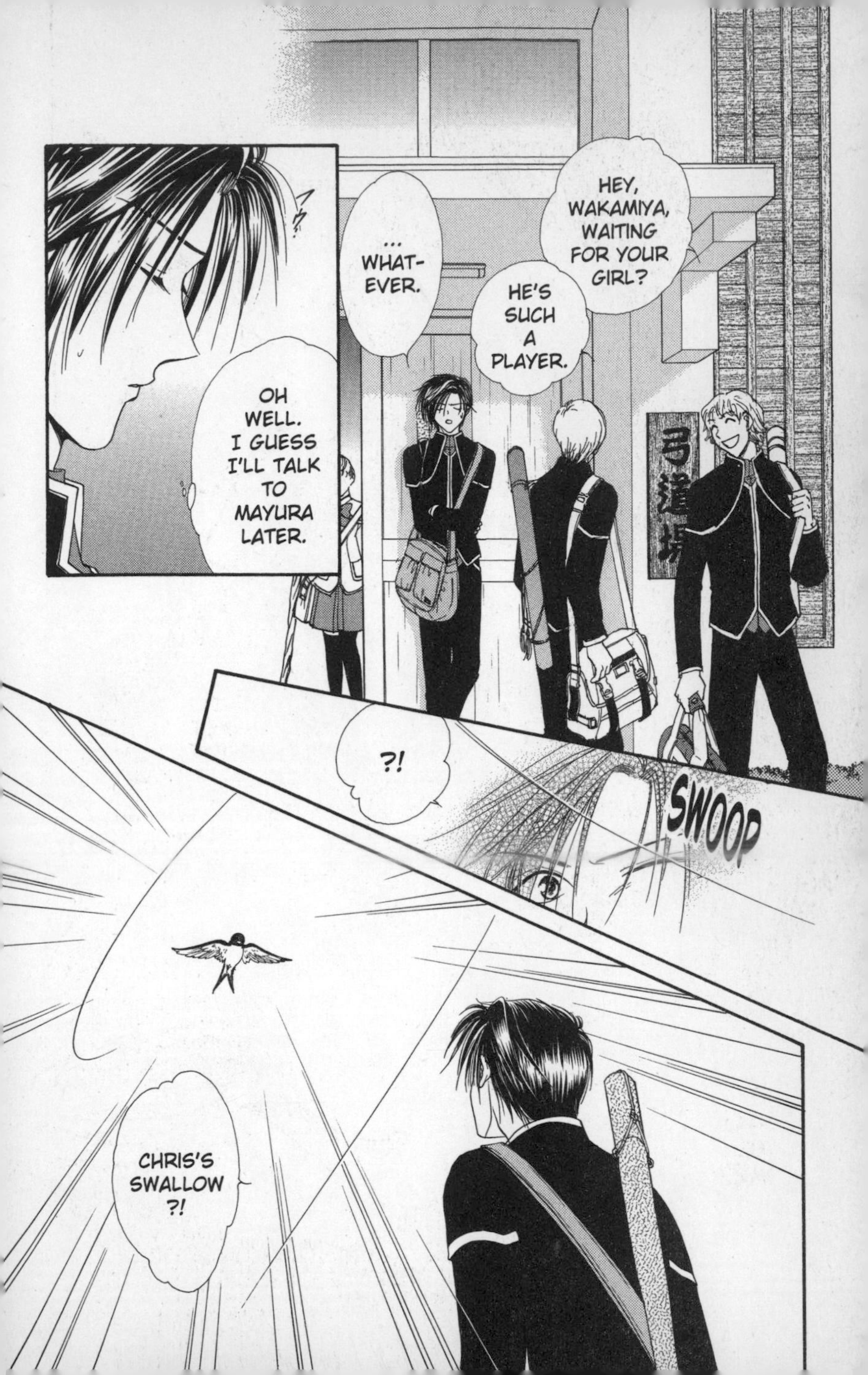
HEY, WAKAMIYA, WAITING FOR YOUR GIRL?
HE'S SUCH A PLAYER.
... WHAT-EVER.
弓道場
OH WELL. I GUESS I'LL TALK TO MAYURA LATER.
?!
SWOOP
CHRIS'S SWALLOW ?!

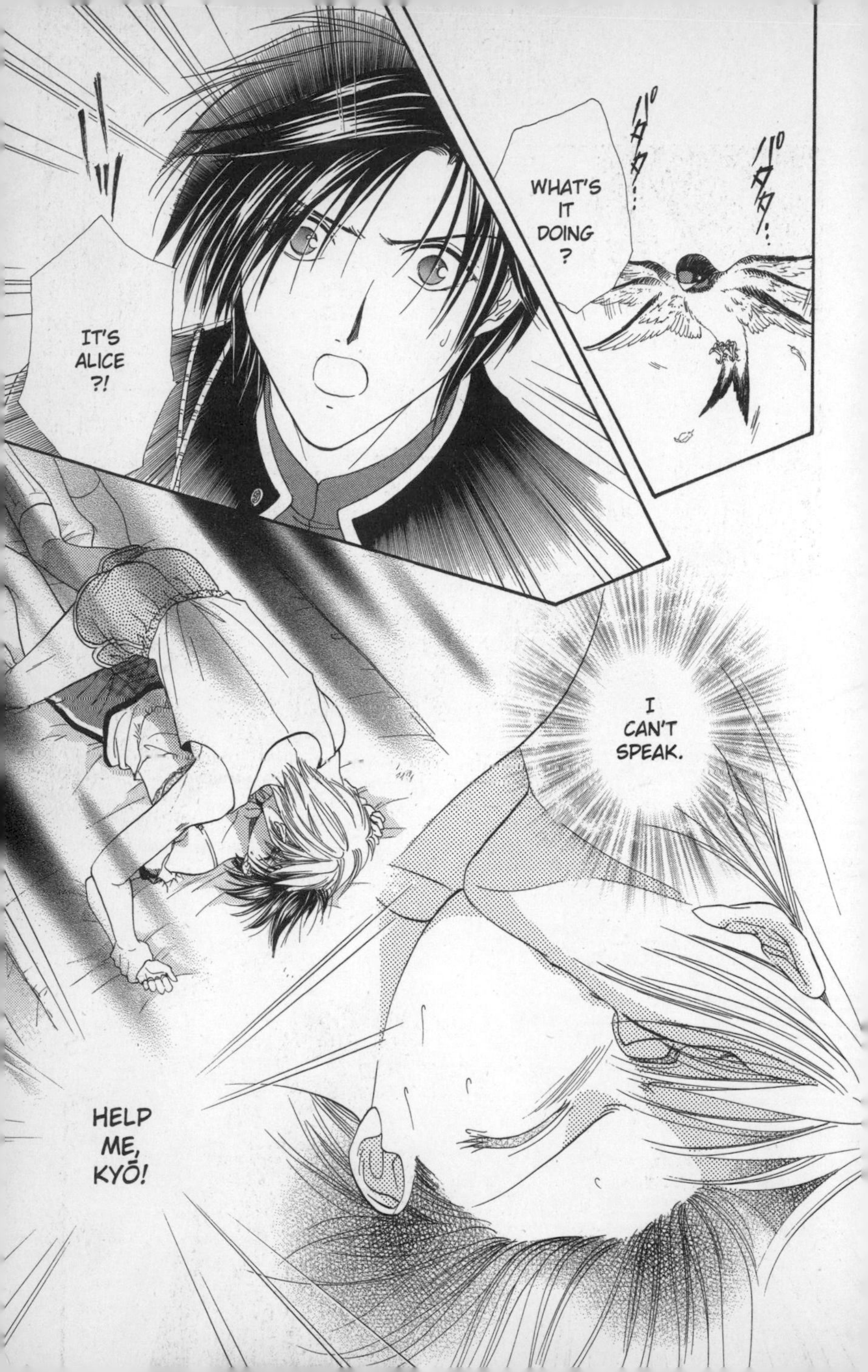
パタタ…
パタタ…
WHAT'S IT DOING?
IT'S ALICE?!
I CAN'T SPEAK.
HELP ME, KYŌ!

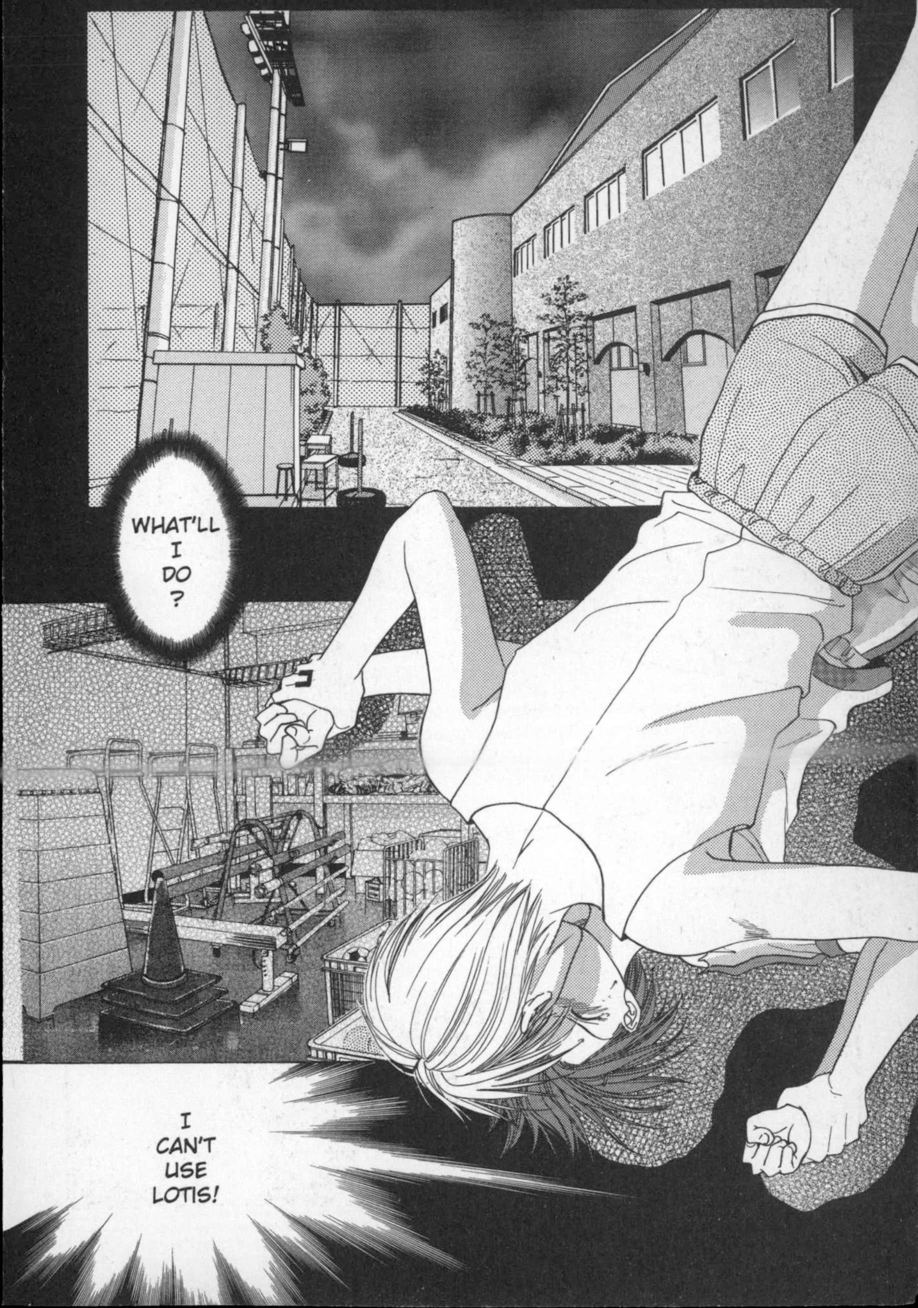
WHAT'LL I DO?
I CAN'T USE LOTIS!

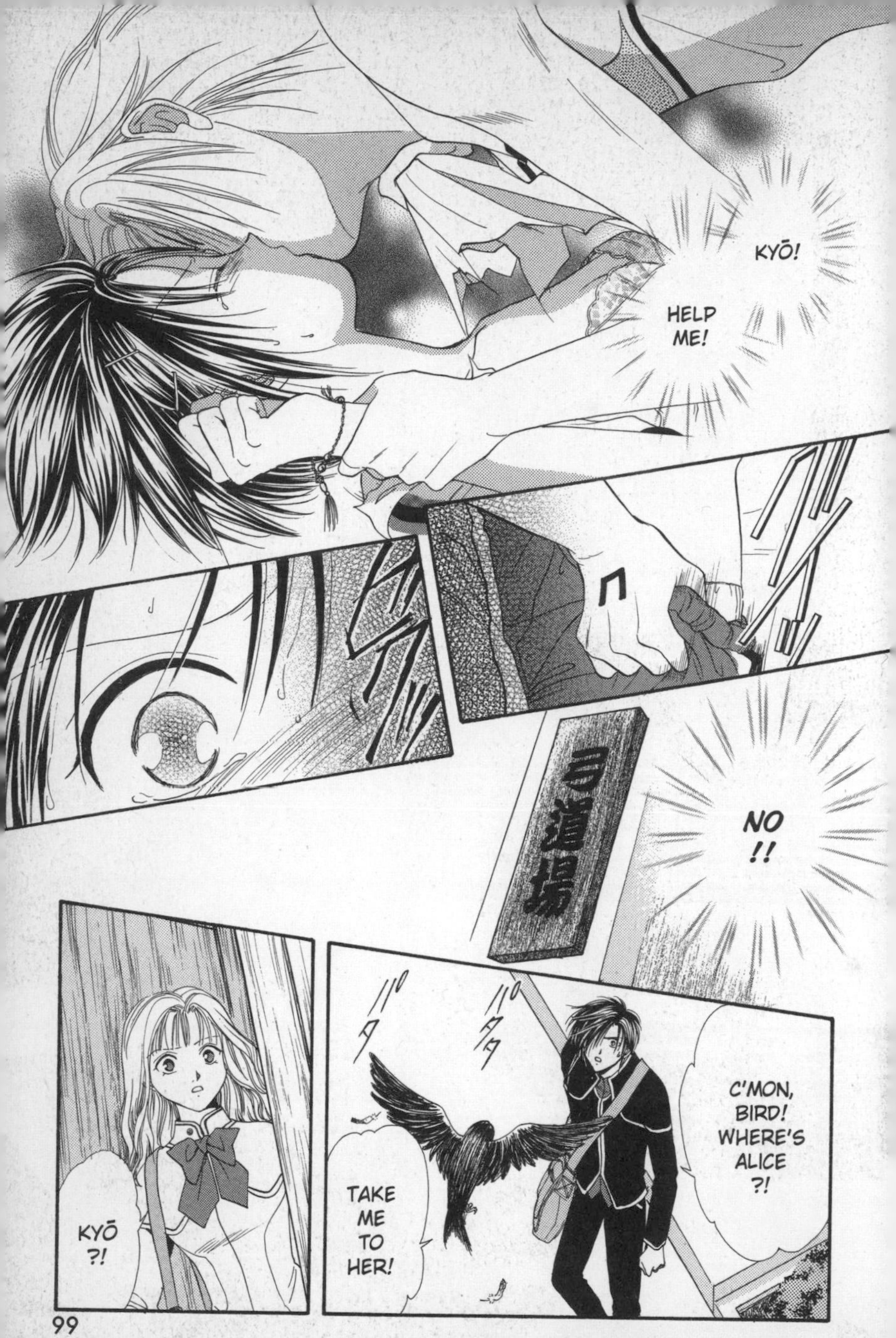
KYŌ!
HELP ME!
弓道場
NO !!
C'MON, BIRD! WHERE'S ALICE ?!
パタ
パタ
TAKE ME TO HER!
KYŌ ?!

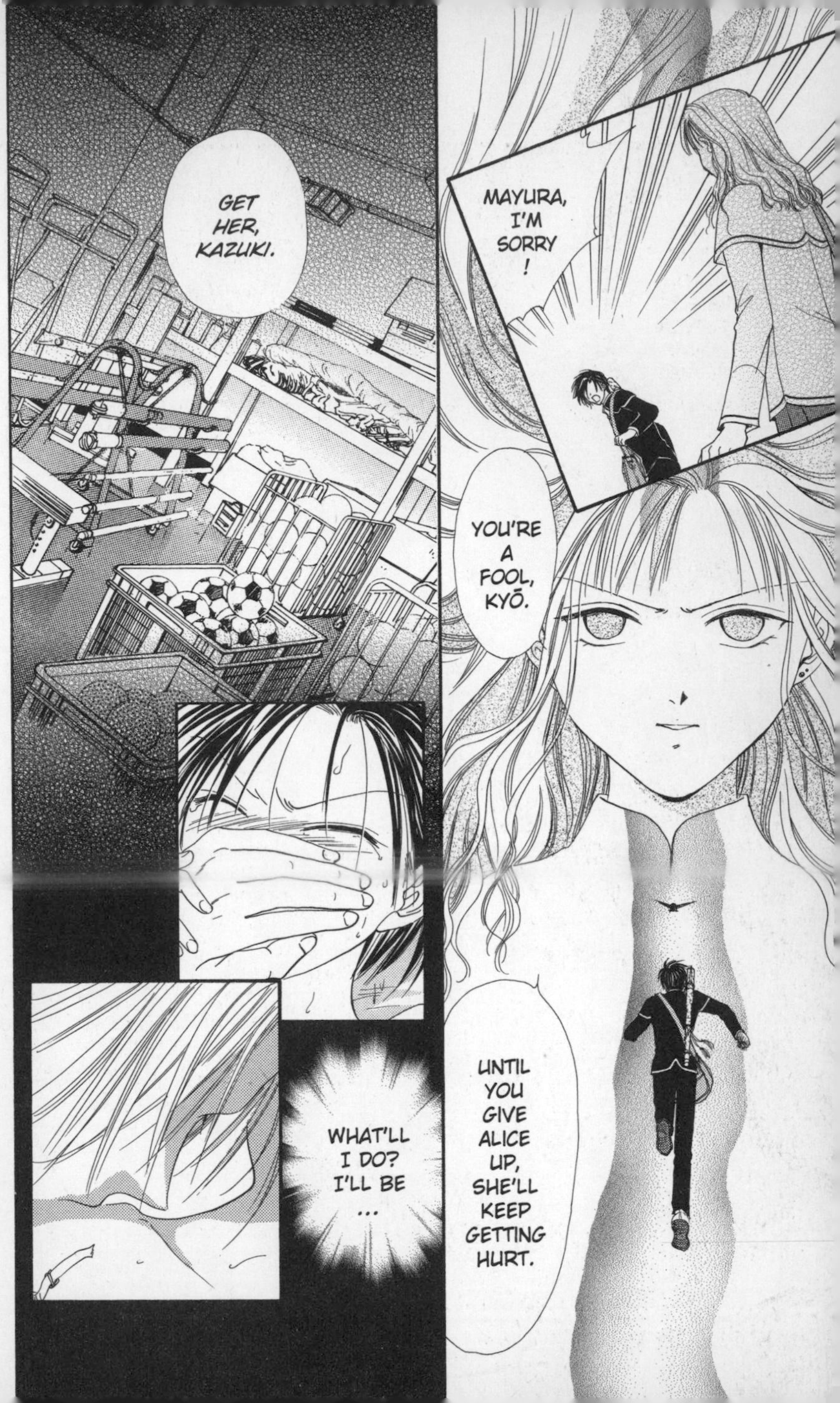
MAYURA, I'M SORRY !
YOU'RE A FOOL, KYŌ.
UNTIL YOU GIVE ALICE UP, SHE'LL KEEP GETTING HURT.
GET HER, KAZUKI.
WHAT'LL I DO? I'LL BE ...

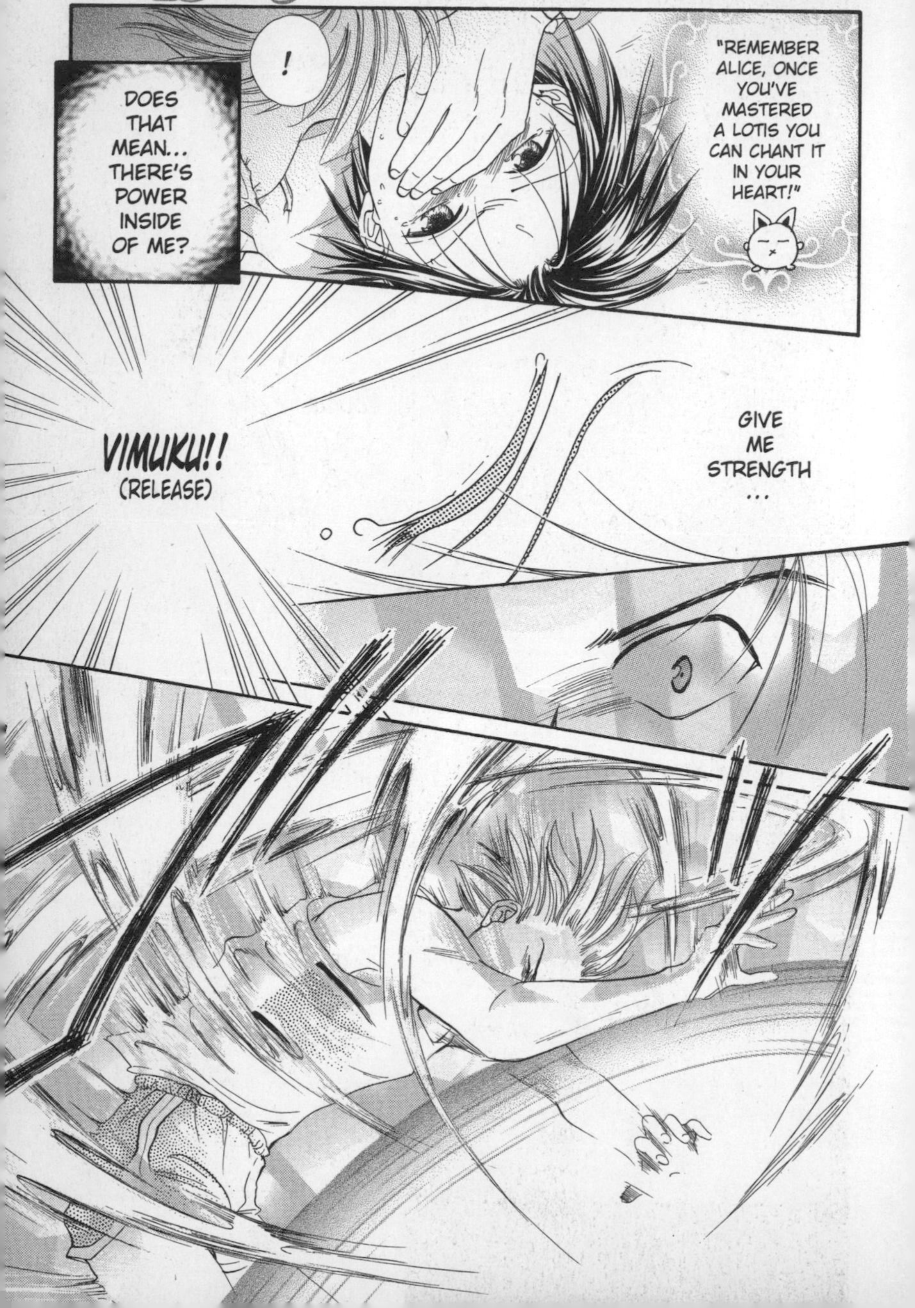
"REMEMBER ALICE, ONCE YOU'VE MASTERED A LOTIS YOU CAN CHANT IT IN YOUR HEART!"
!
DOES THAT MEAN... THERE'S POWER INSIDE OF ME?
GIVE ME STRENGTH ...
VIMUKU!!
(RELEASE)

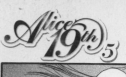

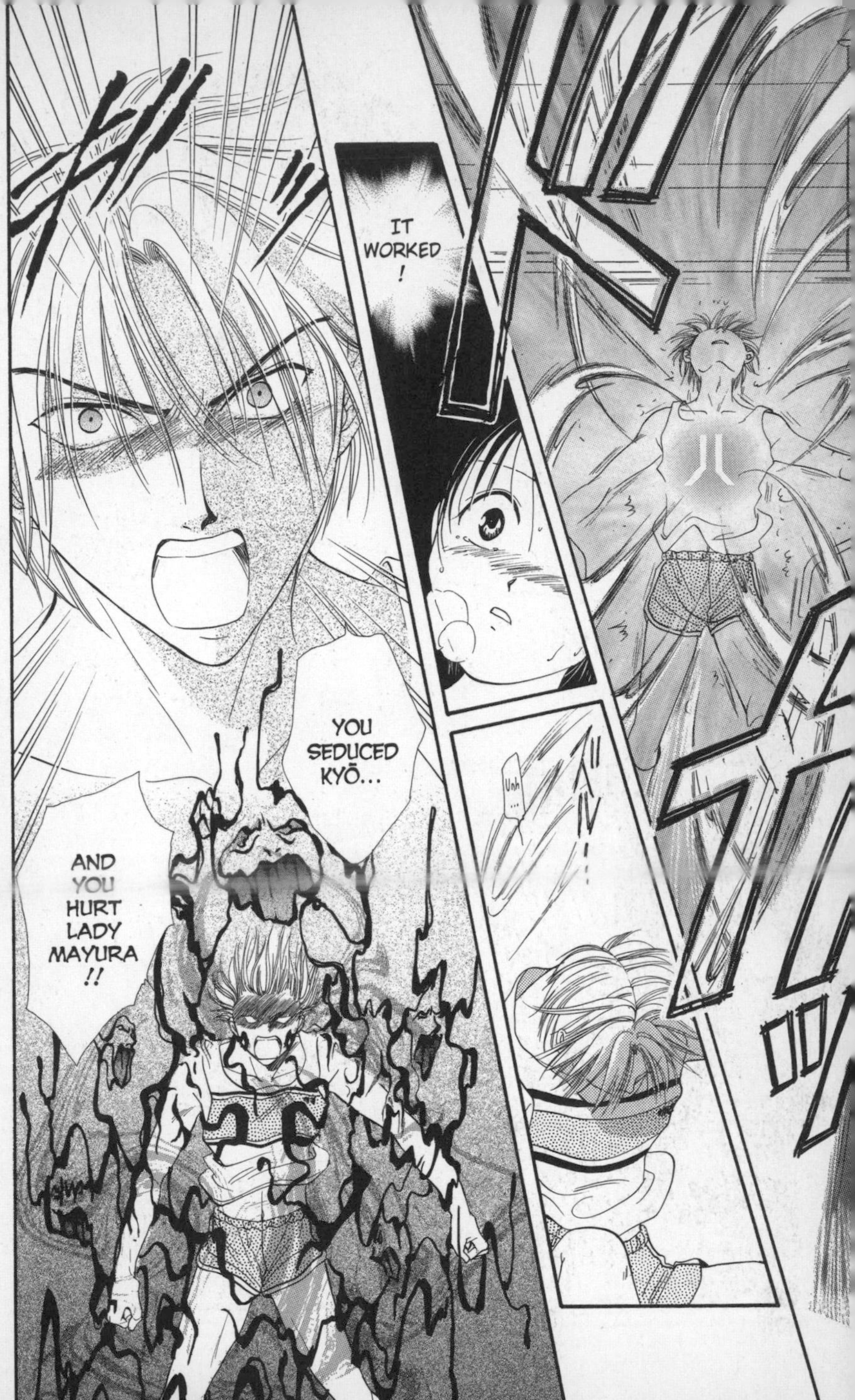
IT WORKED!
Unh...
YOU SEDUCED KYŌ...
AND YOU HURT LADY MAYURA!!

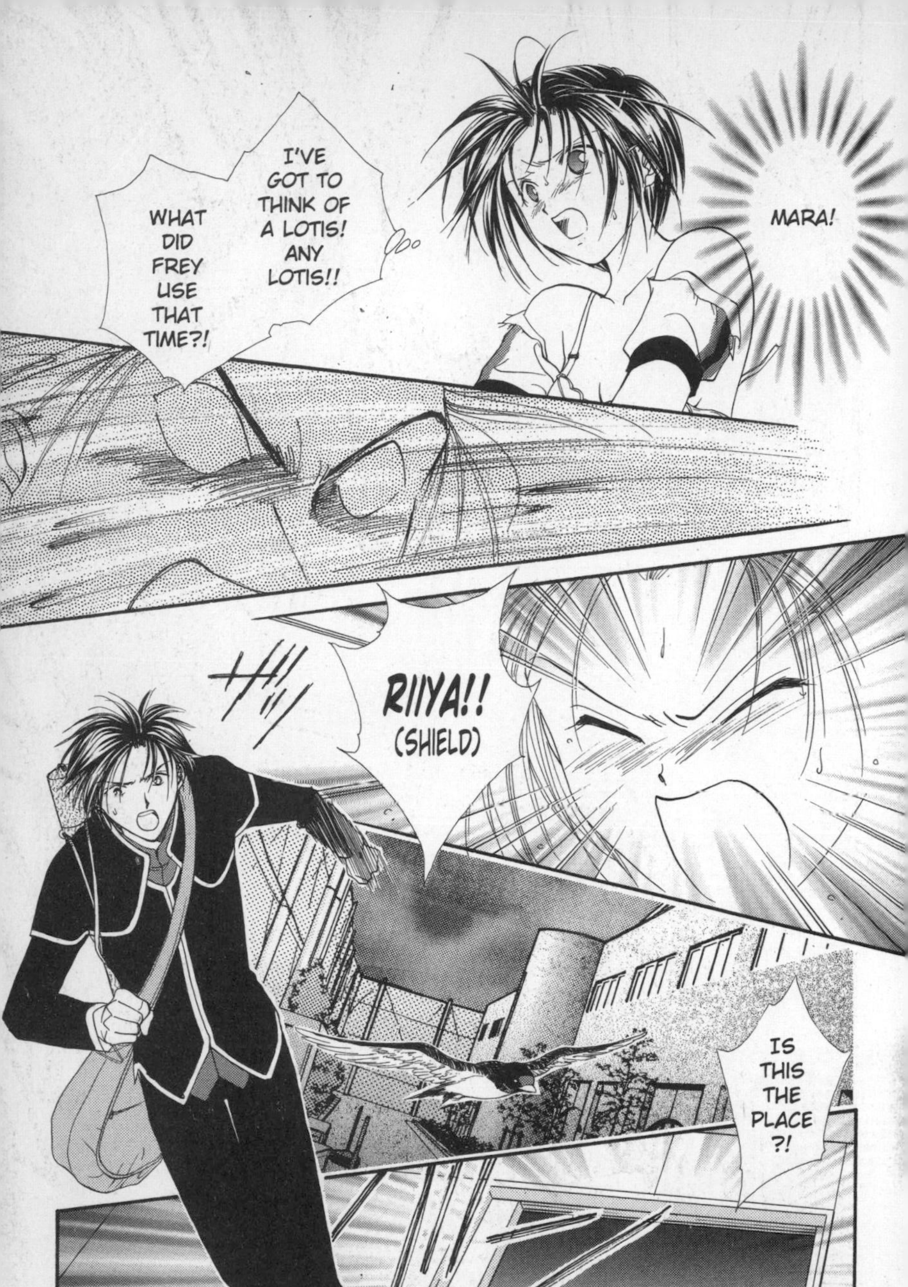
MARA!
I'VE GOT TO THINK OF A LOTIS! ANY LOTIS!!
WHAT DID FREY USE THAT TIME?!
RIIYA!! (SHIELD)
IS THIS THE PLACE?!

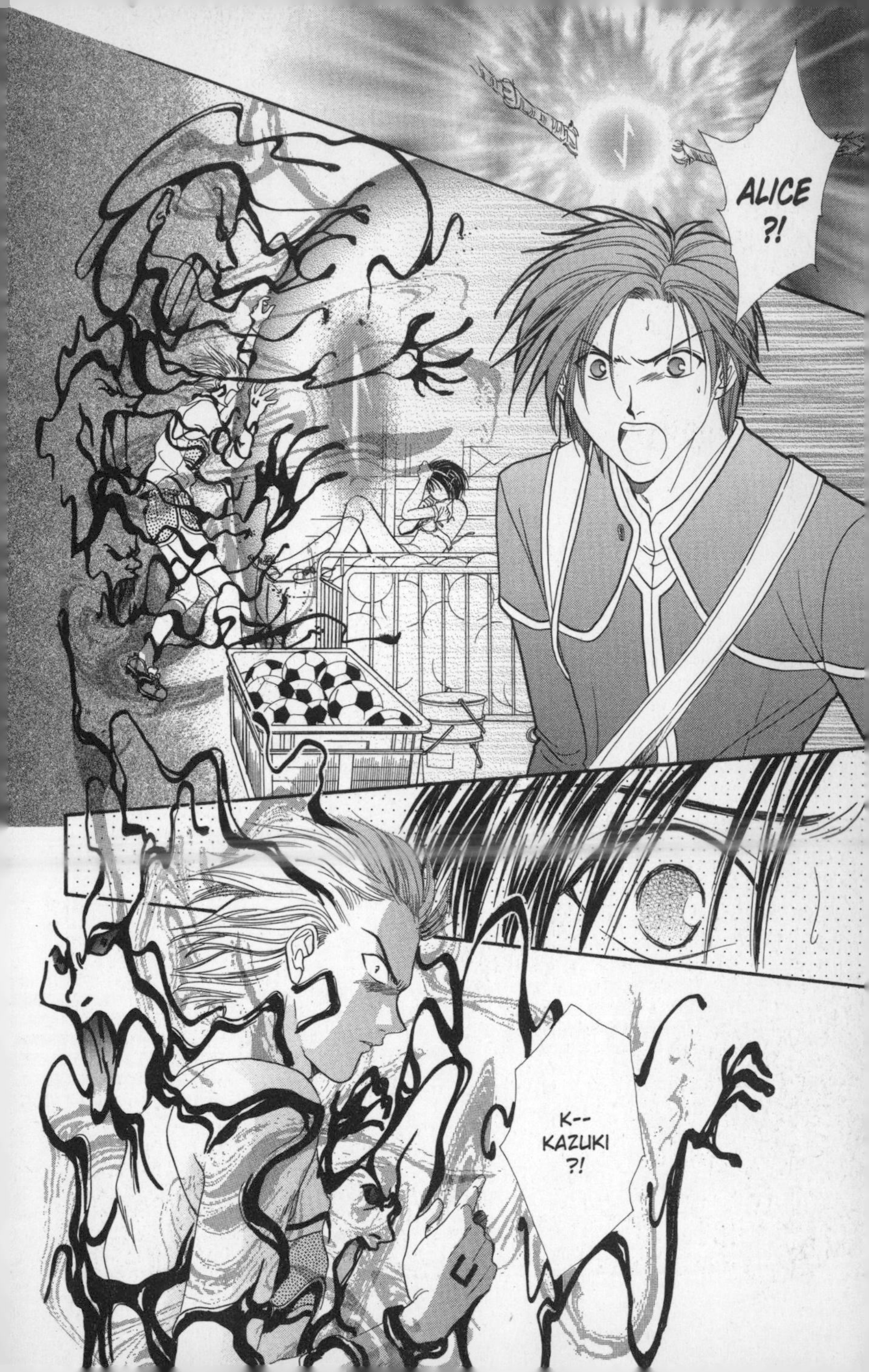
ALICE ?!
K-- KAZUKI ?!

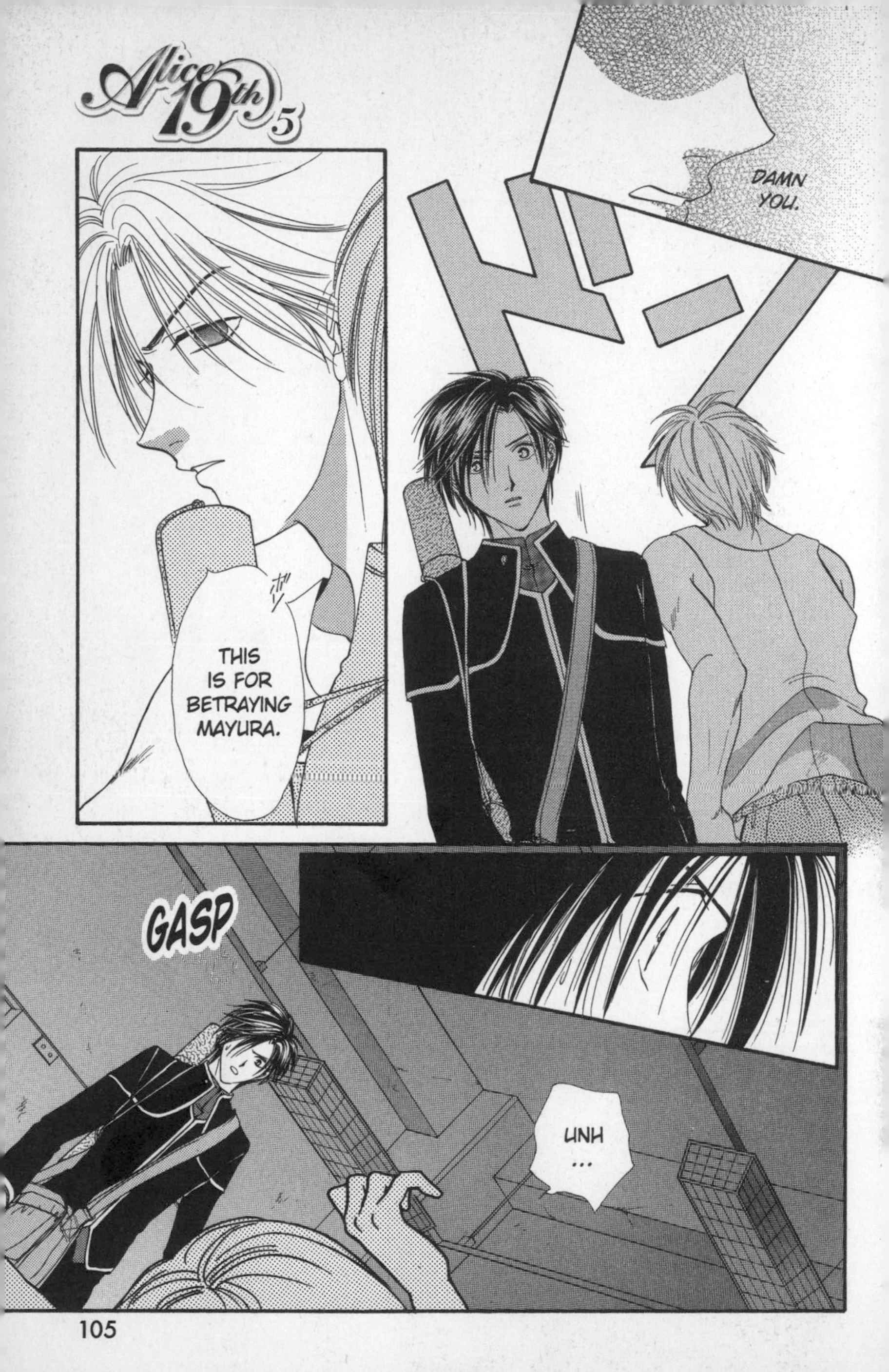
DAMN YOU.
THIS IS FOR BETRAYING MAYURA.
GASP
UNH ...

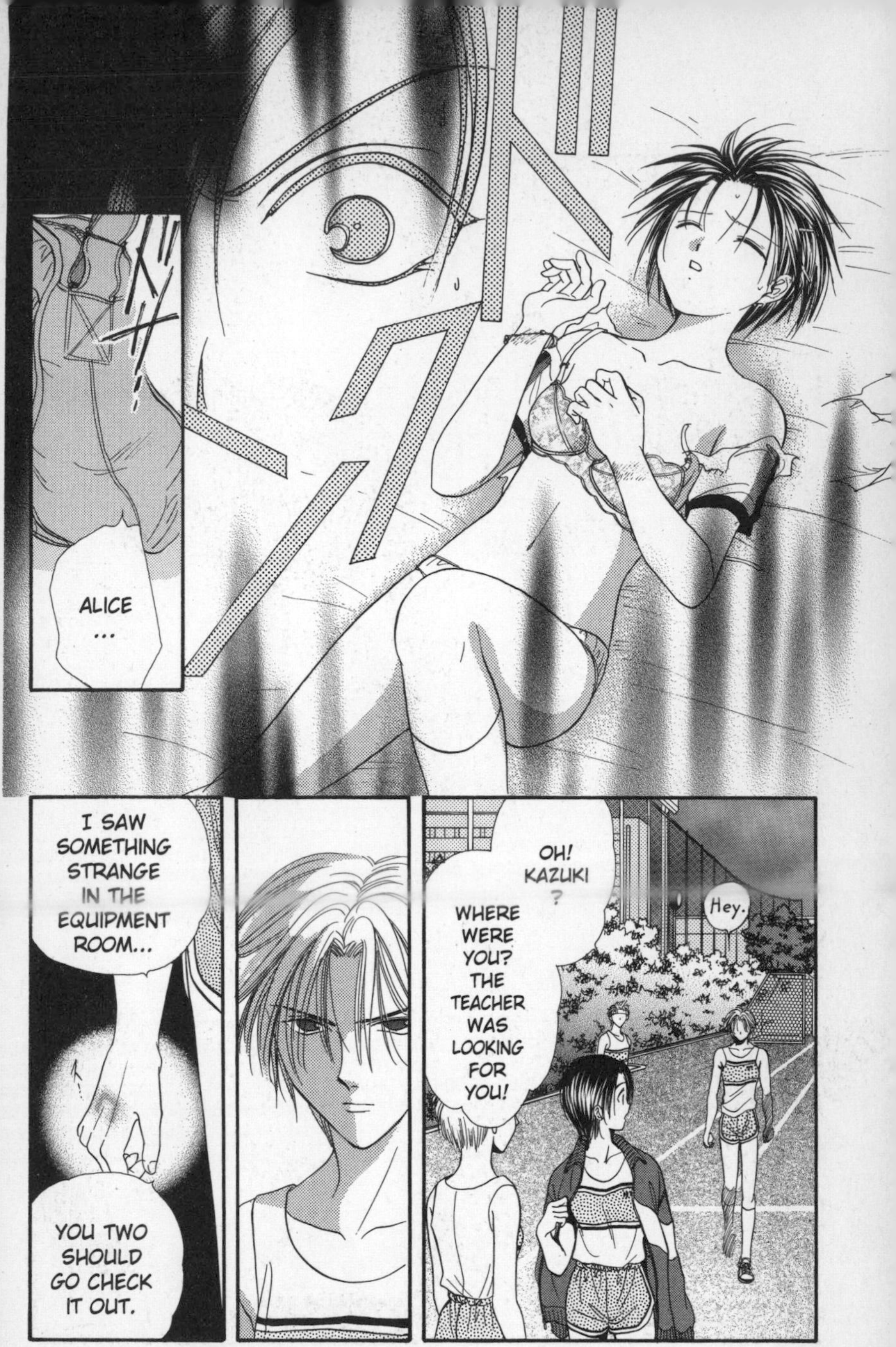
ALICE ...
OH! KAZUKI?
Hey.
WHERE WERE YOU? THE TEACHER WAS LOOKING FOR YOU!
I SAW SOMETHING STRANGE IN THE EQUIPMENT ROOM...
YOU TWO SHOULD GO CHECK IT OUT.

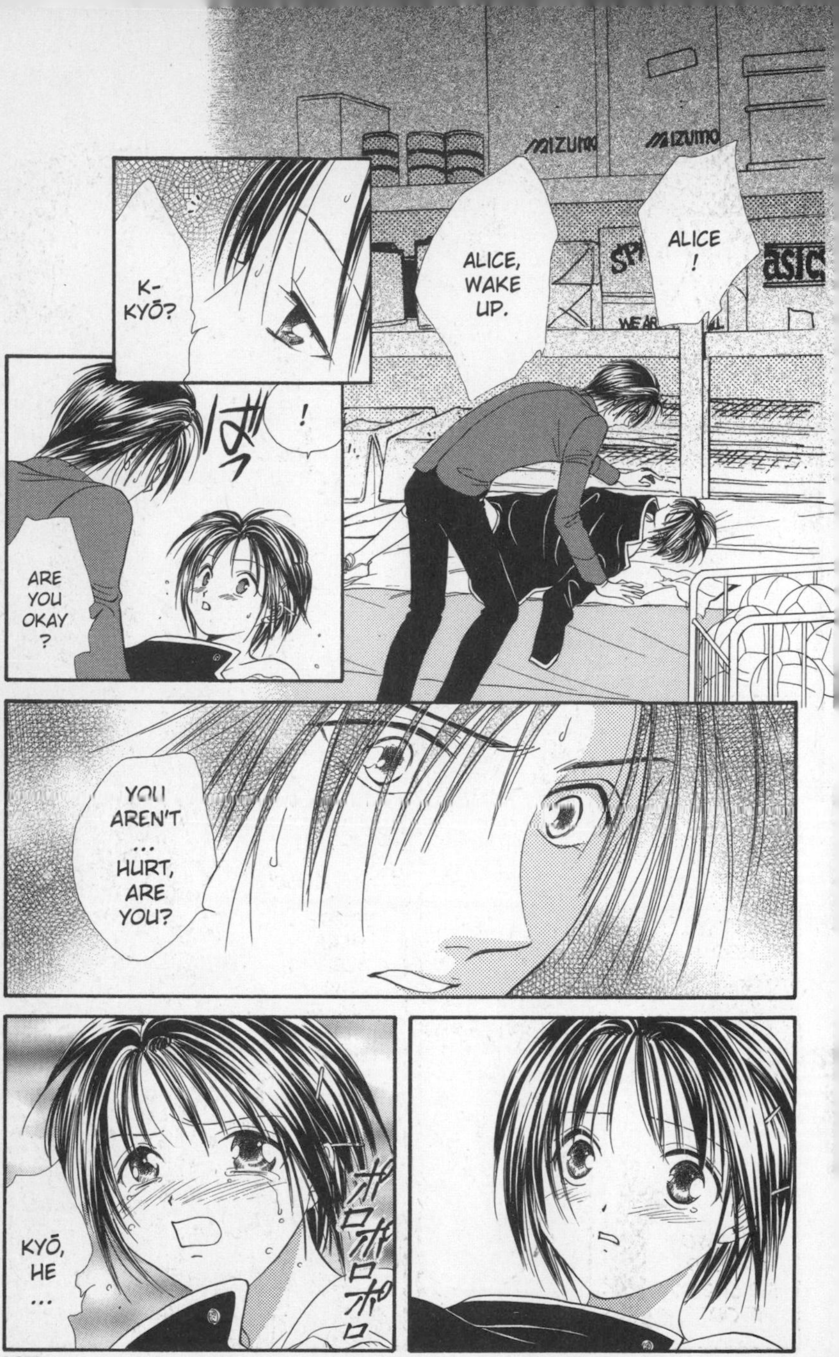
ALICE !
ALICE, WAKE UP.
K-KYŌ?
!
ぱっ
ARE YOU OKAY ?
YOU AREN'T ... HURT, ARE YOU?
KYŌ, HE ...
ポロポロ

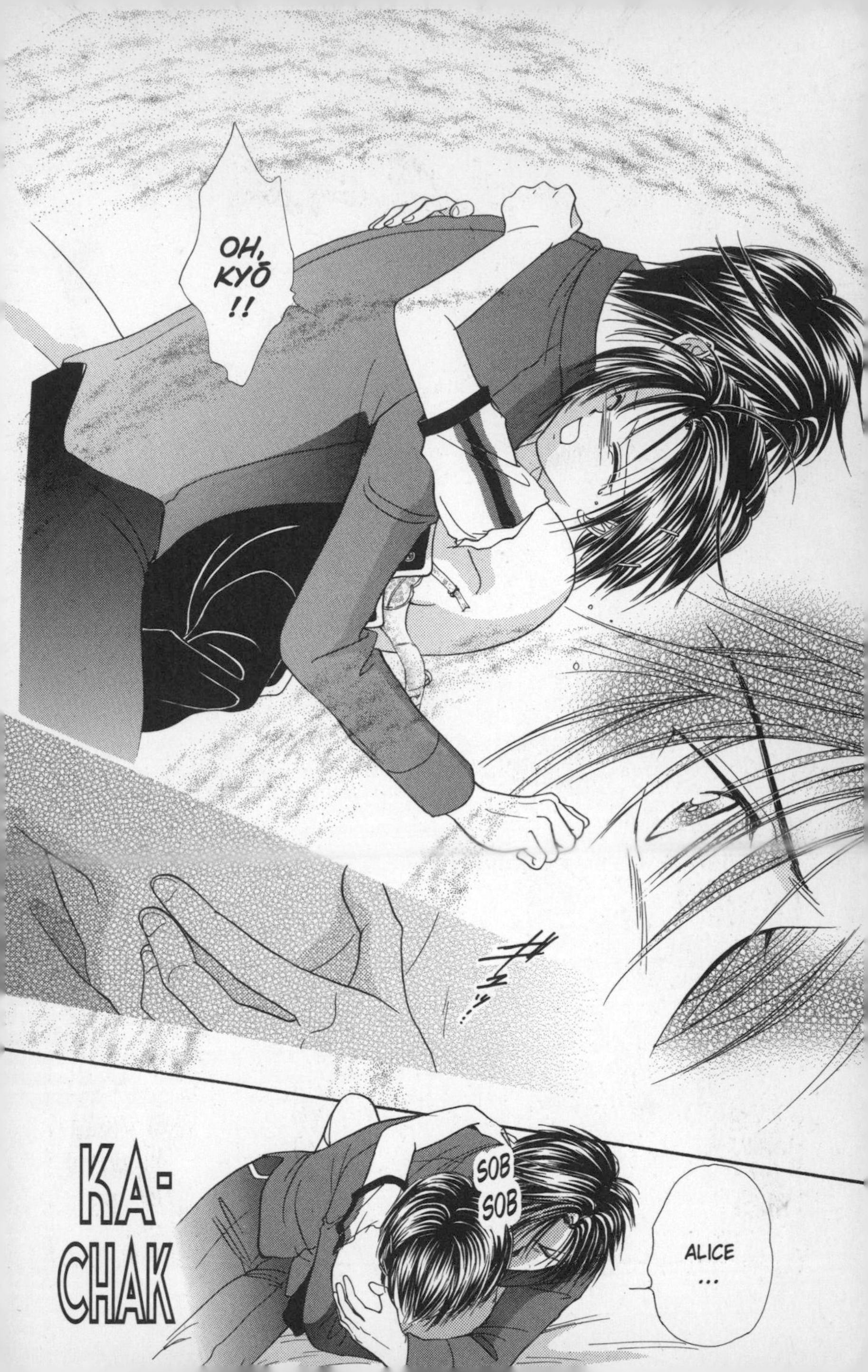
OH, KYŌ !!
ALICE ...
SOB SOB
KA-CHAK

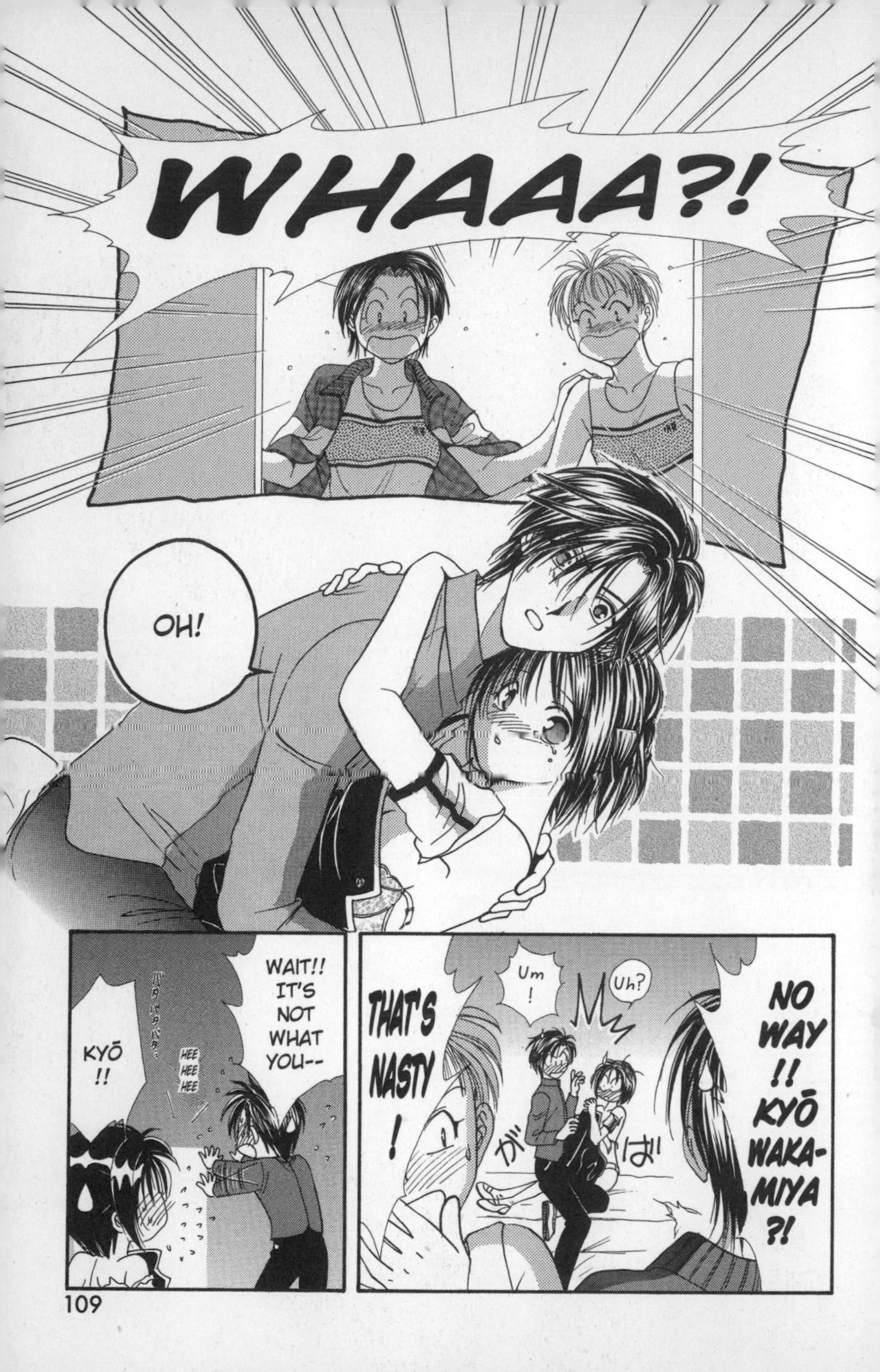
WHAAAA?!
OH!
NO WAY!! KYŌ WAKAMIYA?!
Uh?
Um!
THAT'S NASTY!
ば
が
WAIT!! IT'S NOT WHAT YOU--
HEE HEE HEE
KYŌ!!

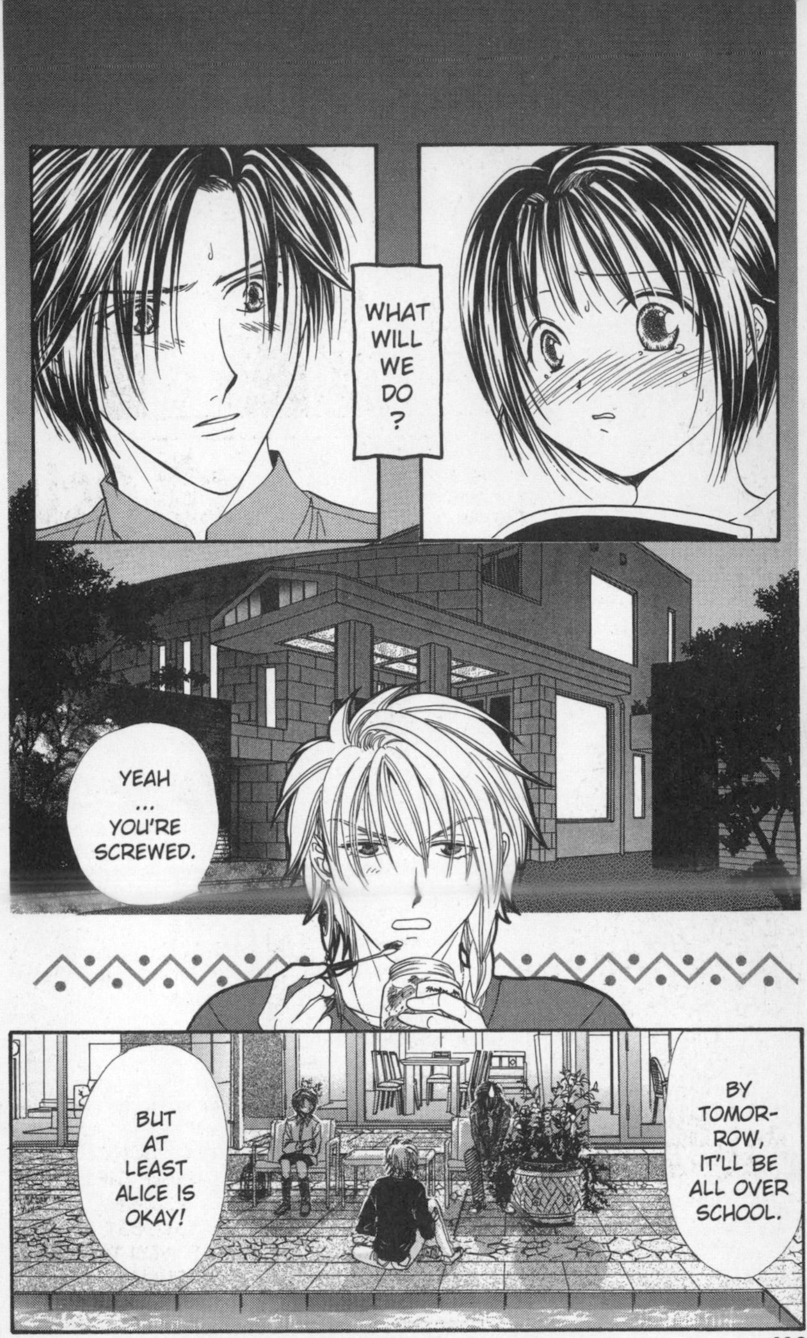
WHAT WILL WE DO?
YEAH ... YOU'RE SCREWED.
BY TOMOR-ROW, IT'LL BE ALL OVER SCHOOL.
BUT AT LEAST ALICE IS OKAY!

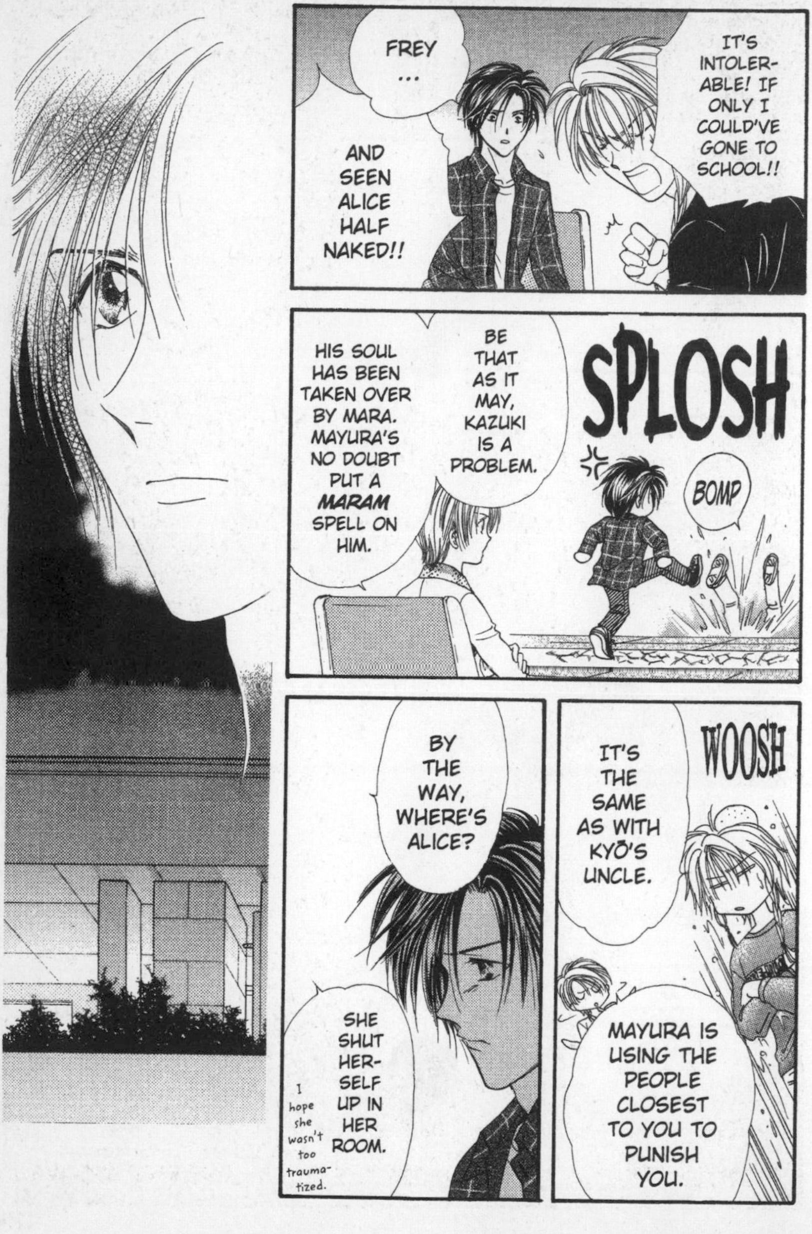
IT'S INTOLERABLE! IF ONLY I COULD'VE GONE TO SCHOOL!!
FREY ...
AND SEEN ALICE HALF NAKED!!
SPLOSH
BOMP
BE THAT AS IT MAY, KAZUKI IS A PROBLEM.
HIS SOUL HAS BEEN TAKEN OVER BY MARA. MAYURA'S NO DOUBT PUT A ***MARAM*** SPELL ON HIM.
WOOSH
IT'S THE SAME AS WITH KYŌ'S UNCLE.
MAYURA IS USING THE PEOPLE CLOSEST TO YOU TO PUNISH YOU.
BY THE WAY, WHERE'S ALICE?
SHE SHUT HERSELF UP IN HER ROOM.
I hope she wasn't too traumatized.

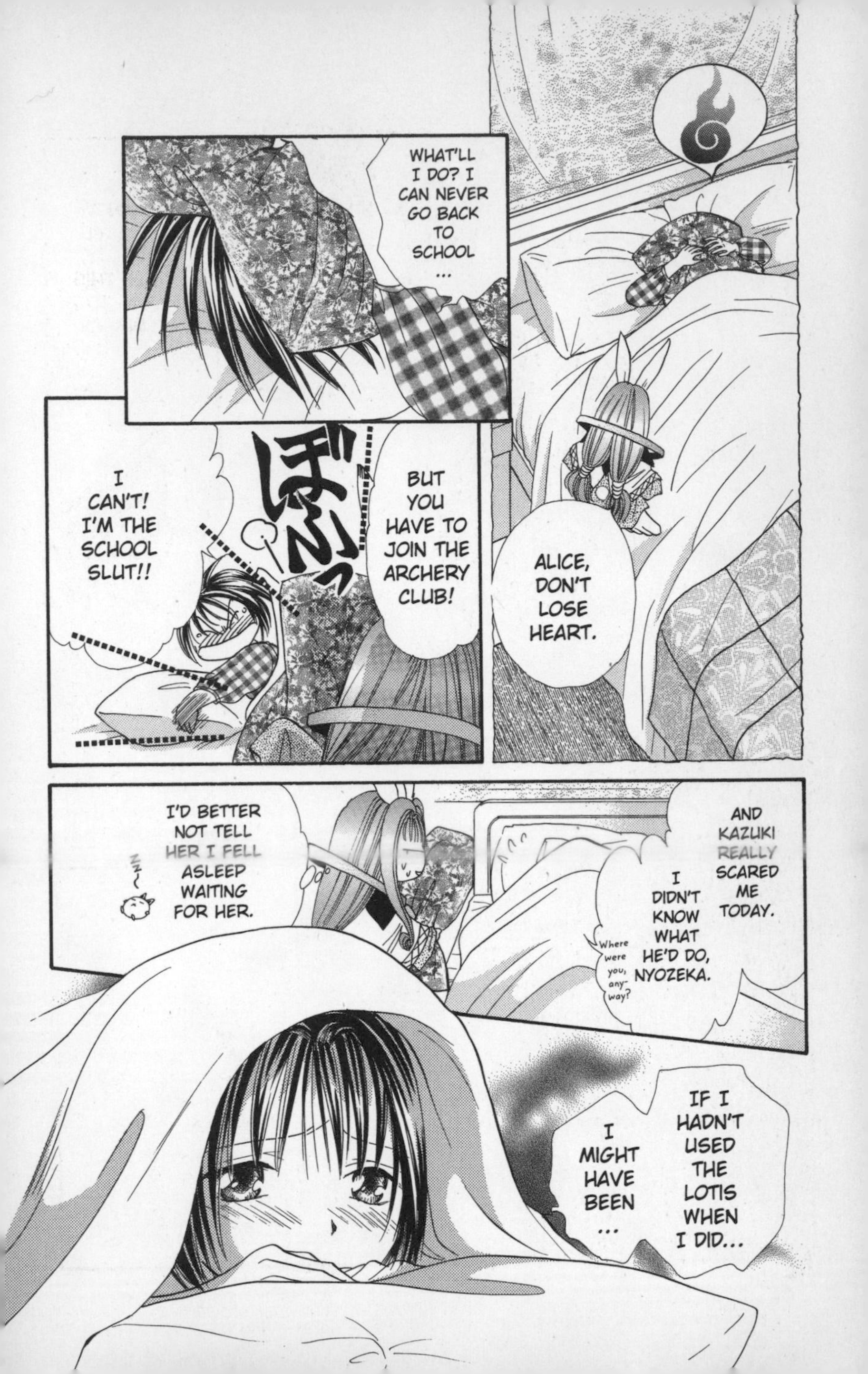
ALICE, DON'T LOSE HEART.
WHAT'LL I DO? I CAN NEVER GO BACK TO SCHOOL ...
BUT YOU HAVE TO JOIN THE ARCHERY CLUB!
ぼふんっ
I CAN'T! I'M THE SCHOOL SLUT!!
AND KAZUKI REALLY SCARED ME TODAY.
I DIDN'T KNOW WHAT HE'D DO, NYOZEKA.
Where were you, any-way?
I'D BETTER NOT TELL HER I FELL ASLEEP WAITING FOR HER.
IF I HADN'T USED THE LOTIS WHEN I DID...
I MIGHT HAVE BEEN ...

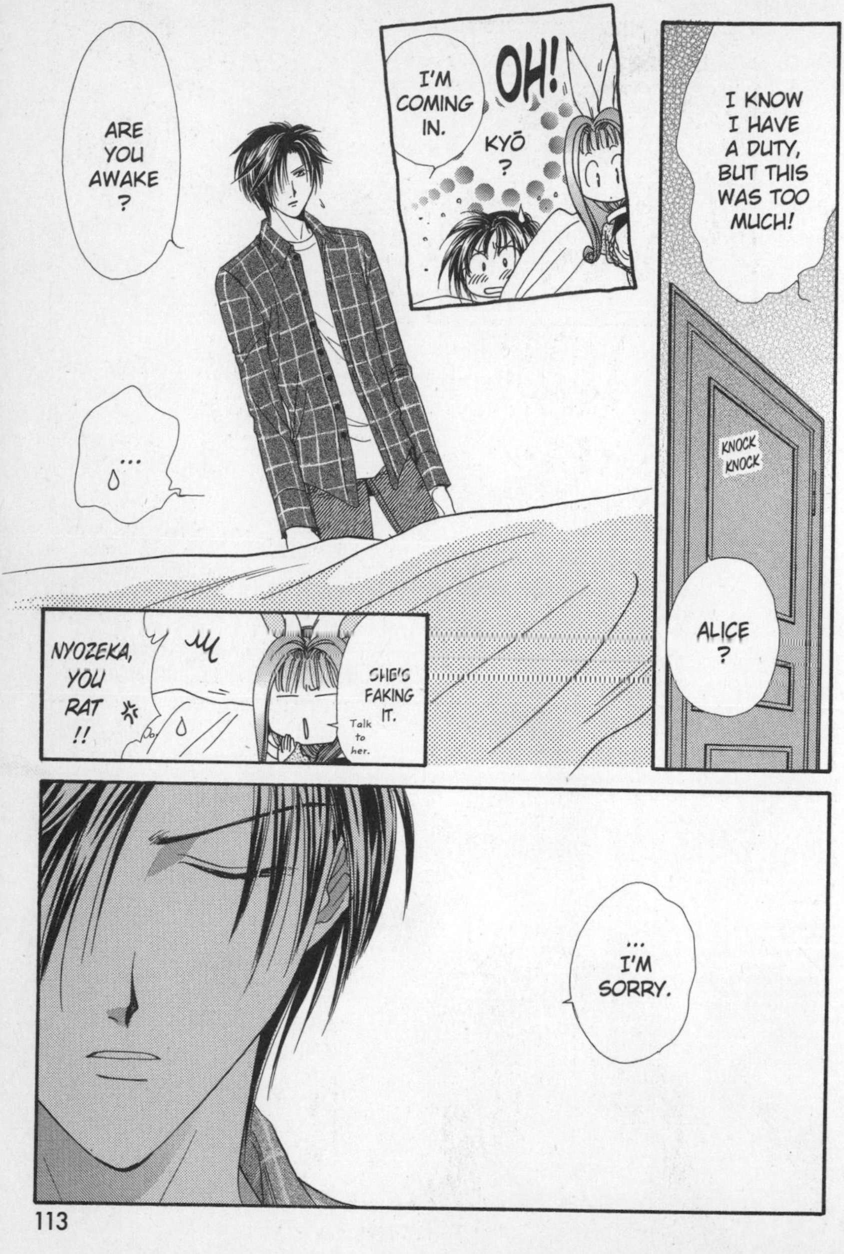
I KNOW I HAVE A DUTY, BUT THIS WAS TOO MUCH!
KNOCK KNOCK
ALICE?
I'M COMING IN.
OH!
KYŌ?
ARE YOU AWAKE?
...
SHE'S FAKING IT.
Talk to her.
NYOZEKA, YOU RAT!!
... I'M SORRY.

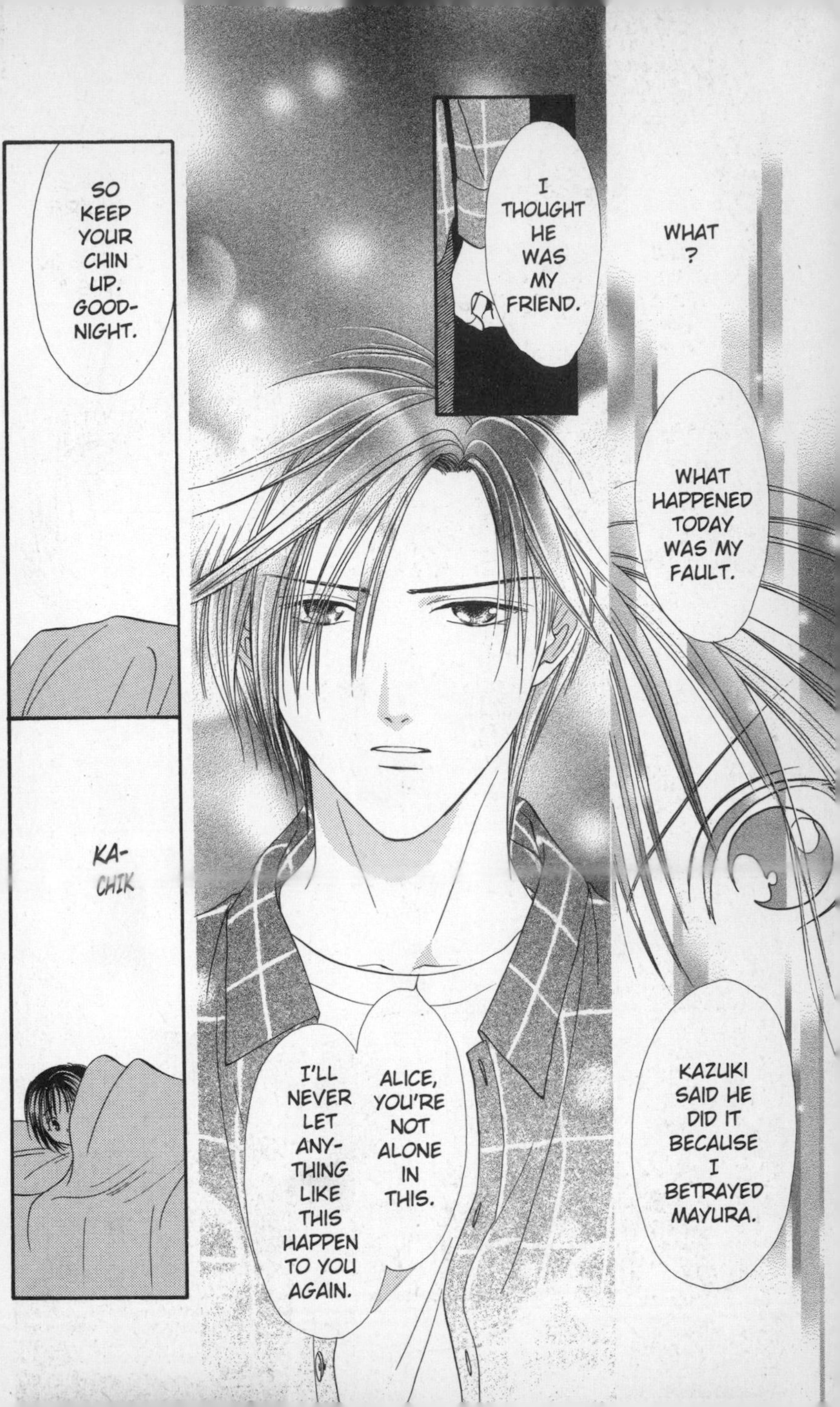
WHAT?
WHAT HAPPENED TODAY WAS MY FAULT.
KAZUKI SAID HE DID IT BECAUSE I BETRAYED MAYURA.
I THOUGHT HE WAS MY FRIEND.
ALICE, YOU'RE NOT ALONE IN THIS.
I'LL NEVER LET ANY-THING LIKE THIS HAPPEN TO YOU AGAIN.
SO KEEP YOUR CHIN UP. GOOD-NIGHT.
KA-CHIK

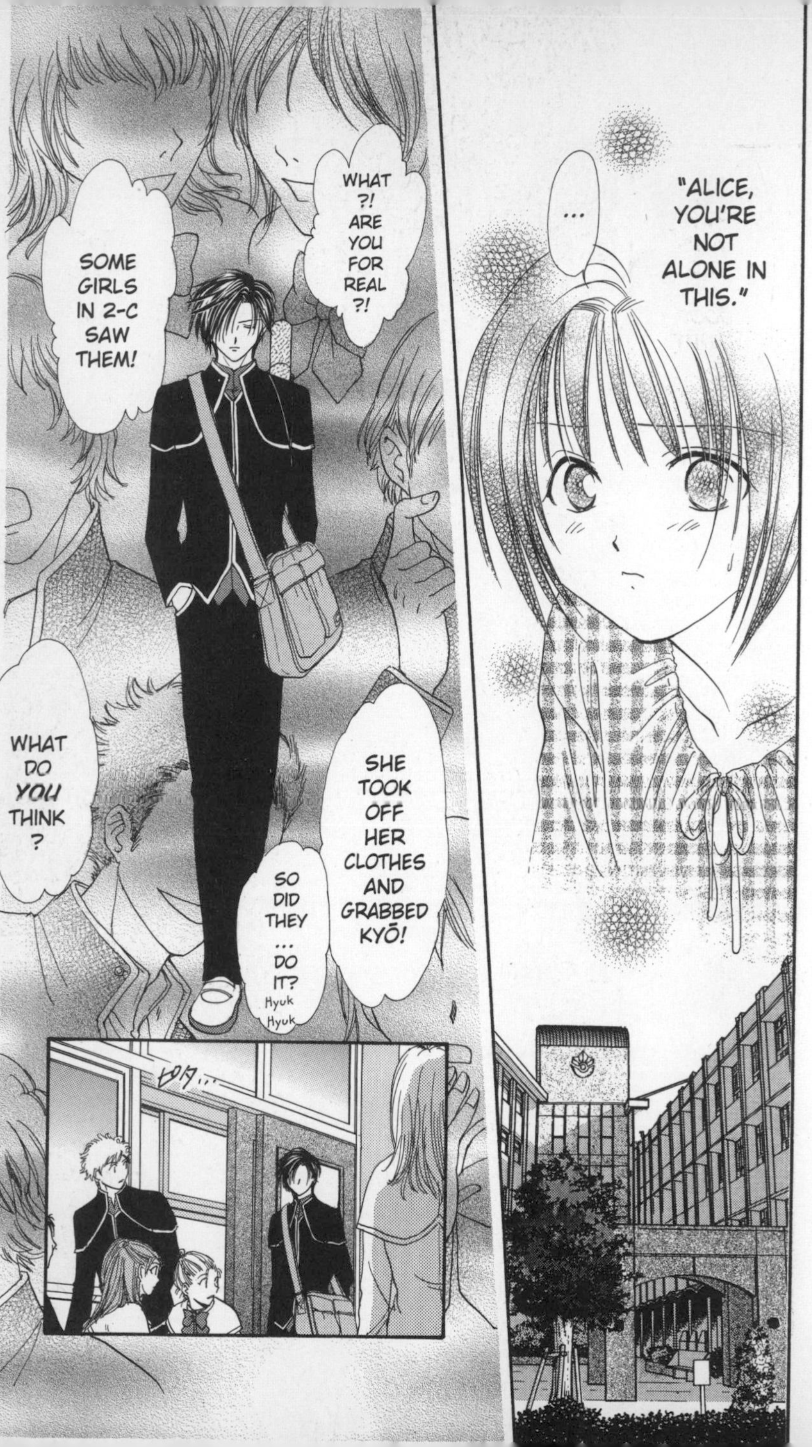
"ALICE, YOU'RE NOT ALONE IN THIS."
...
WHAT?! ARE YOU FOR REAL?!
SOME GIRLS IN 2-C SAW THEM!
SHE TOOK OFF HER CLOTHES AND GRABBED KYŌ!
SO DID THEY... DO IT?
Hyuk Hyuk
WHAT DO YOU THINK?

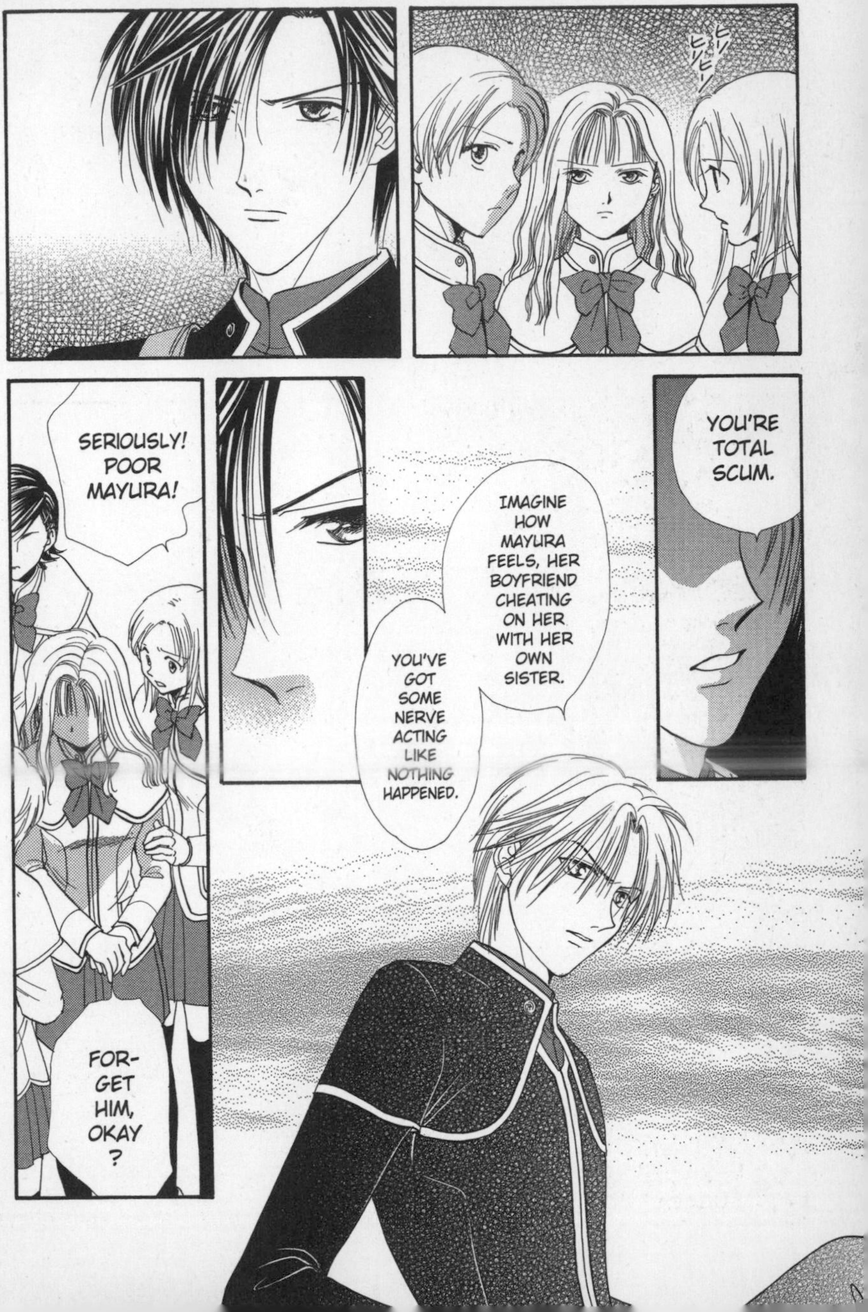
YOU'RE TOTAL SCUM.
IMAGINE HOW MAYURA FEELS, HER BOYFRIEND CHEATING ON HER WITH HER OWN SISTER.
YOU'VE GOT SOME NERVE ACTING LIKE NOTHING HAPPENED.
SERIOUSLY! POOR MAYURA!
FOR-GET HIM, OKAY?

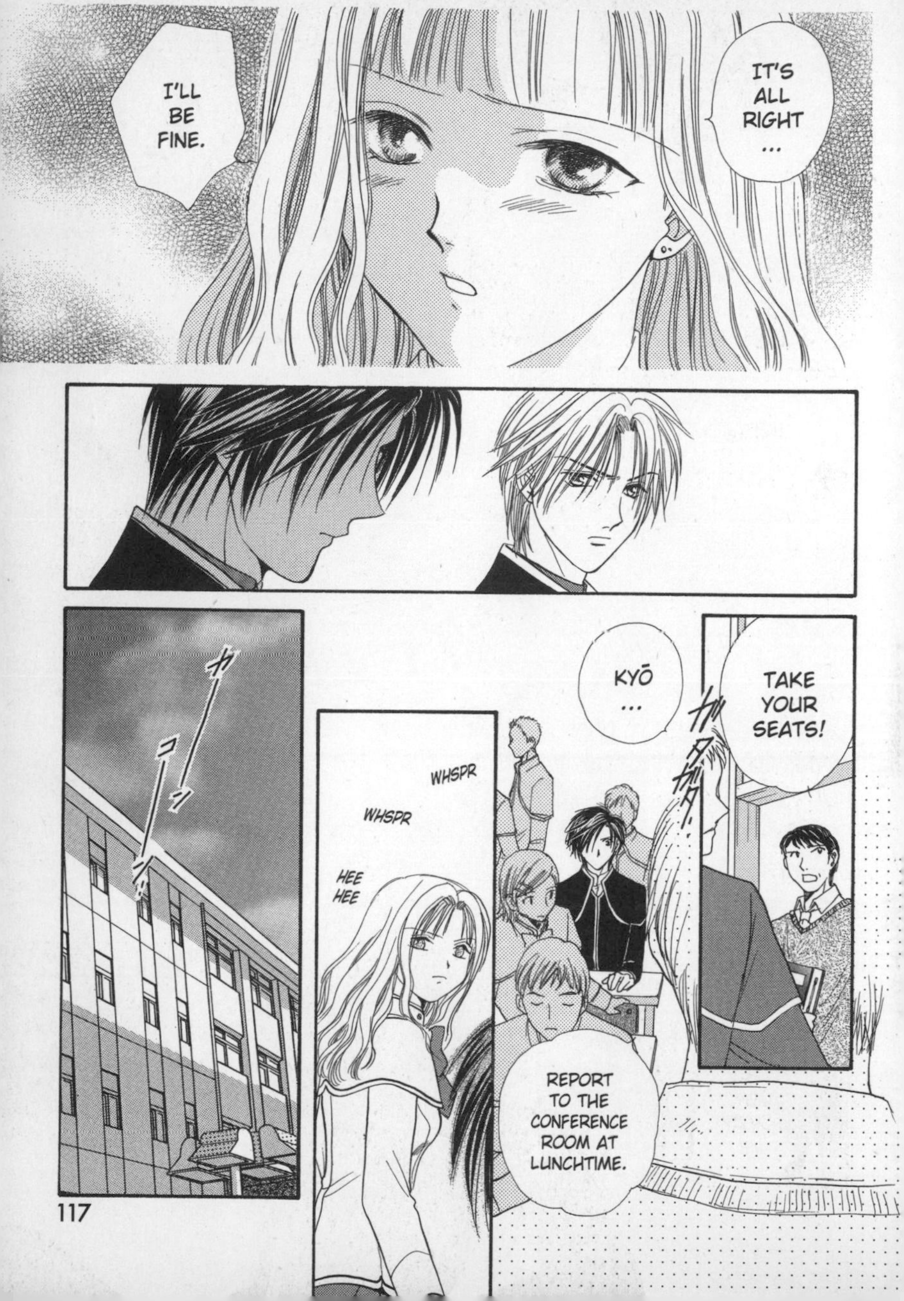
IT'S ALL RIGHT ...
I'LL BE FINE.
TAKE YOUR SEATS!
KYŌ ...
WHSPR
WHSPR
HEE HEE
REPORT TO THE CONFERENCE ROOM AT LUNCHTIME.

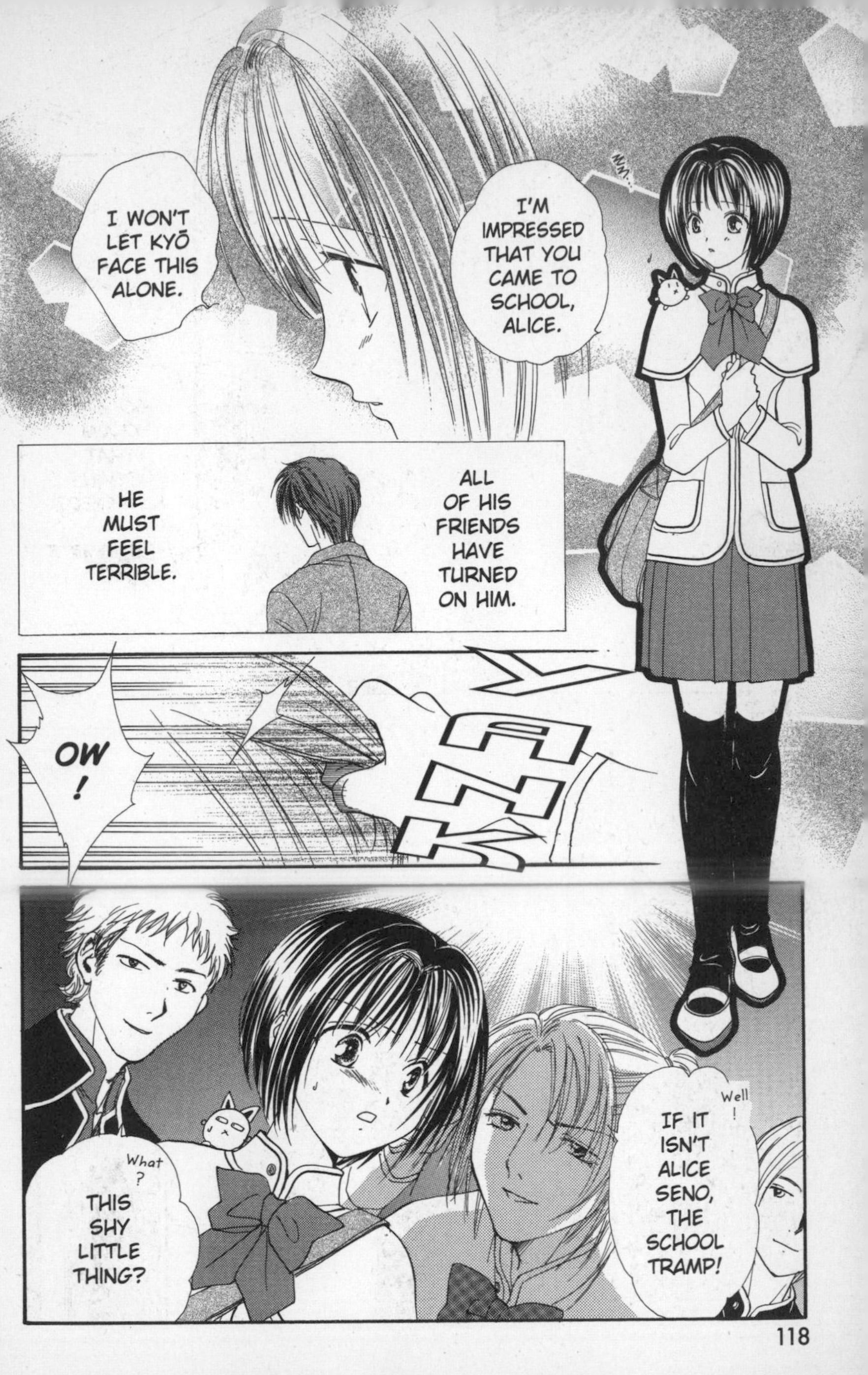
I'M IMPRESSED THAT YOU CAME TO SCHOOL, ALICE.
I WON'T LET KYŌ FACE THIS ALONE.
ALL OF HIS FRIENDS HAVE TURNED ON HIM.
HE MUST FEEL TERRIBLE.
OW!
Well!
IF IT ISN'T ALICE SENO, THE SCHOOL TRAMP!
What?
THIS SHY LITTLE THING?

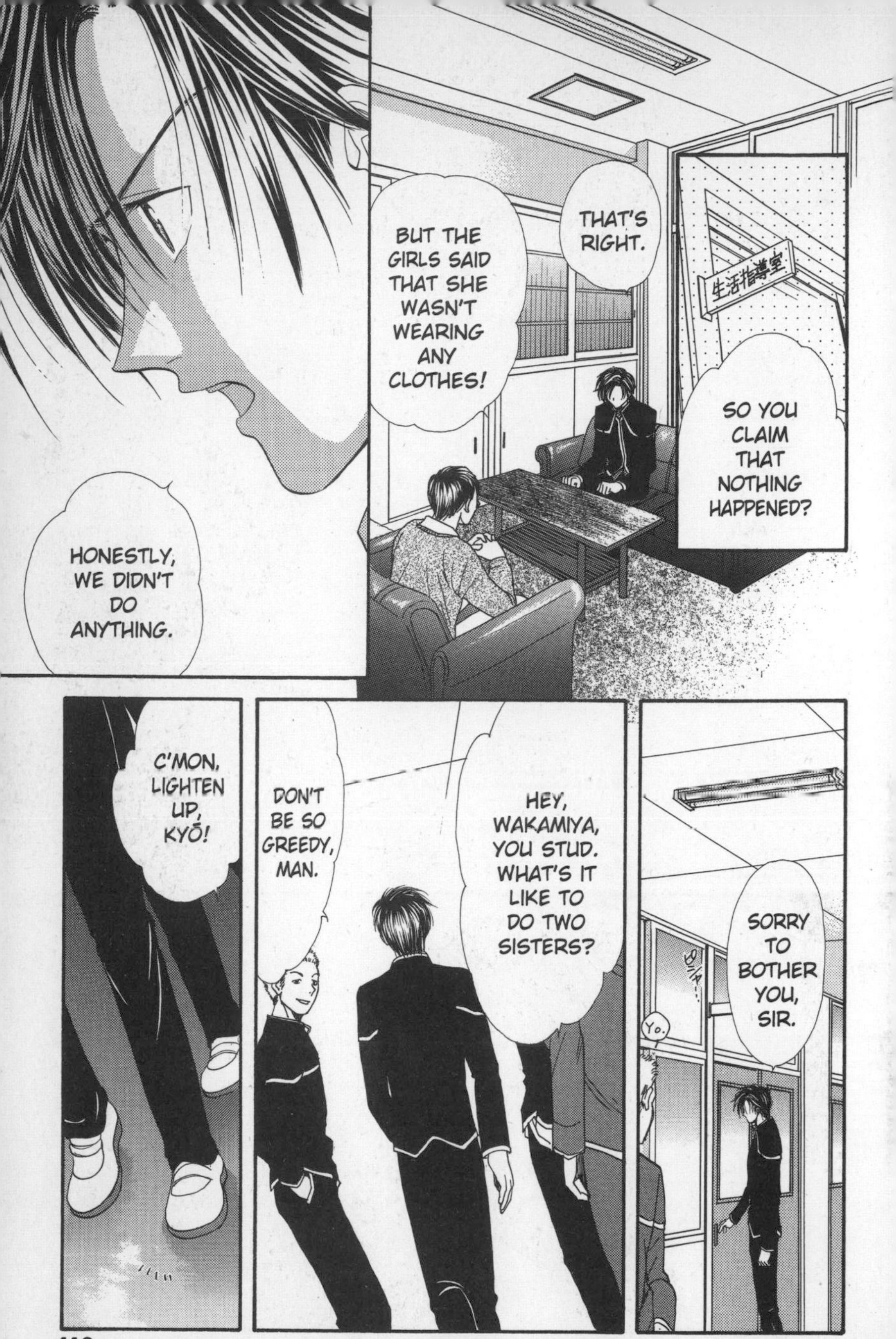
生活指導室
SO YOU CLAIM THAT NOTHING HAPPENED?
THAT'S RIGHT.
BUT THE GIRLS SAID THAT SHE WASN'T WEARING ANY CLOTHES!
HONESTLY, WE DIDN'T DO ANYTHING.
SORRY TO BOTHER YOU, SIR.
Yo.
HEY, WAKAMIYA, YOU STUD. WHAT'S IT LIKE TO DO TWO SISTERS?
DON'T BE SO GREEDY, MAN.
C'MON, LIGHTEN UP, KYŌ!

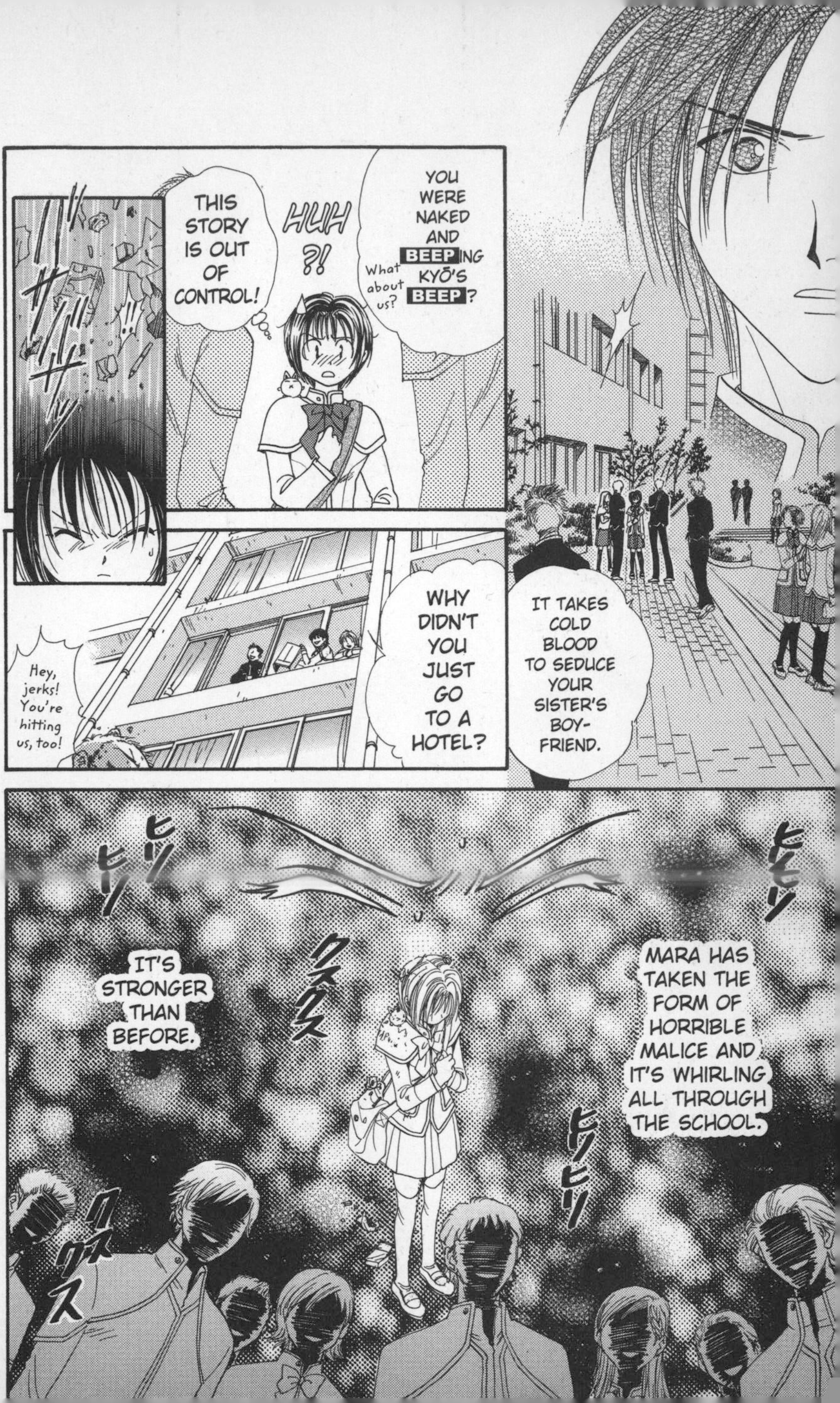
IT TAKES COLD BLOOD TO SEDUCE YOUR SISTER'S BOY-FRIEND.
YOU WERE NAKED AND BEEPING KYŌ'S BEEP?
What about us?
HUH ?!
THIS STORY IS OUT OF CONTROL!
WHY DIDN'T YOU JUST GO TO A HOTEL?
Hey, jerks! You're hitting us, too!
MARA HAS TAKEN THE FORM OF HORRIBLE MALICE AND IT'S WHIRLING ALL THROUGH THE SCHOOL.
IT'S STRONGER THAN BEFORE.

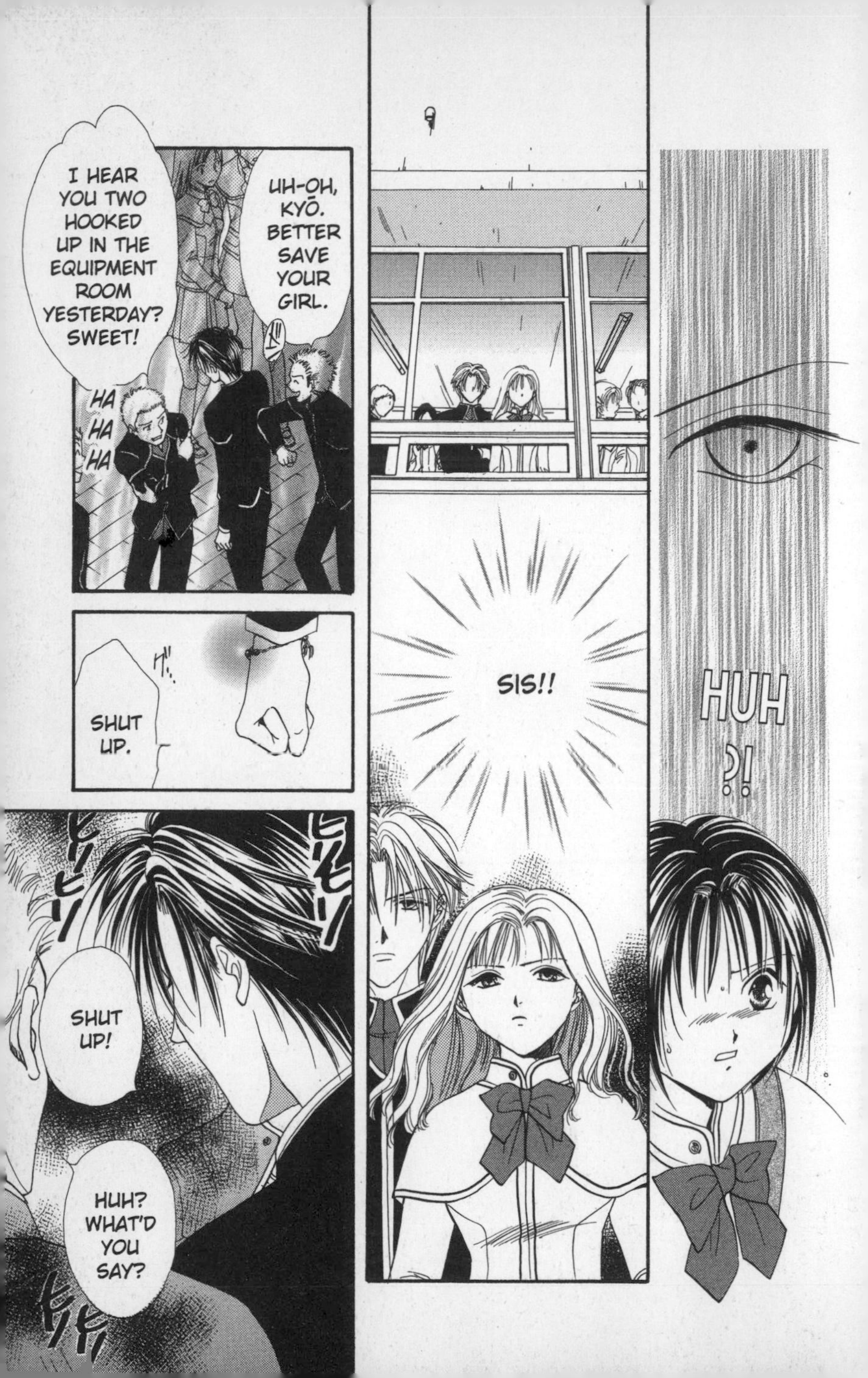
HUH ?!
SIS!!
UH-OH, KYŌ. BETTER SAVE YOUR GIRL.
I HEAR YOU TWO HOOKED UP IN THE EQUIPMENT ROOM YESTERDAY? SWEET!
HA HA HA
SHUT UP.
SHUT UP!
HUH? WHAT'D YOU SAY?

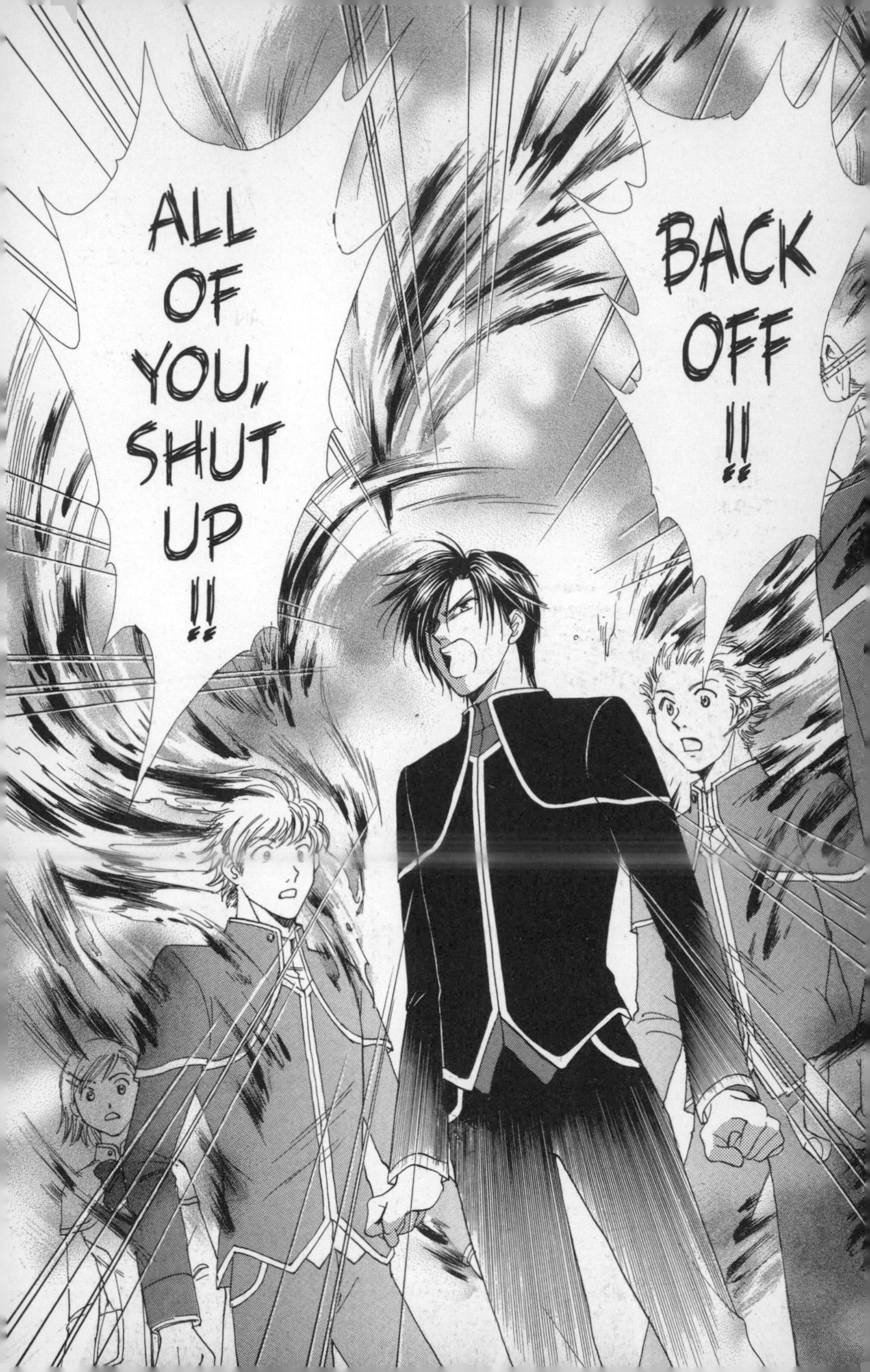
BACK OFF !!
ALL OF YOU, SHUT UP !!

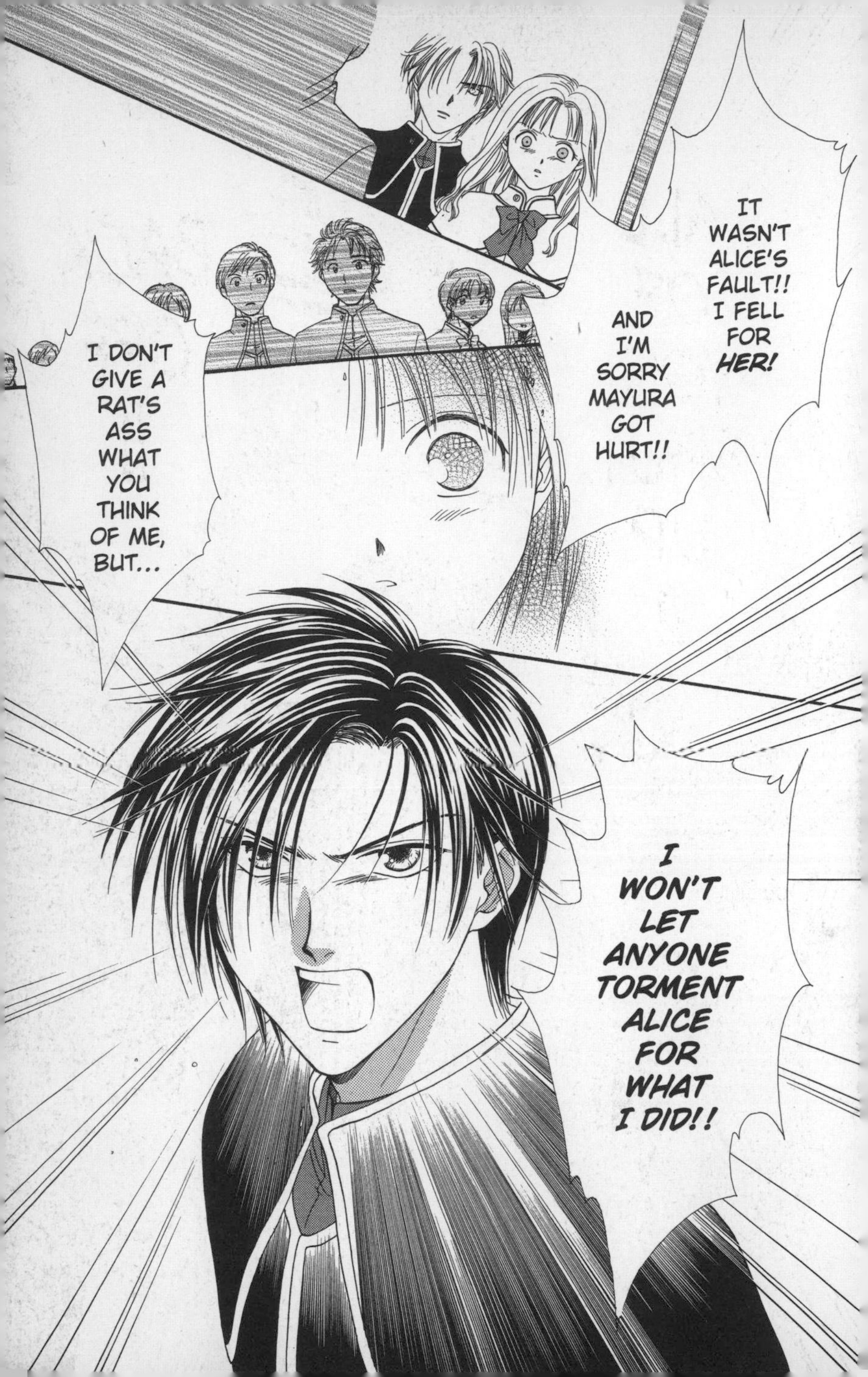
IT WASN'T ALICE'S FAULT!! I FELL FOR *HER!*
AND I'M SORRY MAYURA GOT HURT!!
I DON'T GIVE A RAT'S ASS WHAT YOU THINK OF ME, BUT...
I WON'T LET ANYONE TORMENT ALICE FOR WHAT I DID!!

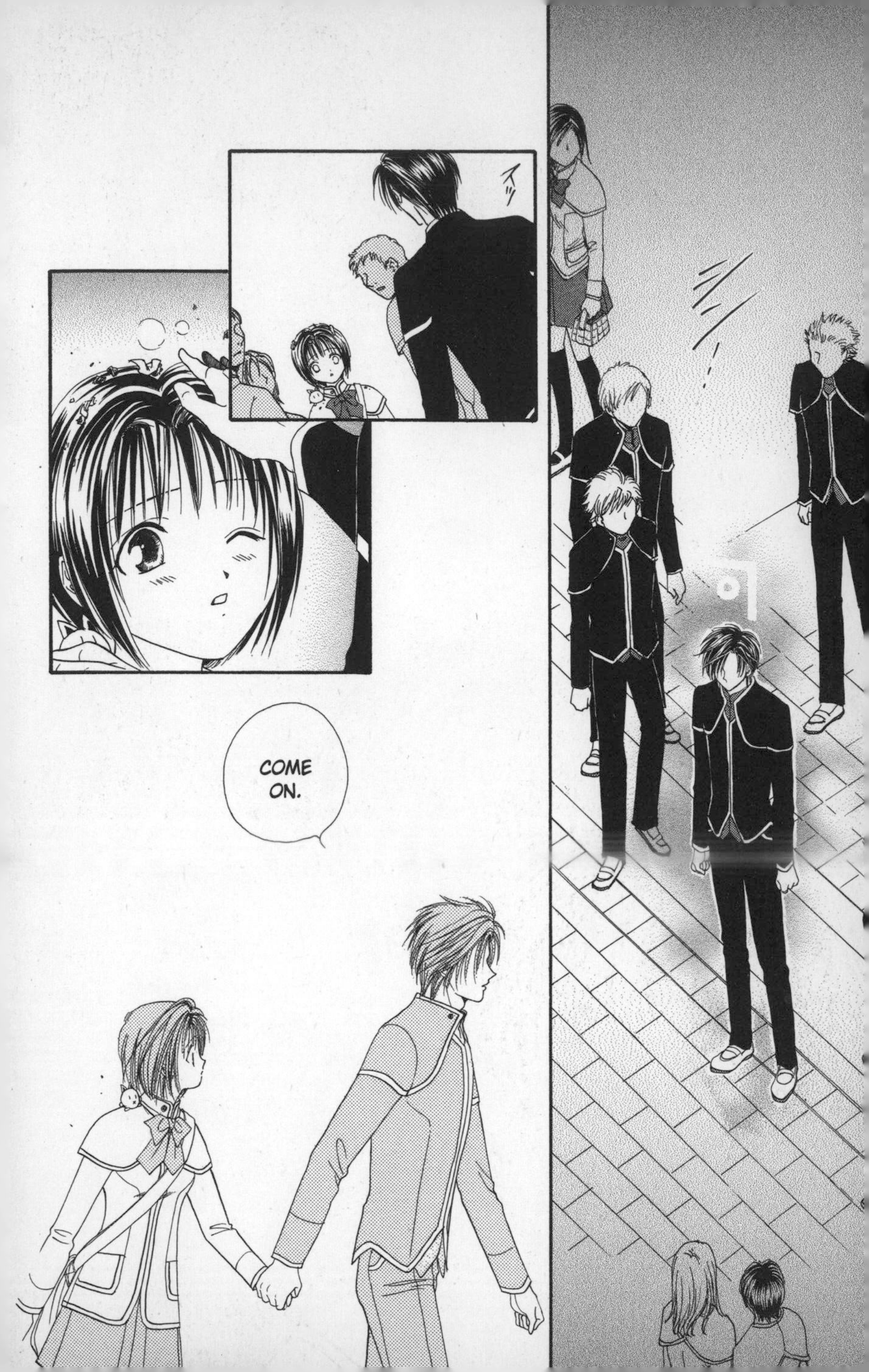
ズッ
COME ON.

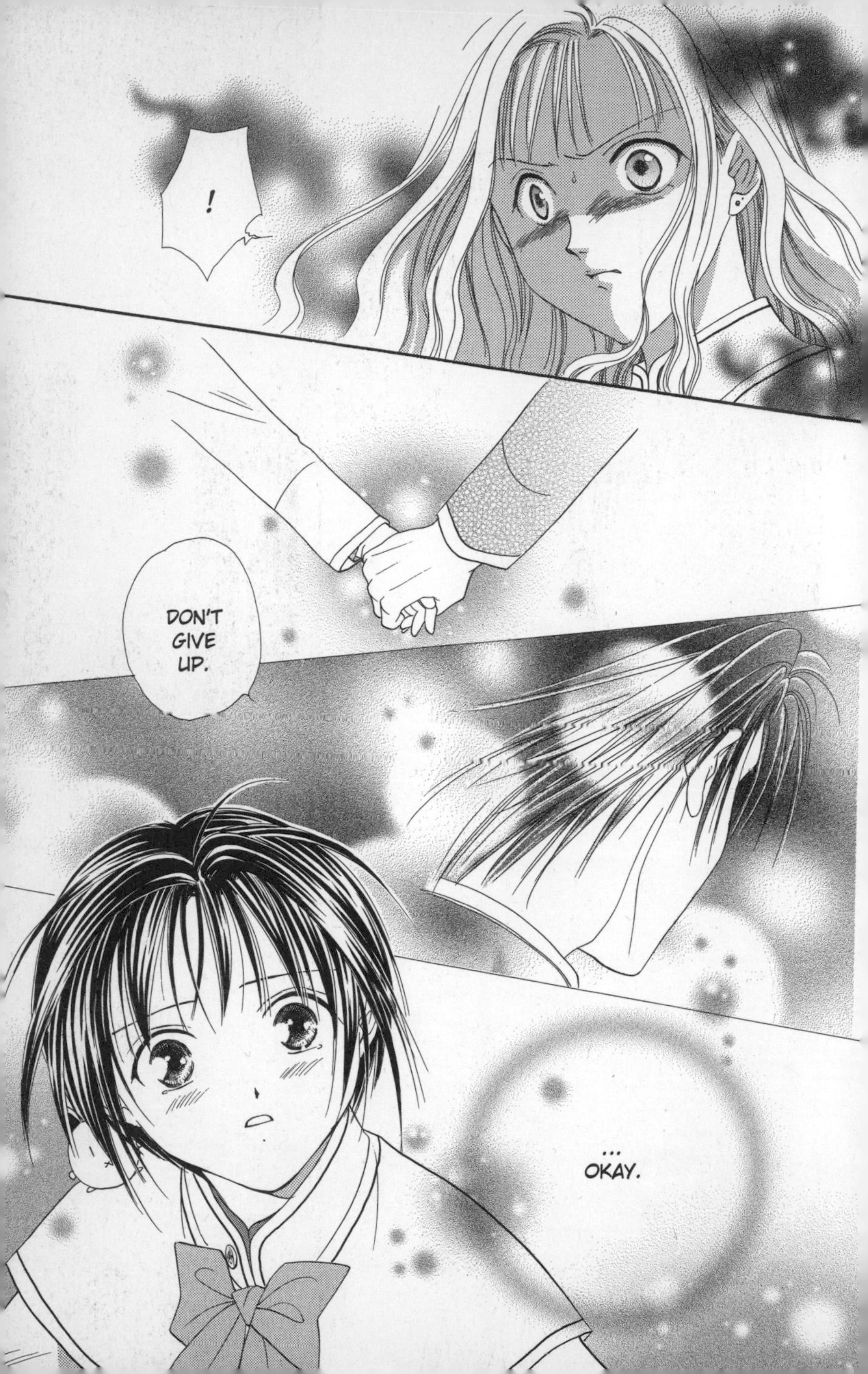
!
DON'T GIVE UP.
... OKAY.

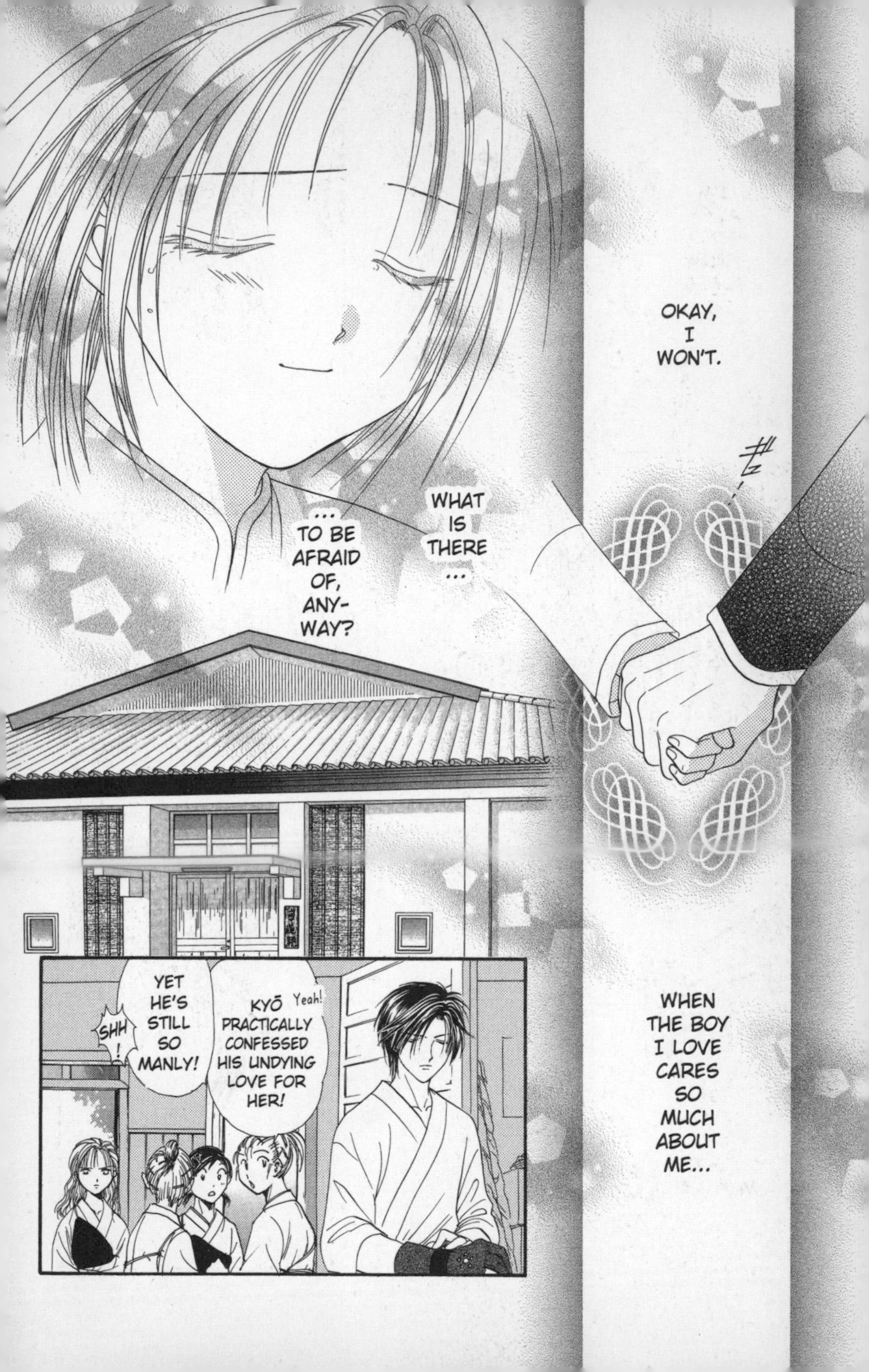
OKAY, I WON'T.
WHEN THE BOY I LOVE CARES SO MUCH ABOUT ME...
WHAT IS THERE...
...TO BE AFRAID OF, ANYWAY?
Yeah!
KYŌ PRACTICALLY CONFESSED HIS UNDYING LOVE FOR HER!
YET HE'S STILL SO MANLY!
SHH!

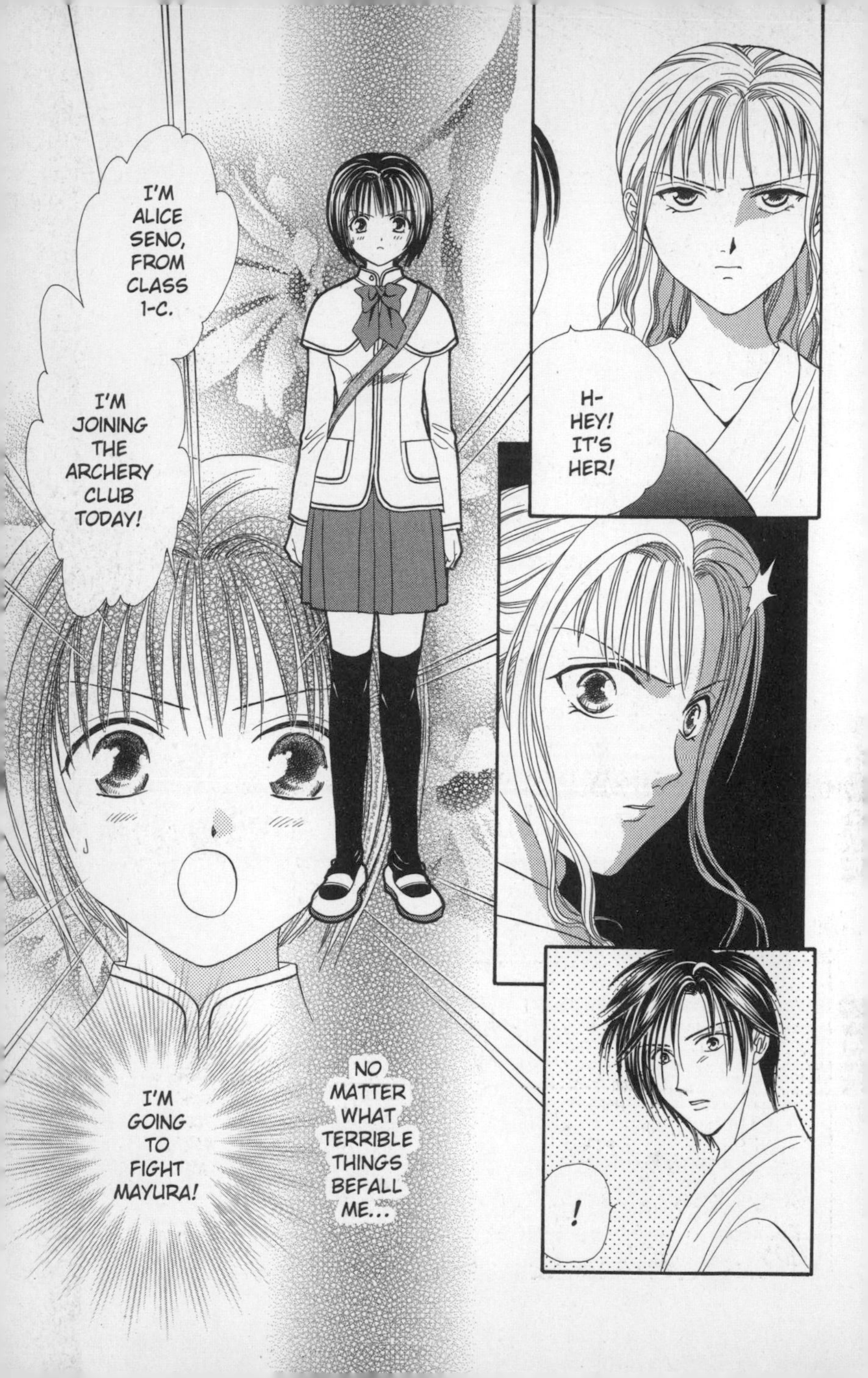
H-HEY! IT'S HER!
!
I'M ALICE SENO, FROM CLASS 1-C.
I'M JOINING THE ARCHERY CLUB TODAY!
NO MATTER WHAT TERRIBLE THINGS BEFALL ME...
I'M GOING TO FIGHT MAYURA!

NYOZEKA'S MINI-MINI LOTIS CLASS

NUMBER 8

 DANA

THE 3RD LOTIS MEANS "BLESSING" OR "WATER." FREY USED IT WHEN HE ENTERED ŌISHI'S INNER HEART. CAN BE USED TO ATTACK OR DEFEND.

darn!

DANA !!

NUMBER 9

 RAJEI

A WORD FREY CAN USE. THE 17TH LOTIS MEANS "LIGHT" OR "SUN." IT WAS USED TO REPEL MAYURA.

RAJEI !

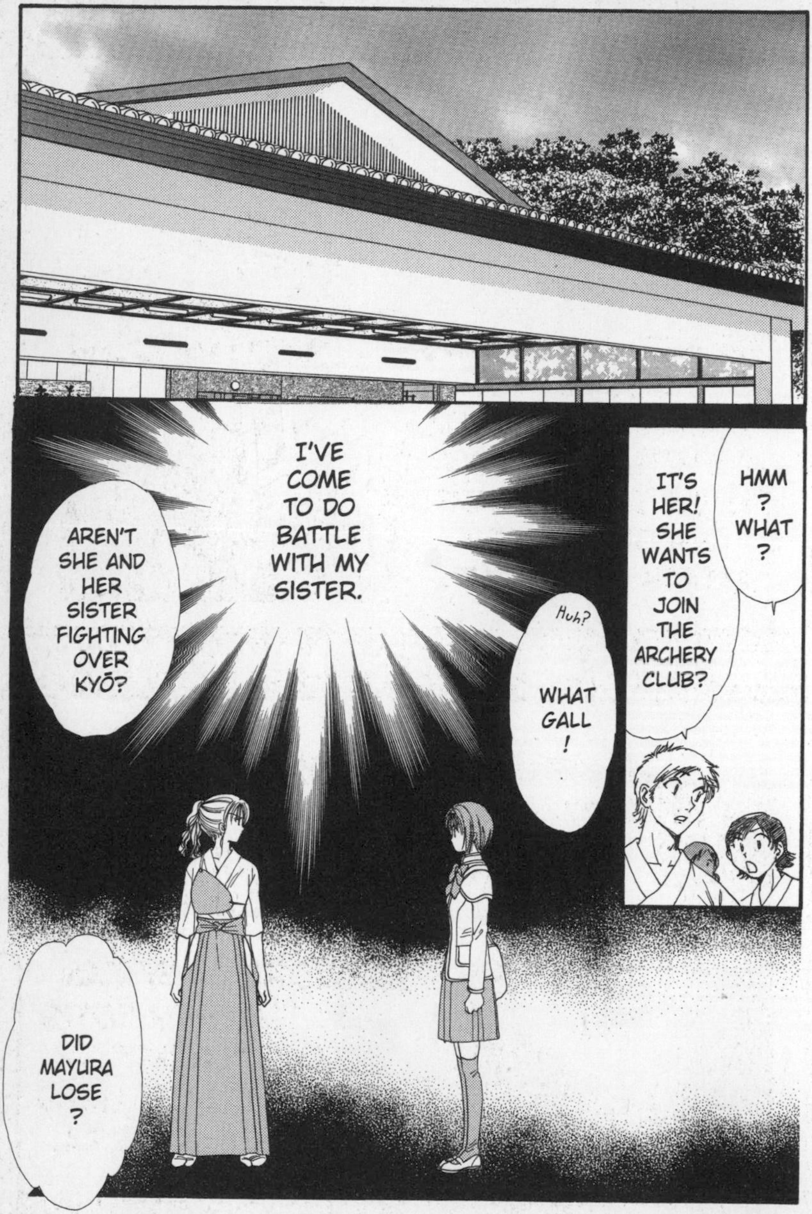
HMM? WHAT?
IT'S HER! SHE WANTS TO JOIN THE ARCHERY CLUB?
Huh?
WHAT GALL!
I'VE COME TO DO BATTLE WITH MY SISTER.
AREN'T SHE AND HER SISTER FIGHTING OVER KYŌ?
DID MAYURA LOSE?

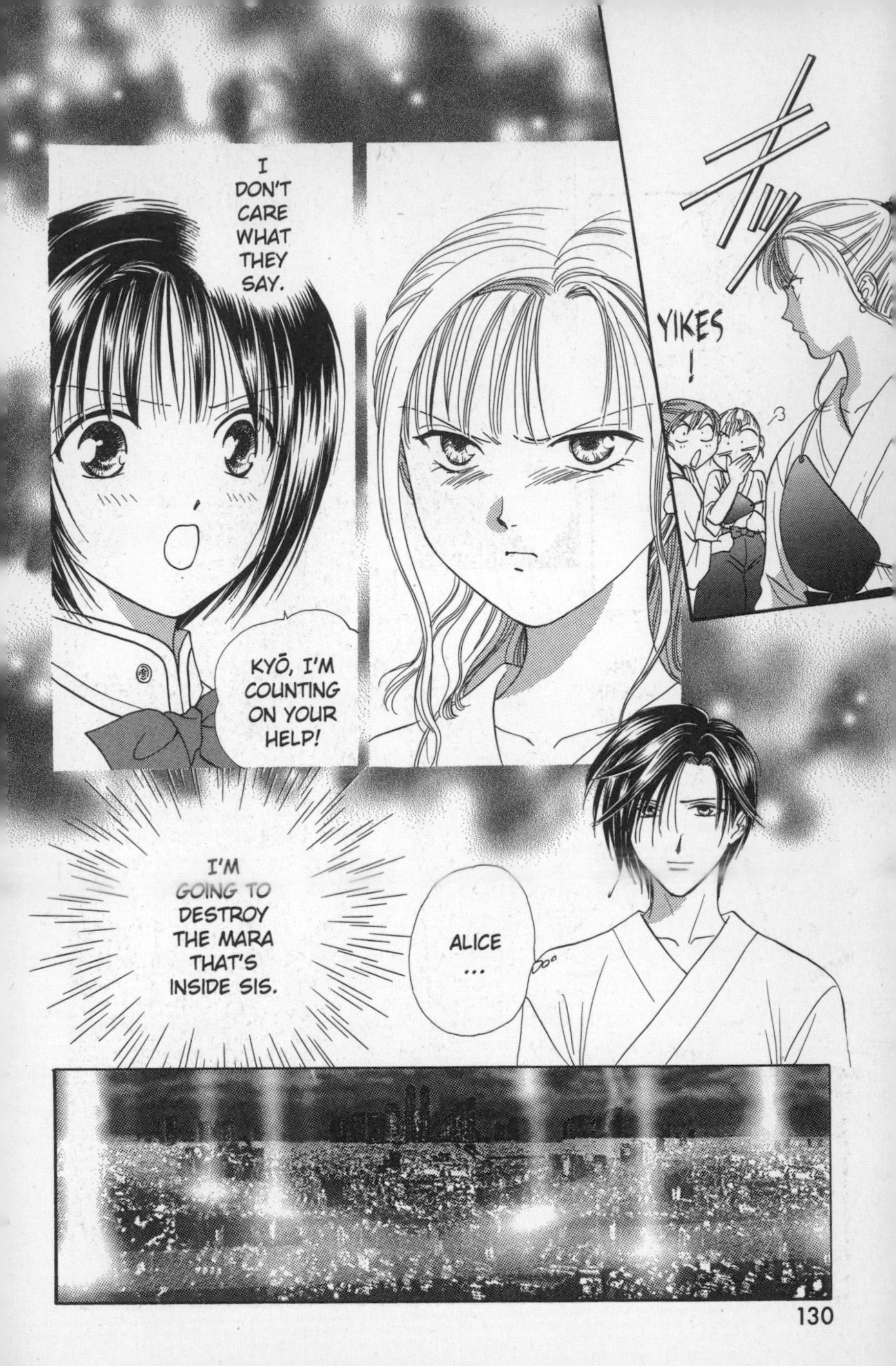
YIKES !
I DON'T CARE WHAT THEY SAY.
KYŌ, I'M COUNTING ON YOUR HELP!
ALICE ...
I'M GOING TO DESTROY THE MARA THAT'S INSIDE SIS.

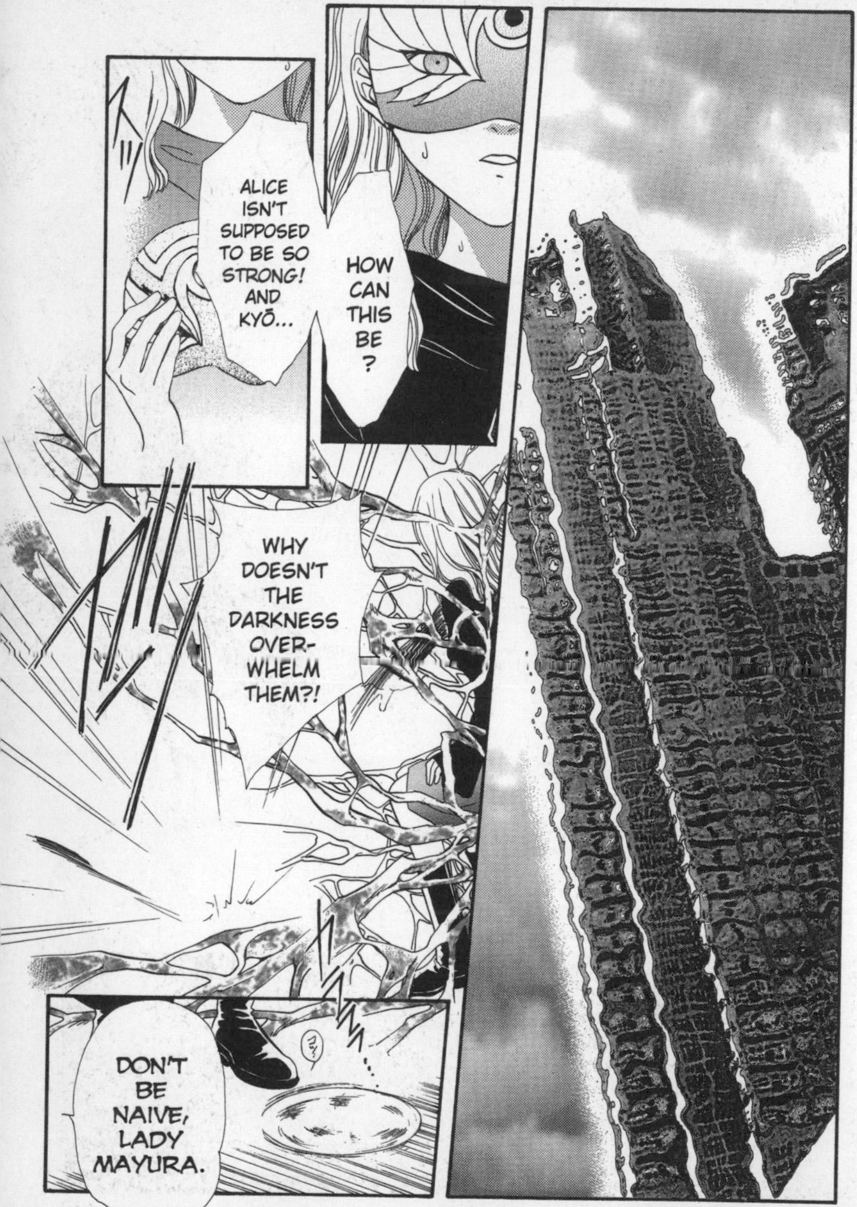
HOW CAN THIS BE?
ALICE ISN'T SUPPOSED TO BE SO STRONG! AND KYŌ...
WHY DOESN'T THE DARKNESS OVER-WHELM THEM?!
DON'T BE NAIVE, LADY MAYURA.

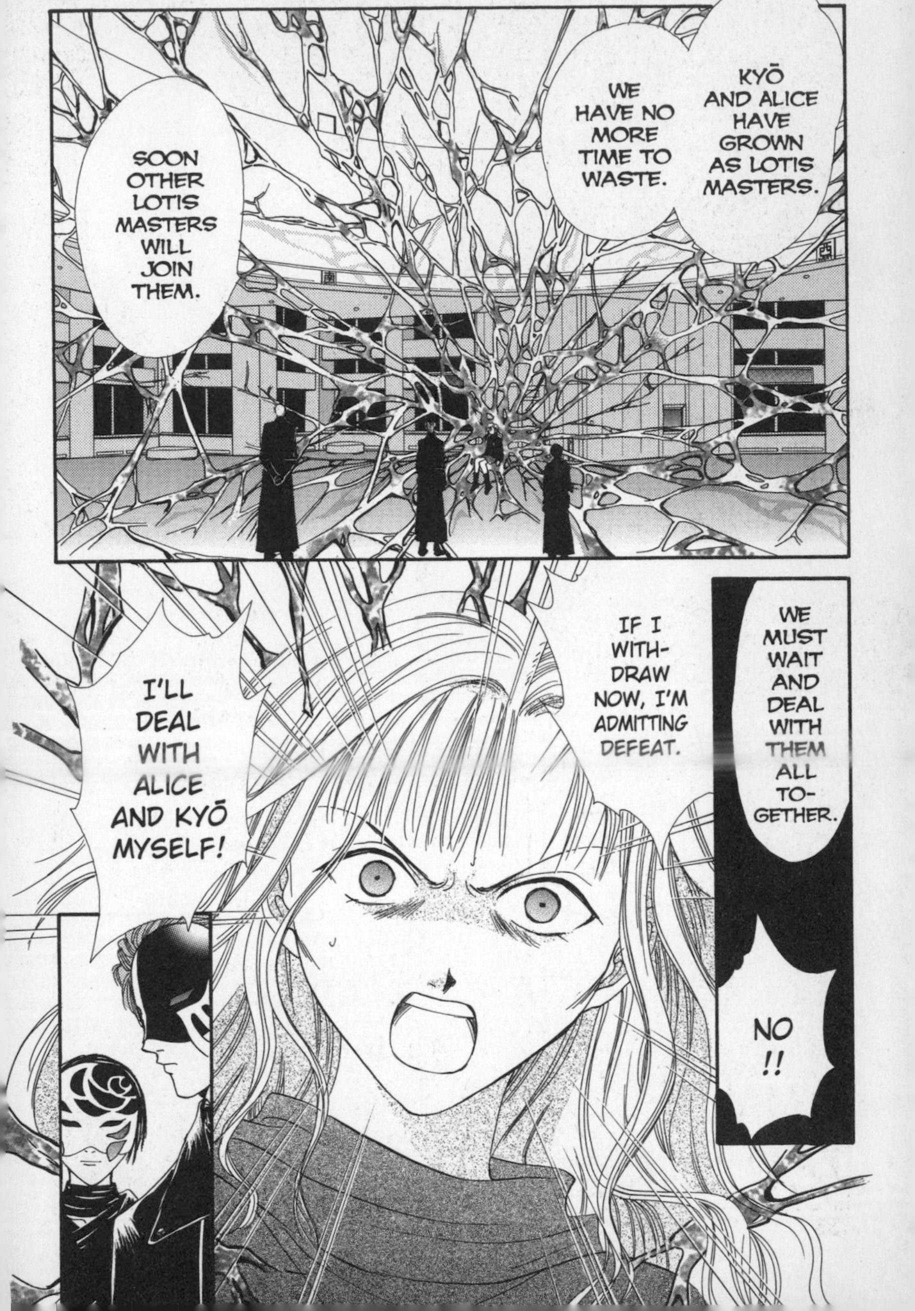
KYŌ AND ALICE HAVE GROWN AS LOTIS MASTERS.
WE HAVE NO MORE TIME TO WASTE.
SOON OTHER LOTIS MASTERS WILL JOIN THEM.
WE MUST WAIT AND DEAL WITH THEM ALL TO-GETHER.
NO !!
IF I WITH-DRAW NOW, I'M ADMITTING DEFEAT.
I'LL DEAL WITH ALICE AND KYŌ MYSELF!

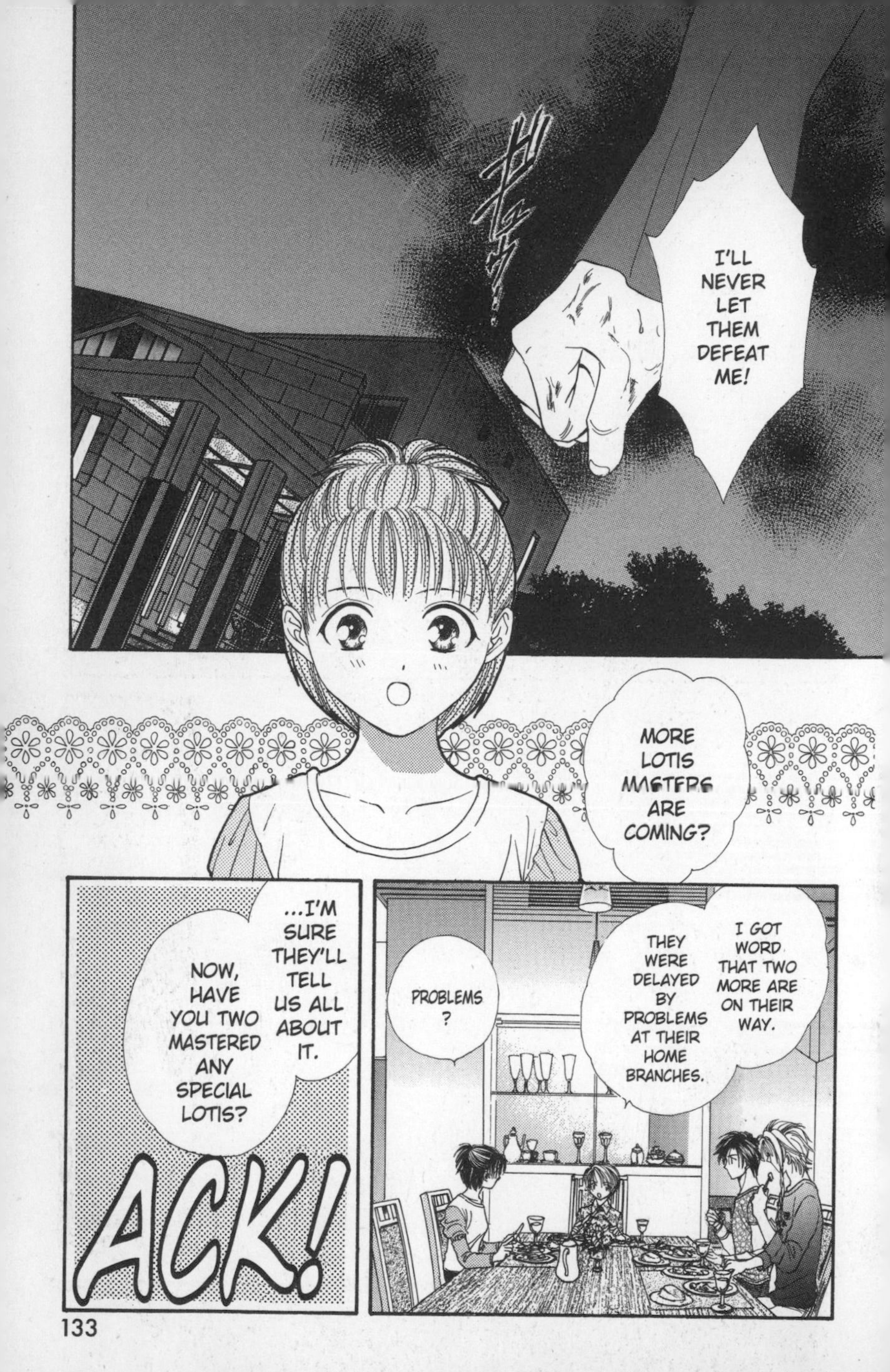
I'LL NEVER LET THEM DEFEAT ME!
MORE LOTIS MASTERS ARE COMING?
I GOT WORD THAT TWO MORE ARE ON THEIR WAY.
THEY WERE DELAYED BY PROBLEMS AT THEIR HOME BRANCHES.
PROBLEMS?
...I'M SURE THEY'LL TELL US ALL ABOUT IT.
NOW, HAVE YOU TWO MASTERED ANY SPECIAL LOTIS?
ACK!

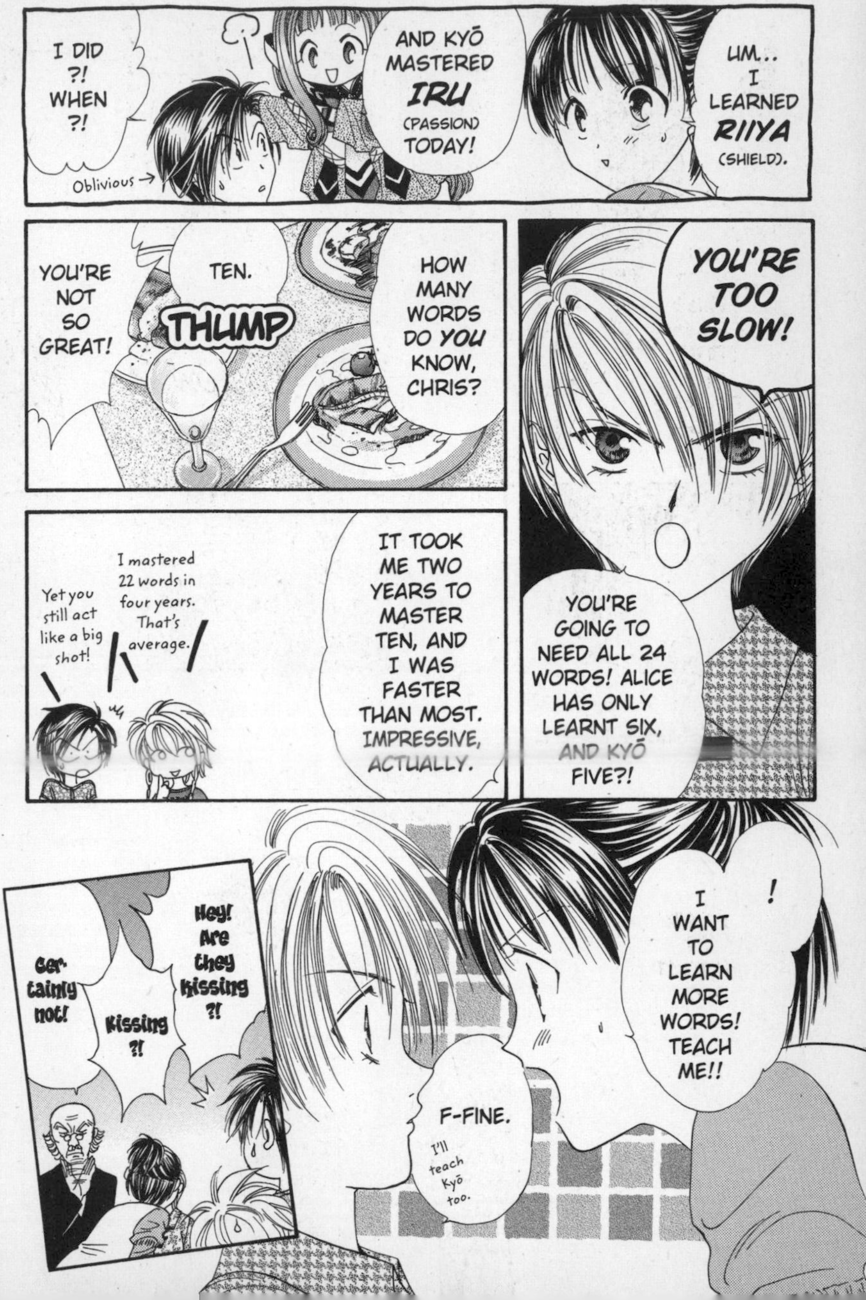
UM.. I LEARNED RIIYA (SHIELD).
AND KYŌ MASTERED IRU (PASSION) TODAY!
I DID ?! WHEN ?!
Oblivious →
YOU'RE TOO SLOW!
YOU'RE GOING TO NEED ALL 24 WORDS! ALICE HAS ONLY LEARNT SIX, AND KYŌ FIVE?!
HOW MANY WORDS DO YOU KNOW, CHRIS?
TEN.
THUMP
YOU'RE NOT SO GREAT!
IT TOOK ME TWO YEARS TO MASTER TEN, AND I WAS FASTER THAN MOST. IMPRESSIVE, ACTUALLY.
I mastered 22 words in four years. That's average.
Yet you still act like a big shot!
!
I WANT TO LEARN MORE WORDS! TEACH ME!!
F-FINE.
I'll teach Kyō too.
Hey! Are they kissing?!
Kissing?!
Certainly not!

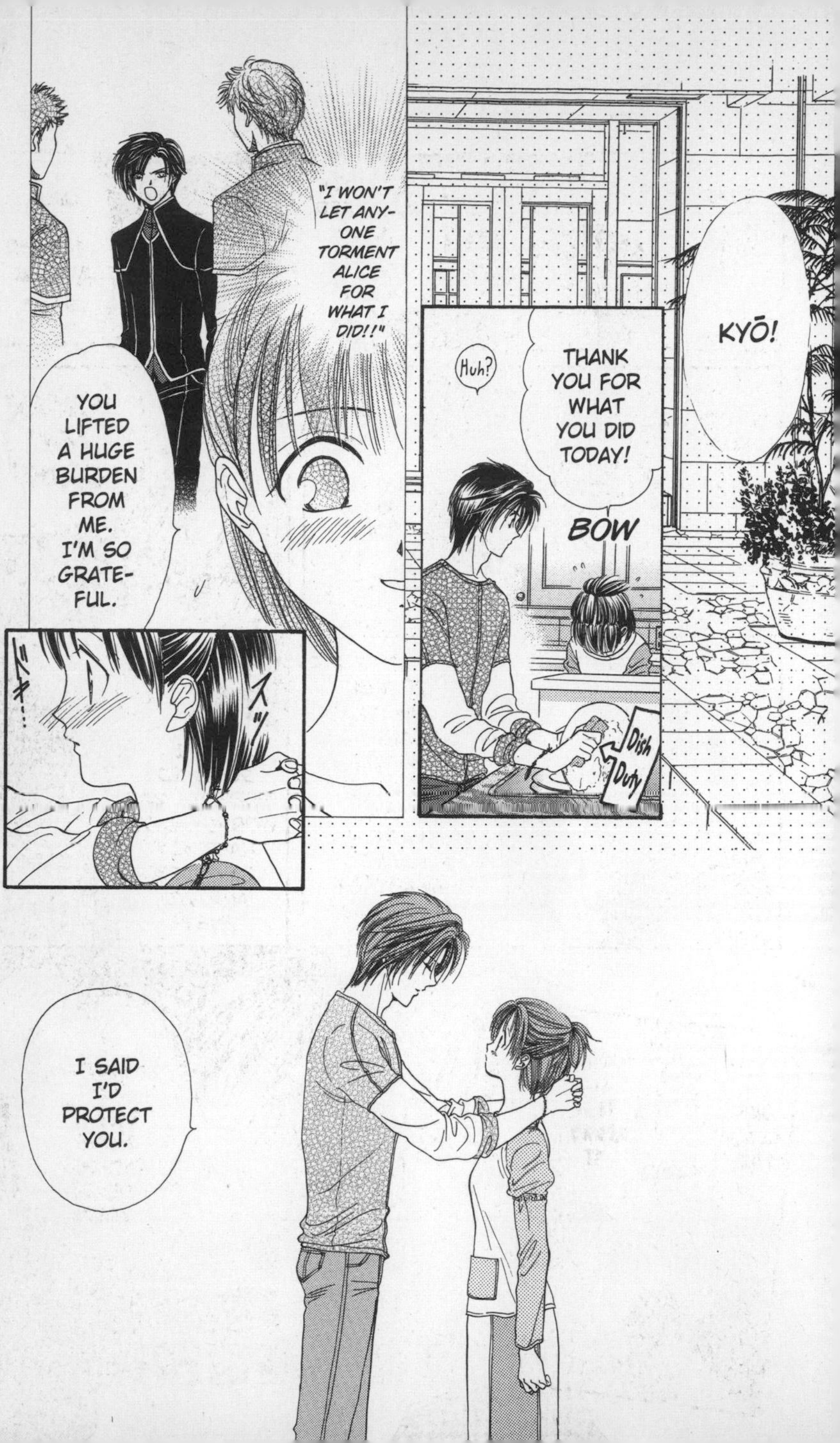
KYŌ!
THANK YOU FOR WHAT YOU DID TODAY!
Huh?
BOW
Dish Duty
"I WON'T LET ANY-ONE TORMENT ALICE FOR WHAT I DID!!"
YOU LIFTED A HUGE BURDEN FROM ME. I'M SO GRATE-FUL.
スッ
ドキ…
I SAID I'D PROTECT YOU.

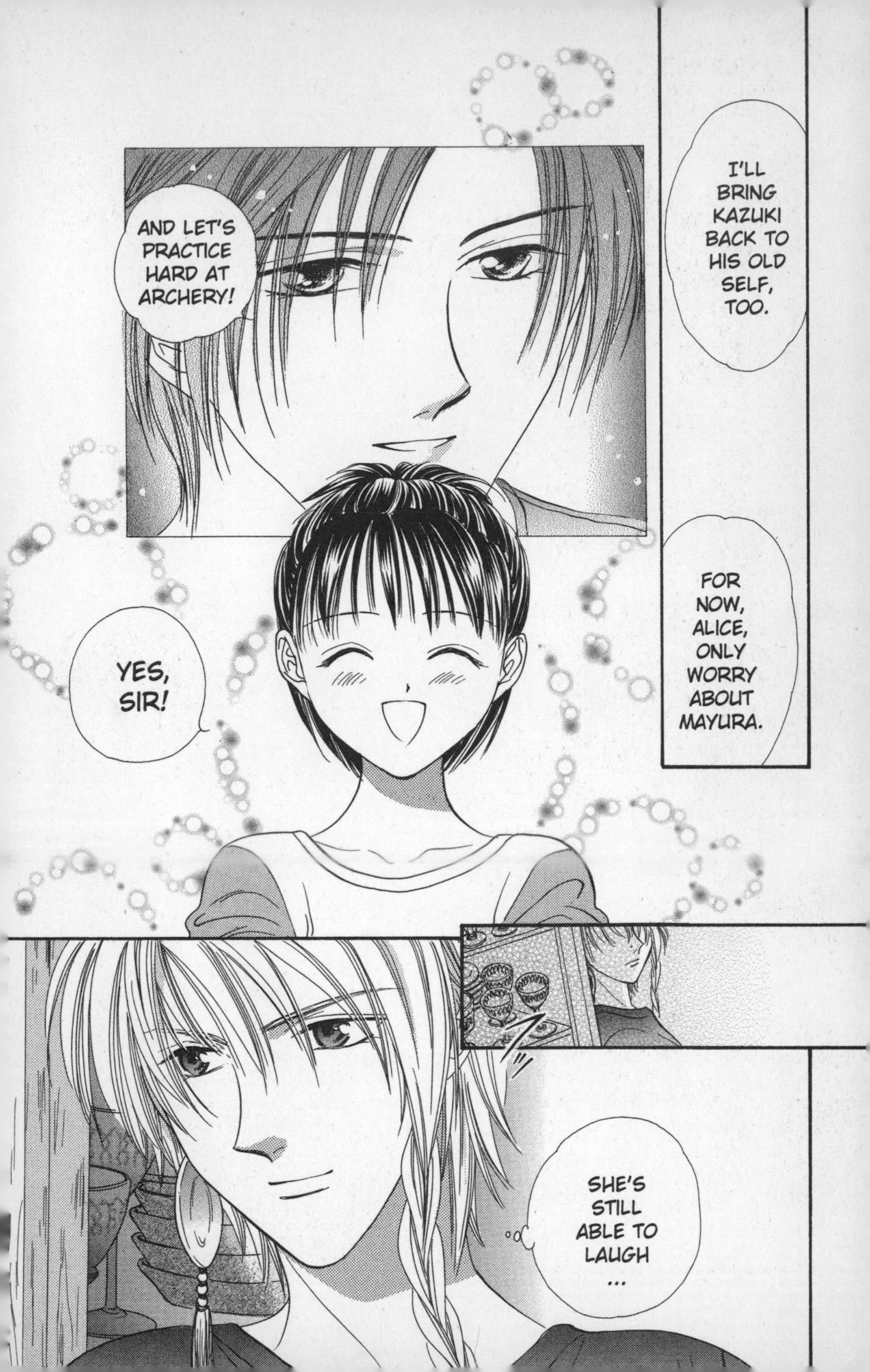
I'LL BRING KAZUKI BACK TO HIS OLD SELF, TOO.
FOR NOW, ALICE, ONLY WORRY ABOUT MAYURA.
AND LET'S PRACTICE HARD AT ARCHERY!
YES, SIR!
SHE'S STILL ABLE TO LAUGH ...

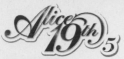

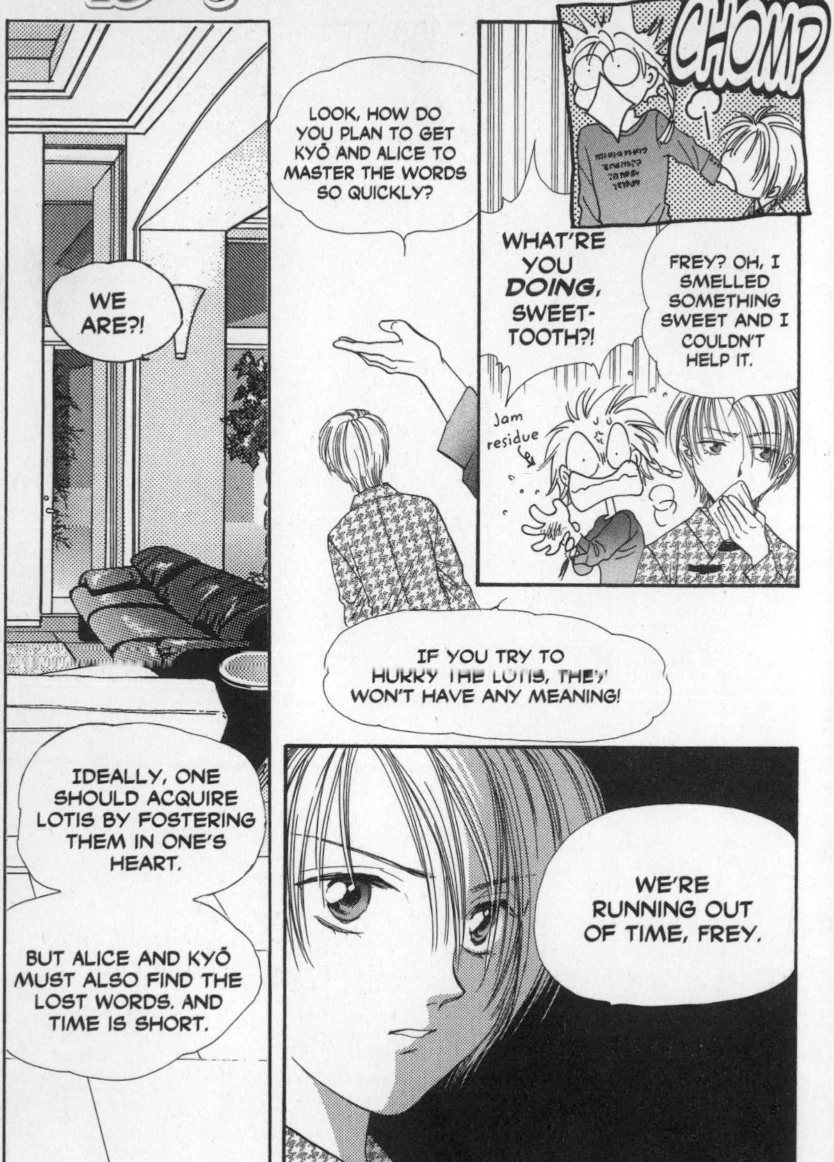
CHOMP
WHAT'RE YOU *DOING*, SWEET-TOOTH?!
FREY? OH, I SMELLED SOMETHING SWEET AND I COULDN'T HELP IT.
Jam residue
LOOK, HOW DO YOU PLAN TO GET KYŌ AND ALICE TO MASTER THE WORDS SO QUICKLY?
IF YOU TRY TO HURRY THE LOTIS, THEY WON'T HAVE ANY MEANING!
WE'RE RUNNING OUT OF TIME, FREY.
WE ARE?!
IDEALLY, ONE SHOULD ACQUIRE LOTIS BY FOSTERING THEM IN ONE'S HEART.
BUT ALICE AND KYŌ MUST ALSO FIND THE LOST WORDS. AND TIME IS SHORT.

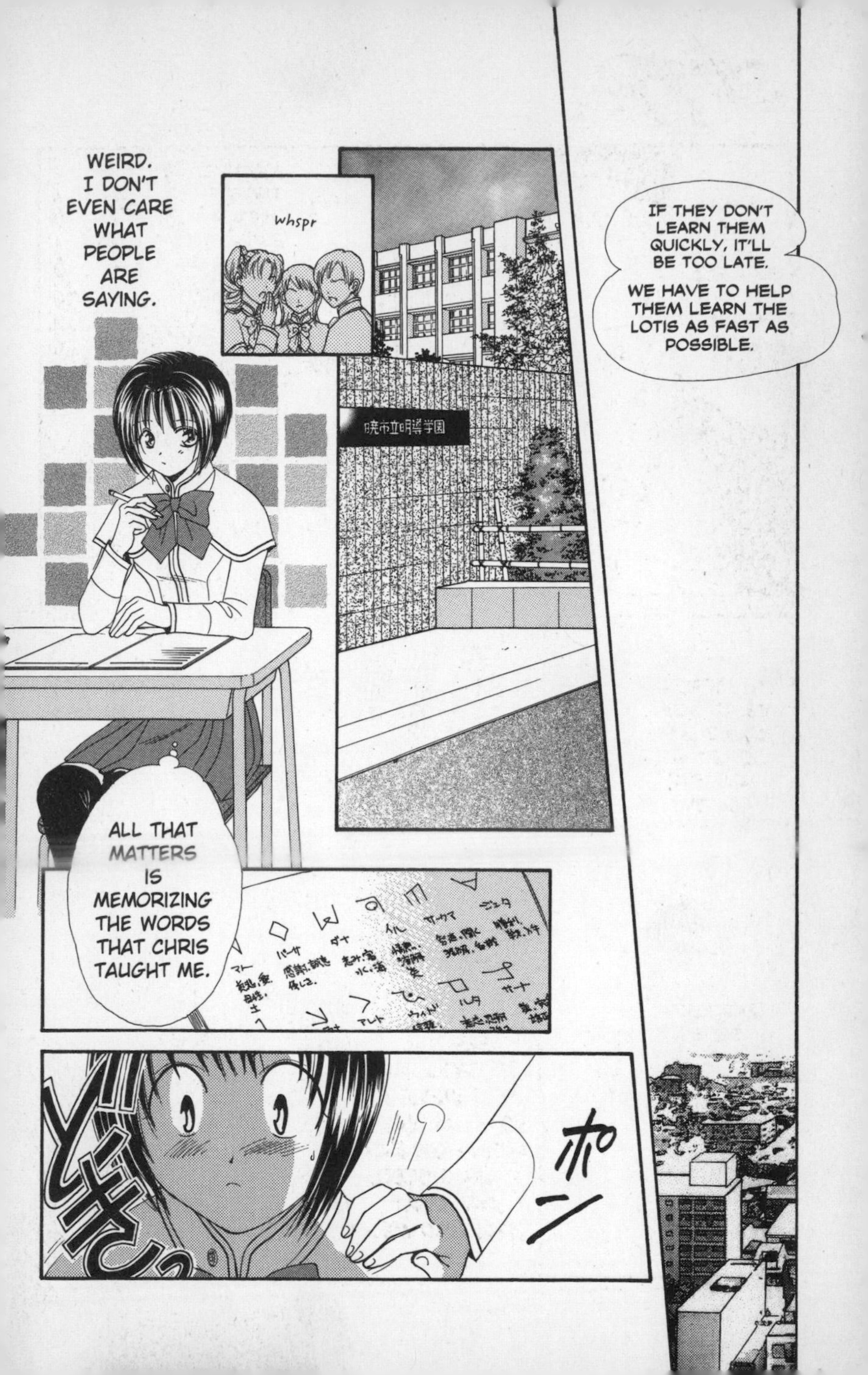
IF THEY DON'T LEARN THEM QUICKLY, IT'LL BE TOO LATE.
WE HAVE TO HELP THEM LEARN THE LOTIS AS FAST AS POSSIBLE.
暁市立明導学園
whspr
WEIRD. I DON'T EVEN CARE WHAT PEOPLE ARE SAYING.
ALL THAT MATTERS IS MEMORIZING THE WORDS THAT CHRIS TAUGHT ME.
ポーン

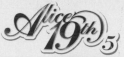

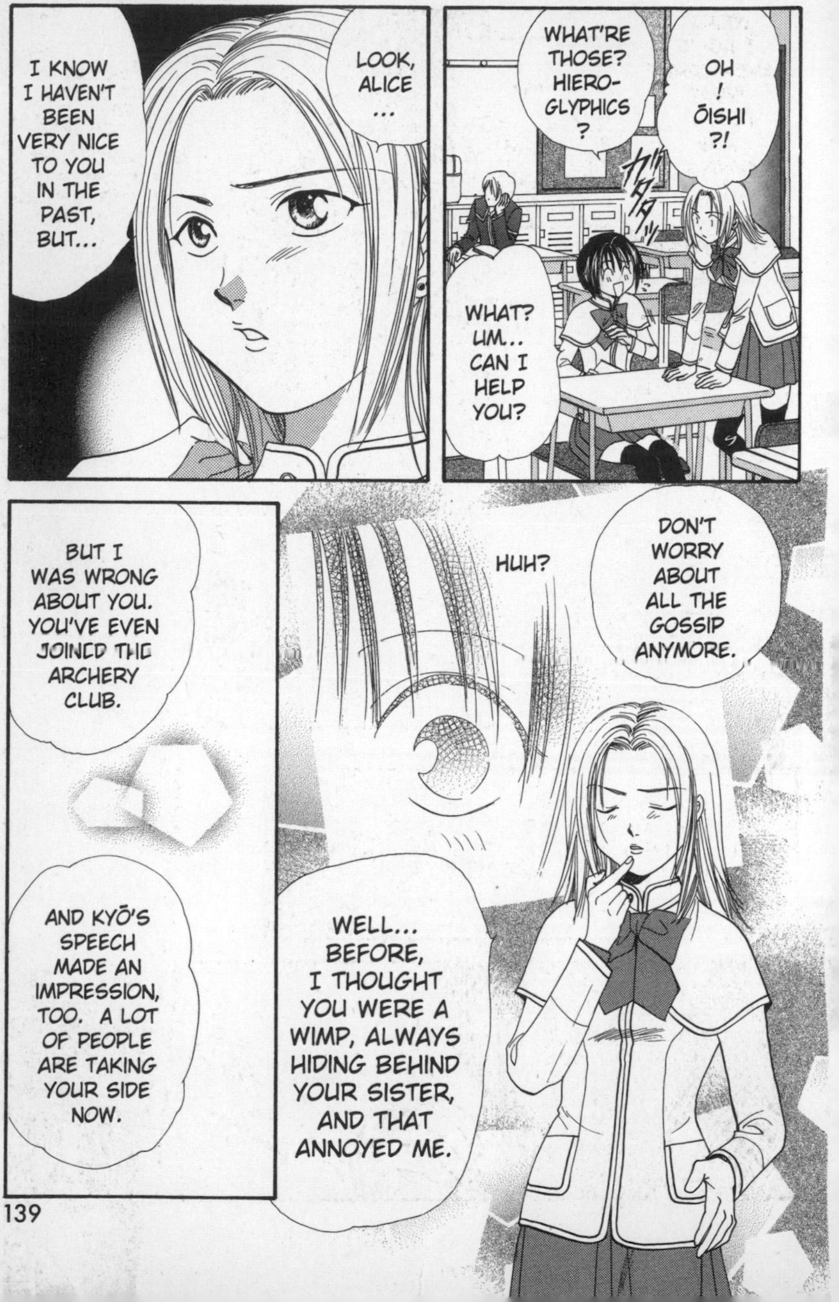
OH! ŌISHI?!
WHAT'RE THOSE? HIERO-GLYPHICS?
WHAT? UM... CAN I HELP YOU?
LOOK, ALICE...
I KNOW I HAVEN'T BEEN VERY NICE TO YOU IN THE PAST, BUT...
DON'T WORRY ABOUT ALL THE GOSSIP ANYMORE.
HUH?
WELL... BEFORE, I THOUGHT YOU WERE A WIMP, ALWAYS HIDING BEHIND YOUR SISTER, AND THAT ANNOYED ME.
BUT I WAS WRONG ABOUT YOU. YOU'VE EVEN JOINED THE ARCHERY CLUB.
AND KYŌ'S SPEECH MADE AN IMPRESSION, TOO. A LOT OF PEOPLE ARE TAKING YOUR SIDE NOW.

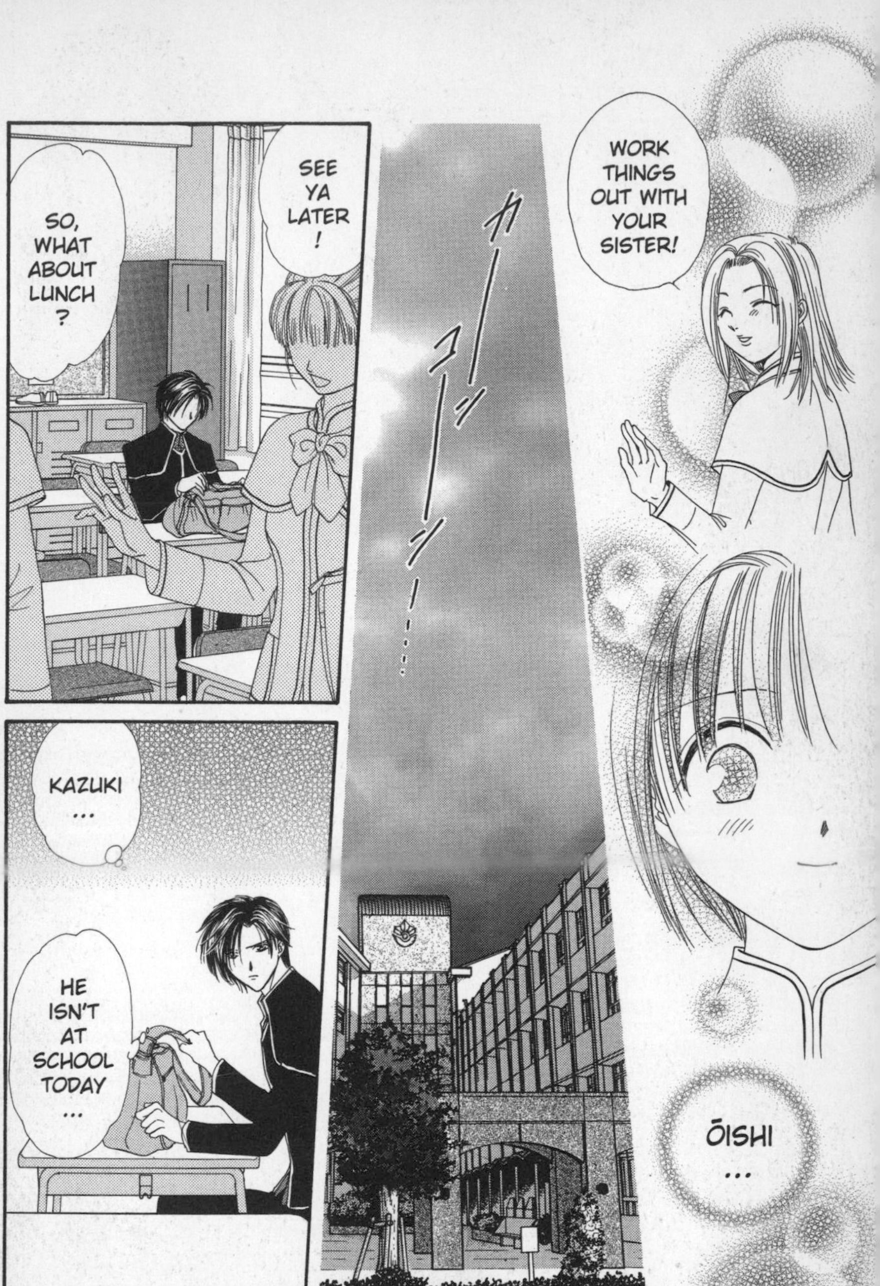
WORK THINGS OUT WITH YOUR SISTER!
ŌISHI ...
SEE YA LATER!
SO, WHAT ABOUT LUNCH?
KAZUKI ...
HE ISN'T AT SCHOOL TODAY ...

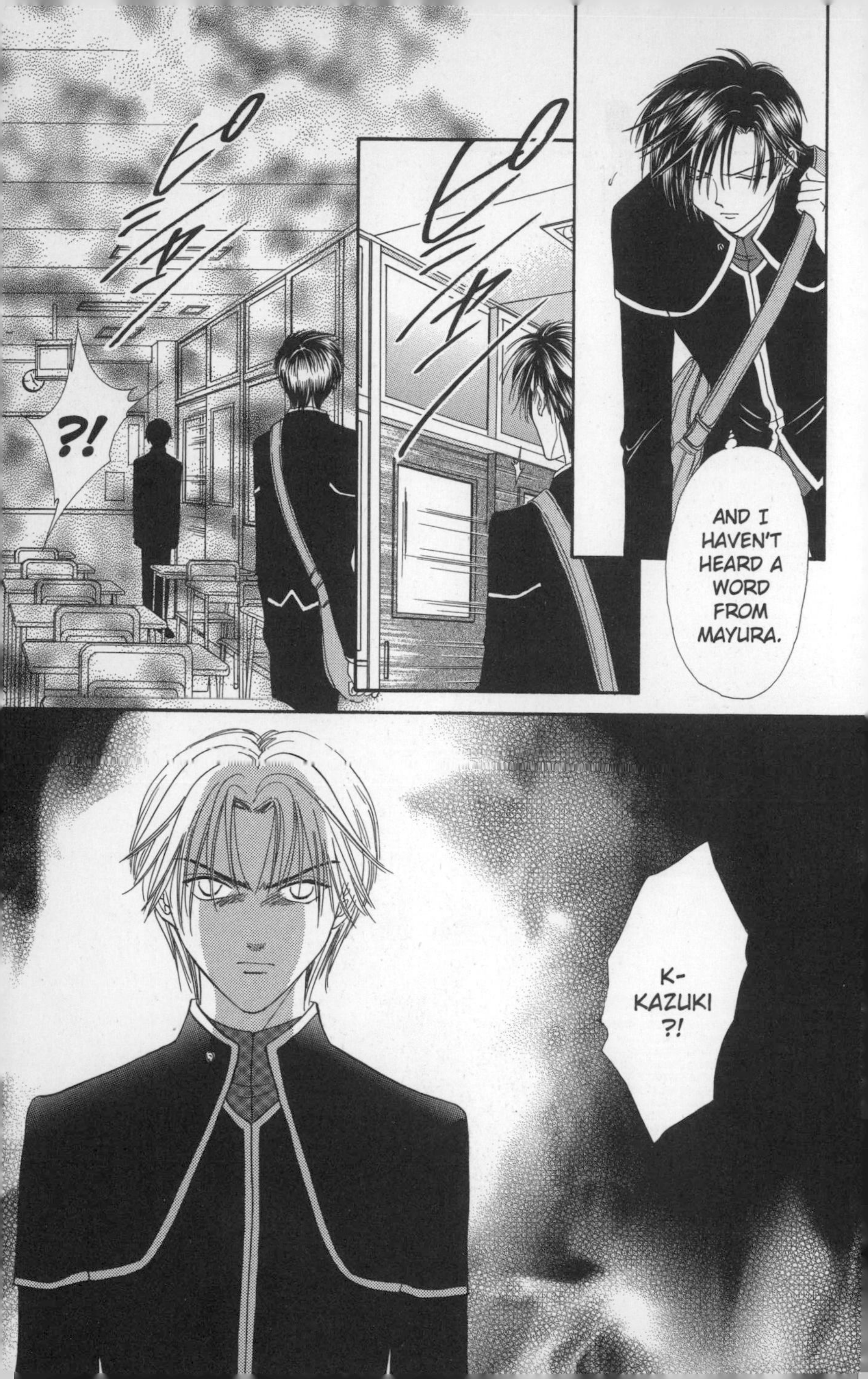
AND I HAVEN'T HEARD A WORD FROM MAYURA.
?!
K-KAZUKI ?!

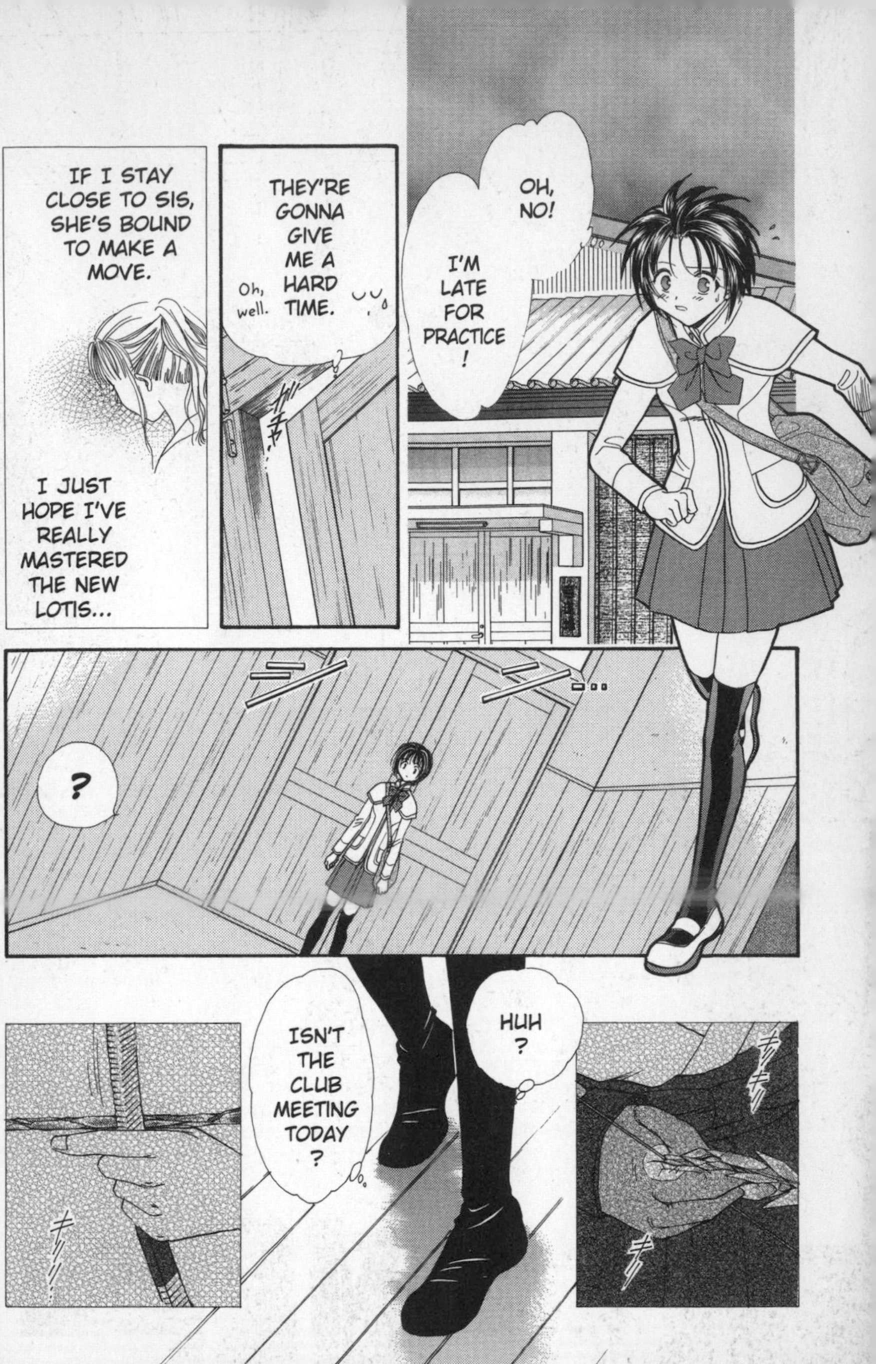
OH, NO!
I'M LATE FOR PRACTICE!
THEY'RE GONNA GIVE ME A HARD TIME.
Oh, well.
IF I STAY CLOSE TO SIS, SHE'S BOUND TO MAKE A MOVE.
I JUST HOPE I'VE REALLY MASTERED THE NEW LOTIS...
?
HUH?
ISN'T THE CLUB MEETING TODAY?

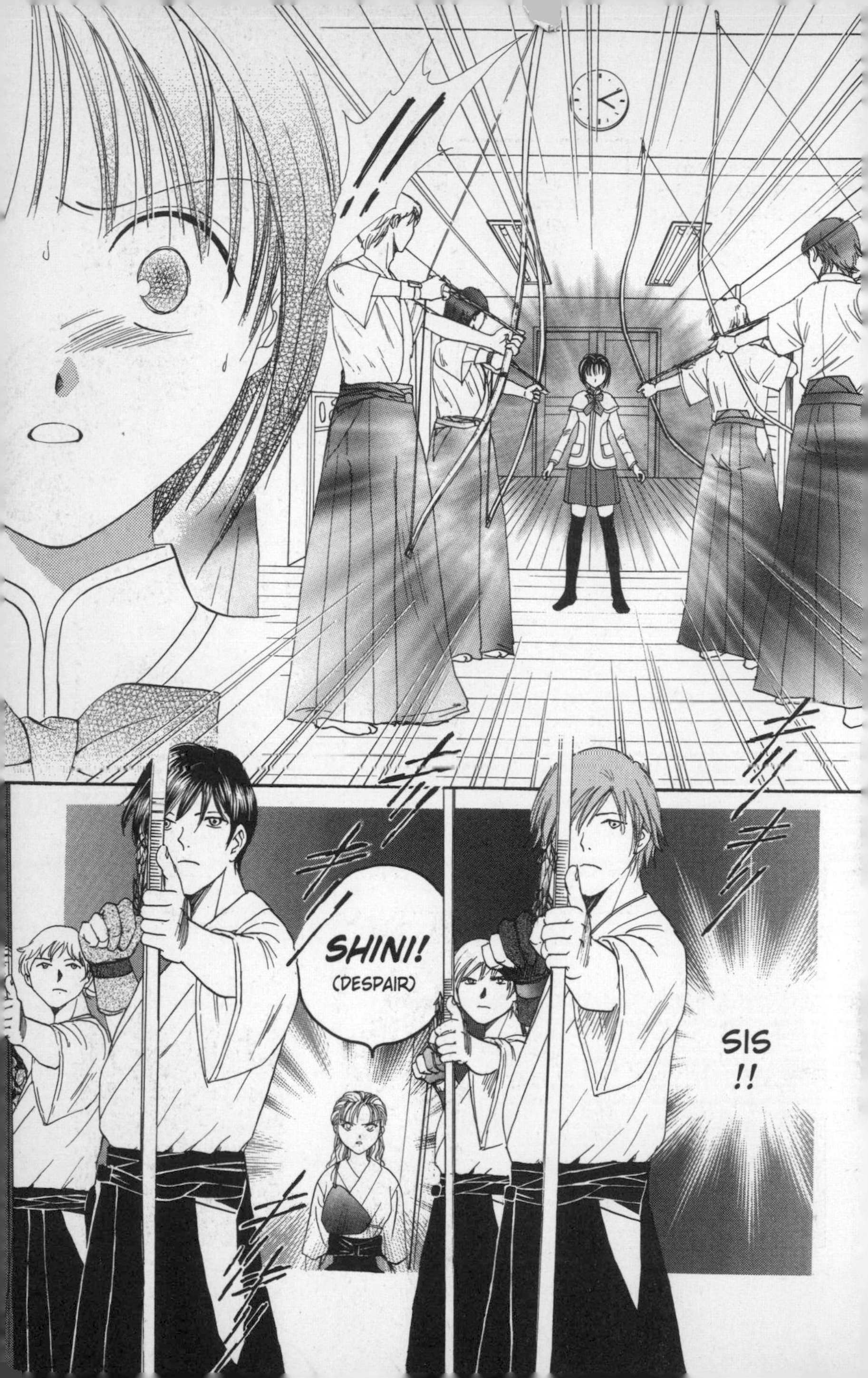
SIS !!
SHINI!
(DESPAIR)

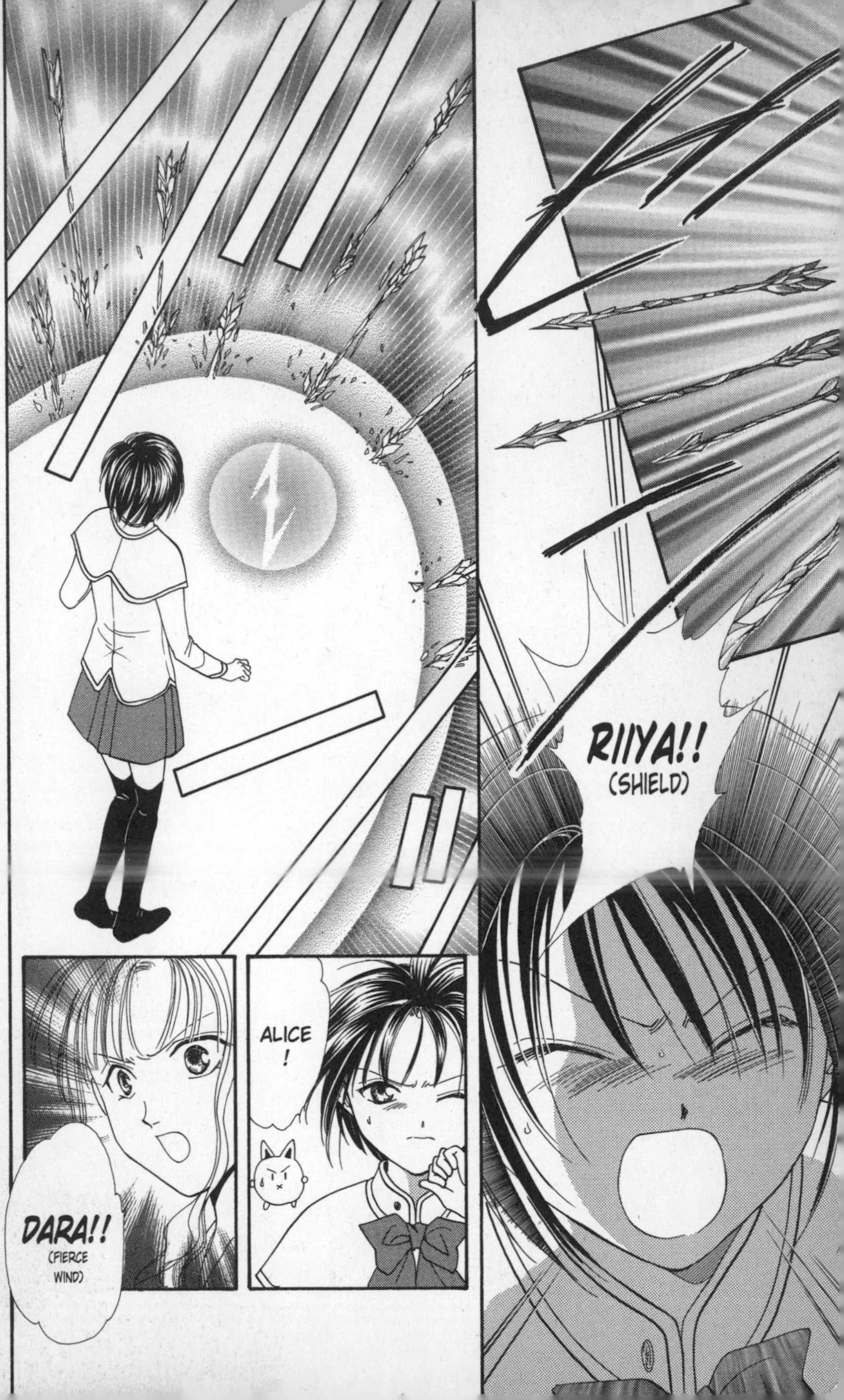
RIIYA!!
(SHIELD)
ALICE
!
DARA!!
(FIERCE WIND)

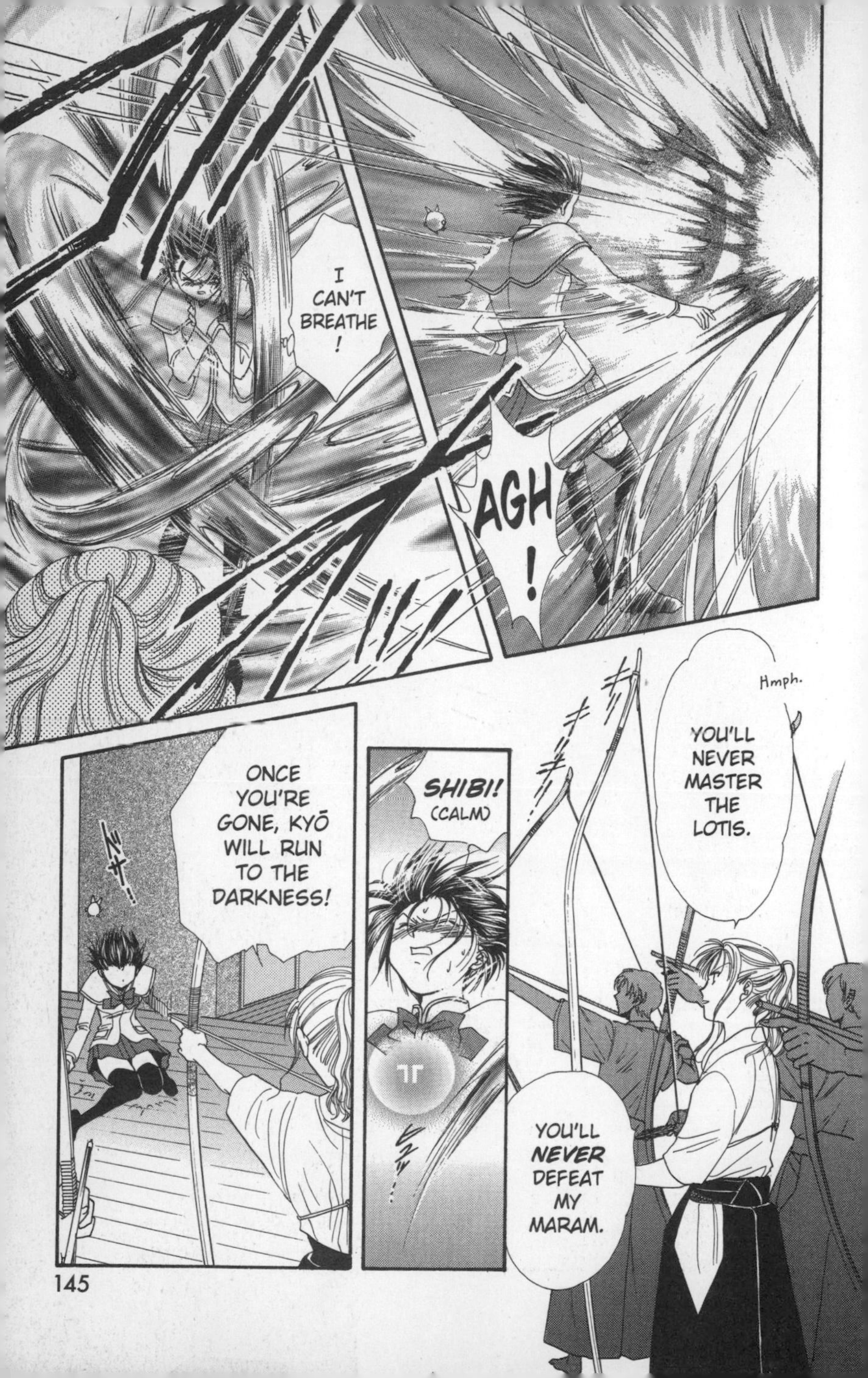
AGH!
I CAN'T BREATHE!
Hmph.
YOU'LL NEVER MASTER THE LOTIS.
YOU'LL **NEVER** DEFEAT MY MARAM.
SHIBI!
(CALM)
ONCE YOU'RE GONE, KYŌ WILL RUN TO THE DARKNESS!

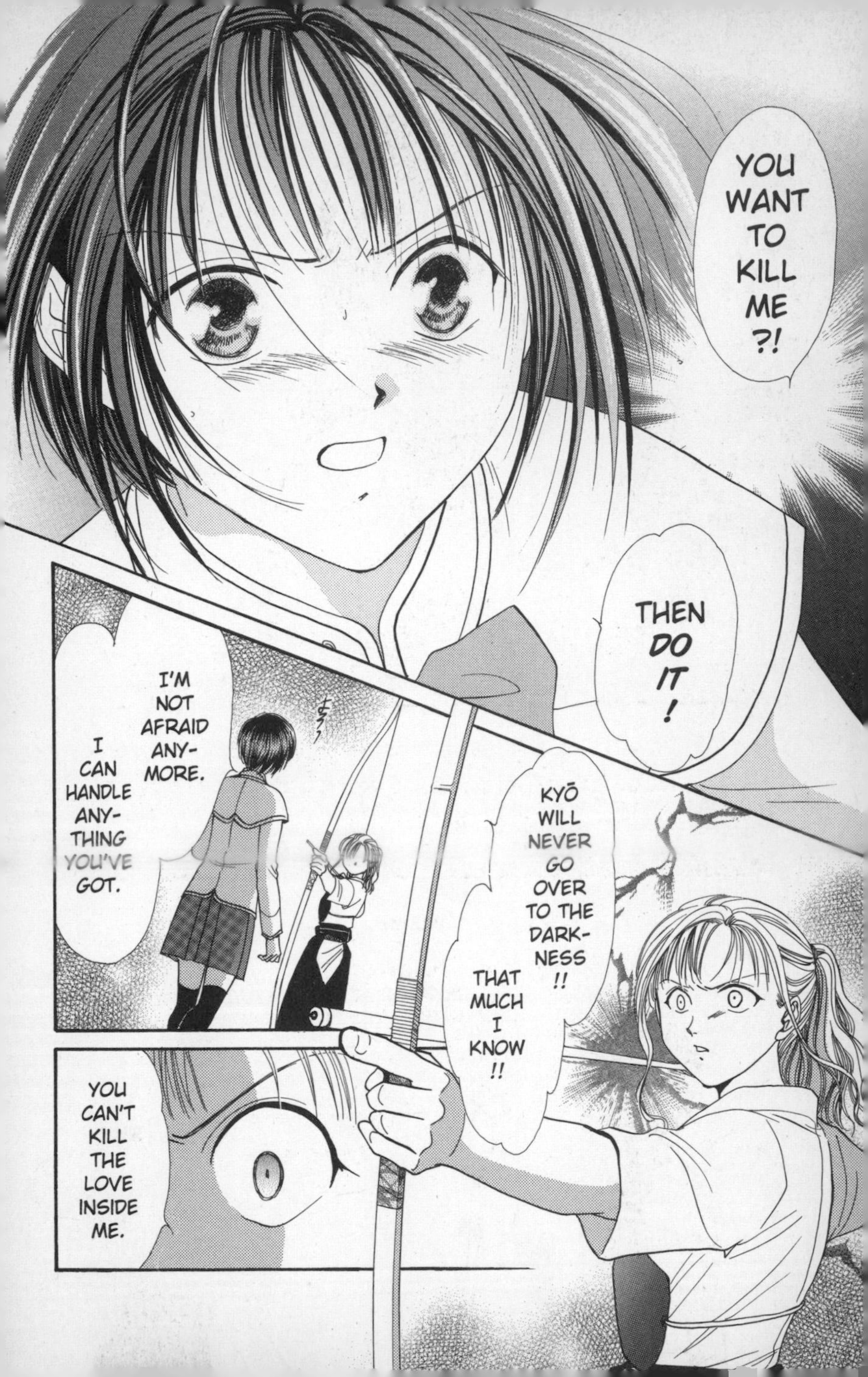
YOU WANT TO KILL ME ?!
THEN DO IT!
KYŌ WILL NEVER GO OVER TO THE DARKNESS !!
THAT MUCH I KNOW !!
I'M NOT AFRAID ANYMORE.
I CAN HANDLE ANYTHING YOU'VE GOT.
YOU CAN'T KILL THE LOVE INSIDE ME.

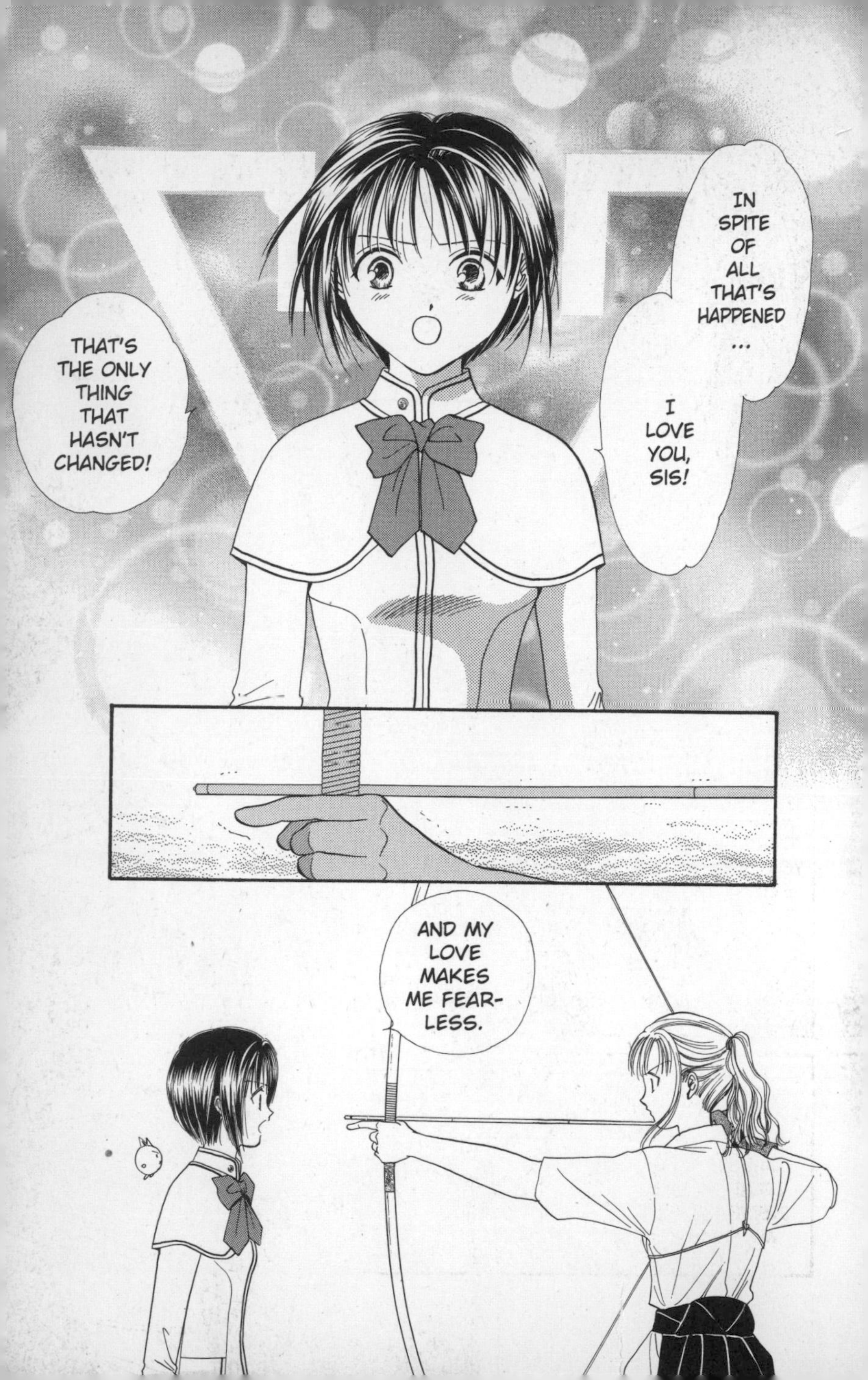
IN SPITE OF ALL THAT'S HAPPENED ...
I LOVE YOU, SIS!
THAT'S THE ONLY THING THAT HASN'T CHANGED!
AND MY LOVE MAKES ME FEAR-LESS.

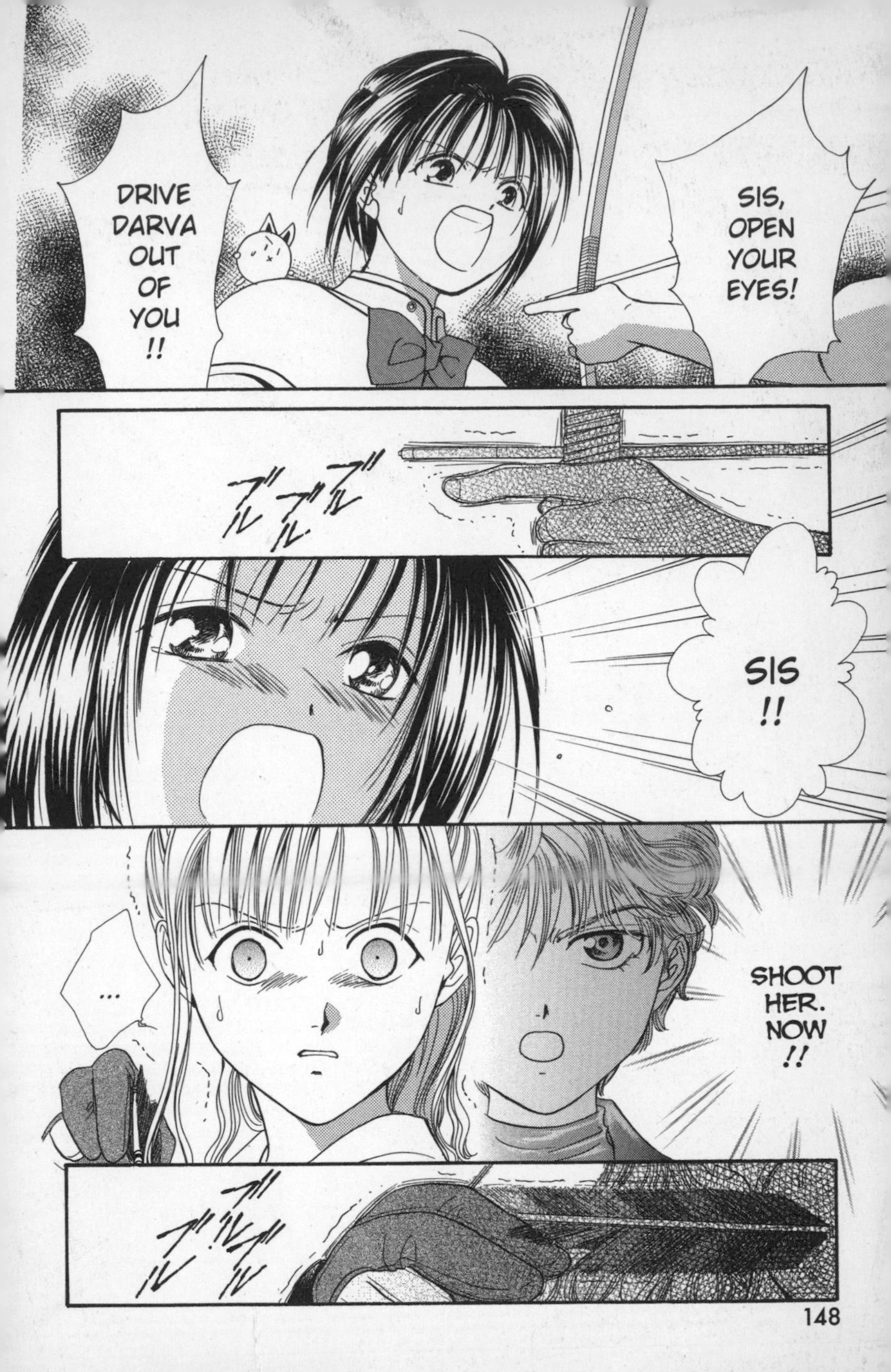
SIS, OPEN YOUR EYES!
DRIVE DARVA OUT OF YOU !!
ブルブル
SIS !!
SHOOT HER. NOW !!
...
ブルブル
ブルブル

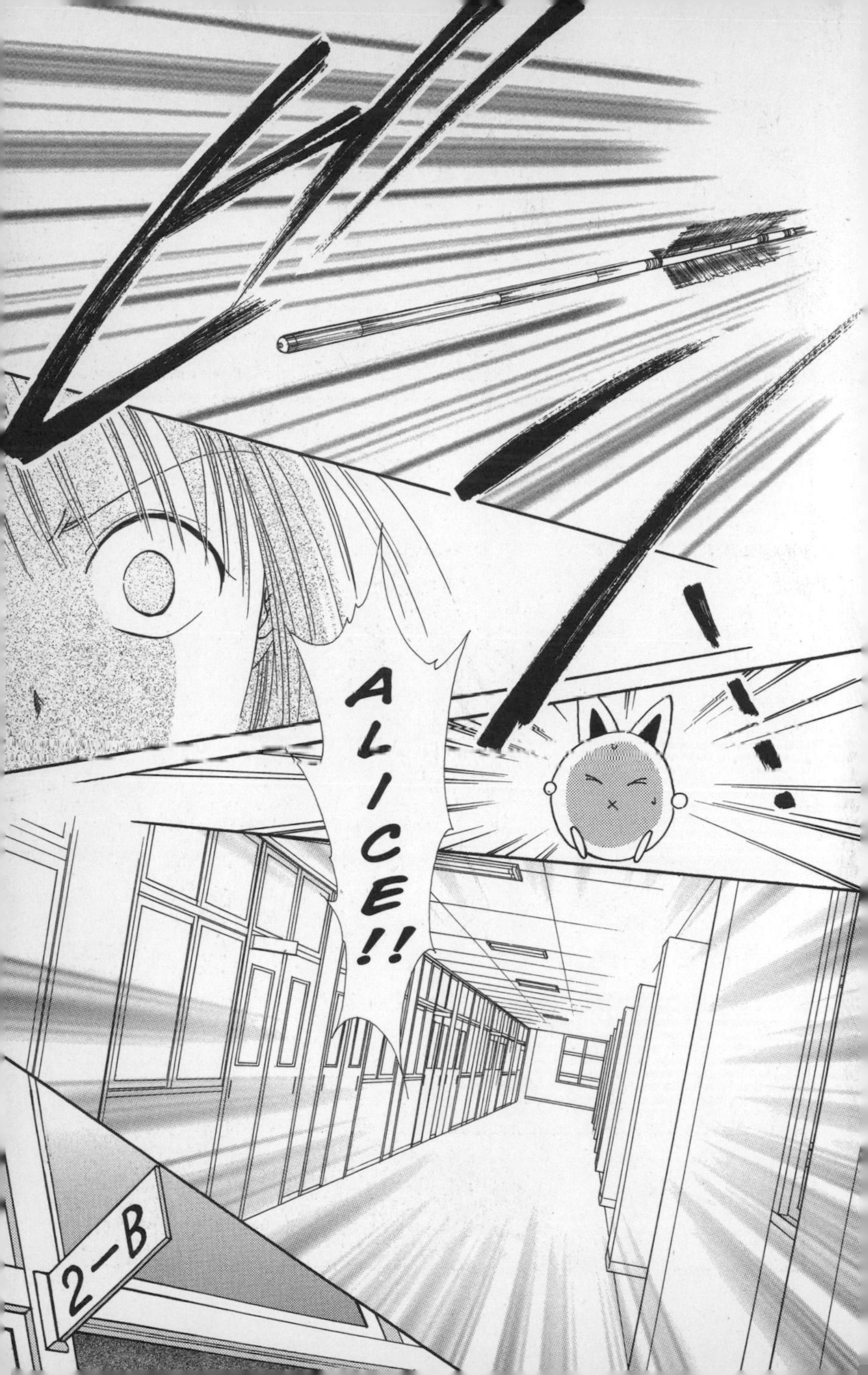
ALICE!!
2-B

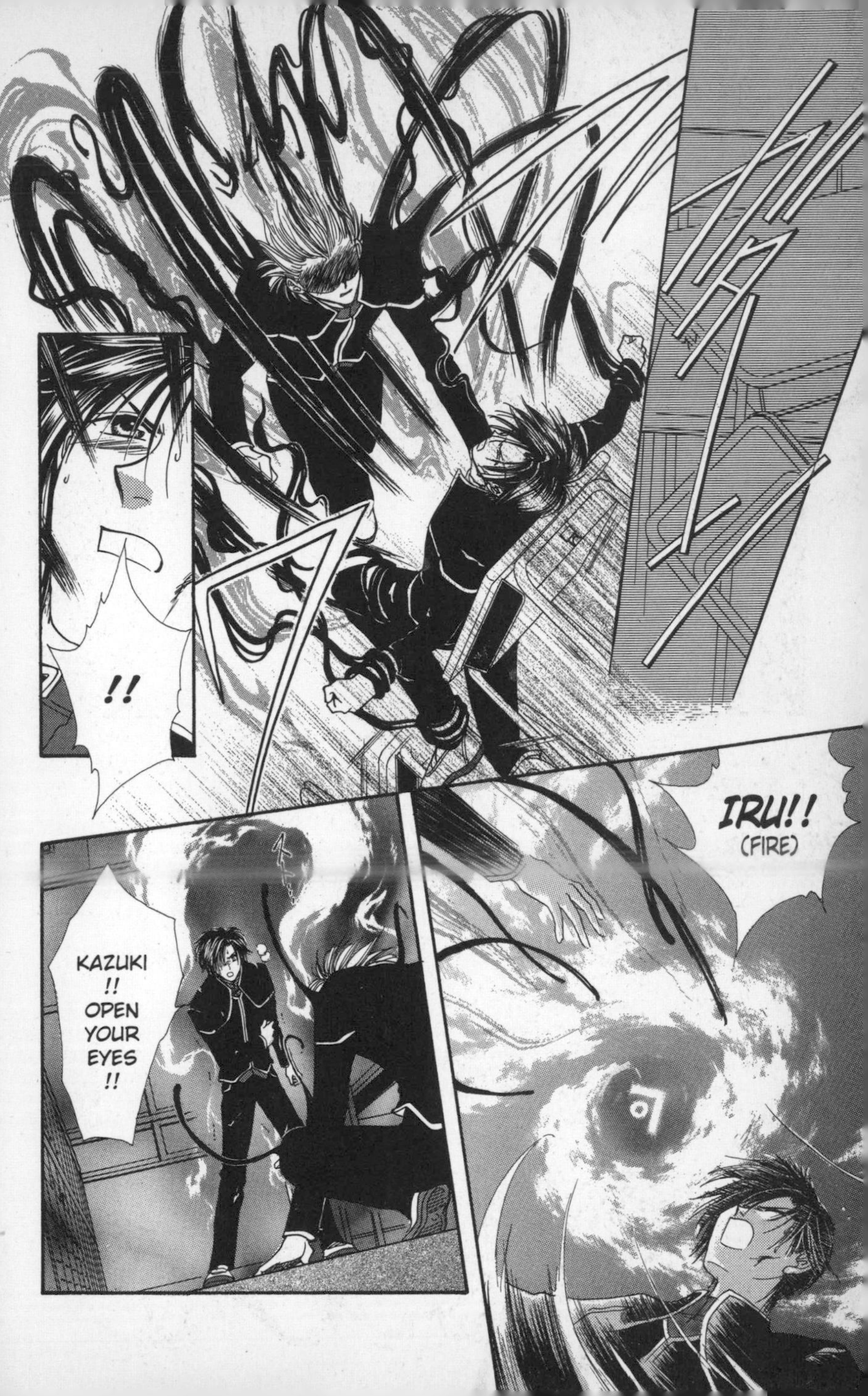
!!
IRU!!
(FIRE)
KAZUKI !! OPEN YOUR EYES !!

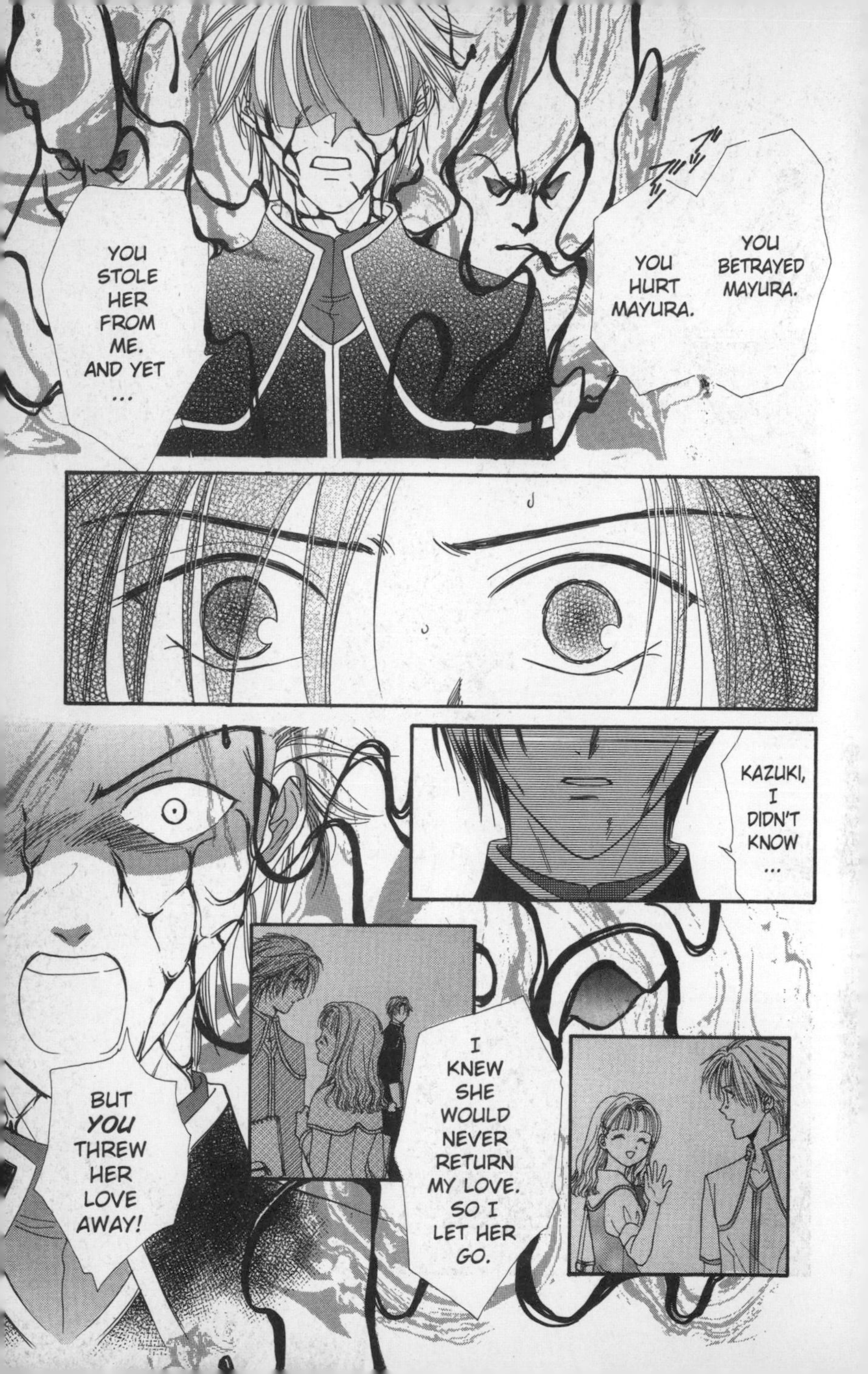
YOU BETRAYED MAYURA.
YOU HURT MAYURA.
YOU STOLE HER FROM ME. AND YET ...
KAZUKI, I DIDN'T KNOW ...
I KNEW SHE WOULD NEVER RETURN MY LOVE. SO I LET HER GO.
BUT *YOU* THREW HER LOVE AWAY!

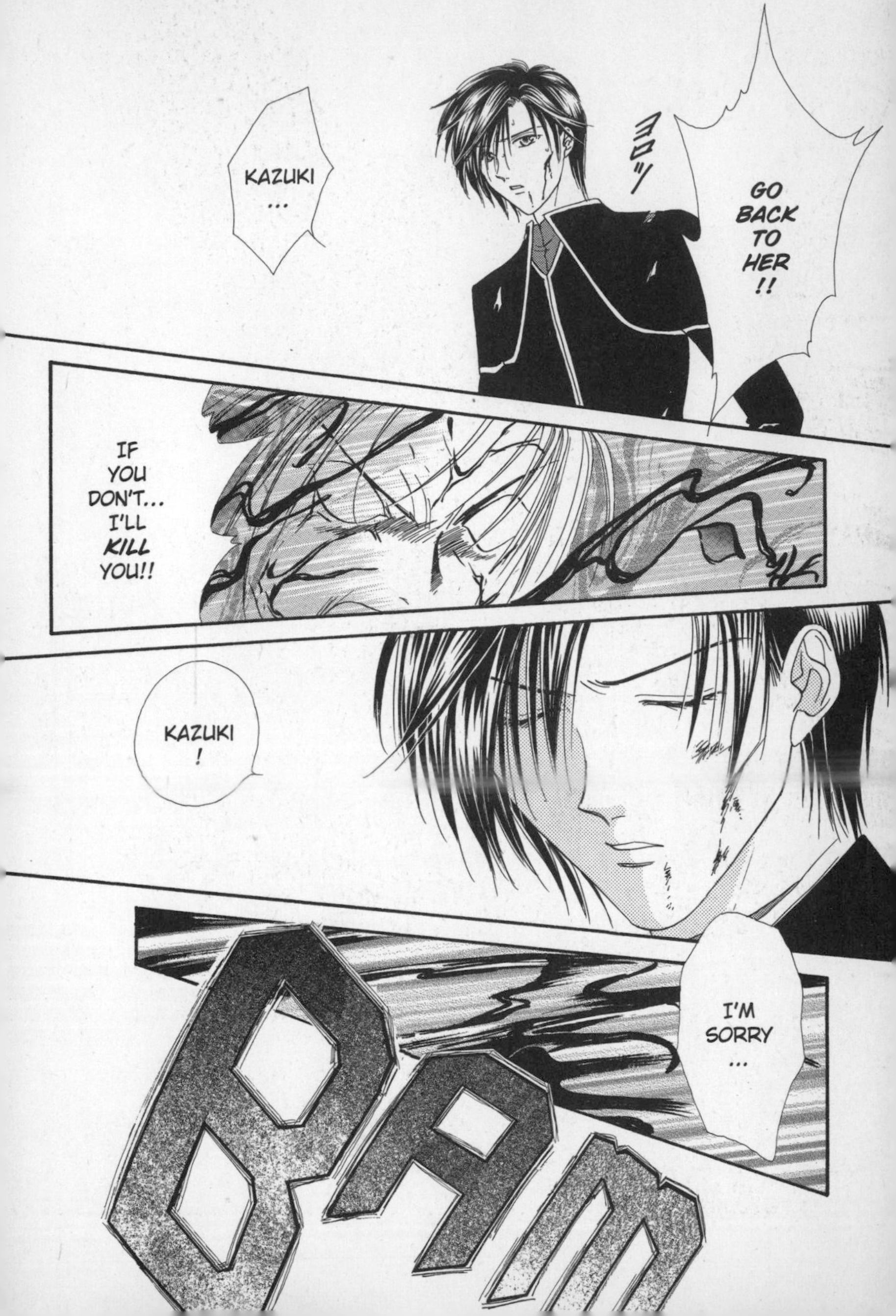
GO BACK TO HER!!
ヨロッ
KAZUKI...
IF YOU DON'T... I'LL KILL YOU!!
KAZUKI!
I'M SORRY...
BAM

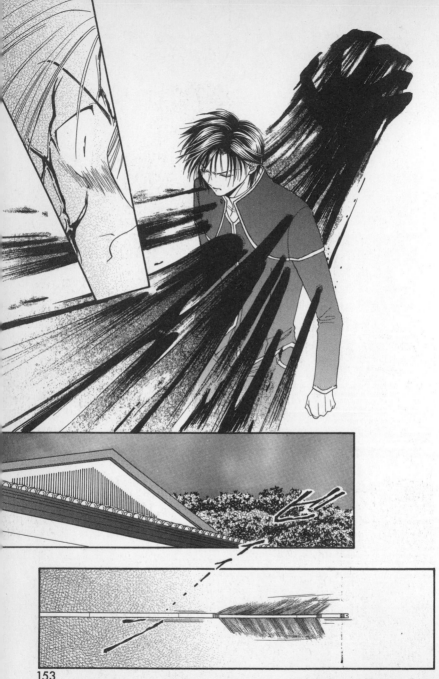

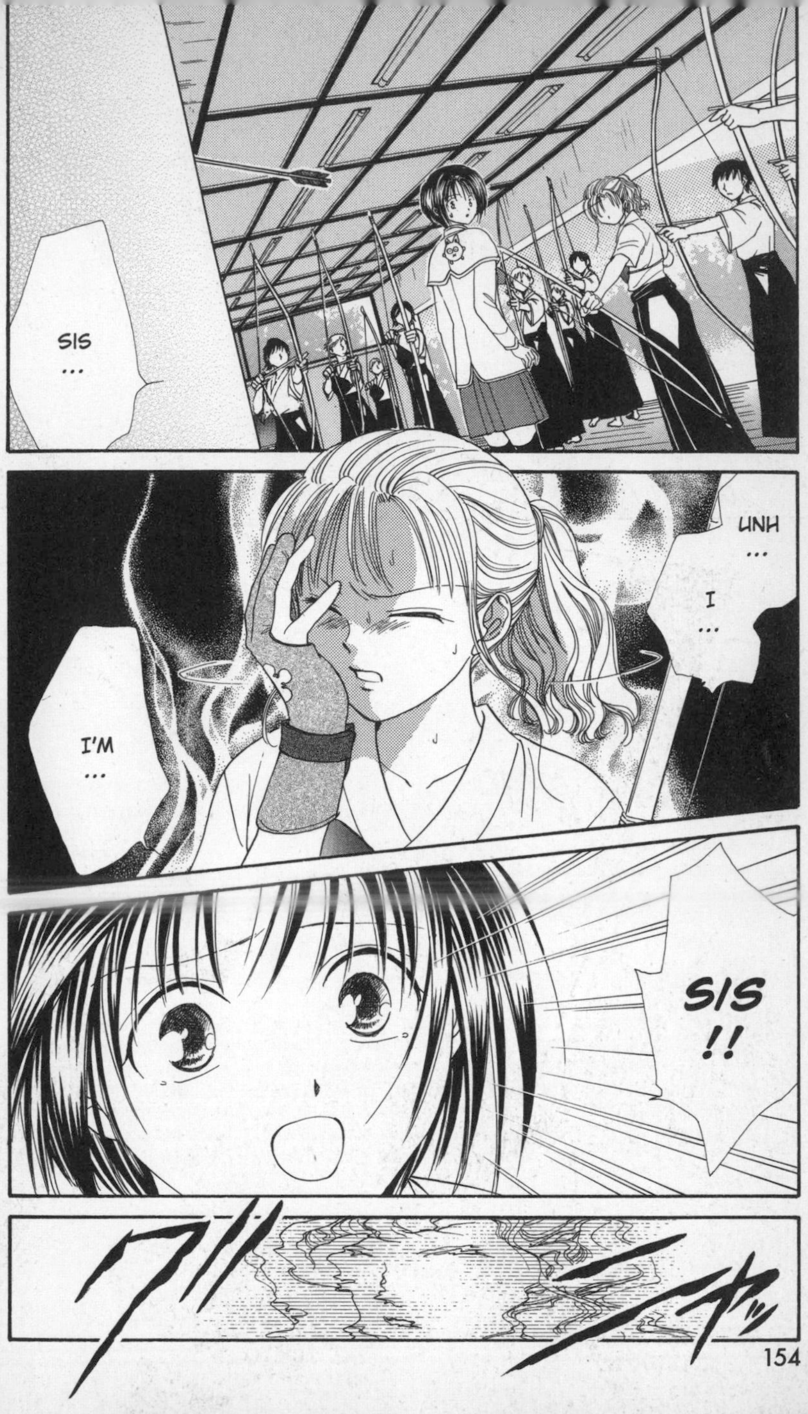
SIS ...
UNH ... I ...
I'M ...
SIS !!

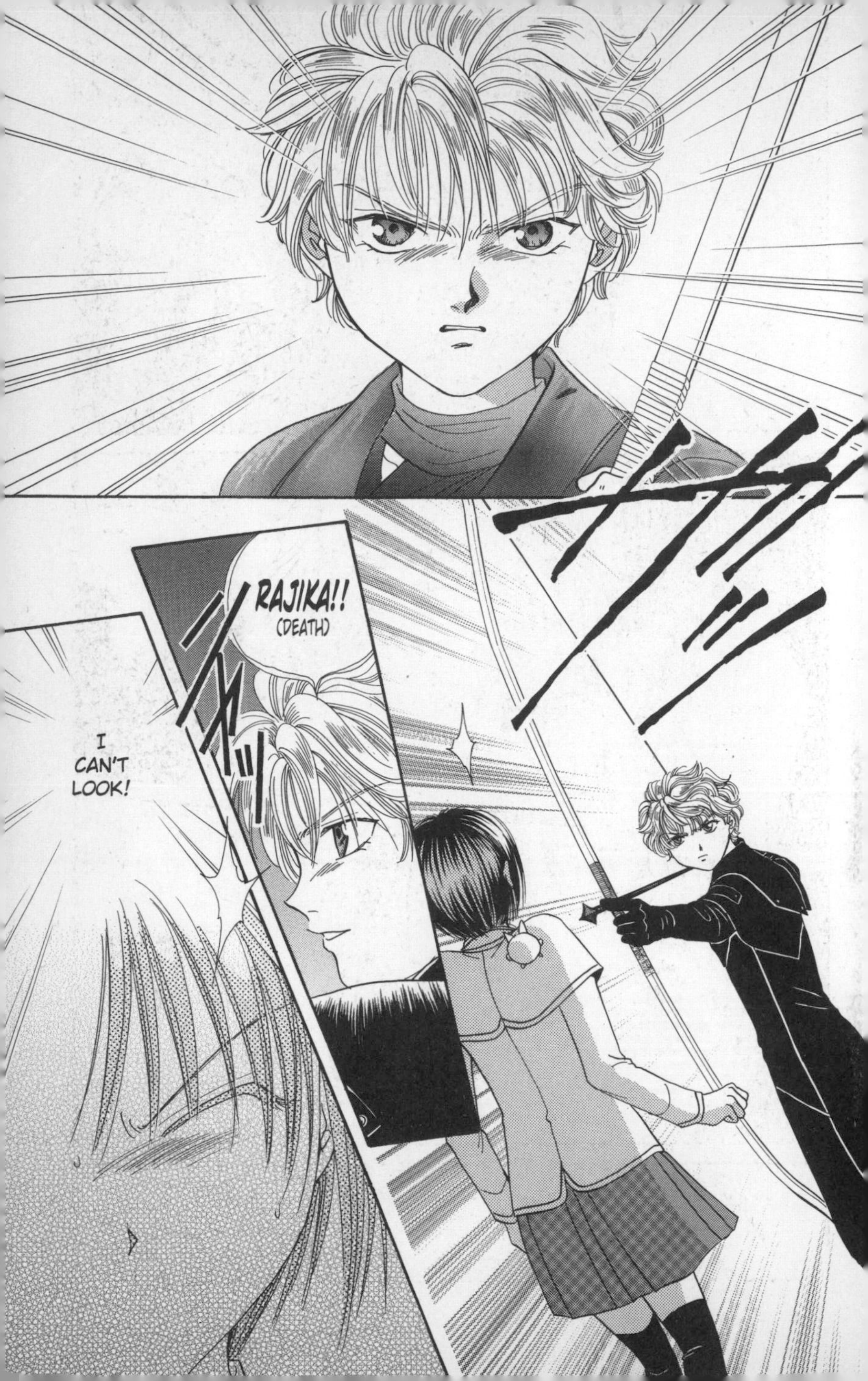
RAJIKA!!
(DEATH)
I CAN'T LOOK!

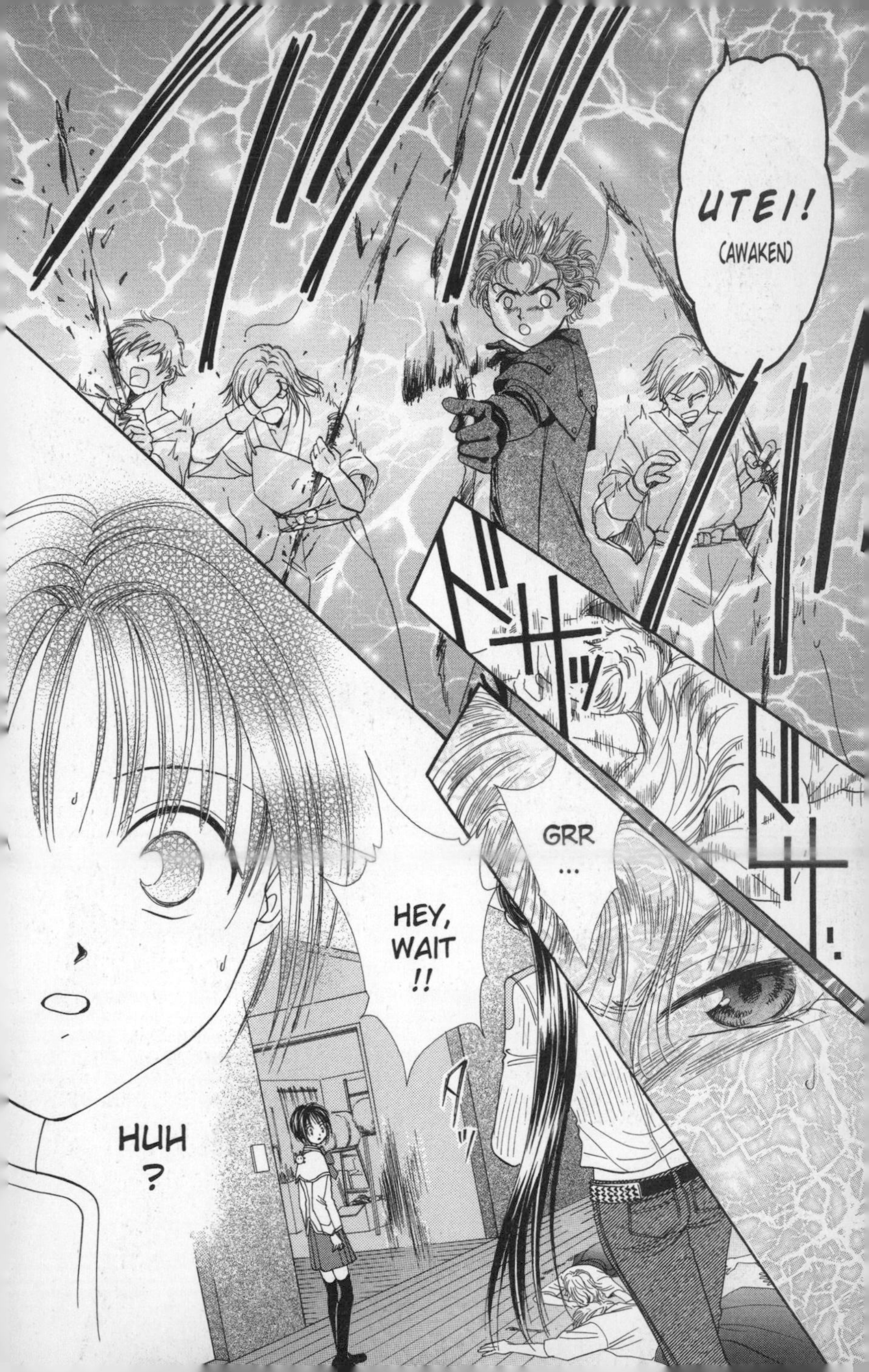
UTEI!
(AWAKEN)
GRR ...
HEY, WAIT !!
HUH ?

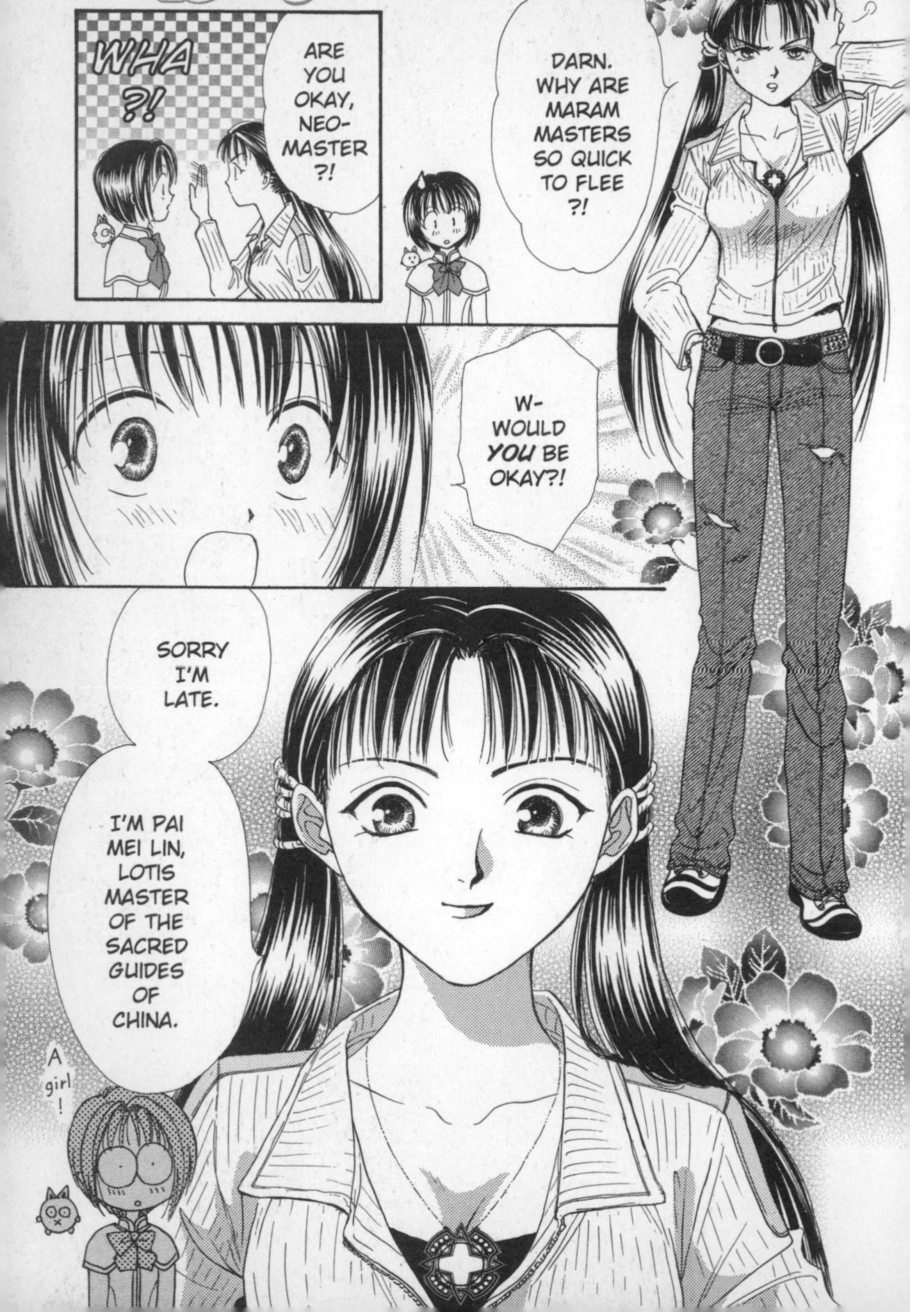
DARN. WHY ARE MARAM MASTERS SO QUICK TO FLEE ?!
WHA ?!
ARE YOU OKAY, NEO-MASTER ?!
W-WOULD *YOU* BE OKAY?!
SORRY I'M LATE.
I'M PAI MEI LIN, LOTIS MASTER OF THE SACRED GUIDES OF CHINA.
A girl !

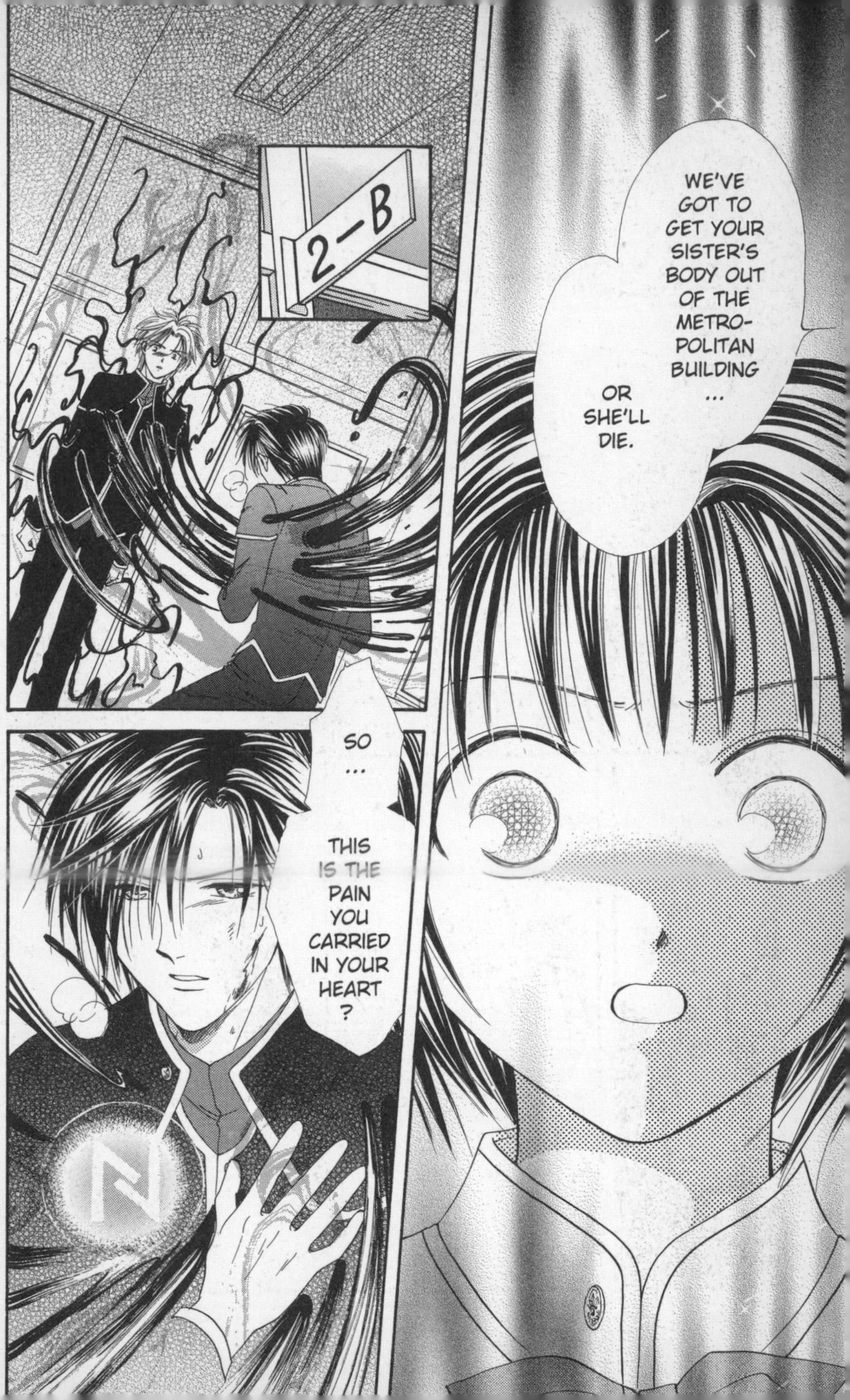
WE'VE GOT TO GET YOUR SISTER'S BODY OUT OF THE METRO-POLITAN BUILDING ...
OR SHE'LL DIE.
2-B
SO ...
THIS IS THE PAIN YOU CARRIED IN YOUR HEART ?

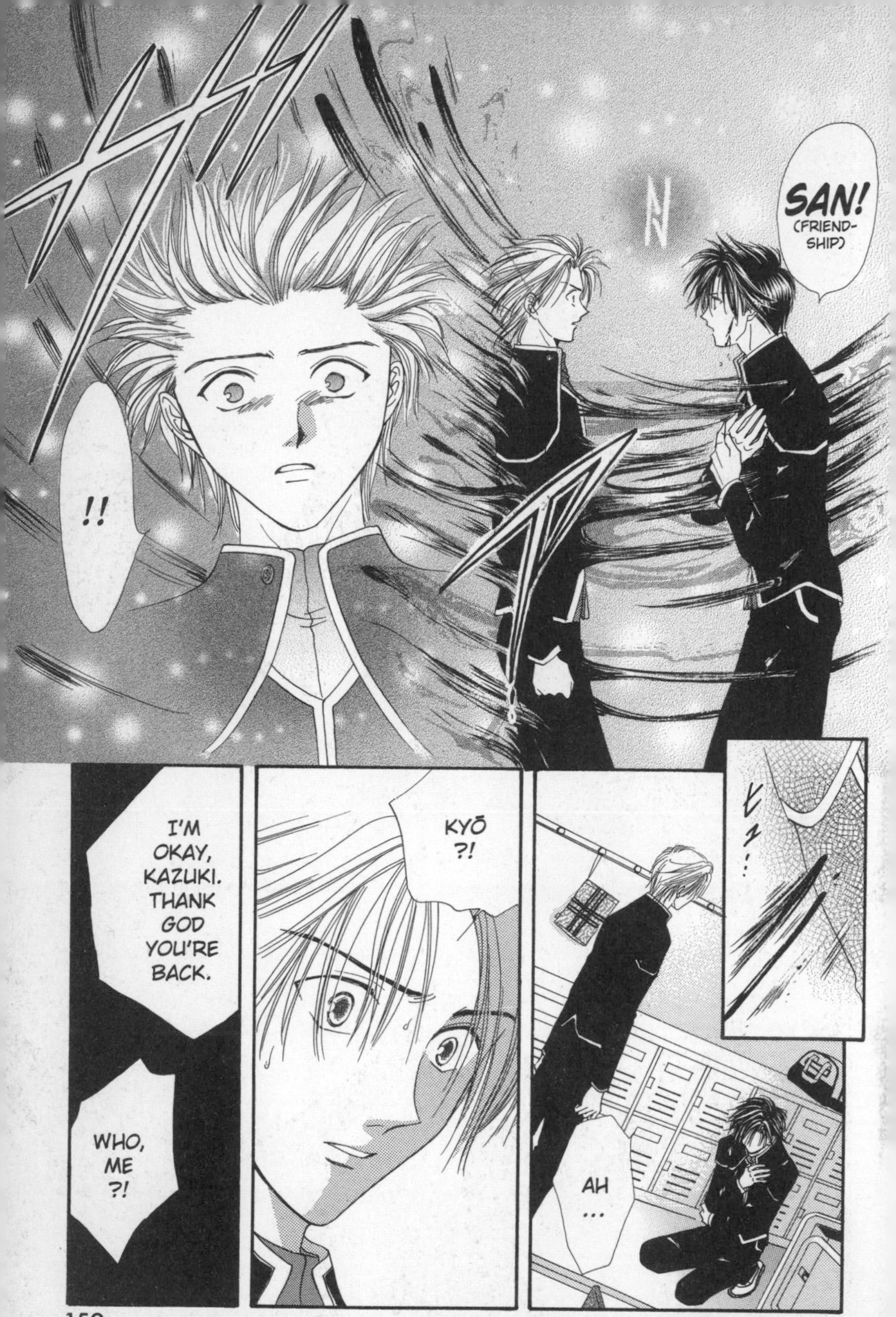
SAN! (FRIEND-SHIP)
!!
AH ...
KYŌ ?!
I'M OKAY, KAZUKI. THANK GOD YOU'RE BACK.
WHO, ME ?!

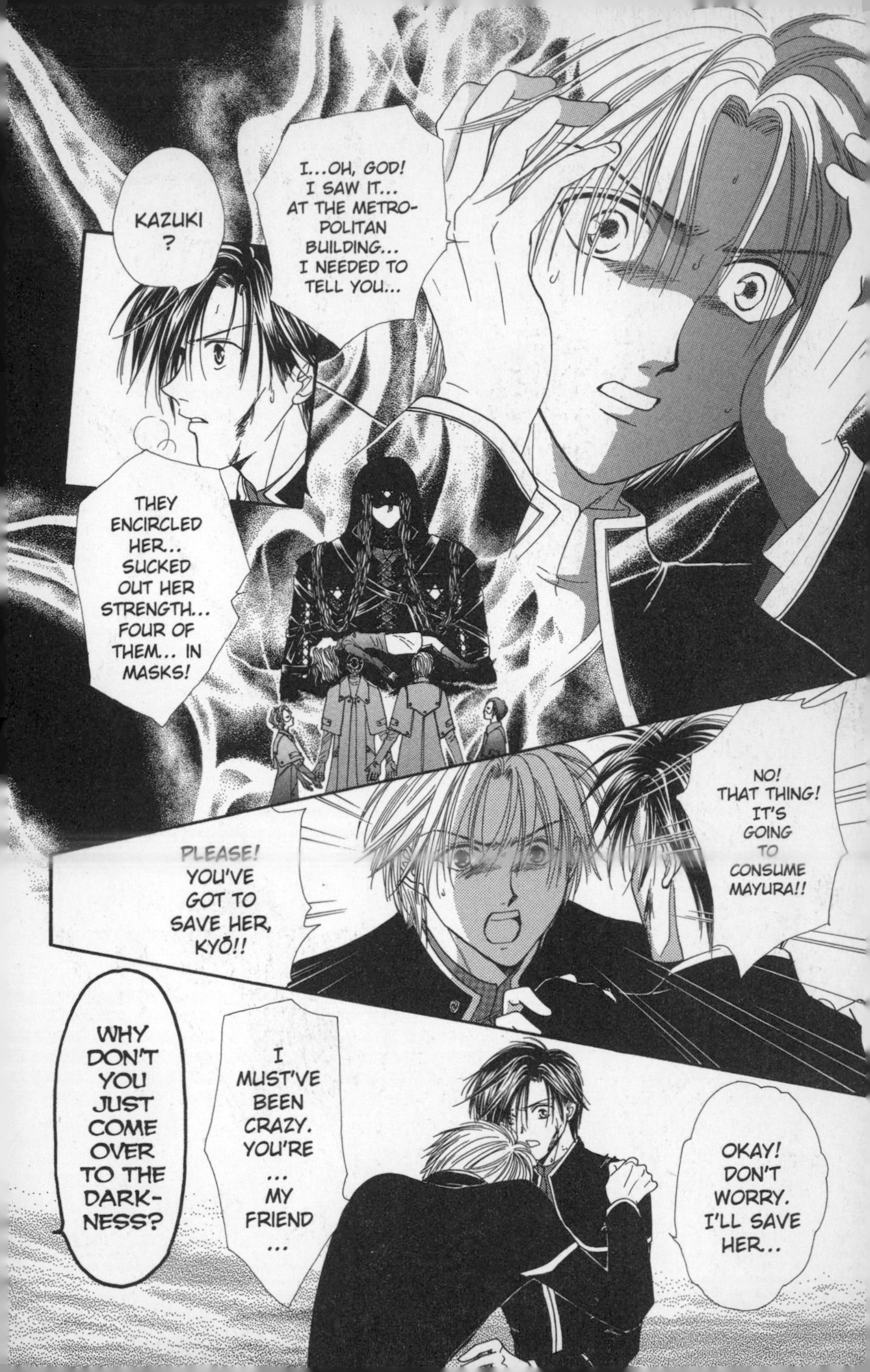
I...OH, GOD! I SAW IT... AT THE METRO-POLITAN BUILDING... I NEEDED TO TELL YOU...
KAZUKI ?
THEY ENCIRCLED HER... SUCKED OUT HER STRENGTH... FOUR OF THEM... IN MASKS!
NO! THAT THING! IT'S GOING TO CONSUME MAYURA!!
PLEASE! YOU'VE GOT TO SAVE HER, KYŌ!!
OKAY! DON'T WORRY. I'LL SAVE HER..
I MUST'VE BEEN CRAZY. YOU'RE ... MY FRIEND ...
WHY DON'T YOU JUST COME OVER TO THE DARK-NESS?

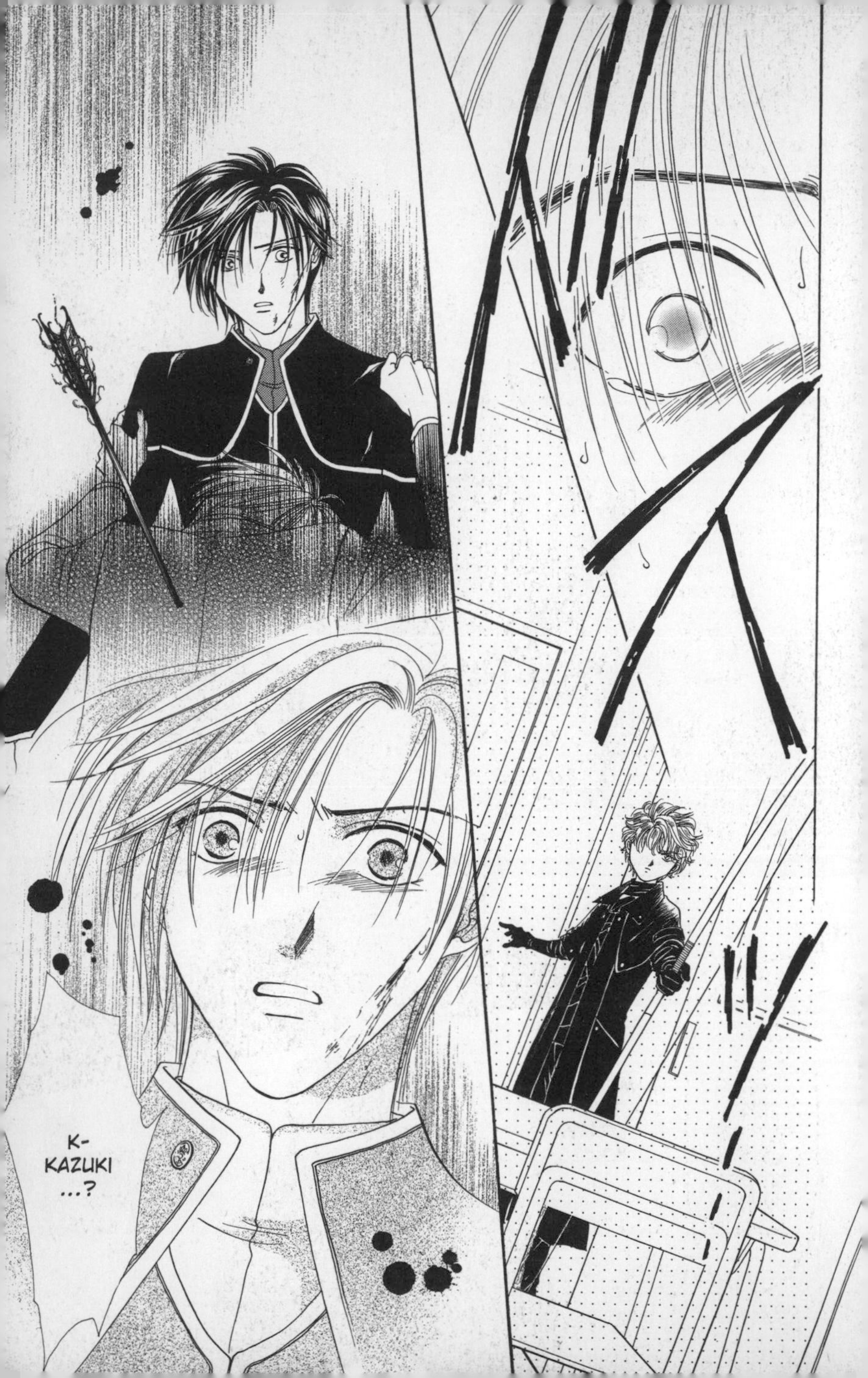
K-KAZUKI ...?

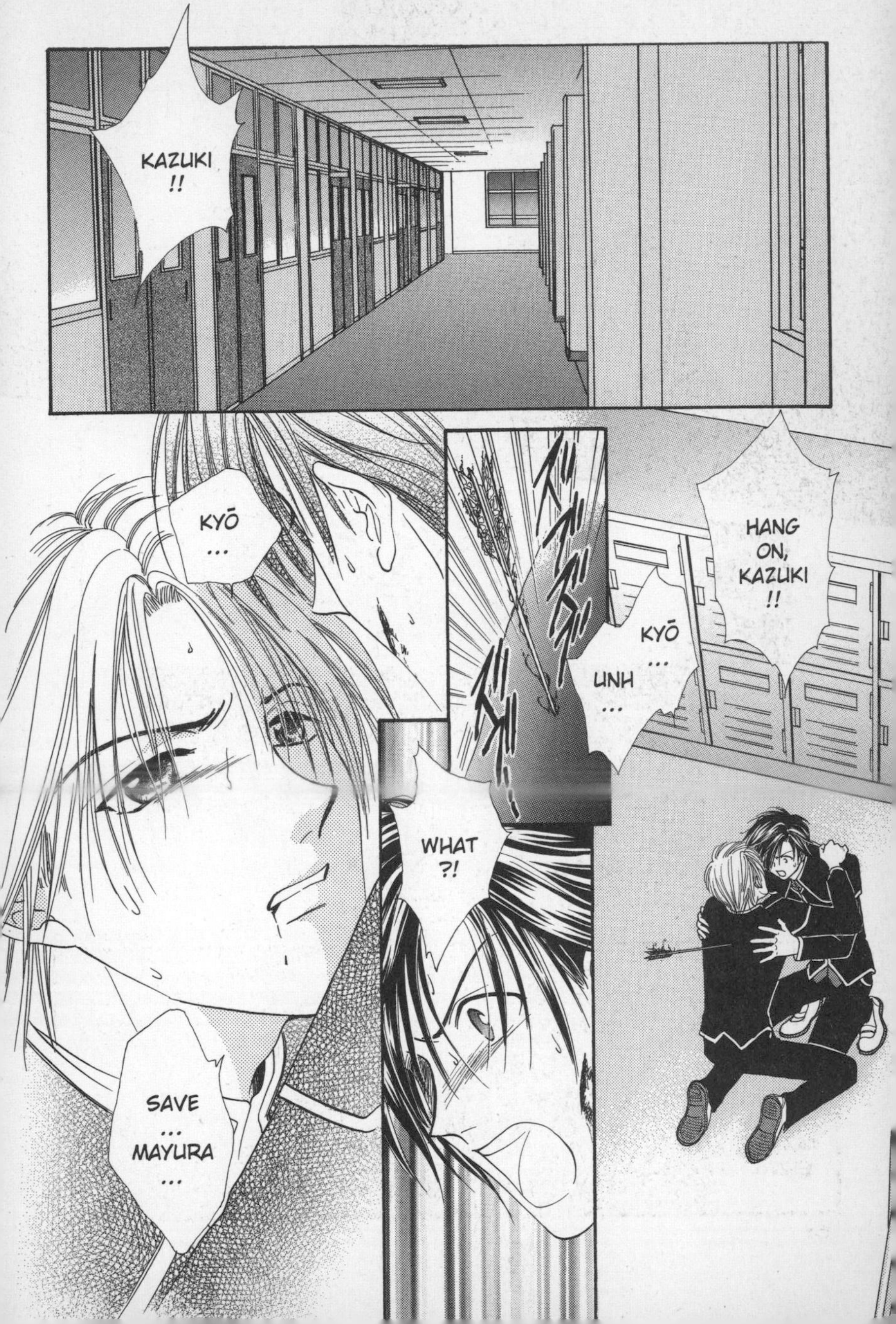
KAZUKI !!
HANG ON, KAZUKI !!
KYŌ ...
UNH ...
WHAT ?!
KYŌ ...
SAVE ... MAYURA ...

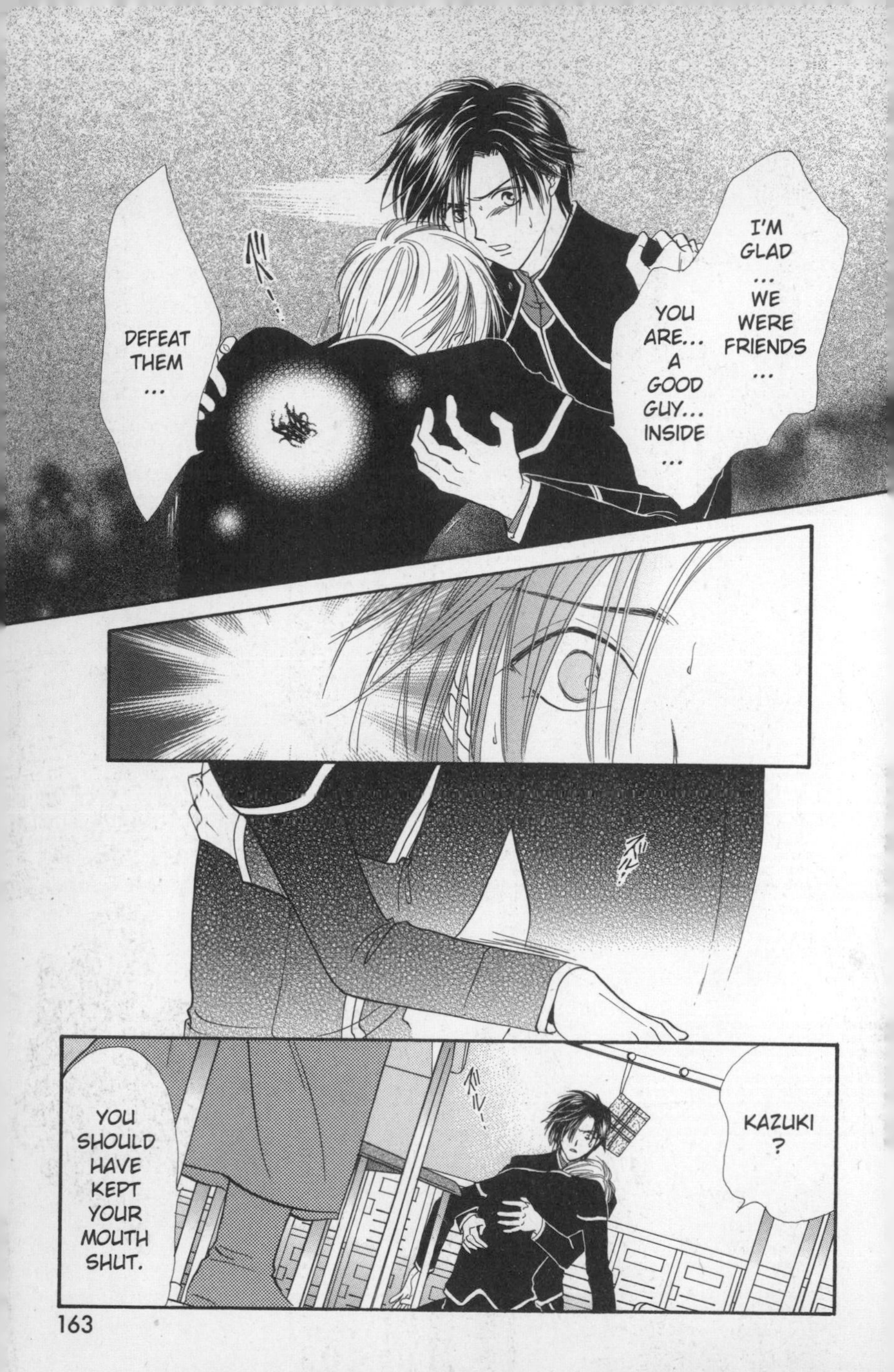
I'M GLAD ... WE WERE FRIENDS ...
YOU ARE... A GOOD GUY... INSIDE ...
DEFEAT THEM ...
KAZUKI ?
YOU SHOULD HAVE KEPT YOUR MOUTH SHUT.

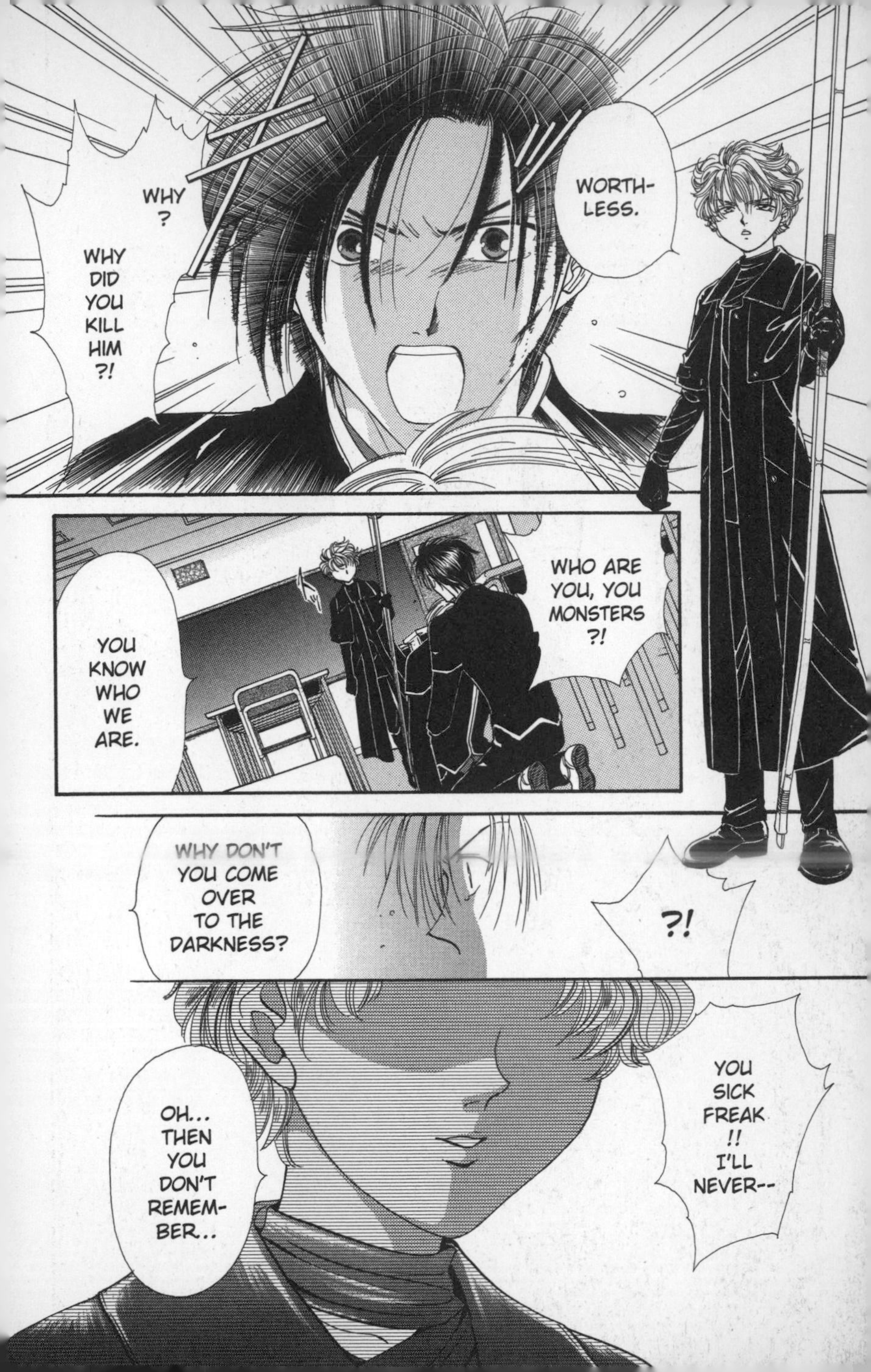
WORTH-LESS.
WHY?
WHY DID YOU KILL HIM?!
WHO ARE YOU, YOU MONSTERS?!
YOU KNOW WHO WE ARE.
?!
WHY DON'T YOU COME OVER TO THE DARKNESS?
YOU SICK FREAK!! I'LL NEVER--
OH... THEN YOU DON'T REMEM-BER...

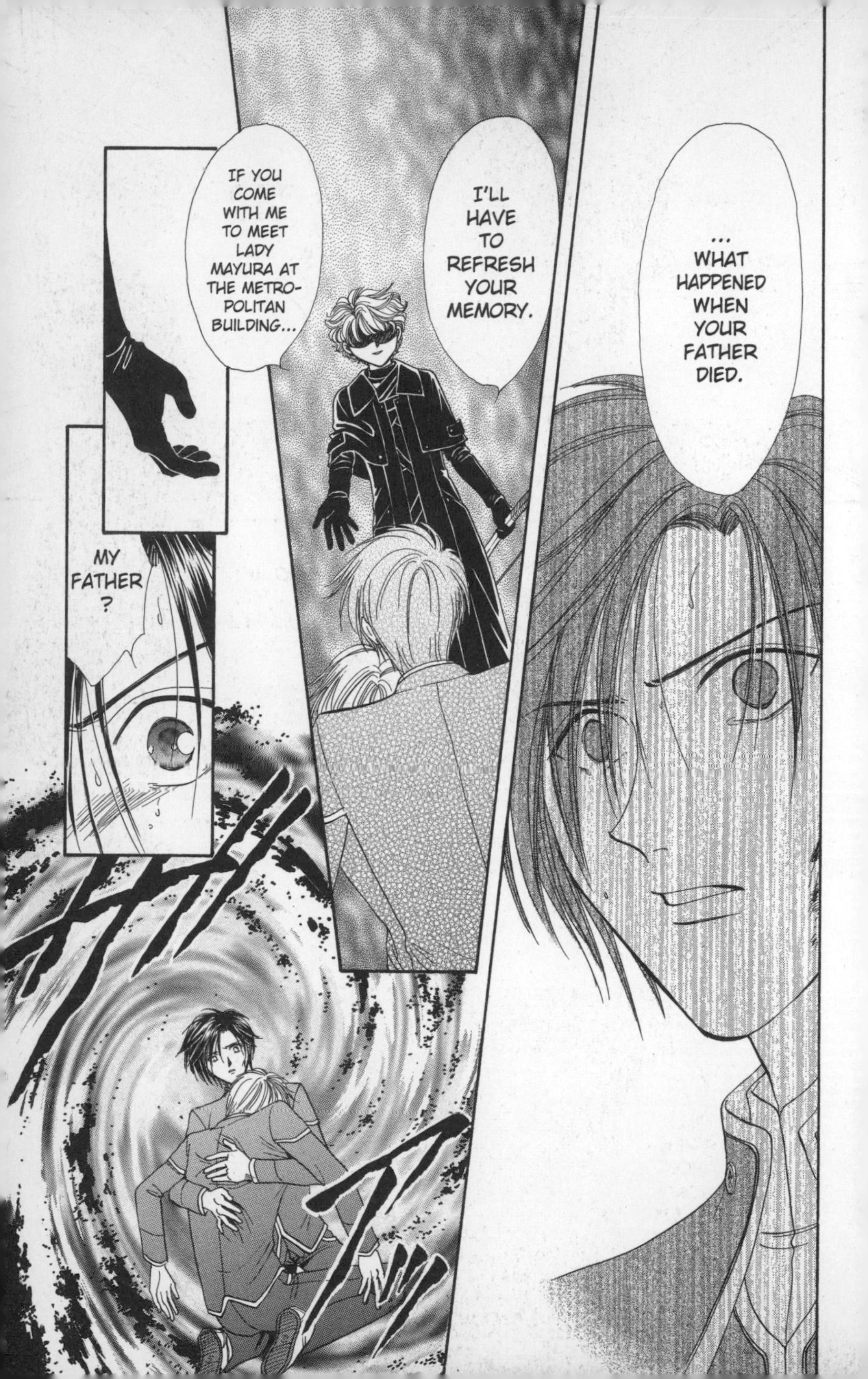
... WHAT HAPPENED WHEN YOUR FATHER DIED.
I'LL HAVE TO REFRESH YOUR MEMORY.
IF YOU COME WITH ME TO MEET LADY MAYURA AT THE METRO-POLITAN BUILDING...
MY FATHER ?

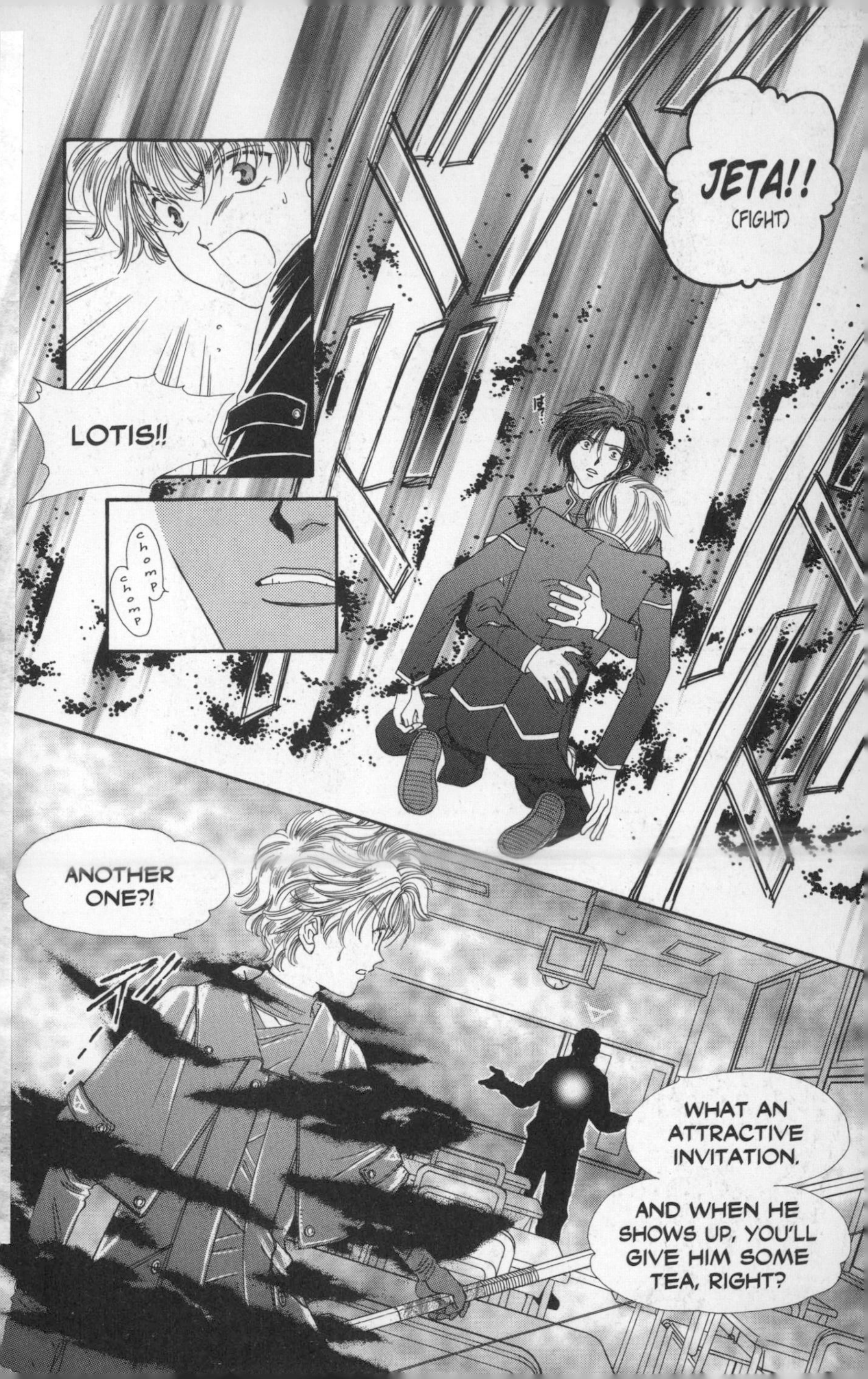
JETA!!
(FIGHT)
LOTIS!!
chomp chomp
ANOTHER ONE?!
WHAT AN ATTRACTIVE INVITATION,
AND WHEN HE SHOWS UP, YOU'LL GIVE HIM SOME TEA, RIGHT?

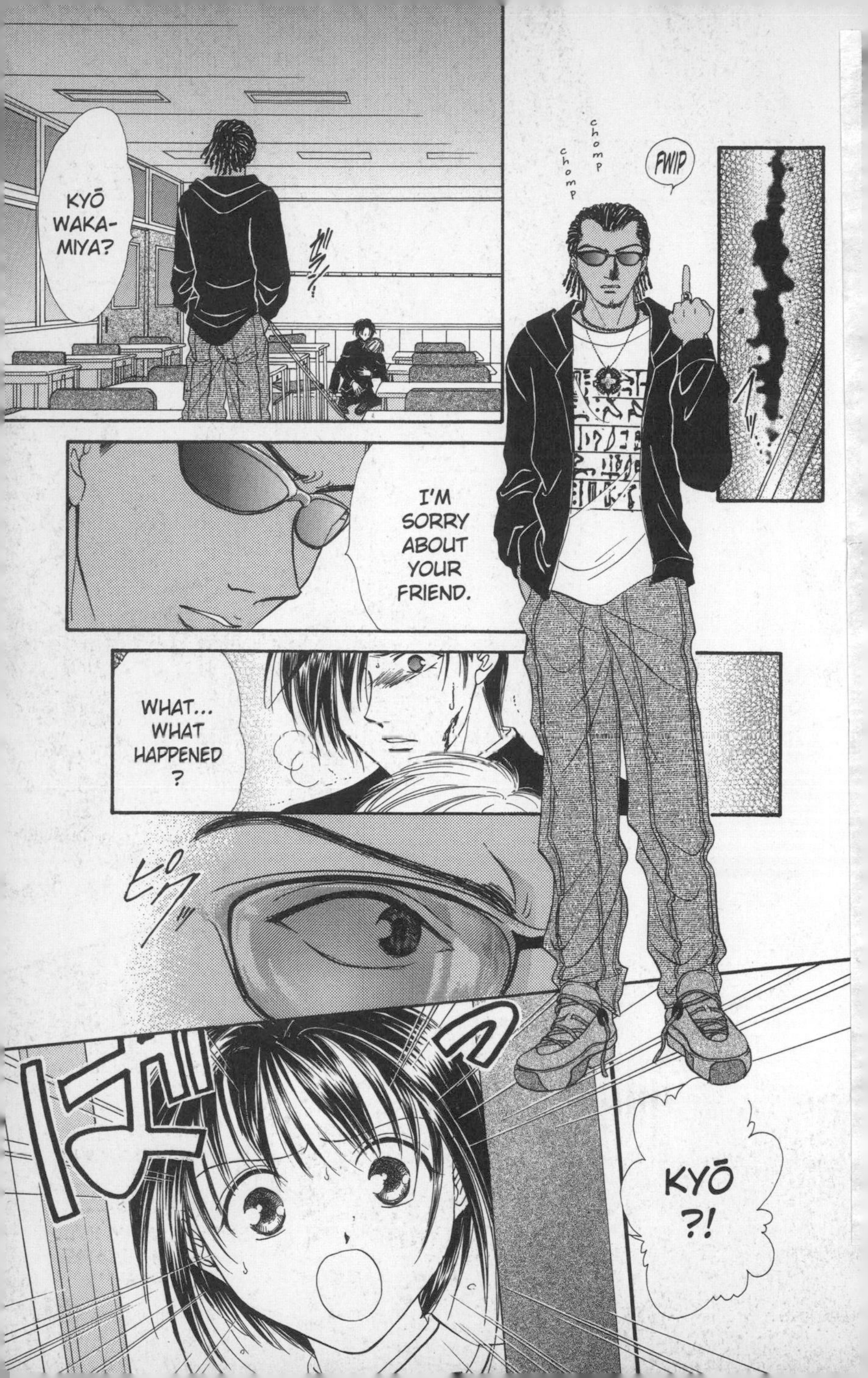
chomp chomp
FWIP
KYŌ WAKA-MIYA?
I'M SORRY ABOUT YOUR FRIEND.
WHAT... WHAT HAPPENED ?
KYŌ ?!

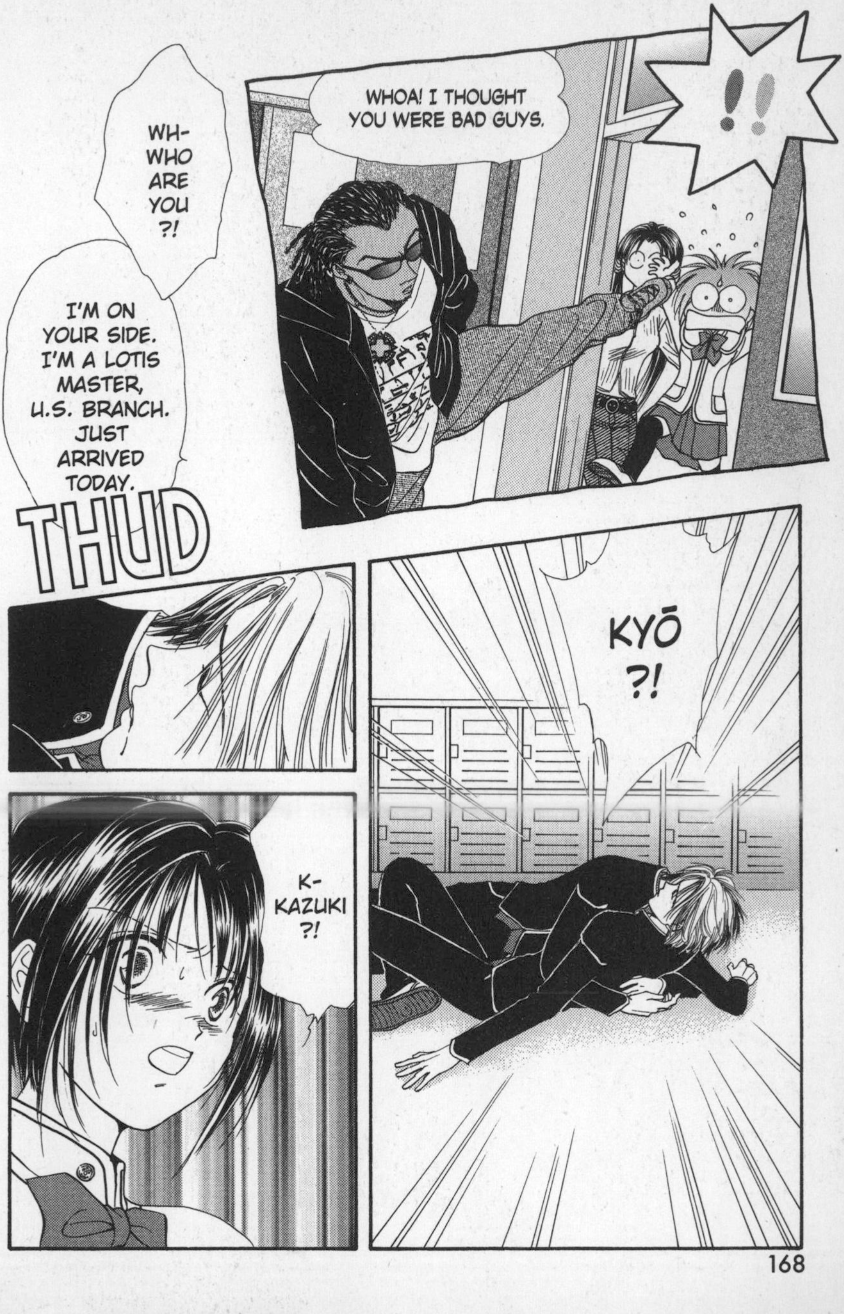
!!
WHOA! I THOUGHT YOU WERE BAD GUYS.
WH-WHO ARE YOU?!
I'M ON YOUR SIDE. I'M A LOTIS MASTER, U.S. BRANCH. JUST ARRIVED TODAY.
THUD
KYŌ?!
K-KAZUKI?!

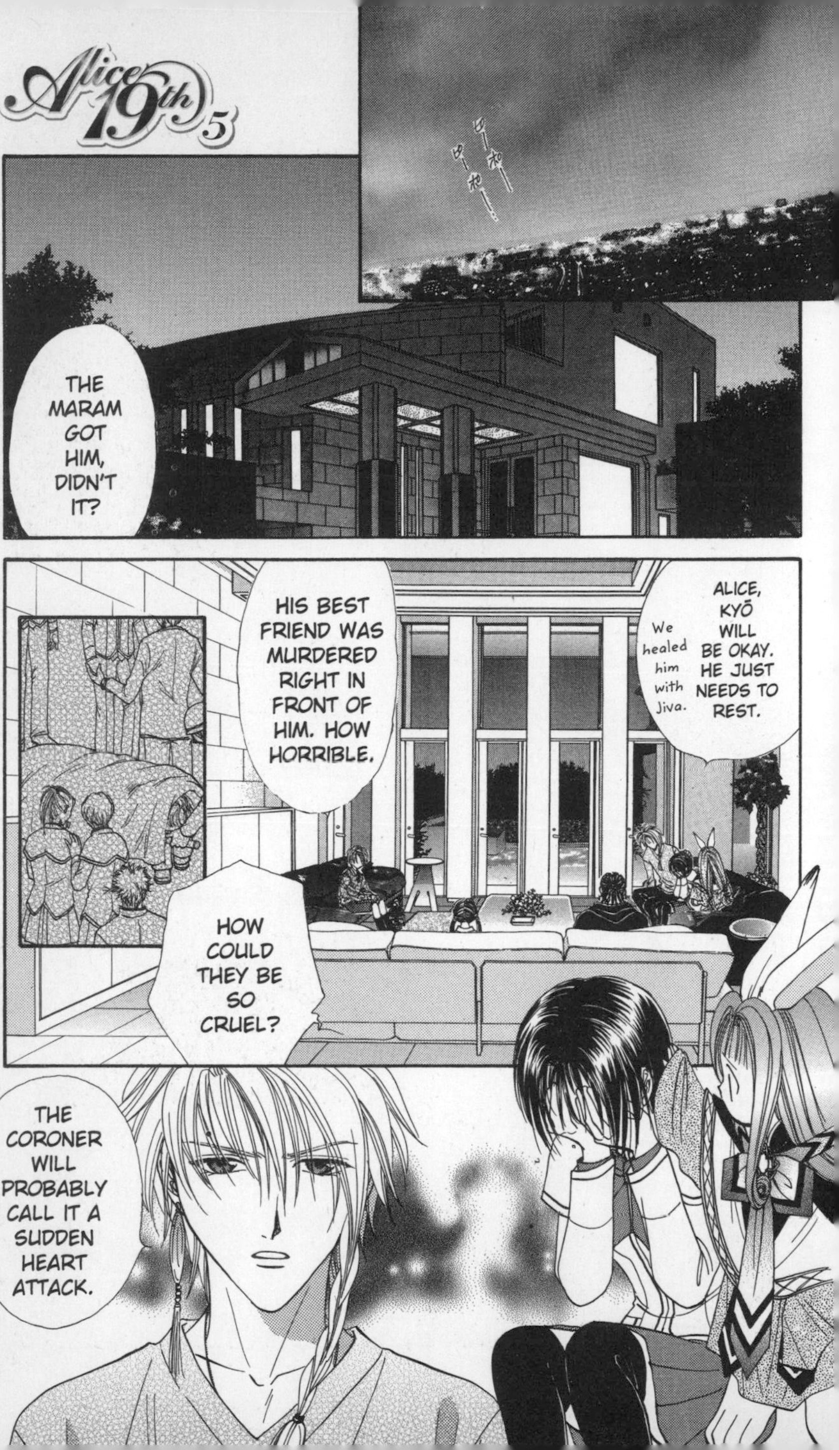
ピーポー ピーポー…
THE MARAM GOT HIM, DIDN'T IT?
ALICE, KYŌ WILL BE OKAY. HE JUST NEEDS TO REST.
We healed him with Jiva.
HIS BEST FRIEND WAS MURDERED RIGHT IN FRONT OF HIM. HOW HORRIBLE.
HOW COULD THEY BE SO CRUEL?
THE CORONER WILL PROBABLY CALL IT A SUDDEN HEART ATTACK.

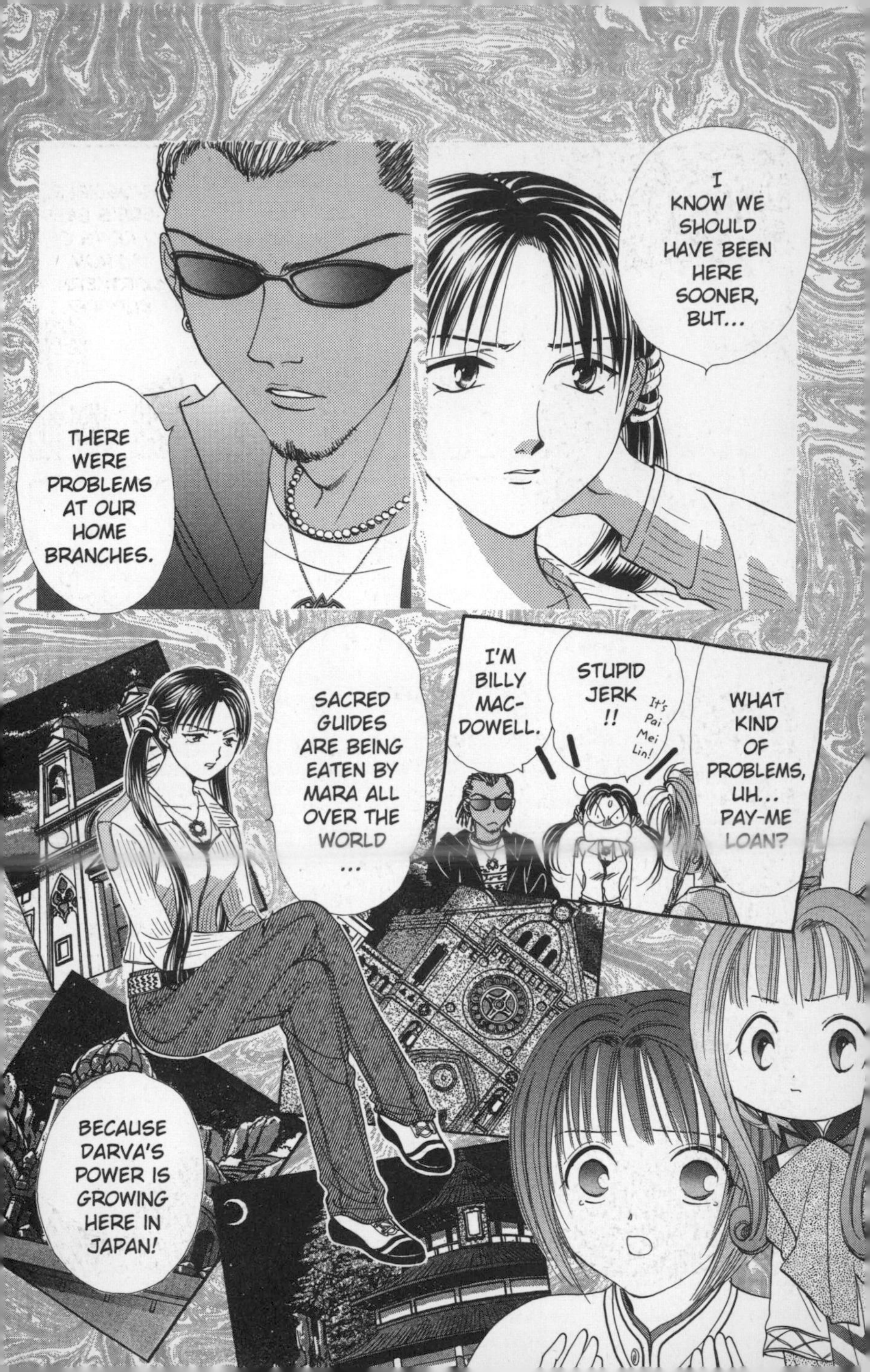
I KNOW WE SHOULD HAVE BEEN HERE SOONER, BUT...
THERE WERE PROBLEMS AT OUR HOME BRANCHES.
WHAT KIND OF PROBLEMS, UH... PAY-ME LOAN?
It's Pai Mei Lin!
STUPID JERK !!
I'M BILLY MAC-DOWELL.
SACRED GUIDES ARE BEING EATEN BY MARA ALL OVER THE WORLD ...
BECAUSE DARVA'S POWER IS GROWING HERE IN JAPAN!

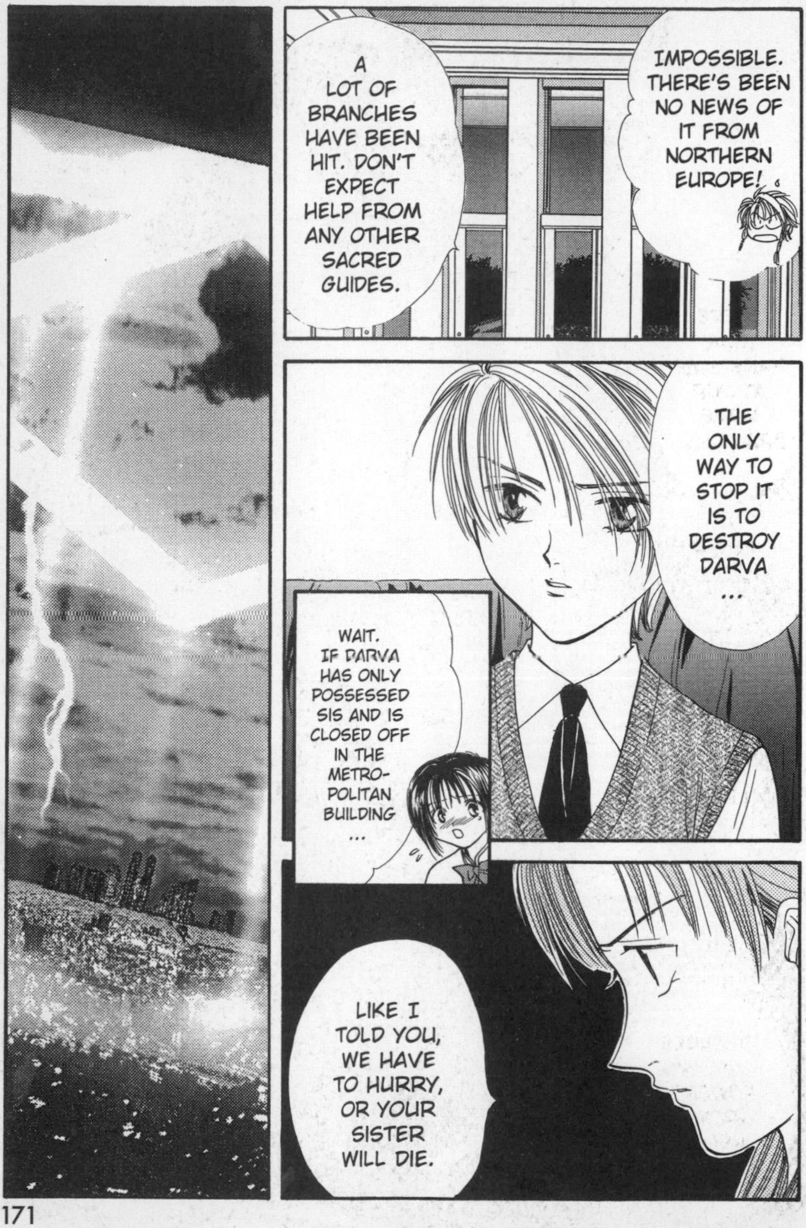
IMPOSSIBLE. THERE'S BEEN NO NEWS OF IT FROM NORTHERN EUROPE!
A LOT OF BRANCHES HAVE BEEN HIT. DON'T EXPECT HELP FROM ANY OTHER SACRED GUIDES.
THE ONLY WAY TO STOP IT IS TO DESTROY DARVA ...
WAIT. IF DARVA HAS ONLY POSSESSED SIS AND IS CLOSED OFF IN THE METRO-POLITAN BUILDING ...
LIKE I TOLD YOU, WE HAVE TO HURRY, OR YOUR SISTER WILL DIE.

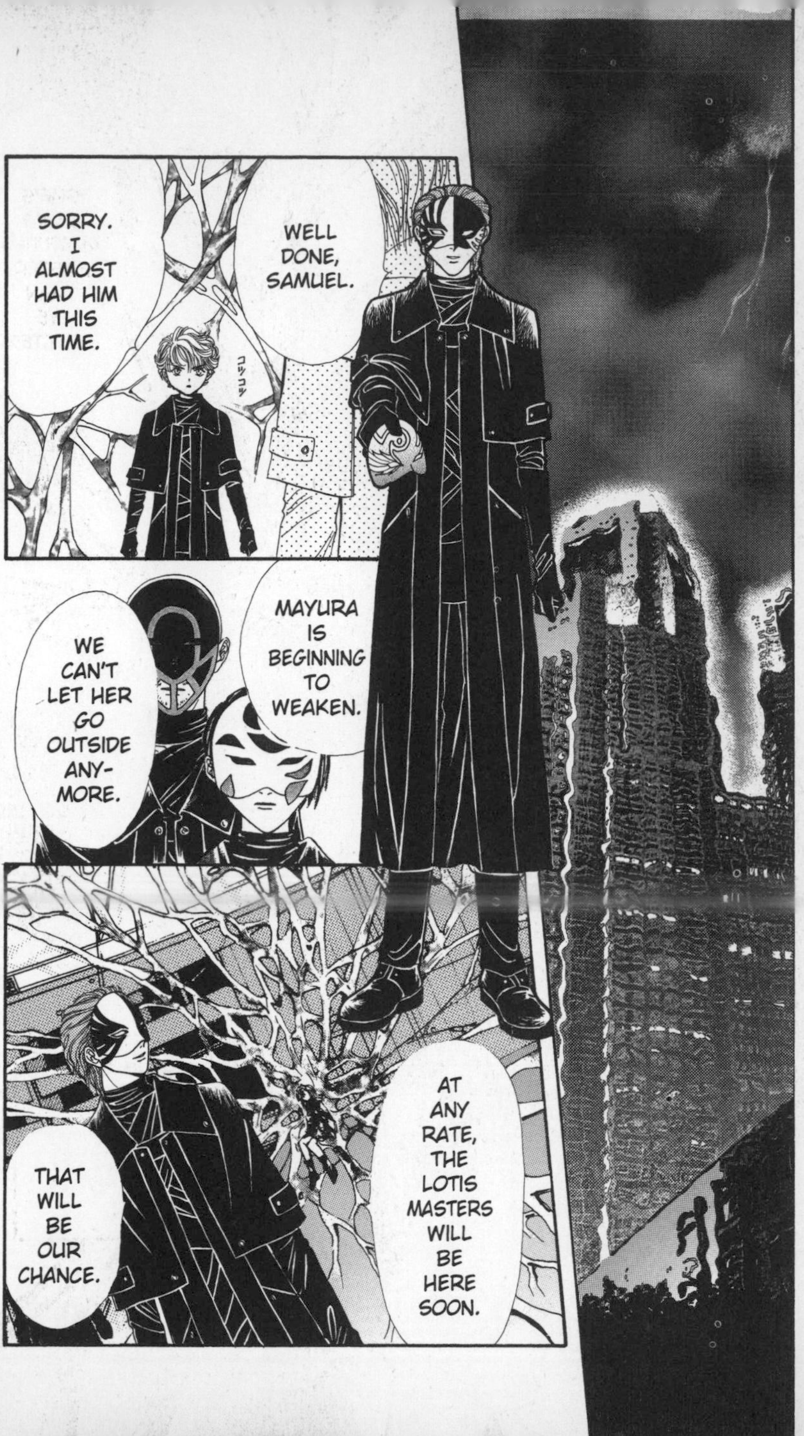
WELL DONE, SAMUEL.
コツコツ
SORRY. I ALMOST HAD HIM THIS TIME.
MAYURA IS BEGINNING TO WEAKEN.
WE CAN'T LET HER GO OUTSIDE ANY-MORE.
AT ANY RATE, THE LOTIS MASTERS WILL BE HERE SOON.
THAT WILL BE OUR CHANCE.

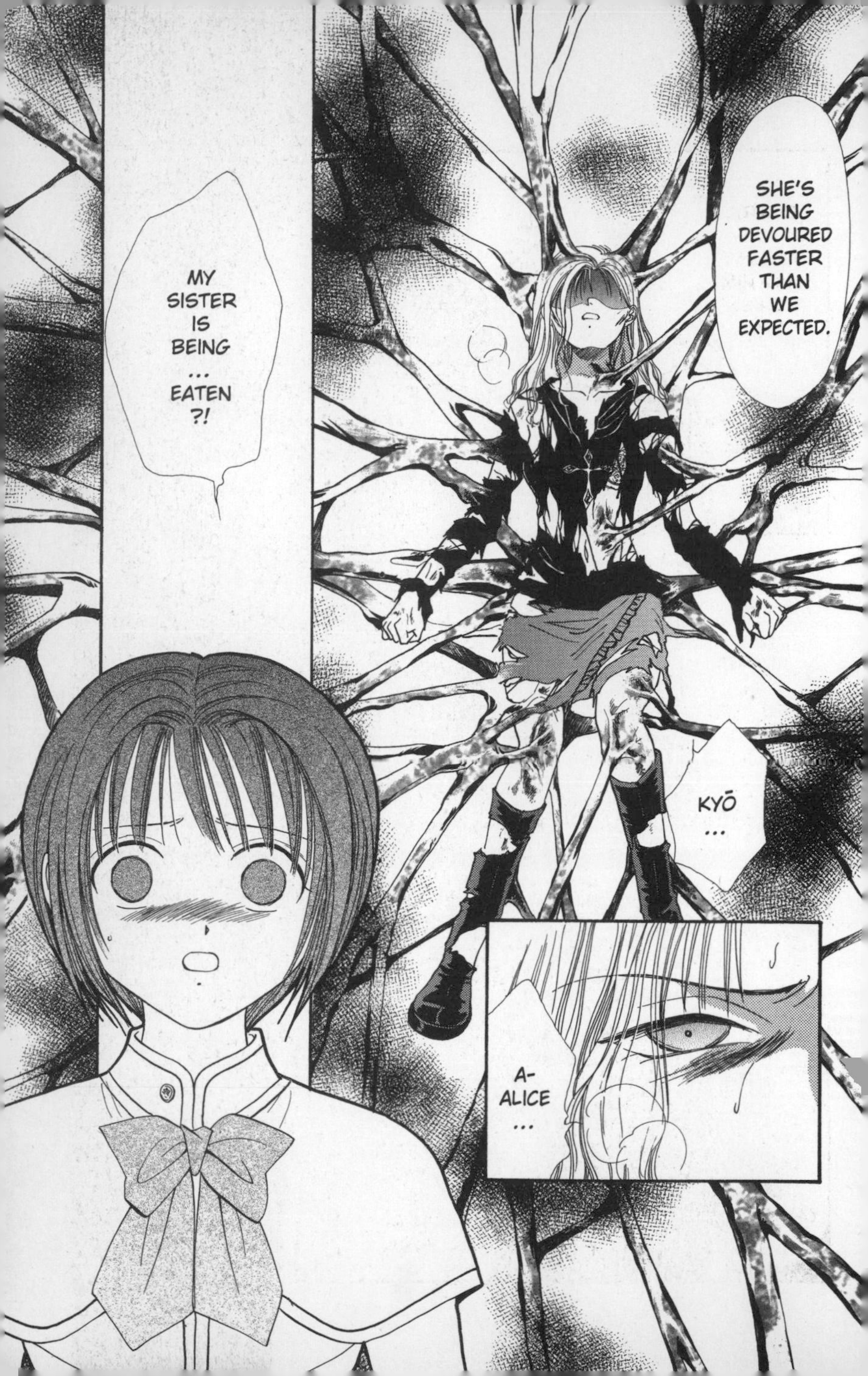
SHE'S BEING DEVOURED FASTER THAN WE EXPECTED.
KYŌ ...
MY SISTER IS BEING ... EATEN ?!
A-ALICE ...

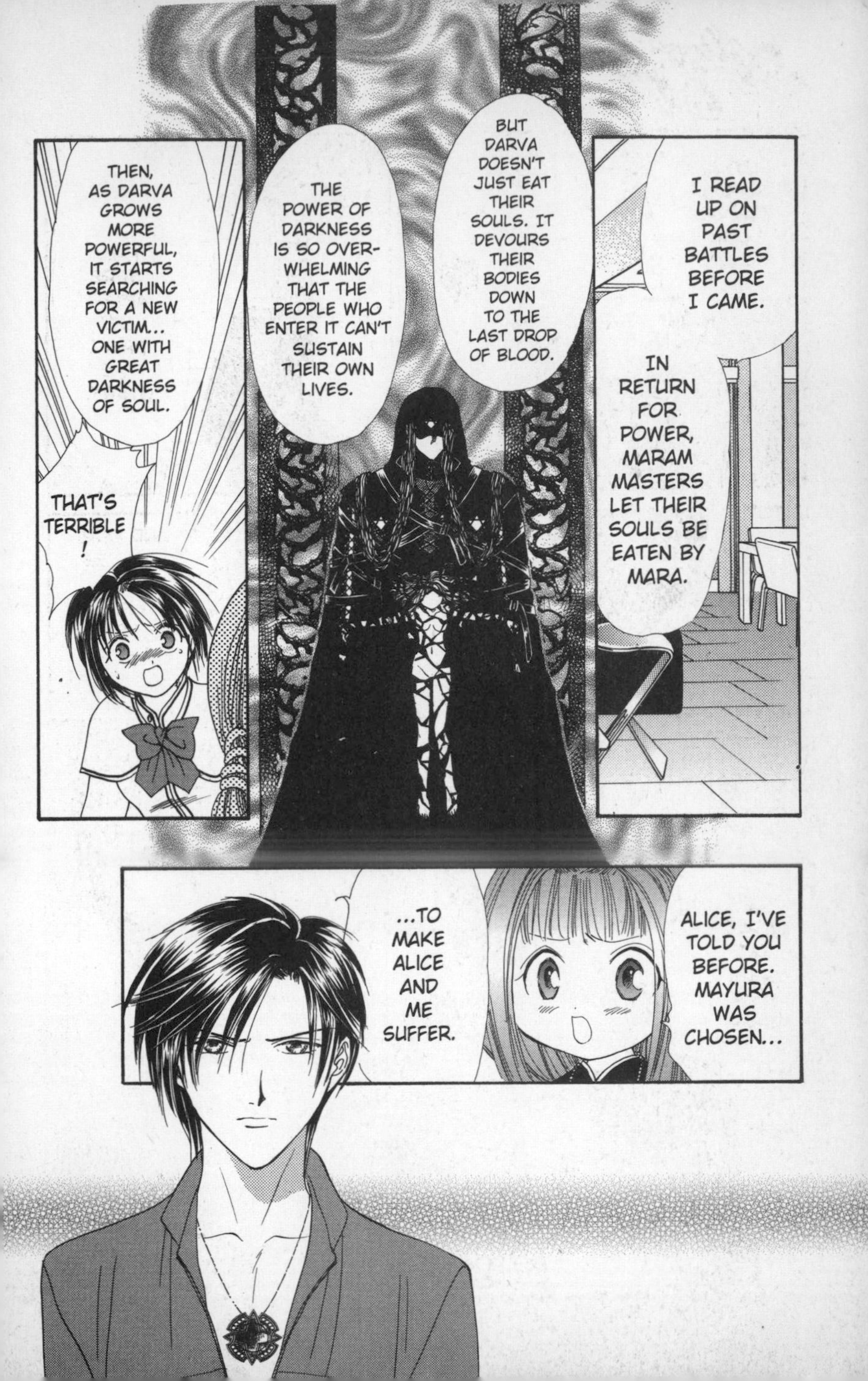
I READ UP ON PAST BATTLES BEFORE I CAME.
IN RETURN FOR POWER, MARAM MASTERS LET THEIR SOULS BE EATEN BY MARA.
BUT DARVA DOESN'T JUST EAT THEIR SOULS. IT DEVOURS THEIR BODIES DOWN TO THE LAST DROP OF BLOOD.
THE POWER OF DARKNESS IS SO OVER-WHELMING THAT THE PEOPLE WHO ENTER IT CAN'T SUSTAIN THEIR OWN LIVES.
THEN, AS DARVA GROWS MORE POWERFUL, IT STARTS SEARCHING FOR A NEW VICTIM... ONE WITH GREAT DARKNESS OF SOUL.
THAT'S TERRIBLE!
ALICE, I'VE TOLD YOU BEFORE. MAYURA WAS CHOSEN...
...TO MAKE ALICE AND ME SUFFER.

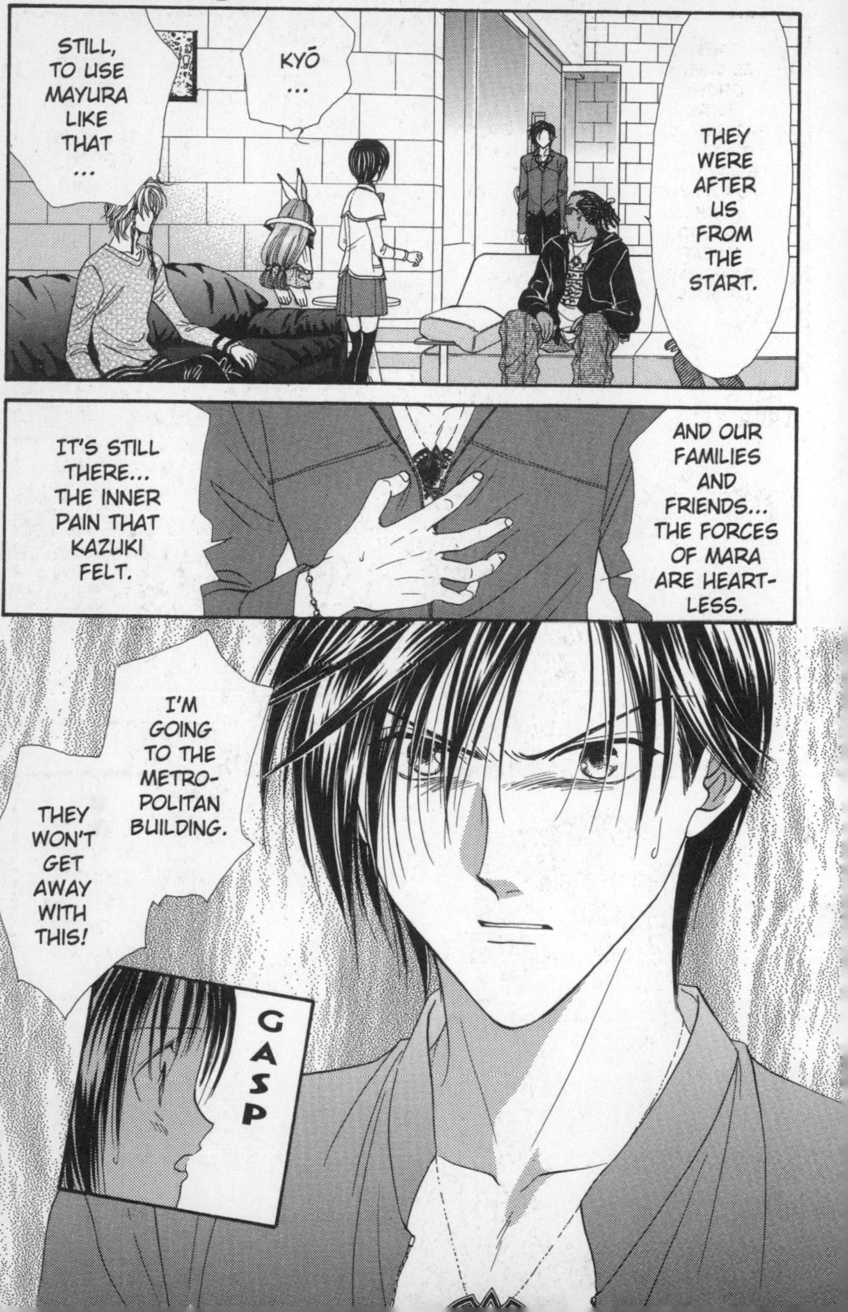
THEY WERE AFTER US FROM THE START.
KYŌ ...
STILL, TO USE MAYURA LIKE THAT ...
AND OUR FAMILIES AND FRIENDS... THE FORCES OF MARA ARE HEART-LESS.
IT'S STILL THERE... THE INNER PAIN THAT KAZUKI FELT.
I'M GOING TO THE METRO-POLITAN BUILDING.
THEY WON'T GET AWAY WITH THIS!
GASP

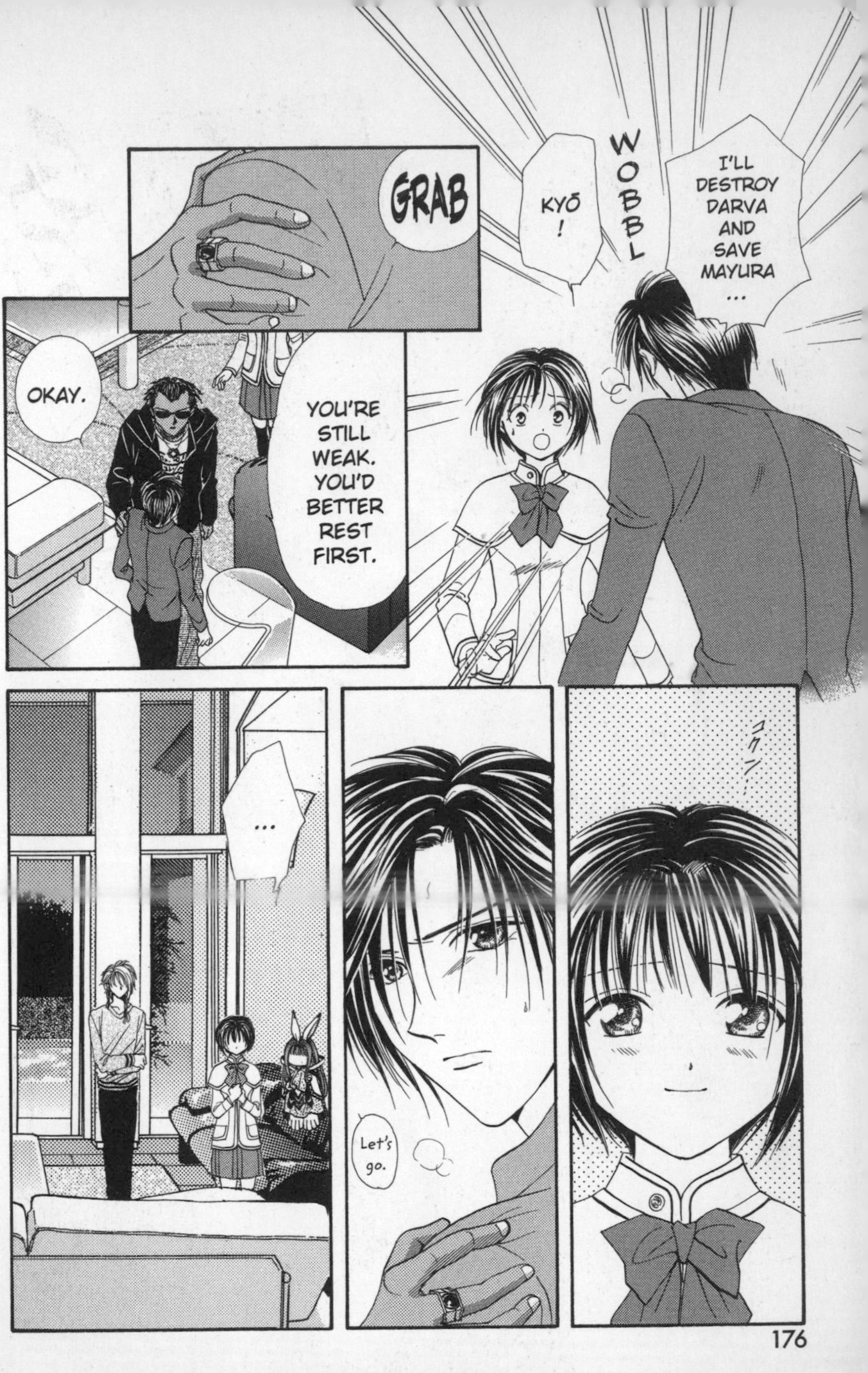
I'LL DESTROY DARVA AND SAVE MAYURA ...
WOBBL
KYŌ!
GRAB
YOU'RE STILL WEAK. YOU'D BETTER REST FIRST.
OKAY.
Let's go.
...

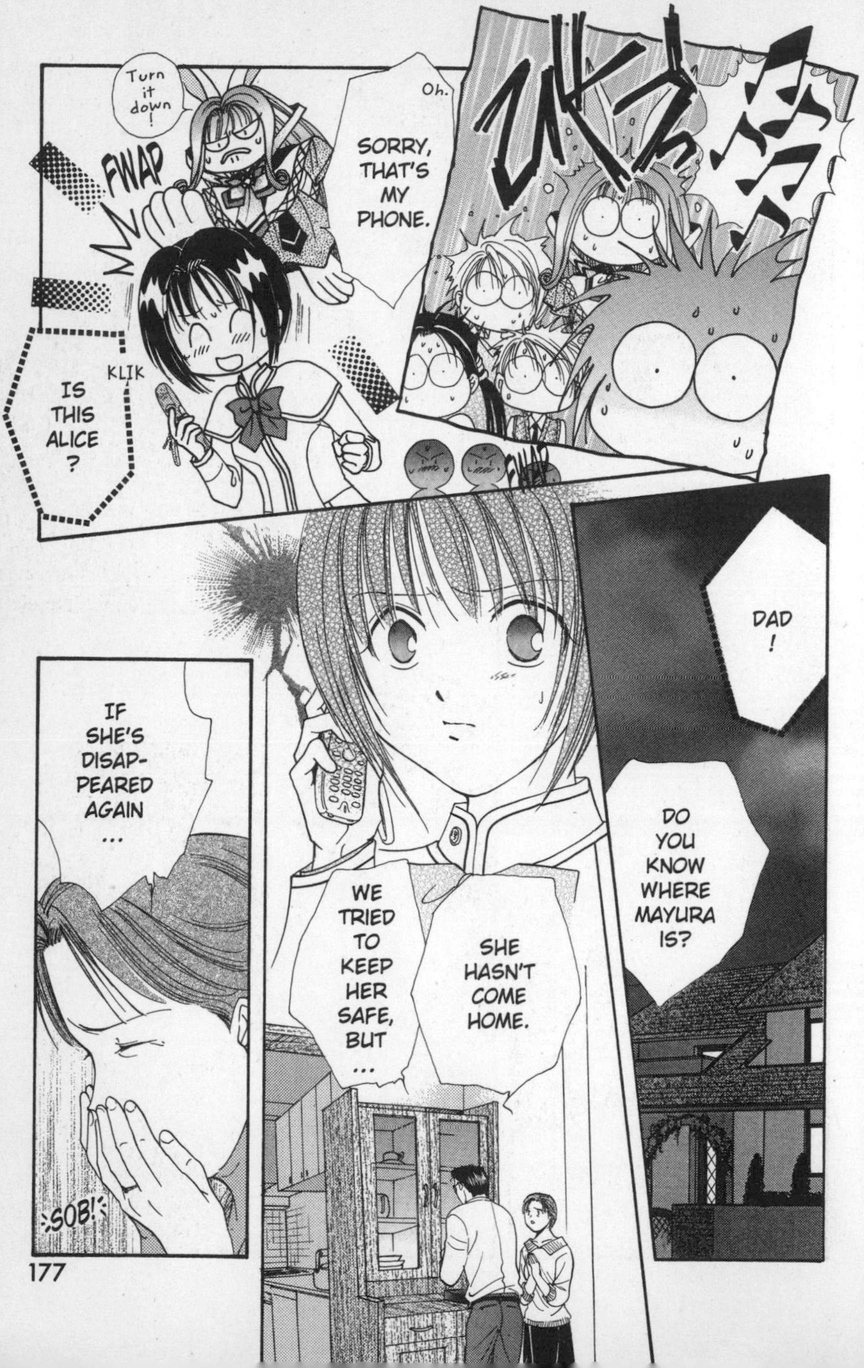
FWAP
Oh.
SORRY, THAT'S MY PHONE.
Turn it down!
FWAP
KLIK
IS THIS ALICE?
DAD!
DO YOU KNOW WHERE MAYURA IS?
SHE HASN'T COME HOME.
WE TRIED TO KEEP HER SAFE, BUT ...
IF SHE'S DISAP-PEARED AGAIN ...
SOB!

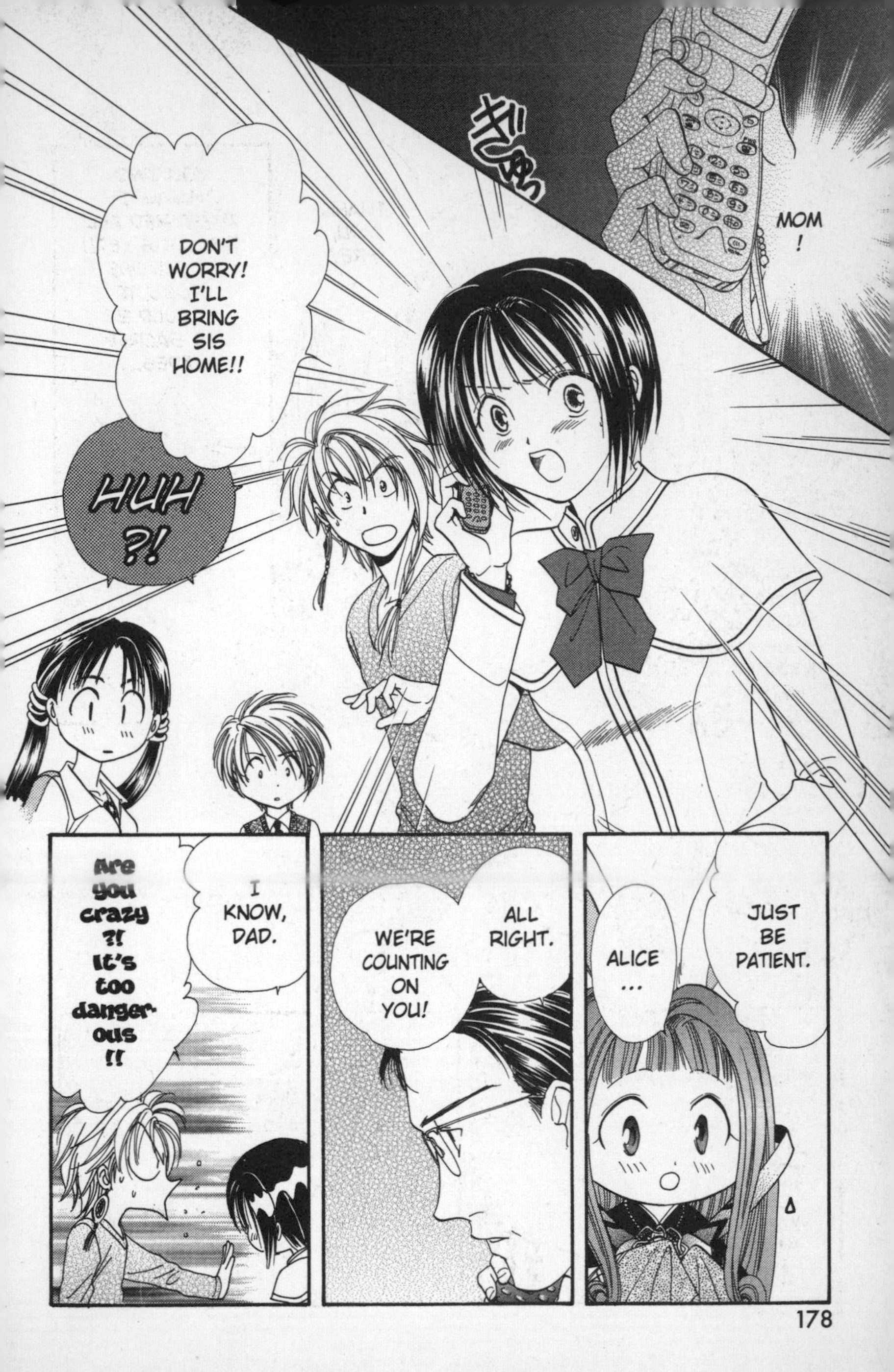
MOM!
DON'T WORRY! I'LL BRING SIS HOME!!
HUH ?!
JUST BE PATIENT.
ALICE ...
ALL RIGHT.
WE'RE COUNTING ON YOU!
I KNOW, DAD.
Are you crazy?! It's too danger-ous!!

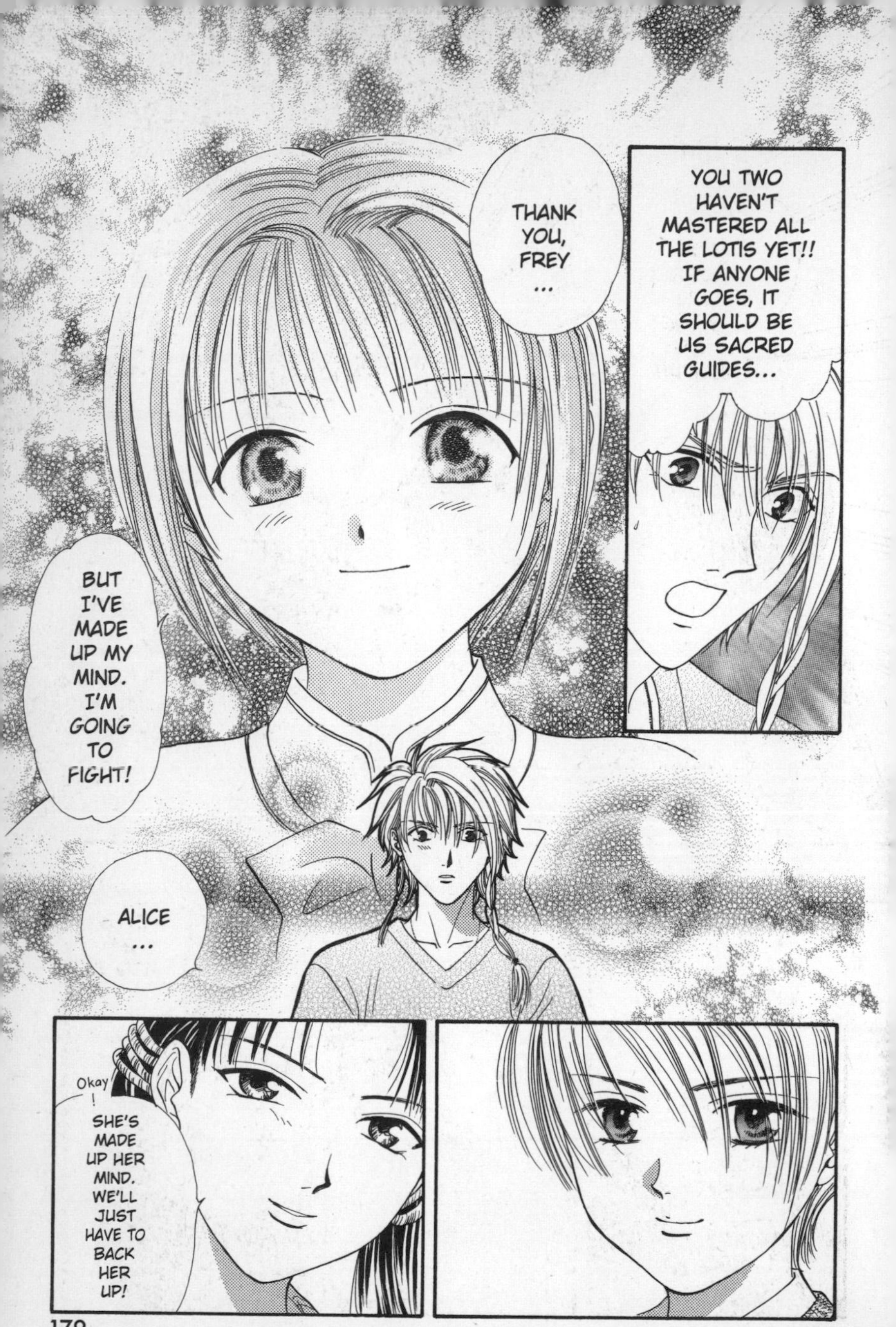
YOU TWO HAVEN'T MASTERED ALL THE LOTIS YET!! IF ANYONE GOES, IT SHOULD BE US SACRED GUIDES...
THANK YOU, FREY ...
BUT I'VE MADE UP MY MIND. I'M GOING TO FIGHT!
ALICE ...
Okay!
SHE'S MADE UP HER MIND. WE'LL JUST HAVE TO BACK HER UP!

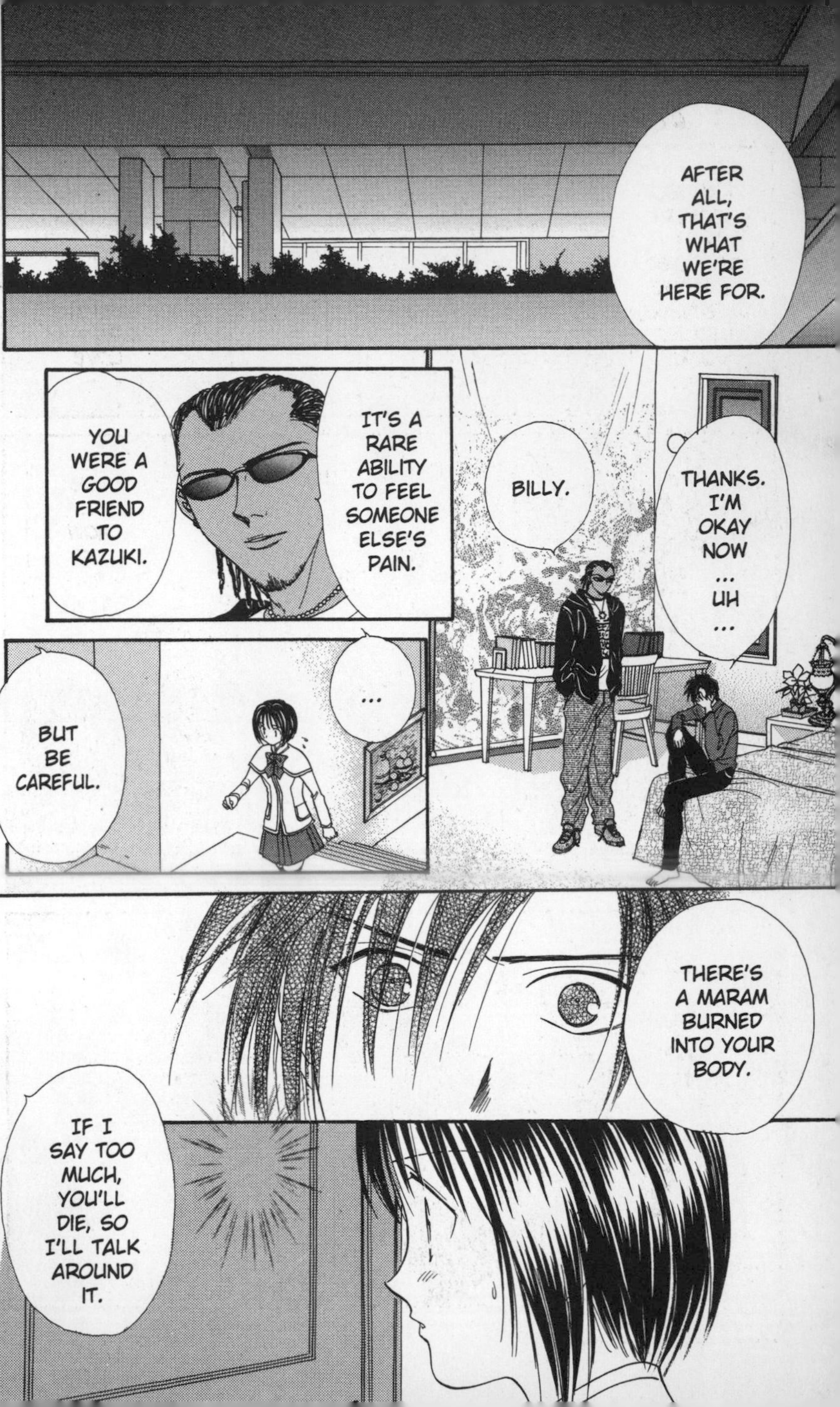
AFTER ALL, THAT'S WHAT WE'RE HERE FOR.
THANKS. I'M OKAY NOW ... UH ...
BILLY.
IT'S A RARE ABILITY TO FEEL SOMEONE ELSE'S PAIN.
YOU WERE A GOOD FRIEND TO KAZUKI.
...
BUT BE CAREFUL.
THERE'S A MARAM BURNED INTO YOUR BODY.
IF I SAY TOO MUCH, YOU'LL DIE, SO I'LL TALK AROUND IT.

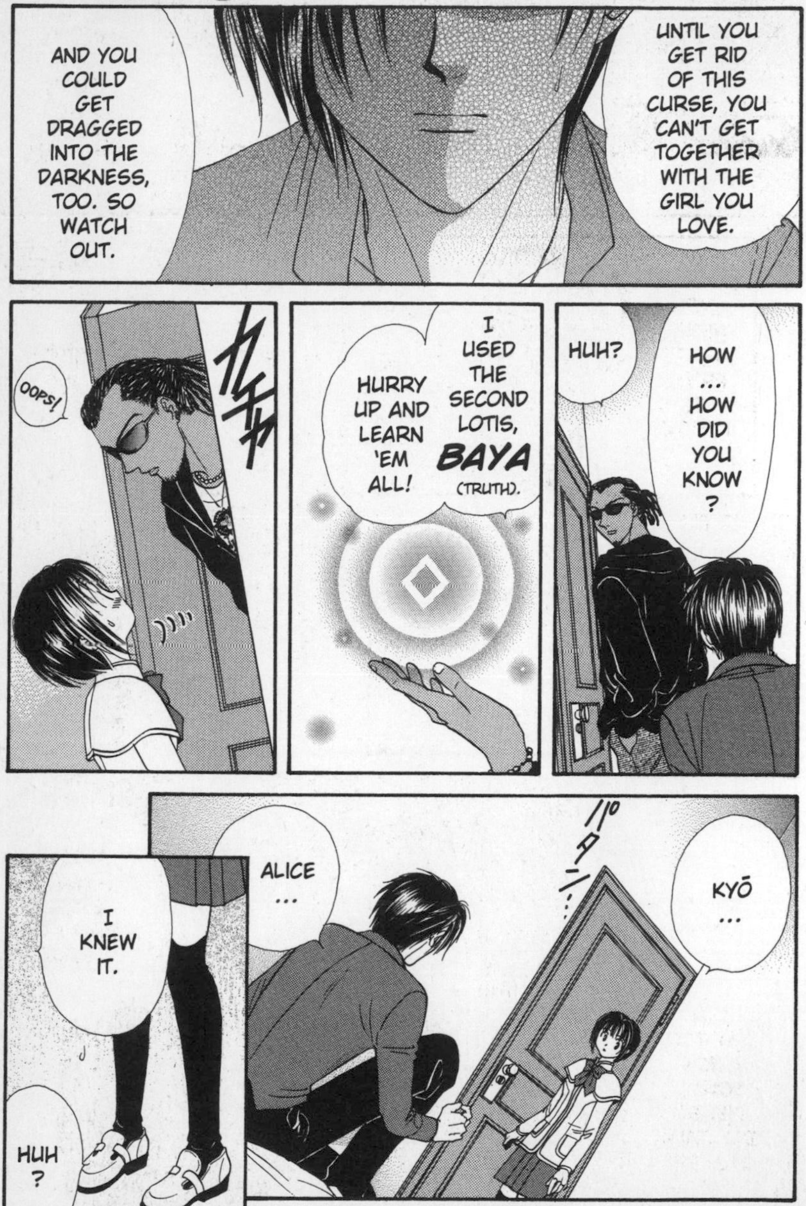
UNTIL YOU GET RID OF THIS CURSE, YOU CAN'T GET TOGETHER WITH THE GIRL YOU LOVE.
AND YOU COULD GET DRAGGED INTO THE DARKNESS, TOO. SO WATCH OUT.
HOW ... HOW DID YOU KNOW ?
HUH?
I USED THE SECOND LOTIS, BAYA (TRUTH).
HURRY UP AND LEARN 'EM ALL!
カチャ
OOPS!
KYŌ ...
パタン
ALICE ...
I KNEW IT.
HUH ?

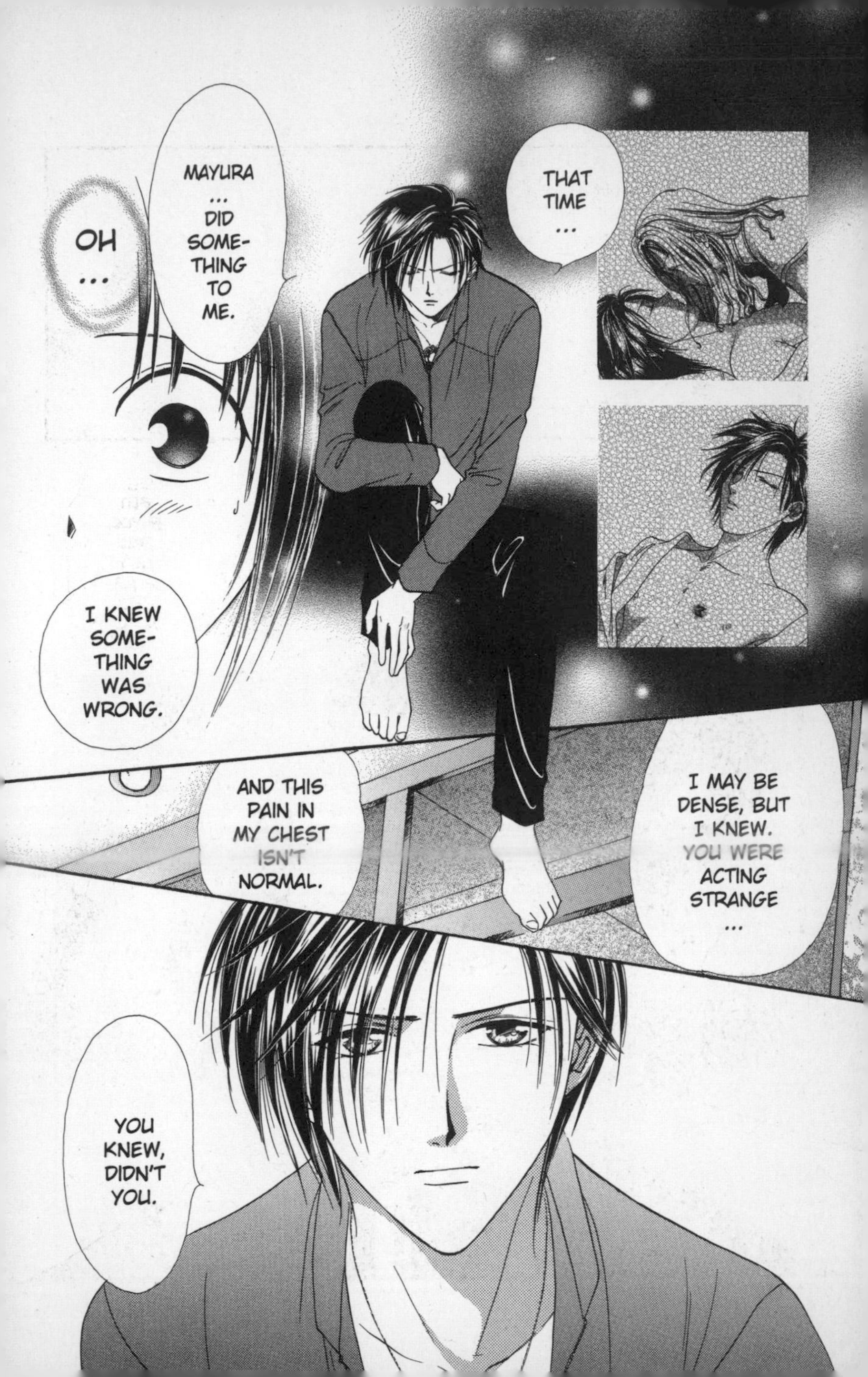
THAT TIME ...
MAYURA ... DID SOMETHING TO ME.
OH ...
I KNEW SOMETHING WAS WRONG.
I MAY BE DENSE, BUT I KNEW. YOU WERE ACTING STRANGE ...
AND THIS PAIN IN MY CHEST ISN'T NORMAL.
YOU KNEW, DIDN'T YOU.

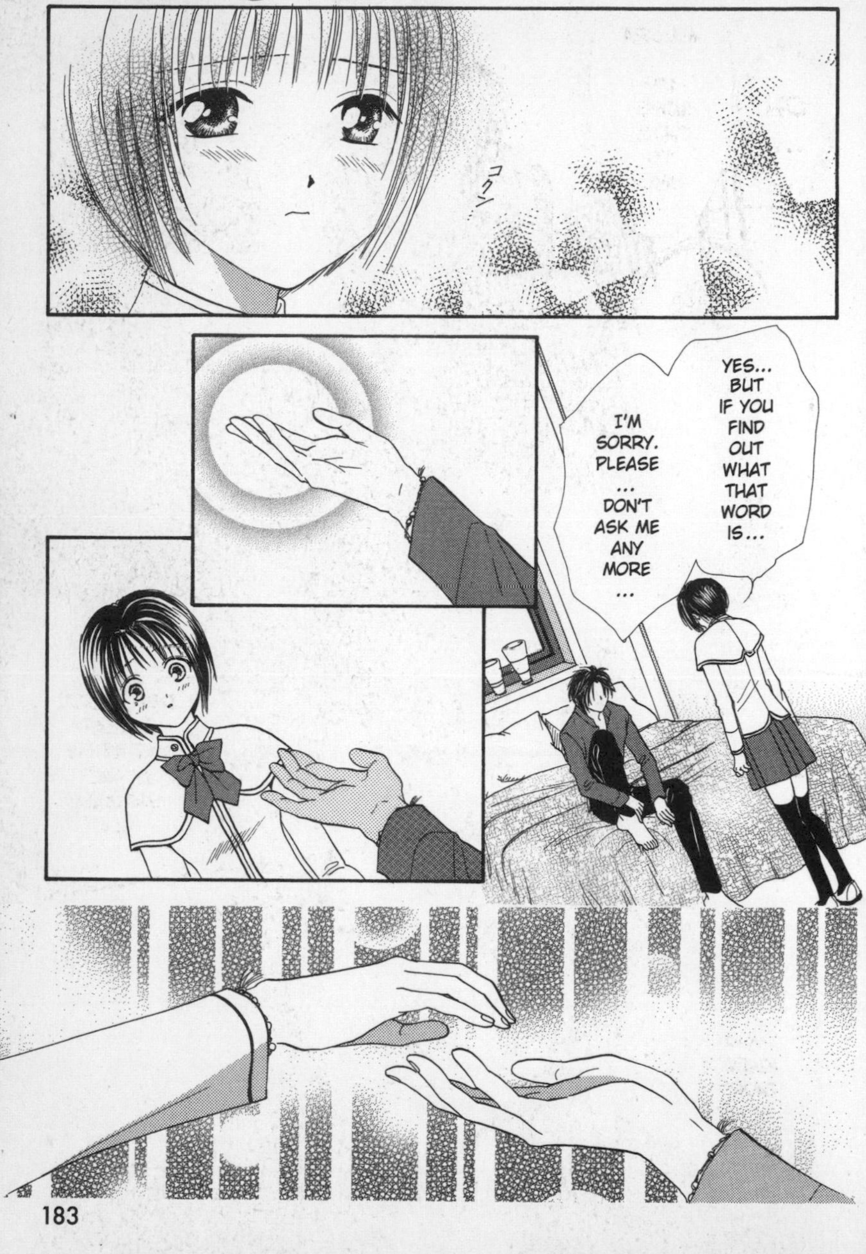
コクン
YES... BUT IF YOU FIND OUT WHAT THAT WORD IS...
I'M SORRY. PLEASE ... DON'T ASK ME ANY MORE ...

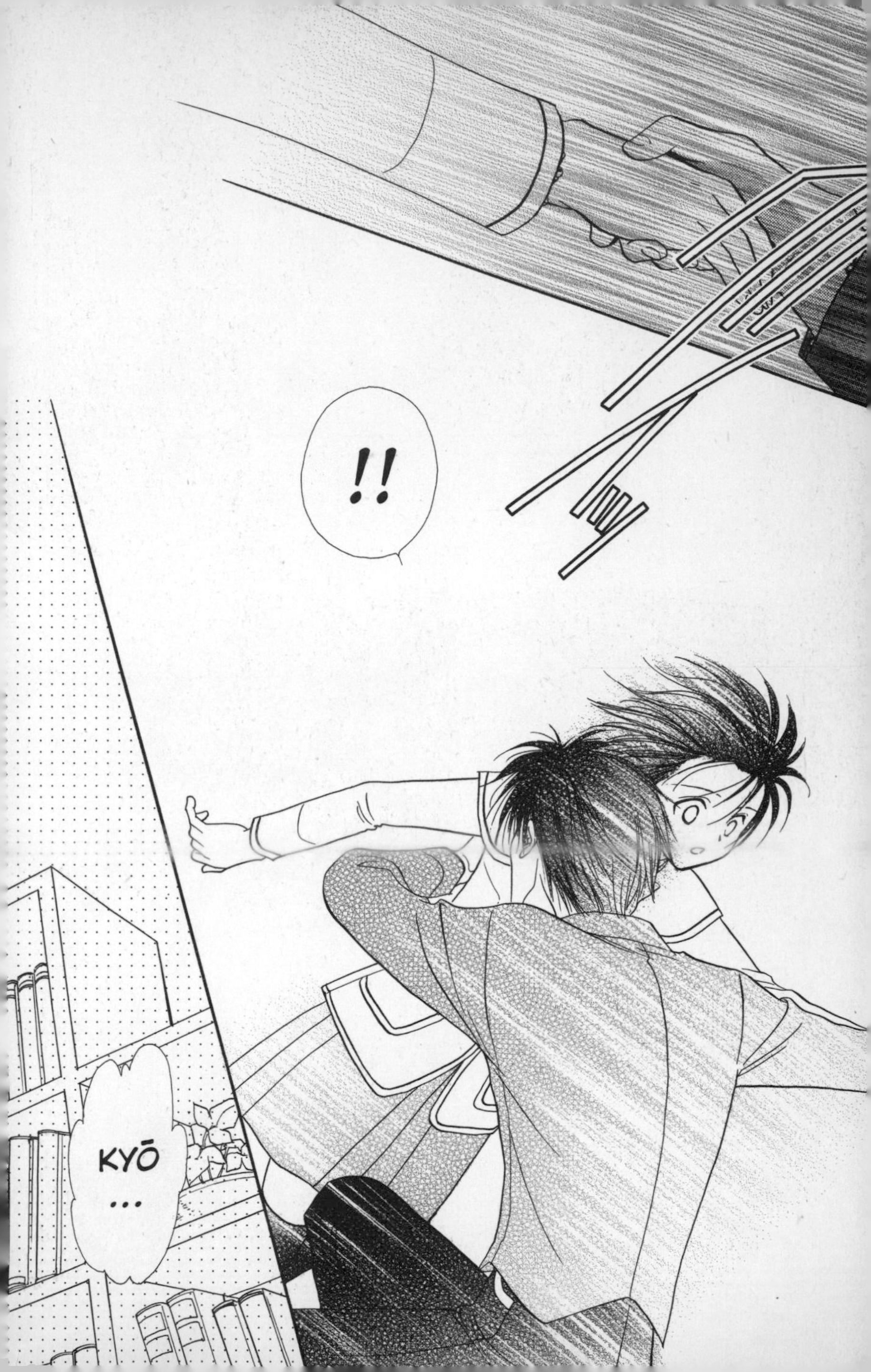
!!
KYŌ
...

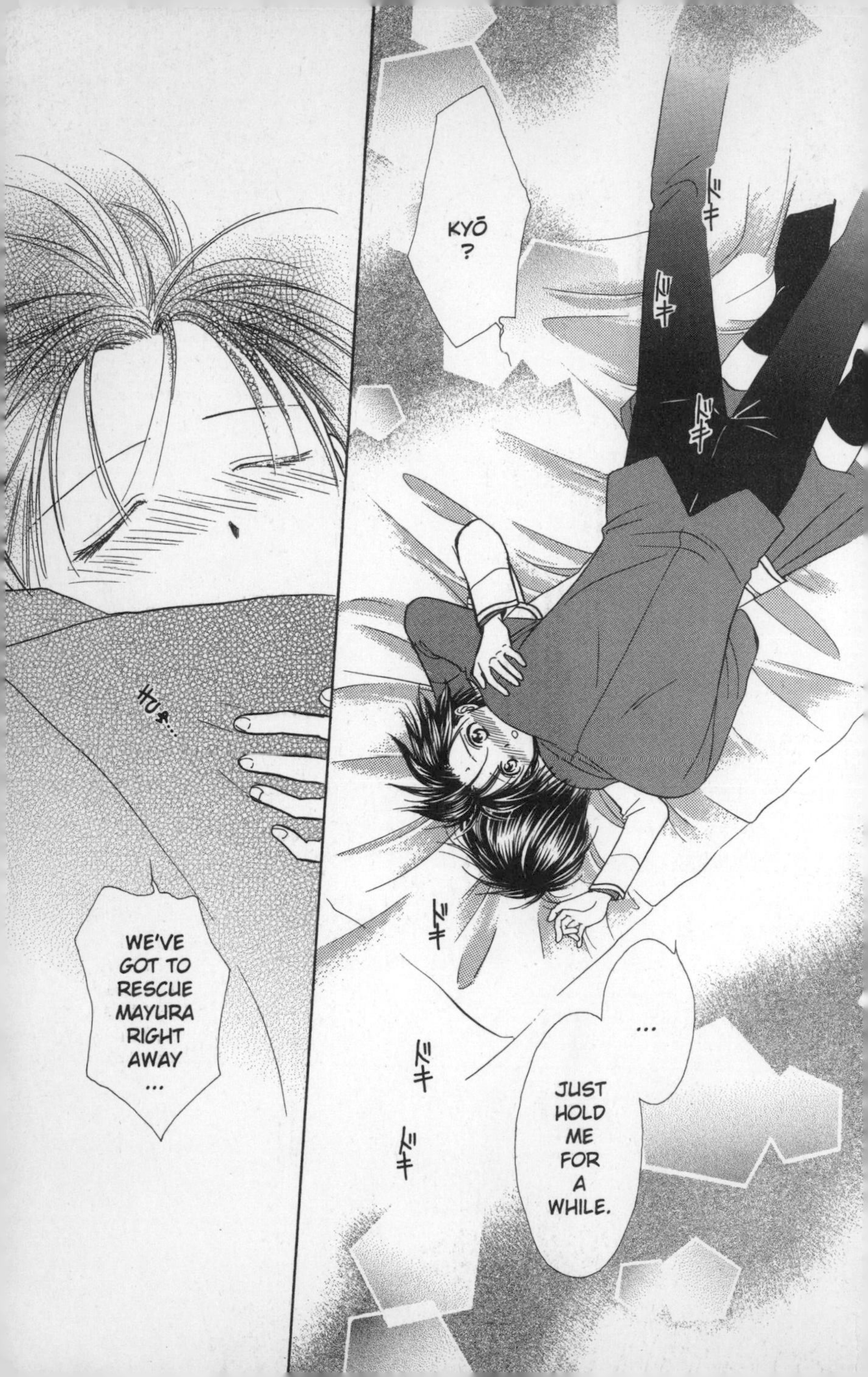
KYŌ?
... JUST HOLD ME FOR A WHILE.
WE'VE GOT TO RESCUE MAYURA RIGHT AWAY...

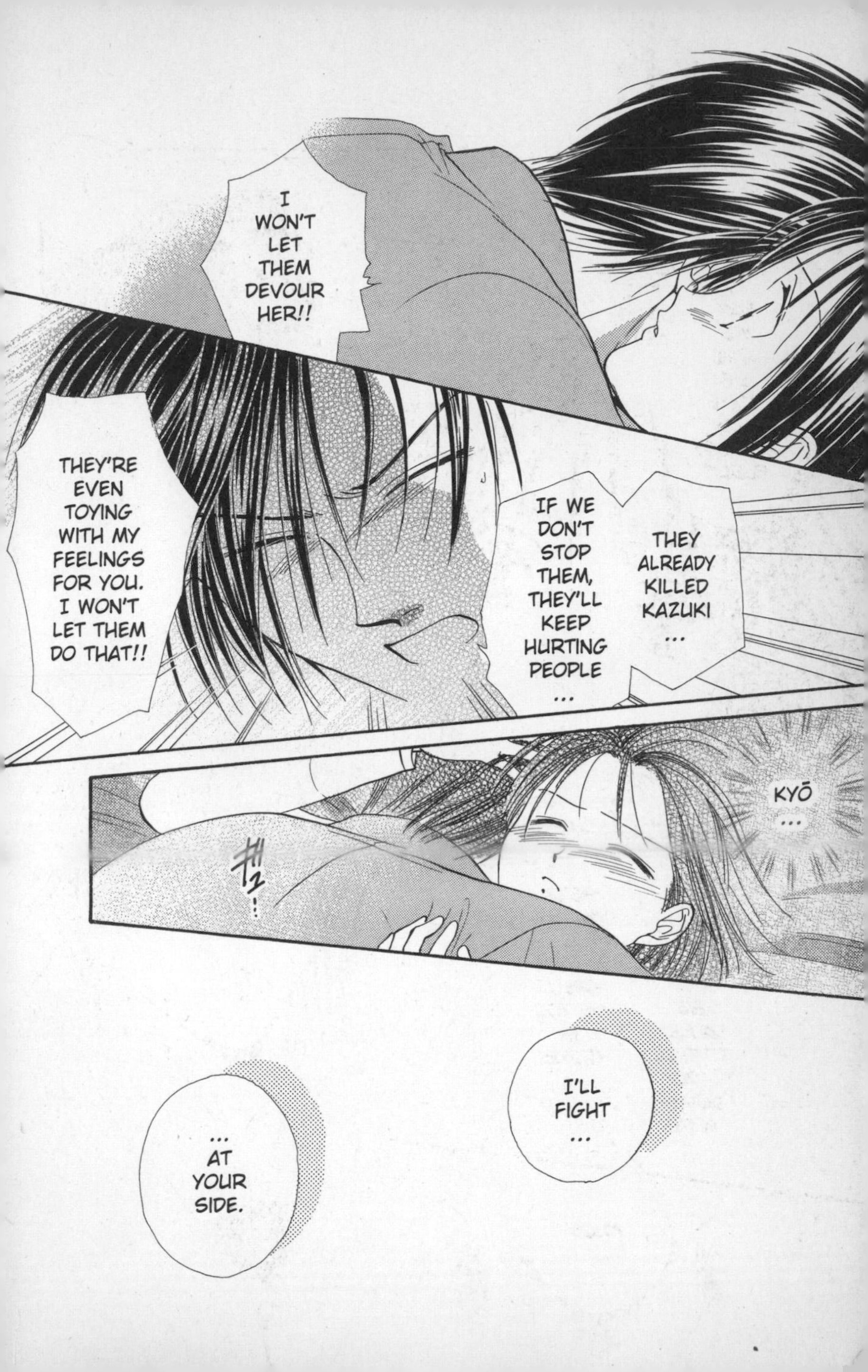
I WON'T LET THEM DEVOUR HER!!
THEY ALREADY KILLED KAZUKI ...
IF WE DON'T STOP THEM, THEY'LL KEEP HURTING PEOPLE ...
THEY'RE EVEN TOYING WITH MY FEELINGS FOR YOU. I WON'T LET THEM DO THAT!!
KYŌ ...
I'LL FIGHT ...
... AT YOUR SIDE.

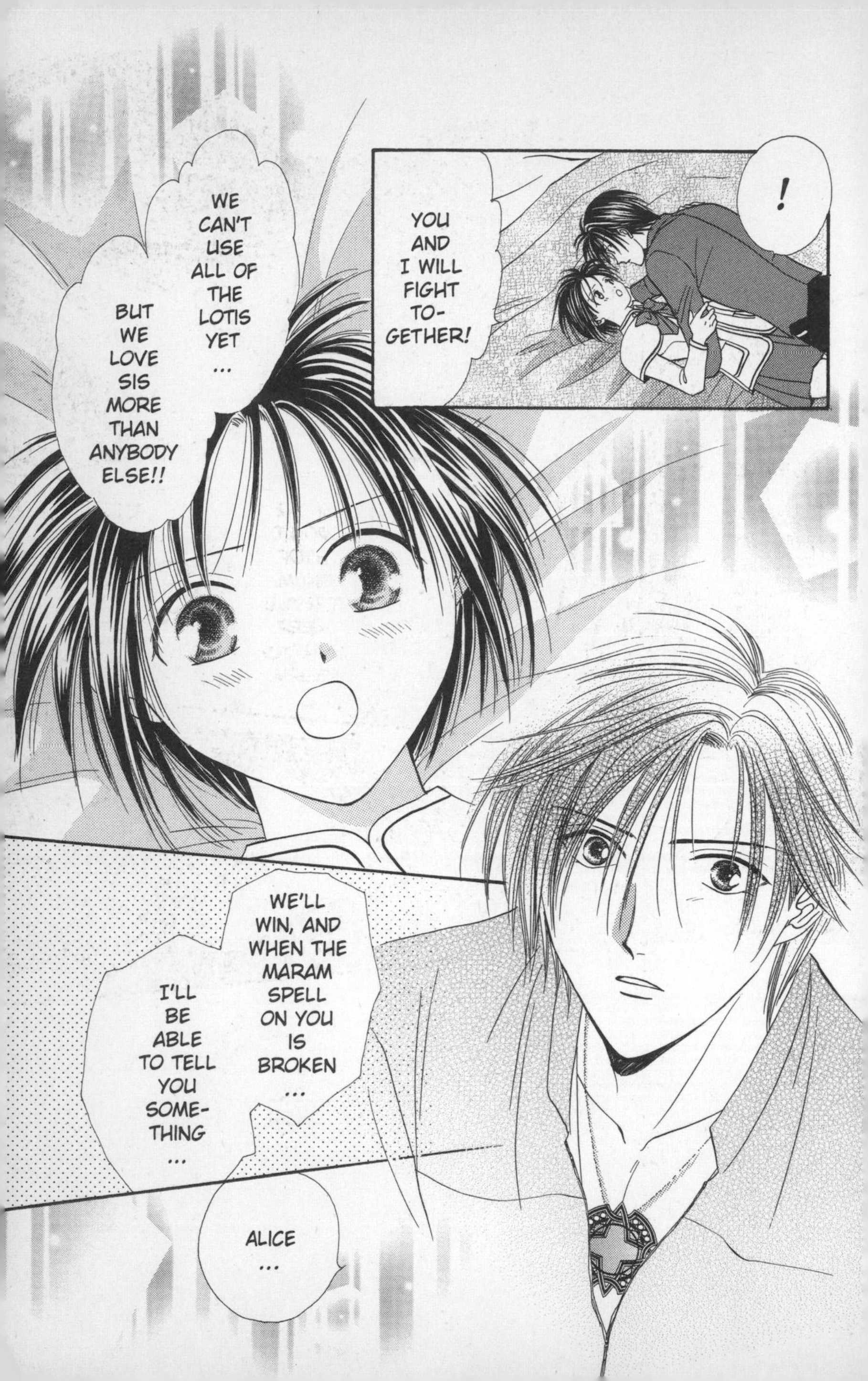
!
YOU AND I WILL FIGHT TO-GETHER!
WE CAN'T USE ALL OF THE LOTIS YET ...
BUT WE LOVE SIS MORE THAN ANYBODY ELSE!!
WE'LL WIN, AND WHEN THE MARAM SPELL ON YOU IS BROKEN ...
I'LL BE ABLE TO TELL YOU SOME-THING ...
ALICE ...

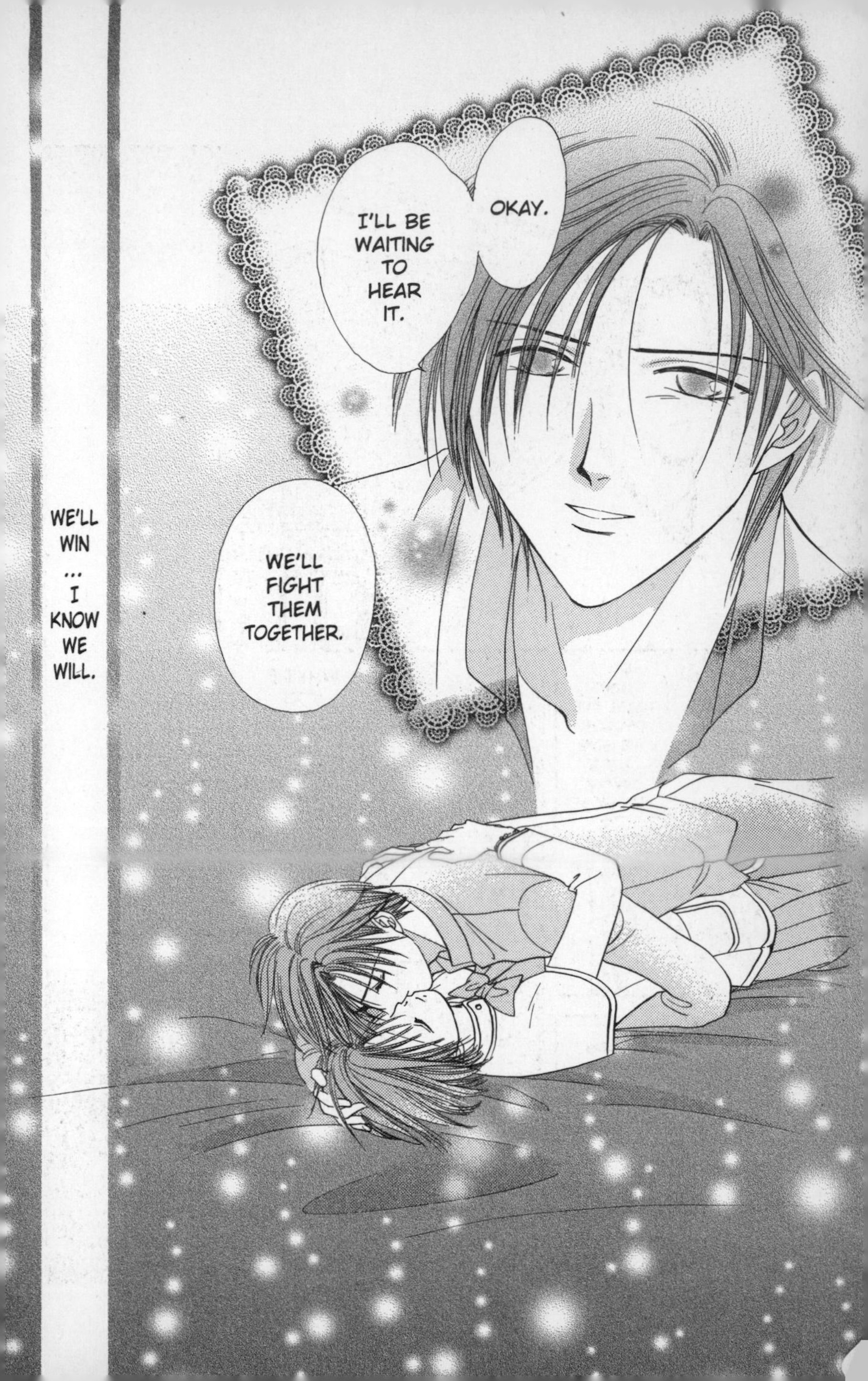
OKAY.
I'LL BE WAITING TO HEAR IT.
WE'LL FIGHT THEM TOGETHER.
WE'LL WIN ... I KNOW WE WILL.

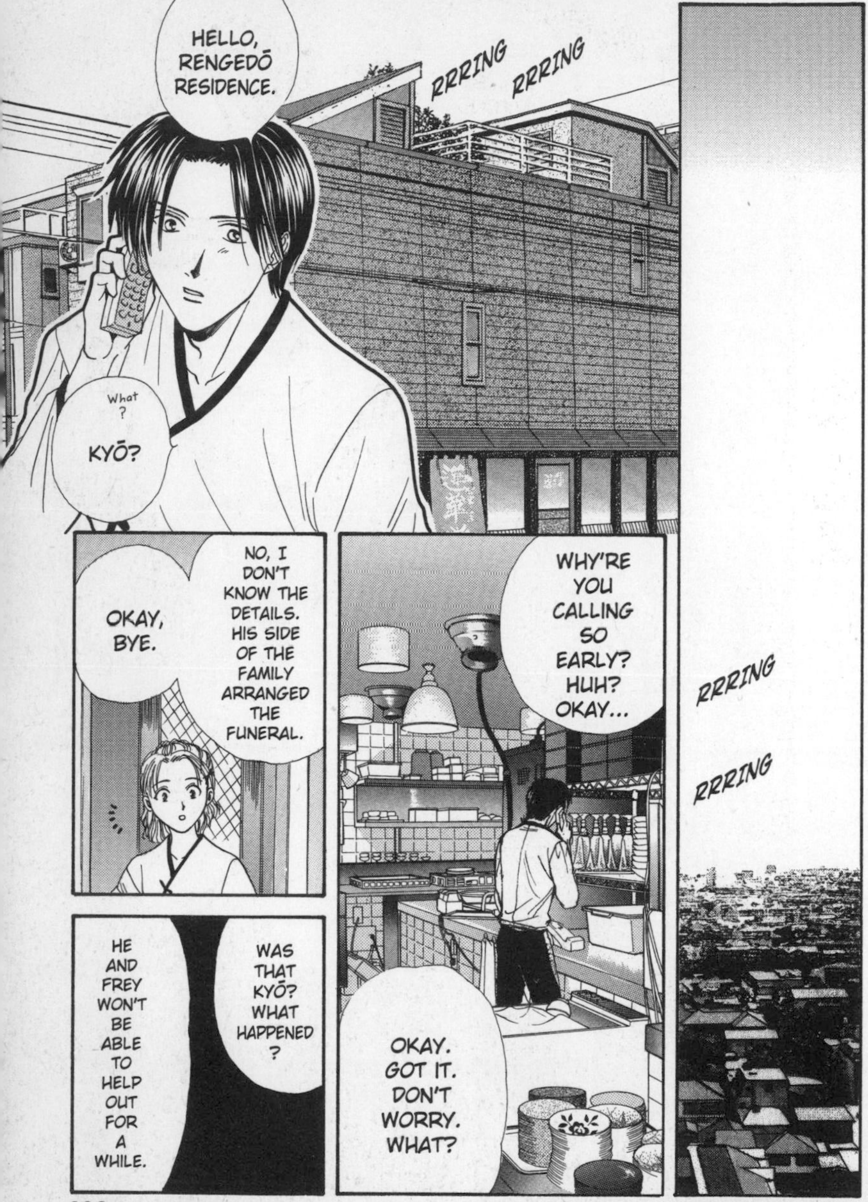
RRRING
RRRING
RRRING
RRRING
HELLO, RENGEDŌ RESIDENCE.
What?
KYŌ?
WHY'RE YOU CALLING SO EARLY? HUH? OKAY...
OKAY. GOT IT. DON'T WORRY. WHAT?
NO, I DON'T KNOW THE DETAILS. HIS SIDE OF THE FAMILY ARRANGED THE FUNERAL.
OKAY, BYE.
WAS THAT KYŌ? WHAT HAPPENED?
HE AND FREY WON'T BE ABLE TO HELP OUT FOR A WHILE.

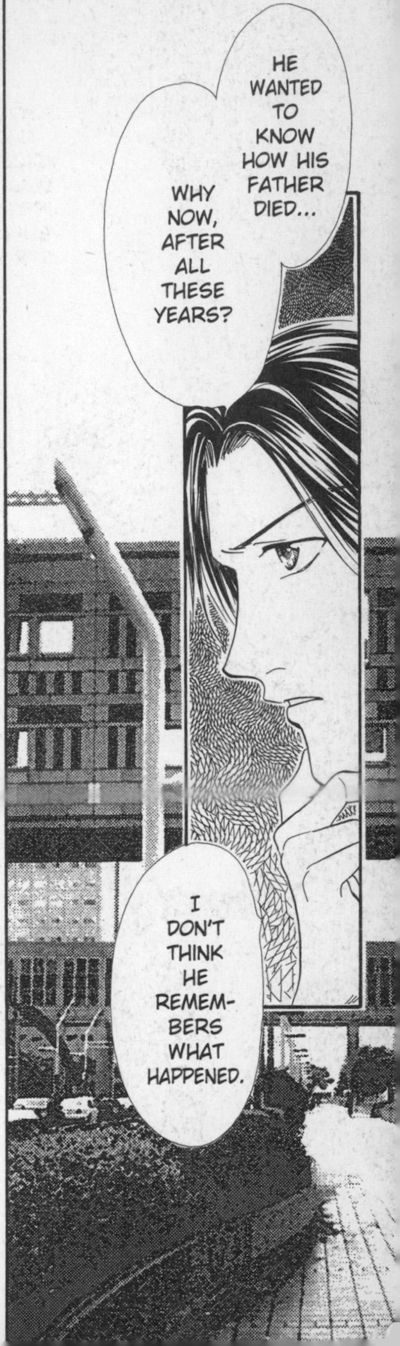
HE WANTED TO KNOW HOW HIS FATHER DIED...
WHY NOW, AFTER ALL THESE YEARS?
I DON'T THINK HE REMEMBERS WHAT HAPPENED.
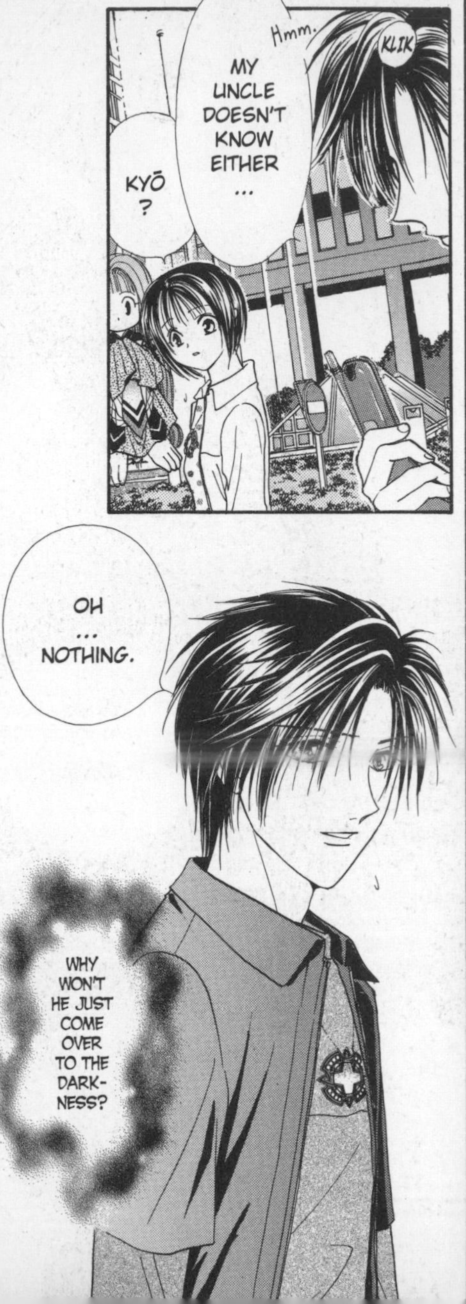
KLIK
Hmm.
MY UNCLE DOESN'T KNOW EITHER ...
KYŌ ?
OH ... NOTHING.
WHY WON'T HE JUST COME OVER TO THE DARKNESS?

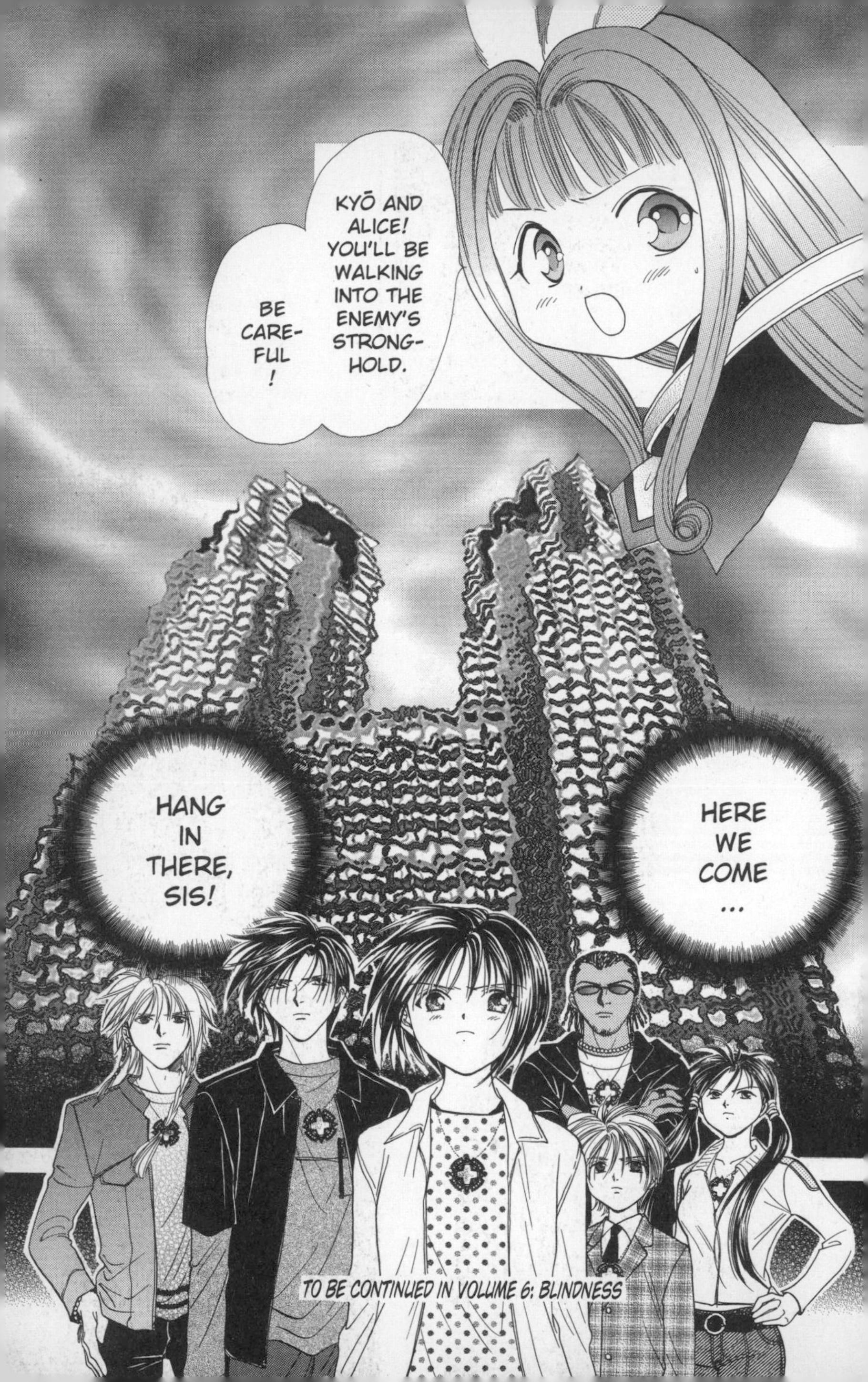
KYŌ AND ALICE! YOU'LL BE WALKING INTO THE ENEMY'S STRONGHOLD.
BE CAREFUL!
HERE WE COME ...
HANG IN THERE, SIS!
TO BE CONTINUED IN VOLUME 6: BLINDNESS

EDITOR'S NOTE

Everyone knows the old adage, "sticks and stones may break my bones, but words will never hurt me," but most people would agree that it's hardly true. Words are capable of causing deep emotional injuries, and that inner pain can take much longer to recover from than physical blows. The power of the Maram and Lotis in *Alice 19th* show us – metaphorically – that words are capable not only of wounding, but of healing as well. Alice's experiences inspire us to speak out with messages of encouragement and love, and to think twice before saying things that are vindictive, petty, and cruel. (Oops, I sound like a saccharine schoolmarm – maybe this is a heretofore hidden part of my personality that's finally revealing itself!)

Alice's relationship with Mayura reminds me a little of the troubles my older sister and I had when I was in junior high. We never fought over a guy, and of course I never sent my sister into the clutches of a demonic presence, but I did struggle with feelings of jealousy and alienation as my sister began to grow up and date boys. It seemed like she was leaving me behind, and I sometimes felt that she must be under the control of dark forces! We're now good friends, but I think I had to become an adult on my own before we could learn to appreciate one another again.

—Frances E. Wall
Editor, *Alice 19th*

If you're enjoying this story and are in the mood for more, here are three manga titles that you should check out:

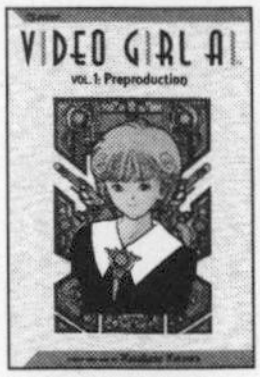

VIDEO GIRL AI
VOL. 1: Preproduction

VIDEO GIRL AI When Moemi, the object of Yota's incurable crush, turns out to be in love with the dashing and popular Takashi, poor Yota is devastated. He rents a video to distract himself, but Ai, the hottie featured on the tape, magically bursts out of the TV and into Yota's world. Ai's mission is to fix Yota's hopeless love life, but when Ai develops romantic feelings towards Yota, things get complicated. A true manga classic, sweet and hilarious!

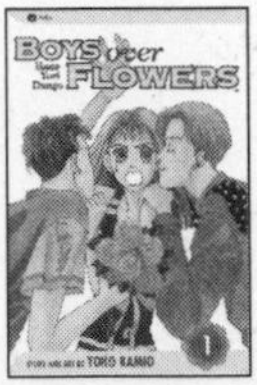

BOYS over FLOWERS

BOYS OVER FLOWERS (Hana yori Dango) Tsukishi Makino is a young girl who is entering a prestigious high school that only the richest, most elite students attend. She's from a middle-class family, though, and feels more than a little out of place. Tsukishi is happy being a fly on the wall until one day, when she sticks up for her friend to the coolest, most influential gang at the school, known as the F4. Now on their hit list, the entire school rejects her! Rather than flee the scene, Tsukishi fights back and discovers her own inner strength.

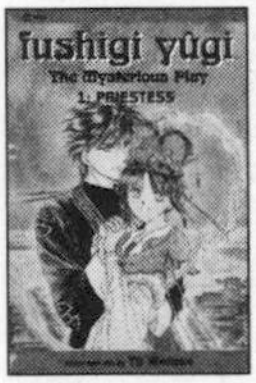

fushigi yûgi
The Mysterious Play
1: PRIESTESS

FUSHIGI YÛGI An innocent girl named Miaka Yûki is magically transported to the Universe of the Four Gods by opening up an ancient book. Helpless and in danger in this ancient world, she is rescued by the handsome Tamahome, whom she will fall in love with. This magical world is based in ancient Chinese legend, and is filled with action, romance, and love triangles unimaginable. Another fantasy Shôjo brought to you by Yû Watase!

Glossary of Sound Effects, Signs, and other Miscellaneous Notes

Each entry includes: the location, indicated by page number and panel number (so 3.1 means page 3, panel number 1); the phonetic romanization of the original Japanese; and our English "translation"—we offer as close an English equivalent as we can.

47.4——FX: Gui! (grab)

49.2——FX: Bishi (crack)

49.3——FX: Doki–! (heartbeat)

50.1——FX: Ji–n... (stunned silence)

51.1——FX: Kusha (fingers ruffling hair)

53.3——FX: Kira–n (gleaming with joy)

55.4——FX: Dohn! (whap)

65.3——Sign: Akatsuki Public School, Meido Campus

66.3——FX: Dokin (heartbeat)

68.2——FX: Dokun (heartbeat)

68.3——FX: Piku! (twitch)

69——FX: Dokun dokun dokun (heartbeats)

71.3——FX: Zuzazazaza (footsteps running away)

72.1——FX: Doki doki doki (fast heartbeats)

73.1——FX: Sui... (turning away)

73.4——Signs: Ramen shop, Yoshinoya Beef Bowl restaurant

78.2——FX: Ban (bang)

78.4——FX: Za! (thud)

79.1——FX: Pi–! (someone flying through the air)

79.3——FX: Pi–! (flying through the air)

79.4——FX: Da! (dash)

5.4——FX: Ga! (hand grabbing counter)

6.4/5——FX: Dokun (heartbeat)

7.1——FX: Dokun (heartbeat)

7.2——FX: Dokun (heartbeat)

7.3——FX: Zawa! (ooooh)

7.3——FX: Dokun (heartbeat)

8.1——FX: Gataan! (crash)

10.3——FX: Bashi (boom)

13.1——FX: Gu! (clenching fist)

16.3——FX: Koku... (nod)

22.1——FX: Gal (grab)

22.2——FX: Doka (crash)

22.3——FX: Za! (doom)

24.5——FX: Gacha (door opening)

24.6——FX: Ga! (smack/punch)

26.4——FX: Doka! (crash)

35.3——FX: Koh! Koh! (rronk, rronk)

35.4——FX: Koh... (rrronk)

39.1——FX: Gabah! (thrashing awake)

39.5——FX: Pokan... (confusion)

40.4——FX: Su... (releasing shirt from grip)

45.4——FX: Chira (glance)

46.5——FX: Kokun... (nod)

80—FX: Ta–n (sproing)

81.1—FX: Suta... (soft landing)

82.1—FX: Dowa! (shock!)

82.2—FX: Byun! (fwoosh)

85.2—FX: Ka–n ko–n (clanging of school bell)

85.3—FX: Pon (grasping shoulder)

85.4—FX: Gakkuri (sobbing)

86.1—FX: Zaaa (water running)

86.2—FX: Basha basha basha (splashing water)

86.4—FX: Haah! (gasp)

87.1—FX: Zoku! (startle)

88.1—FX: Supan (thunk of arrow in target)

89.3—FX: Pi–... (someone flying through the air)

89.4—FX: Za! (thud)

89.6—FX: Dosun (collapse)

91.3—FX: Su... (door slides open)

93.1—FX: Dokun dokun dokun (heartbeats)

93.2—FX: Dokun dokun (heartbeats)

93.4—FX: Dokun dokun (heartbeats)

94.3—FX: Gui (turning her head forcefully)

96.2—FX: Fuu... (sigh)

97.1—FX: Patata patata (wings flapping)

97.2—FX: Ha! (sharp intake of breath)

99.2—FX: Gui! (yank)

99.3—FX: Biku! (eyes widen in horror)

99.5—FX: Patata pata (wings flapping)

101.5—FX: Goh! (bang)

102.1—FX: Doka! (crashing into wall)

102.3—FX: Zuru... (sliding to the floor)

102.4—FX: Gi! (fierce glare)

103.4—FX: Za! (dashing off)

103.5—FX: Ban! (door flung open)

105.2—FX: Dohn (bumping shoulders)

106.1—FX: Dokun (heartbeat)

106.2—FX: Dosa... (bag slides to floor)

106.5—FX: Su... (Maram mark fades from his hand)

107.3—FX: Ba! (jolted upright)

107.6—FX: Poro poro poro (tears falling)

108.2—FX: Gyu...! (squeezing each other)

109.3—FX: Gaba (bolting up and away from each other)

109.4—FX: Bata bata bata (footsteps running away)

112.3—FX: Bofu! (pillow smacks Nyozeka)

115.3—FX: Pita... (silence and stunned staring)

116.1—FX: Hiso hiso hiso (whispering)

117.4—FX: Gata gata... (chairs scraping across floor as students get seated)

117.6—FX: Ka–n ko–n... (ringing of school bells)

118.1—FX: Soro... (slowly turning)

119.1—Sign: Conference Room

119.4—FX: Pisha... (door clicks shut)

120.3—FX: Basa basa!
(trash falls on her head)

120.5—FX: Hiso hiso hiso hiso hiso hiso
(whispering)

120.5—FX: Kusu kusu kusu kusu (snickering)

121.3—FX: Dohn (nudge)

121.4—FX: Gu... (clenching fist)

121.5—FX: Hiso hiso hiso hiso hiso hiso
(whispering)

124.1 —FX: Shin... (utter silence)

124.2—FX: Su! (Alice shows up)

126.2—FX: Gyu... (grip tightens)

130.1 —FX: Ki! (intense glare)

131.3—FX: Su! (removing mask)

131.4—FX: Gan (smash)

131.5—FX: Kararara...
(mask rattling on the ground)

131.5—FX: Kotsu... (mask clinks to a stop)

133.1 —FX: Gyuu... (clenching fist)

135.4—FX: Su! (hands slip around her neck)

135.4—FX: Doki... (heartbeat)

136.4—FX: Fu! (sneaking around corner)

138.2—Sign: Akatsuki Public School,
Meido Campus

138.6—FX: Pon
(hand claps down on shoulder)

138.6—FX: Doki! (heartbeat)

139.1 —FX: Gatata!
(putting Lotis word notes away hastily)

140.2—FX: Ka–n ko–n (school bells ringing)

141.2—FX: Pishan (door slamming shut)

141.3—FX: Pishan (door slamming shut)

142.2—FX: Gacha (door clicks open)

142.4—FX: Shin... (silence)

142.5—FX: Kiri kiri kiri
(bowstring being pulled back)

142.7—FX: Kiriri
(bowstring being pulled back)

143.2—FX: Kiri kiri
(bowstrings being held taut)

143.3—FX: Kiri kiri kiri kiri
(bowstrings being held taut)

144.2—FX: Bin
(arrows being released and flying)

144.3—FX: Ban! (arrows hitting Alice's shield)

145.2—FX: Gohh! (roaring wind)

145.3—FX: Kiri kiri kiri...
(bowstrings being pulled)

145.4—FX: Hyu...! (winds disperse)

145.5—FX: Dosa... (falling to her knees)

146.2—FX: Yoro! (wobble)

148.2—FX: Buru buru buru
(hand and bow trembling)

148.5—FX: Buru buru buru (trembling)

149.1 —FX: Bin... (arrow flying)

150.1 —FX: Gata–n (crash)

150.2—FX: Buwa (wham)

151.1 —FX: Butsu butsu (rumbling)

152.1 —FX: Yoro! (staggering)

153.3/4 FX: Biii–n (arrow flying)

167.7—FX: Pa! (she bursts into the room)

169.1—FX: Pi– po– pi– po–
(ambulance siren)

172.2—FX: Kotsu kotsu (walking briskly)

176.4—FX: Kokun... (nod)

177.1—FX: Biku! (startled out of their wits)

178.1—FX: Gyu! (squeezes phone)

181.4—FX: Kacha (door opens)

181.5—FX: Patan... (door closes)

183.1—FX: Kokun (nod)

184.1—FX: Gui! (grabbing hands)

185.1—FX: Doki doki doki doki doki doki
(heartbeats)

185.2—FX: Kyu... (squeeze)

186.3—FX: Gyu... (squeezing more tightly)

154.4—FX: Gunya! (image of Mayura blurring
and shifting)

155.2—FX: Za! (bow and arrow being aimed)

155.3—FX: Nya! (evil smirk)

156.1—FX: Ba ba ba! (blam - bows exploding)

156.2—FX: Dosa dosa!
(people hitting the floor)

156.4—FX: Ta! (Maram master disappears)

157.1—FX: Pokan... (dazed and confused)

159.2—FX: Zaa (evil blowing away)

159.3—FX: Hyu... (Kyô collapses)

161.1—FX: Dosu...! (arrow hits)

162.3—FX: Zubu zubu zubu
(arrow grinding deeper into his back)

163.1—FX: Zu... (arrow disappears completely
into his body)

163.3—FX: Zuru...
(his arm slides as it goes limp)

163.4—FX: Zuru...
(his body goes limp and slides further)

164.1—FX: Ki! (eyes flashing with anger)

164.2—FX: Su!
(the Maram master approaches)

165.5—FX: Zaa! (vortex appears)

166.1—FX: Doh doh doh doh
(bang bang bang)

166.4—FX: Zu... (evil forces disperse)

167.1—FX: Fu...!
(the Maram master disappears)

167.3—FX: Garan... (room becomes silent)

167.6—FX: Piku! (blink)

About the Author:

Yû Watase was born on March 5 in a town near Osaka, Japan, and she was raised there before moving to Tokyo to follow her dream of creating manga. In the decade since her debut short story, **PAJAMA DE OJAMA** ("An Intrusion in Pajamas"), she has produced more than 50 compiled volumes of short stories and continuing series. Her latest series, **ZETTAI KARESHI** ("He'll Be My Boyfriend"), is currently running in the anthology magazine **SHÔJO COMIC**. Watase's long-running horror/romance story **Ceres: Celestial Legend** and her most recent completed series, **ALICE 19TH**, are now available in North America, published by VIZ. She loves science fiction, fantasy and comedy.

COMPLETE OUR SURVEY AND LET US KNOW WHAT YOU THINK!

☐ Please do NOT send me information about VIZ products, news and events, special offers, or other information.

☐ Please do NOT send me information from VIZ's trusted business partners.

Name: _____

Address: _____

City: _____ **State:** _____ **Zip:** _____

E-mail: _____

☐ Male ☐ Female   Date of Birth (mm/dd/yyyy): ___/___/___   (Under 13? Parental consent required)

What race/ethnicity do you consider yourself? (please check one)

☐ Asian/Pacific Islander ☐ Black/African American ☐ Hispanic/Latino

☐ Native American/Alaskan Native ☐ White/Caucasian ☐ Other: _____

What VIZ product did you purchase? (check all that apply and indicate title purchased)

☐ DVD/VHS _____

☐ Graphic Novel _____

☐ Magazines _____

☐ Merchandise _____

Reason for purchase: (check all that apply)

☐ Special offer ☐ Favorite title ☐ Gift

☐ Recommendation ☐ Other _____

Where did you make your purchase? (please check one)

☐ Comic store ☐ Bookstore ☐ Mass/Grocery Store

☐ Newsstand ☐ Video/Video Game Store ☐ Other: _____

☐ Online (site: _____)

What other VIZ properties have you purchased/own? _____

_____

CLAYTON

How many anime and/or manga titles have you purchased in the last year? How many were VIZ titles? (please check one from each column)

ANIME
- ☐ None
- ☐ 1-4
- ☐ 5-10
- ☐ 11+

MANGA
- ☐ None
- ☐ 1-4
- ☐ 5-10
- ☐ 11+

VIZ
- ☐ None
- ☐ 1-4
- ☐ 5-10
- ☐ 11+

I find the pricing of VIZ products to be: (please check one)

- ☐ Cheap
- ☐ Reasonable
- ☐ Expensive

What genre of manga and anime would you like to see from VIZ? (please check two)

- ☐ Adventure
- ☐ Comic Strip
- ☐ Science Fiction
- ☐ Fighting
- ☐ Horror
- ☐ Romance
- ☐ Fantasy
- ☐ Sports

What do you think of VIZ's new look?

- ☐ Love It
- ☐ It's OK
- ☐ Hate It
- ☐ Didn't Notice
- ☐ No Opinion

Which do you prefer? (please check one)

- ☐ Reading right-to-left
- ☐ Reading left-to-right

Which do you prefer? (please check one)

- ☐ Sound effects in English
- ☐ Sound effects in Japanese with English captions
- ☐ Sound effects in Japanese only with a glossary at the back

THANK YOU! Please send the completed form to:

NJW Research
42 Catharine St.
Poughkeepsie, NY 12601

All information provided will be used for internal purposes only. We promise not to sell or otherwise divulge your information.